Propositions for Museum Education

Artwork Scholarship:
International Perspectives in Education

Series editors: Anita Sinner and Rita L. Irwin
Print ISSN: 2632-7872 | **Online ISSN:** 2632-9182

The aim of the Artwork Scholarship series is to invite debate on, and provide an essential resource for transnational scholars engaged in creative research involving visual, literary and performative arts. Approaches may include arts-based, practice-based, a/r/tography, artistic, research creation and more, and explore pedagogical and experimental perspectives, reflective and evaluative assessments, methodological deliberations, and ethical issues and concerns in relation to a host of topic areas in education.

In this series:
Provoking the Field: International Perspectives on Visual Arts PhDs in Education, edited by Anita Sinner, Rita L. Irwin and Jeff Adams (2019)
Living Histories: Global Perspectives in Art Education, edited by Dustin Garnet and Anita Sinner (2022)
Community Arts Education: Transversal Global Perspectives, edited by Ching-Chiu Lin, Anita Sinner and Rita L. Irwin (2023)
Art Education in Canadian Museums: Practices in Action, edited by Anita Sinner, Patricia Osler and Boyd White (2024)
Walking in Art Education: Ecopedagogical and A/r/tographical Encounters, edited by Nicole Rallis, Ken Morimoto, Michele Sorensen, Valerie Triggs and Rita L. Irwin (2024)
A/r/tography: Essential Readings and Conversations, edited by Rita L. Irwin, Alexandra Lasczik, Anita Sinner and Valerie Triggs (2024)
Art, Sustainability and Learning Communities: Call to Action, edited by Raphael Vella and Victoria Pavlou (2024)
Propositions for Museum Education: International Art Educators in Conversation, edited by Anita Sinner, Patricia Osler and Boyd White (2024)

Propositions for Museum Education
INTERNATIONAL ART EDUCATORS IN CONVERSATION

Edited by
Anita Sinner, Patricia Osler and Boyd White

Bristol, UK / Chicago, USA

First published in the UK in 2024 by
Intellect, The Mill, Parnall Road, Fishponds, Bristol, BS16 3JG, UK

First published in the USA in 2024 by
Intellect, The University of Chicago Press, 1427 E. 60th Street,
Chicago, IL 60637, USA

Copyright © 2024 Intellect Ltd

All rights reserved. No part of this publication may be reproduced, stored in a retrieval system or transmitted, in any form or by any means, electronic, mechanical, photocopying, recording or otherwise, without written permission.

A catalogue record for this book is available from the
British Library.

Cover designer: Holly Rose
Cover image: Photo, Anita Sinner, Artist's Palette, Wai-O-Tapu, New Zealand
Production editor: Laura Christopher
Series: Artwork Scholarship: International Perspectives in Education
Series editors: Anita Sinner and Rita L. Irwin
Typesetting: MPS Limited

Hardback ISBN: 978-1-78938-913-5
Paperback ISBN: 978-1-78938-912-8
ePDF ISBN: 978-1-78938-915-9
ePUB ISBN: 978-1-78938-914-2
Series ISSN 2632-7872 / Online ISSN 2632-9182

Printed and bound by CMP, UK.

Contents

Land Acknowledgement	ix
Acknowledgement	xi
Preface-*ing* Anita Sinner, Patricia Osler and Boyd White	xiii
The Promise of Museums: An Introduction Dónal O'Donoghue	1

Part I	**Decolonizing Museums**	**11**
Chapter 1	Displays of Inhumanity and the Inhumanity of Displays: Dialogue at the Junctures of Contemporary Art, Museum Collections and Hate Speech Raphael Vella and Shaun Grech	13
Chapter 2	Museums as Intersectional Spaces for Artivist Solidarity Riikka Haapalainen, Anniina Suominen, Tiina Pusa, Jasmin Järvinen and Melanie Orenius	25
Chapter 3	Decolonizing Benjamin Franklin House Through Comics: Reflections and Potential Kremena Dimitrova	37
Chapter 4	Community Museums: Dialogical Spaces for Knowledge Creation, Mobilization and Income Generation for Marginalized Citizens in Brazil Bruno de Oliveira Jayme	49
Chapter 5	"Becoming Ecological" for Nature Conservation: Insights From Two Museums in the Island State of lutruwita/Tasmania, Australia Abbey MacDonald, Annalise Rees, Jan Hogan and Benjamin J. Richardson	61

| Chapter 6 | On the Possibility of Reconstructing a Contested Past Through Memory Museums in Turkey
Esra Yildiz | 75 |

| **Part II** | **Museums of Purpose** | **87** |

| Chapter 7 | Disrupting Museum Education: Counter-Monument as a Pedagogical Space
Susana Vargas-Mejía | 89 |

| Chapter 8 | Korundi Recreated: Participatory Experience Creates a Dialogue Between Past and Present
Anniina Koivurova and Tatiana Kravtsov | 101 |

| Chapter 9 | Be the Nature: Enhancing Nature Connectedness Through Art Museum Pedagogy
Timo Jokela, Maria Huhmarniemi and Tanja Mäkitalo | 111 |

| Chapter 10 | Interpretation Design at a Crossroads With Museum Education
Richard Lachapelle | 123 |

| Chapter 11 | The Portuguese Contemporary Art Museum Today
João Pedro Fróis | 137 |

| Chapter 12 | Museum-School Partnership: Synergizing Paradigmatic Engagements
Attwell Mamvuto | 149 |

| Chapter 13 | Every School Is a Museum: The Case of "Art for Learning Art" in Tegucigalpa, Honduras
Joaquín Roldán, Andrea Rubio-Fernández and Ángela Moreno-Córdoba | 161 |

| **Part III** | **Pedagogic Pivots** | **173** |

| Chapter 14 | Not-Knowing: Creating Spaces for Co-curation
Deborah Riding | 175 |

| Chapter 15 | Children's Voices: Making Children's Perspectives Visible in Gallery Spaces
Lilly Blue and Sue Girak | 187 |

| Chapter 16 | The Art of Learning Art
Paloma Palau-Pellicer, Maria Avariento-Adsuara and Paola Ruiz-Moltó | 199 |

Contents

Chapter 17	Out of the Museum Into the Art Lise Sattrup and Lars Emmerik Damgaard Knudsen	207
Chapter 18	Thinking Ahead in Art Education... Rolf Laven and Wolfgang Weinlich	221
Chapter 19	Social Functions of Museum Education in Double Peripheries: Between Museology and Sociology Dominik Porczyński	233
Chapter 20	The Role of the University Museum in Museum Education: The Example of the University of Tartu Museum Jaanika Anderson	245
Part IV	**Sites of Sensorial Practice**	**259**
Chapter 21	"You Have to Form Your Mediators. It's a Series": On Mediation, Encounters and Deleuze in the Art Museum Marie-France Berard	261
Chapter 22	Learning Changes the Museum Ricardo Marín-Viadel and Joaquín Roldán	273
Chapter 23	Encounters on the Fringe of a Museum Tour: *Trailing Behind* as a Site of Affective Intensities Keven Lee, Melissa Park and Marilyn Lajeunesse	285
Chapter 24	The Educational Turn and A/r/tography: An Interplay Between Curating, Education and Artmaking Jaime Mena and Guadalupe Pérez-Cuesta	297
Chapter 25	Redescribing Territories: Inhabiting the Continuum of Art Production and Education Lene Crone Jensen and Hilde Østergaard	305
Chapter 26	Senses and Sensibility: Finding the Balance in Sensory Museum Education Emilie Sitzia	317
Chapter 27	Towards a More Human-Centred Museum: A Narrative of an Imagined Visit to a Trauma-Aware Art Museum Jackie Armstrong, Laura Evans, Stephen Legari, Ronna Tulgan Ostheimer, Andrew Palamara and Emily Wiskera	329

Part V	**Virtual Museums**	**341**
Chapter 28	The Art of Teaching in the Museum: A Proposition for Pedagogy of Dissensus Lisbet Skregelid	343
Chapter 29	The Virtual of Abstract Art: Museum Educational Encounters with Concrete Abstraction Heidi Kukkonen	357
Chapter 30	Projection-Based Augmented Reality for Visual Learning and Creation in Contemporary Art Museums Rocío Lara-Osuna and Xabier Molinet	369
Chapter 31	Co-imagining the Museum of the Future: Meaningful Interactions Among Art(efacts), Visitors and Technology in Museum Spaces Priscilla Van Even, Annika Wolff, Stefanie Steinbeck, Anne Pässilä and Kevin Vanhaelewijn	379
Chapter 32	Immersive Museum Technologies in Turkey and Future Projections in the Field Ceren Güneröz and Ayşem Yanar	393
Chapter 33	A New Pedagogy of Museology? Innovative Changes in Museum Education for Cultural Heritage, Social Communication and Participation: A Case Study Renata Pater	405
Biographies		417
Index		427

Land Acknowledgment

As is our practice in Canada, we offer a land acknowledgement to recognize that Canada is a land of many, many nations.

Anita Sinner learns and teaches on land that is the traditional, ancestral and unceded territory of the xʷməθkʷəy̓əm (Musqueam) People at The University of British Columbia in Vancouver, British Columbia, Canada.

Boyd White, as a long-time member of McGill University, acknowledges the traditional territory of the Haudenosaunee and Anishinabeg nations, a place which has historically served as a site of meeting and exchange amongst nations.

Patricia Osler honours the Mississaugas of the Credit First Nation as current treaty holders of Toronto, where she resides. Tkaronto has been caretaken by the Anishinabek Nation, the Haudenosaunee Confederacy and the Huron-Wendat. This territory accords with the Dish with One Spoon Wampum Belt Covenant, an agreement to peaceably share and care for the Canadian Great Lakes region.

In accordance with the United Nations Declaration on The Rights of Indigenous Peoples, we join with all authors in this book to recognize the many places where we reside, and the rights of all Indigenous Peoples globally, to ensure the dignity, freedom and well-being of all peoples, and to share and protect the lands, territories and resources, respectfully.

Acknowledgement

This book was published with the support of an Insight Grant from the Social Sciences and Humanities Research Council of Canada (435-2019-1138: CREATION of the Self: A Museum-University Collaboration).

Preface-*ing*

Anita Sinner, Patricia Osler and Boyd White

Ongoing conversations about dynamic, educative movements now underway in museums prompted our curiosity to invite artful "xchanges" among educators in this collection. Our goal was twofold: to exchange views and attend to the incremental "x," for we suggest there is an unknown qualitative shift underway that is magnifying, and indeed multiplying, our understandings of museums today. By attending to such between spaces, we invoke in this collection an interplay of situations, conditions, bodies, spaces and artworks, co-creating together an unpredictable yet discernable change. Much like neo-phenomenologists, we adopt a position that the intensification of the felt body in relation to museums moves us to "thinking in constellations," where we mediate our "embodied happenings" as openings to engage with works of art in new ways (Gugutzer, 2019, p. 189).

As art educators preoccupied with pedagogic intention, we sought to bring together diverse worldviews with contributors sharing candid perspectives that survey, investigate, prompt and propose possibilities for museums as contiguous sites of learning. Dónal O'Donoghue creates the conditions to enliven this conversation with a thoughtful introduction and commentary, storying how we live with museums as sites of educative transformation. The chapters that follow deliberate decolonizing museums, with emphasis on social, cultural, historical and ecological justice as a relational act and action. Extending from decolonizing practices, museums of purpose – be that peace, heritage, history, memory, science, participatory, or otherwise shifting in purpose (e.g. museums joining with community or school partnerships) – are at crossroads of change. Such movements advance pedagogic pivots by attending to how we mediate art, and why multimodal methods as creative catalysts enhance what it means to know and not know. Building upon these sections, sites of sensorial practice invoke affect and explore presence, body traces, and health and well-being. This brings us to the conversation in our last section, where authors unpack virtual museums as immersive iterations of technologies and digital delivery.

Reflecting constellations of thought shared among authors, it is important to note that chapters blur and overlap discrete sections, often addressing multiple themes, and so may be read differently depending on one's positionality. The dispositions, definitions and practices offered in these 33 chapters from 19 countries – Zimbabwe, Honduras, Colombia, Estonia, Poland, Malta, Turkey and Brazil, among others – articulate how museums are nuanced and situated as social institutions and why collections enact responsibility in public exchange, leading cultural discourses of empowerment in new ways. To ensure a blended and balanced flow of ideas across each section, we intersperse and mingle chapters that are diverse in issues, challenges, art forms and museum orientations to consider more fully, as Donna Haraway (2016) advocates, how the act of "composting" issues intersects with visual arts, teaching and learning. Our goal in drawing together international perspectives is to facilitate deeper thinking, making and doing practices central to museum engagement, opening an "artful xchange" across global, local and glocal contexts.

Presented within these pages, a wide range of topics and arts-based modes of inquiry imagine new possibilities concerning theory-practice, sustainability of educational partnerships and communities of practice with, in and through artwork scholarship. The individual chapters are well-situated within museum studies and related literature and grounded in creative disciplines while enlarging discussions with *trans*-topographies (transdisciplinary, transnational, translocal, transindividual and more) as critical directions for art educators. Authors rupture predictive discourses of museum education and counter existing museo-narratives in style, order, sequence, framework and structure. This effort brings us to radically different museum education contexts and to emergent knowledge clusters that enfold cultural activism, sustainable practices and experimental teaching and learning alongside transformative exhibitions, while all the time questioning – Who is a learner? What is a museum? Whose art is missing?

International art educators committed to redefining museum education impart collective diversity through richly textured exposés, first-person accounts, essays and visual essays, informed by socio-materiality and more-than-human perspectives, in unison with traditional forms and historical expressions of researching museums. With formal and informal approaches, experiential and systematic inquiry, authors embrace innovations for teaching and learning from museum studies, education, fine arts, curatorial inquiry and philosophy to consider how institutions bring into conversation community activists, change agents and social policymakers. In turn, we see how museums, as cultural brokers within wider society, facilitate public pedagogies among visitor audiences, patrons of museums and tourists alike. From the perspective of art educators, museum education is shifting to a new paradigm, which this collection showcases and marks as threshold moments of change underway internationally.

For this edited collection, curated with movement and reverberation, we deeply appreciate the many ways authors initiate educative potentials from the standpoint of art education, bringing us to lively, vibrant and forceful dialogues in the process. Seldom do we encounter such a uniquely provocative series of propositions. May we continue to welcome and anticipate ever more eloquent conversations beyond these pages.

References

Gugutzer, R. (2019). Beyond Husserl and Schütz: Hermann Schmitz and neophenomenological sociology. *Journal for the Theory of Social Behaviour, 50*(2), 184–202.

Haraway, D. (2016). *Staying with the trouble: Making kin in the Chthulucene*. Duke University Press.

The Promise of Museums: An Introduction

Dónal O'Donoghue

Driving back to Vancouver, Canada, last summer from Bentonville, Arkansas, United States, I stopped off at the Nelson Atkins Museum in Kansas City to visit Andy Goldsworthy's site-specific artwork, *Walking Wall*. At the time, I was writing a short piece on the artwork – an artwork built over a nine-month period and in five distinctive and successive phases, an artwork that presents as a stone wall 100 yards long made from 100 tons of limestone gathered from the Flint Hills of Kansas. In the museum bookstore, while searching for a book that might give an account of how the work came to be, I came across another book: András Szántó's *The Future of the Museum: 28 Dialogues*, published in 2020 by Hatje Cantz Verlag, Berlin. Given that since childhood, I have spent a considerable amount of my time in museums – places that nurture my curiosity, imagination, wonderment and thinking and encourage other interpretations of the world – on that day in July in the bookstore at the Nelson-Atkins Museum, I wondered what Szántó might have to say about the future of such places.

Szántó tells his readers that the content of the book was developed during the pandemic lockdown of 2020. It comprises 28 dialogues between him and 28 museum directors from fourteen countries and six continents, whom he invited into a conversation. While these conversations do not lay claim to being representative of what is on the minds of museum directors across the world, nonetheless, they offer insights – important insights, one might say – into some of the questions, concerns, thoughts, observations and hopes of a sizeable number of directors who lead significant museums across the globe. And as the title of the book suggests, these dialogues also reveal, in part, how these museum directors envision a future for the institutions they lead.

While Szántó asked several questions of his interlocutors – questions specific to the museums in which they work and to their experiences in the museum world thus far – one question common across all conversations related to how they define the term *museum*. Their responses, varied in some respects but strikingly similar in others, suggest that they view the museum as a place of learning and discovery, of encounter and exploration and of confrontation and change, as well as a place that affords opportunities to slow down and take time to become familiar differently with things already thought known. Acknowledging that museums "are the memory banks of our civilization" (Birnbaum, as cited in Szántó, 2020, p. 264) and that they are places in which research is conducted, scholarship produced, and interpretation and engagement of audience members supported and advanced, museum directors describe the museum as a place in which visitors are provoked to think and to pursue thinking that is promiscuous in nature: thinking that is neither bound nor wholly faithful to convention or tradition; thinking that, as Hans Ulrich Obrist, artistic director at the Serpentine Galleries in London, United Kingdom, says, "transcends established systems of thought and looks to the utopian" (as cited in Szántó, 2020, p. 194). Along similar lines, Sandra Jackson-Dumont, director and CEO of the Lucas Museum of Narrative Art in Los Angeles, United States, suggests, "[the museum] is the custodian of critical conversations, objects, and people related to the past, present, and future" (as cited in Szántó, 2020, p. 248).

For some of Szántó's interlocutors, a museum is a place of "contemplation and convergence where ideas and objects intersect to produce meaning and social value" (Kouoh, as cited in Szántó, 2020, p. 112) and a place in which new modes of reality are suggested, gestured towards and at times produced in the Barthian punctum kind of way. As Obrist tells Szántó, the museum is a place where new futures are put on display, including new ways of thinking about how we might live in the world with ourselves and others. New possibilities for living are suggested in the types of perceptual and interpretive demands that artworks can make on our bodies.

For many museum directors, museums function as democratic communal spaces, meeting places where one encounters others – others they might not ordinarily encounter or interact with. As Max Hollein, director of the Metropolitan Museum of Art, New York City, puts it, "museums are where communities should convene for engaged dialogue" (as cited in Szántó, 2020, p. 222). The director of Brooklyn Museum, Anne Pasternak, tells Szántós, "museums are great democratic spaces to learn, debate, and advance social change" (as cited in Szántó, 2020, p. 64), and they ought to continue to function as "public places where you can come to learn, meet other people, share ideas, debate, and even disagree" (p. 65). Expanding on Pasternak's claim, Katrina Sedgwick, director and CEO of the Australian Centre for the Moving Image, argues "it is more important than ever to have these safe democratic spaces to explore ideas together, to look at our past, and to get a glimpse of what the future may bring" (as cited in Szántó, 2020, p. 274).

With this in mind, Maria Mercedes Gonzalez, director-general of Museo de Arts Moderno de Medellin, Columbia, observes that "all museums exist within wider social, political, and economic systems" (as cited in Szántó, 2020, p. 119). Including traditions of showing, displaying, organizing, selecting, creating, looking, interpreting and making sense of objects made by others that are deemed significant and worthy of our attention, museums offer opportunities for studying the world and coming to know aspects of it through one's engagement with the works and objects on a show – works and objects animated not only by the context of their presentation and the conditions of their production but also by the questions and curiosities that audience members bring to them. Thus, several of these directors describe the museum as a place with which audiences engage: where they expand their ways of seeing, sensing and responding to the world in which they live and come to know through their engagement with artworks and the various activities designed to bring them into dialogue with such works.

Most of all, directors defined the museum as a place of education, acknowledging that education is (and ought to be) one of the key values of any museum. Thomas P. Campbell, director and CEO of Fine Arts Museums of San Francisco, tells Szántós that a museum is a place

> where people are presented with objects from the past and the present that allow them to understand their own heritage and that of other people, to better understand the issues of the day, and to empower their creative engagement in their own futures.
> (as cited in Szántó, 2020, p. 157)

Implied here is the idea that viewers are supported in their journeys of reflection, contemplation and contextualization through the conditions created by museum professionals to bring them into a meaningful engagement with objects and collections. Thus, by extension, the museum is a place in which people are encouraged to notice, see or understand something that expands or complicates what they already know. And the museum, says Cecillia Alemani, director and chief curator of the High Line in New York City, is a storyteller – a storyteller that can "tell opposite and oppositional stories" (as cited in Szántó, 2020, p. 232), even though, as Campbell tells Szántó, "all too often, museums tell their stories, uncritically" (p. 152).

The authors of the collection before you, *Propositions for Museum Education: International Art Educators in Conversation*, share many of the concerns and hopes for the museum that the directors in Szántó's collection do, including the desire to make museums ever more relevant to a wider and larger population, and in doing so to attend more closely to the museums' relationships with communities. Like Szántó's interlocutors, the authors of the essays that follow acknowledge and recognize the ongoing work that needs to be done to ensure museums are places that are open to all: places that foster and promote inclusive engagement as well as critical conversations for all. This work involves attending to community engagement and establishing community partnerships that address barriers to accessing museums, especially for members of communities who traditionally might feel excluded and marginalized or see little promise or relevance to the museum. Also, like many of Szántó's interlocutors, many of the authors in this collection recognize that the museum does not exist outside of or apart from the world but is rather very much part of the world, entangled in its systems of operation and structure. This collection introduces some additional concerns as well. Further, like Szántó's book, this collection includes chapters from authors across several continents who are interested in the nature of education within museums today and how such models might find form in other educational sites beyond the museum. They are interested in understanding what museum education does: what it produces, reproduces, interrupts and extends.

The chapters in this collection take many different forms. Some are narrative, some are historical; some are case studies, some are guided by questions, and some are not. Some are visual essays. Others are interview-based. Many share accounts of empirical research studies, while others engage in a study of concepts deemed relevant and important for the field of museum education at this time. Some contributors are curious about what the practice of thinking with others produces as they themselves pursue such a practice. Several chapters are outcomes of collaborative inquiry and pedagogical experiments resulting from partnerships between cultural institutions and educational institutions.

Not surprisingly given the title of this collection, all authors share one common concern: museum education. They focus on what it is, where it occurs, how it occurs, the assumptions, intentions and traditions that underpin and guide it, as well as the expectations that shape it. All, in their own ways, seek to complicate easy understandings of museum education and museum practices more generally. Some, such as Riikka Haapalainen et al., seek to "challenge oppressive practices of museum institutions from an antinormative (queer) and anticolonial stance." Several others quietly encourage an interrogation of current museum education practices by demonstrating how education happens in museums within and beyond what is articulated as the educational mission and practices of museums.

While several authors are interested in the nature of museum education and the role that museum educators occupy within museums (see, for instance, Dominik Porczyński's and João Pedro Fróis' contributions), and while Lisbet Skregelid is interested in how understandings and interpretations of art and art theory inform education practices within museums, others are interested in the educational potential of informal, playful encounters in the museum – encounters that can occur within an exhibition or in the company of an individual artwork. For instance, with interest in what the act of looking at artworks with another produces as each shares what they see, notice, are drawn to and are curious about, Marie-France Berard invites us to think about what chance encounters with strangers in the museum might provoke, especially when such encounters are open, generous and responsive in nature. Focusing on museum encounters with artworks and others in the museum is also of interest to Keven Lee, Melissa Park and Marilyn Lajeunesse; in their contribution, they share accounts of their experience of working in the programme called *Art Links* – established at the Montreal Museum of Fine Arts (MMFA) in Canada, "for caregivers and persons living with Alzheimer's to take a break from their daily schedule and get together, talk, laugh, and create" – and what occurs at the margins of a museum tour, a component of *Art Links*.

Several other chapters give attention to the pedagogical potential of individual objects, artworks and museum collections and one's interactions with them. Susana Vargas-Mejía's contribution focuses on counter-monuments: one in particular, *Fragmentos: Espacio de Arte y Memoria* by the Colombian artist Doris Salcedo. Vargas-Mejía reflects on the distinctive capacity of counter-monuments to cultivate empathy and animate the affective lives of those who engage them.

For many of the authors in this collection interested in the pedagogical potential of interacting with and responding to artworks and artists' practices, place is also important. Artmaking in places similar to the ones in which artists made their works is what interests Lise Sattrup and Lars Emmerik Damgaard Knudsen. Their contribution theorizes a form of museum pedagogy they call "activist art museum pedagogy." Also interested in the relationship between place and pedagogy, Jaanika Anderson explores the educational role of the University of Tartu Museum (UTM) in the context of the national education system of Estonia in an effort to study the potential of university museums to influence and support schools' educational activities. This curiosity about what museums can do when they are located within educational complexes such as universities or schools also informs Joaquín Roldán, Andrea Rubio-Fernández, and Ángela Moreno-Córdoba's contribution to this collection.

Some of the authors here emphasize the need for museums to intentionally nurture and support the participation of communities who do not typically access museums' collections or engage with them. One example is Attwell Mamvuto's essay; another is Ceren Güneröz and Ayşem Yanar's contribution, in which they argue that "accessibility for the museums is the practice of making museum's sections accessible for all peoples and this includes making museum websites usable by as many people as possible." Museum websites, they claim, "can play a crucial role in society by educating the public and representing diverse aspects of culture through their exhibits." Another example is Deborah Riding's chapter, based on their interest in studying the "challenges and benefits of developing new knowledge and understandings of collections" through acts of co-curating museum exhibitions and collections – an approach used to support audience members' exploration and responses to museums' collections. Along similar lines, Jackie Armstrong, Laura Evans, Stephen Legari, Ronna Tulgan Ostheimer, Andrew Palamara and Emily Wiskera argue that museums ought to become more intentional and purposeful about how they support diverse audiences. For instance, Armstrong et al. argue that "our museums must become more purposefully trauma-aware and responsive if we are to be relevant to our visitors' needs," and they advance an approach to museum education they have named "Trauma-Aware Art Museum Education" (T-AAME).

Further, the authors in this collection study a range of museums: from the more traditional ones to memory museums, biographical museums, community museums and school museums. For instance, Esra Yildiz focuses on the role memory museums can play in "defending human rights and democracy through the initiation of different conflict groups and different ethnic parts of society." Bruno de Oliveira Jayme argues that community museums "have the potential to trouble colonialism, racism, and classism" while they also "co-create and mobilize new knowledge, while surfacing hidden or even forgotten stories of local communities."

Other authors in the collection are interested in the work of those employed in museums, who do work that is inherently educational in nature but not articulated as such. For instance, Richard Lachapelle considers the work of museum interpretation designers, who, he argues, "share with museum educators many of the same interests regarding museum visitors and the quality of their experiences." The work of interpretation designers, Lachapelle suggests, has the potential to "encourage extended viewing and careful looking" and complicate viewers' interpretations, reactions and interests in works encountered. An examination of their work, he says, offers insights into how others make sense of objects and artworks through study, research and interpretative practices. Related in some ways to Lachapelle's interest in the work of museum interpretation designers and the educational potential and promise of such work, Lilly Blue and Sue Girak share outcomes from a collaborative study in which they invited children to create labels for a select number of works shown in *The Botanical: Beauty and Peril* exhibition at the Art Gallery of Western Australia in 2019. Given that museums often conceptualize and arrange their educational activities and foci based on what they assume about the populations they serve (for instance, on museum webpages it is not uncommon to find educational programmes designed for families, educators, K–12 teachers and school groups) Blue and Girak's study is particularly interesting as it amplifies the rich potential of exhibition making and museum programming that happens *with* children rather than undertaken *for* children. Finding ways to increase the involvement of youth is also a concern shared by Lene Crone Jensen and Hilde Østergaard in their contribution to this collection. They ask, "How can art institutions and art exhibitions more systematically function as real, democratic spaces for a public dialogue that includes the younger generations: not only in the mediation of content but also in the production and public presentation?" Just as Blue and Girak staged an intervention in a museum with children, Ricardo Marín-Viadel and Joaquín Roldán did something similar in their study with university students, of which they offer an account in this collection.

Other issues are also addressed – issues that include digital technology and the museum and the nature of museum education during the pandemic. Renata Pater has a particular interest in how lockdowns "not only forced museums to establish a presence in cyberspace but also opened new possibilities for diverse groups of visitors, providing much-needed support for maintaining good physical and mental health of the population."

In reading this collection, I was curious about the type of questions that motivated and guided the authors to study museum education, to undertake and pursue their research inquiries and to make a case for expanded and responsive museum education practices. This is likely a curiosity that spilled over from reading Szántó's collection. Not all authors shared the questions that guided their inquiries and interventions, but most did. I will finish this introduction then by listing the questions as I found them in this collection:

- "What happens when we make use of the dissensual characteristics inherent in the art itself to guide the education in the art-museum?" (Lisbet Skregelid)
- "So, if the museum is to behave like a school, what should happen in a school museum?" (Joaquín Roldán, Andrea Rubio-Fernández and Ángela Moreno-Córdoba)
- "In a museum context, what are the possible experiences of a queer youth of immigrant backgrounds in relation to cultural heritage, and how might we overcome the forces of marginalization and repetitive discrimination?" (Riikka Haapalainen, Anniina Suominen, Tiina Pusa, Jasmin Järvinen and Melanie Orenius)
- "What happens when an art museum moves a lesson from the museum itself to a relevant place and instructs the students to use the artist's strategies? How does it affect the positioning of the students? How can it inspire an activist art museum pedagogy?" (Lise Sattrup and Lars Emmerik Damgaard Knudsen)

- "What might it look and feel like for a visitor to move through an idealized trauma-aware museum?" (Jackie Armstrong, Laura Evans, Stephen Legari, Ronna Tulgan Ostheimer, Andrew Palamara and Emily Wiskera)
- "How do the pressing contemporary challenges to morality and responsibility with regard to equality prompt us to rethink the colonial texts and representations in the museum and heritage sector?" (Kremena Dimitrova)
- "How does *Fragmentos* become a different space when we, as spectators, walk through the space?" (Susana Vargas-Mejí)
- "What are the objectives of educational interpretation design? What might such an approach achieve?" (Richard Lachapelle)
- "How can art museum pedagogy enhance nature connectedness?" (Timo Jokela, Maria Huhmarniemi and Tanja Mäkitalo)
- "What is the role of education in art museums today? What are the relationships between curators and education specialists? What can we teach each other?" (João Pedro Fróis)
- "How can art institutions and art exhibitions more systematically function as real, democratic spaces for a public dialogue that includes the younger generations, not only in the mediation of content, but also in the production and public presentation? How can young people's voices become a relevant part of the exhibition content, outweighing an age-based and knowledge-hierarchical imprint of the output available to the public? And what curatorial strategies must be used to maintain artistically and pedagogically high-level engagement when young non-artists are involved in production through participatory processes?" (Lene Crone Jensen and Hilde Østergaard)
- "Instead of asking how do museum artworks provoke learning in their visitors, we are asking – How does the learning of museum visitors provoke changes in the artworks exhibited in the museum? What traces does learning leave on the works of art? How is it possible for the artworks to remain unchanged in the presence of the profound emotional and cognitive experience of their viewers? How can we visualize, through a collaborative artistic intervention, that our learning has transformed the museum's works of art?" (Ricardo Marín-Viadel and Joaquín Roldán)
- "Can the multiplication of sensory stimuli in exhibition spaces become counter-productive to learning? How, then, can museums reconcile our senses and our (varied) sensibilities?" (Emilie Sitzia)
- "What if museums could be thought of as spaces in which bodies – living or nonliving – are appreciated as affecting as much as they are affected?" (Keven Lee, Melissa Park and Marilyn Lajeunesse)
- "The question is, what will be the lingering effects of the pandemic? What new forms of activity will museums initiate in different regions of the world?" (Renata Pater)
- "Will technology change have an impact on the museum concept? How does the museum type (e.g. a natural history museum versus a design museum) have an influence on the use of technology, and would there be different requirements to establish a meaningful

interaction?" (Priscilla Van Even, Annika Wolff, Stefanie Steinbeck, Anne Pässilä and Kevin Vanhaelewijn)

In this short introduction, I haven't addressed all chapters in this collection; my intention was to offer but a glimpse of the richness to follow rather than a comprehensive account of its content. I hope you enjoy reading this collection of essays as much as I did. My thanks to the editors for inviting me to share some thoughts on the collection – a collection that will no doubt be a valuable and provocative contribution to the field of museum education and museum studies. My thanks to the editors for editing and producing such a fine collection, especially to Dr Anita Sinner for her vision and commitment to art education across many educational sites. And finally, my thanks to the authors of the essays in this collection for sharing your work and ideas with us all.

Reference

Szántó, A. (2020). *The future of the museum: 28 dialogues.* Hatje Cantz Verlag.

Part I

Decolonizing Museums

Chapter 1

Displays of Inhumanity and the Inhumanity of Displays: Dialogue at the Junctures of Contemporary Art, Museum Collections and Hate Speech

Raphael Vella and Shaun Grech

This chapter engages artist Shaun Grech and artist/curator Raphael Vella in debate to critically discuss the foundations, directions and contradictions of Grech's recent exhibition called *Dehumaneation*, curated by Raphael Vella. The exhibition was held at Spazju Kreattiv in Valletta, Malta from 15 January to 28 February, 2021. The curatorial process that characterized the setting up of *Dehumaneation* was dialogical in nature, and the conversational mode in this chapter strives to mirror that process. More information about the exhibition can be found here: https://www.kreattivita.org/en/event/dehumaneation/.

Raphael: The title of the exhibition, *Dehumaneation*, revolves around the coining of an awkward word that simultaneously refers to dehumanization, humiliation and nation. By associating the latter term with the other two, the concept of "nation" is immediately problematized because the title implies that political communities are, or could be, complicit with the degrading treatment of other human beings. Connecting the prefix "de" (a privative) with the word "nation" (a word etymologically linked to birth or origin, hence also to biology) also divests the notion of a unified or autonomous people of its moral character and self-regulating powers, perhaps even its right to be born and exist. If this prefix usually undoes the meaning of verbs (to deactivate, for example), we might ask: What would an "undone" nation look like?

Clifford Geertz (1973) describes primordial attachments or "givens," like blood ties, language and religion as assumed foundations of identity and the need to be visible. In the same context, he also describes a second motive in new states: the desire to form modern, civil states which cannot remain attached to ethnic, religious and other affiliations if they need to progress. In Malta, this tension between the two motives has provided fertile ground for political and other controversies for decades. Foundation myths based on Semitic roots, Christianity and aspirations of sovereignty have often led to partisan squabbling about connections with the Arab world, European Union membership and even St. Paul (Gerber, 2000). More than half a century after achieving independence, Malta now often sees itself as being overwhelmed by another "invasion," that of migrants arriving from the African continent. Migrants are perceived as a security threat, leading to the requirement of strengthened borders and various punitive detention measures (Lemaire, 2019).

Unsurprisingly, such a context lends itself well to artistic, curatorial and museological reinterpretations or "undoings" of the concept of nation. Unfortunately, it also corresponds with vicious, dehumanizing behaviour, characterized by hate speech as well as physical violence. This violence has historical roots. This is why I included reproductions of Old Master paintings from our national collection in Valletta in the exhibition: paintings that portray violent religious iconographies involving figures like Judith and Holofernes,

Figure 1.1: Shaun Grech (centre), painting. Flanked (left) by hate speech and (right) a reproduction of *The Martyrdom of St Catherine of Alexandra* by Mattia Preti, painted in 1660.

St. Agatha and St. John the Baptist (Figure 1.1). Art needs to elicit something more than a personal feeling of empathy or identification with victims. Rather, the exhibition addressed violence and derogatory language as issues of social justice with deep historical roots. These were the ingredients that marked the beginnings of *Dehumaneation*.

Shaun: The analysis of this intersectional space (dehumaneation) was indeed inevitable to us, and reflective of key geopolitical dimensions in times of coloniality (see Quijano, 2000), maintained and intensified by neoliberal globalization in the fluid and rapidly changing globalized space, including Malta. This tiny island with multiple post/neocolonial anxieties served as our backdrop. It has one of the highest usages of social media in the world, a newfound sense of national pride propped up by an intensification of Othering – not only of the bodies (darker) that do not belong (embodied in refugees and asylum seekers from the African continent) but also a newfound resistance to ideas that are perceived as "imported" because they challenge the conveniently constructed notion of nation and "Malteseness." Similar patterns are seen in fortress Europe and in the United States, among others, where a reformulated national identity and selective historical memory are constructed through and maintained by an obsession with borders (discursive and material) and the creation of an Other that can seemingly never fit in this fabricated narrative. From refugees and asylum seekers crossing to Europe by boat to those traversing the gruelling US–Mexico border on foot, to activists who push for open borders and actively lobby against racism and hate speech, to those alert to increasing poverty and inequality – the "wretched of the earth," to use Fanon's (1967) words, are not only the Othered bodies regularly subjectified but also

Displays of Inhumanity and the Inhumanity of Displays

those creating alliances with them. Importantly, the idea of "nation" continues to serve as an operative in framing who is human and who is not, or only momentarily; who belongs and who doesn't and who has rights and how these travel across borders – or put another way, the right to rights (Pisani, 2012). Dehumanization bound to nations may be enacted through physical or discursive violence, where humiliation continues to be a consistent weapon of aggression. More specifically, the concept of nation is weaponized, and humiliation is one of the bullets in a growing arsenal of contempt, much of which is expressed online.

Themes of neocoloniality and such discursive violence have long informed my painting, which is an extension of my academic and activist work (see Grech, 2015). Over the years, I have sought to freeze multiple and evolving moments of dehumanization traversing colonial and neocolonial incidences, positions and identities. But with this exhibition, the paintings were not enough, so we used "found" text online to lay it bare without over-intellectualizing and without forsaking the nuances. The ontological and physical borders and the racialization that sustain "nation" were not born overnight and, indeed, have long historical lineages requiring in-depth study and reflection (see Fanon, 1967). This meant the need to also frame and historicize, which we did through a shrine-like installation, emphasizing historical images – some made public, perhaps for the first time (Figure 1.2).

Figure 1.2: Detail of a shrine in Shaun Grech's exhibition – a statuette of St. Sebastian next to framed photos lifted from news outlets.

We also produced a short film using archival material, including content pertinent to Maltese emigration to Australia: an intense short history of racialized Othering. Finally, in *Spark 15*, a group of young refugees collaborated with us to produce their own short film. Their only guideline was the notion of "dehumaneation" as they understood it and wanted to articulate it. Our task as artists and curators was effectively to undo an assumed, homogenized, even sterilized idea of nation in Malta, to strip it and lay it bare. An undone nation is one capable of critically looking at itself and dislocating "fixities."

Raphael: Evidence of these fixities was plastered all over the exhibition, particularly in the assortment of Facebook posts and other internet comments you collected. Putting all that hatred on display next to the paintings created a deliberately dissonant chorus of voices. We wanted art to meet the things we find most appalling about this society head-on. The colourfully designed hate speech quotations were intended to get the public to reflect on the aestheticization of violence, perhaps a nod towards what Peter Osborne (2013) sees as part of the critical legacy of conceptual art and whatever follows it: "Art's ineliminable – but radically insufficient – aesthetic dimension" and the "critical necessity of an anti-aesthetic*ist* use of aesthetic materials" (p. 48). The corporeal dimension or affect generated by the encounter of visitors with strong imagery and texts made it possible for us to conceive of this event as something more than an exhibition *about* inhumanity. It became an emotional encounter.

Philosopher Ronald Dworkin (2006) famously defended the right of free speech as a basic principle in a democratic society, in which any form of coercion or censorship would delegitimize the democratic basis of that society. I think that you and I would argue that not everyone in democratic societies has equal access to this freedom. And if some people equate hate speech with free speech, others have a right, perhaps even an obligation, to react and resist.

The exhibition also made us reflect on the use of institutional art spaces to engage with this hatred. How relevant can museums be to such debates? Was our display of internet hate speech in a gallery space an irrelevant, watered-down version of a contested and even violent social arena? Or was it rather the (necessary) insertion into a relatively "safe" cultural haven, part of a relevant process of institutional critique in the country? And does a display that addresses inhumanity become inhumane by doing so?

Shaun: Context was critical in framing dehumaneation and how everything worked together to construct and respond to a narrative, in an "artistic" space that may not always sit comfortably with the political. This does not mean that people and artists do not complain or seek avenues of marginal resistance. There is plenty of that online, the space of purging. We are all, though, complicit in maintaining this status quo, the ugliness online and offline, the racism, the transphobia, the misogyny […] the hate. The safe sterilized art galleries are no more or less of a reflection of the national mindset and context. Indeed, if asked whether an art gallery was the adequate space for such politically charged material, one is hard pressed to question whether the barren walls in this space are so different from the uncritical space outside. For us, the aestheticization of hatred within

Displays of Inhumanity and the Inhumanity of Displays

the space, drawing profoundly on found text expressed on Maltese social media, was a mere articulation of this ugliness, coming face-to-face with it, outside the relative safety and anonymity of Facebook, outside the illusory and fabricated notion of who we think we are and how we have tried to construct and present ourselves to the world. We have in effect, colonized even the narrative about ourselves: for example, the notion of a welcoming nation. Metaphors (including in art) can easily work "by subverting the need for conscious reflection" (Betcher, 2004, p. 89).

Raphael: The complicity you speak of, particularly that of the relatively safe spaces we construct for the display of art, was one of the reasons why I opted for a trans-historical strategy in the curation of the exhibition, mixing your paintings with reproductions of much older paintings. In the past, anachronistic reinterpretations of biblical narratives were sometimes used to render the event's significance intelligible to a contemporary audience. In contrast, the anachronisms in your exhibition were meant to direct contemporary audiences to the roots of hate speech, misogyny, patriotism and humiliation of the Other (Figure 1.3). This is how, for example, a nineteenth-century painting showing the killing of Dragut, a Muslim Ottoman naval commander (the Other *par excellence*) in the Great Siege of Malta, was re-examined through the lens of contemporary tourism by nailing it over a tacky souvenir napkin printed with the

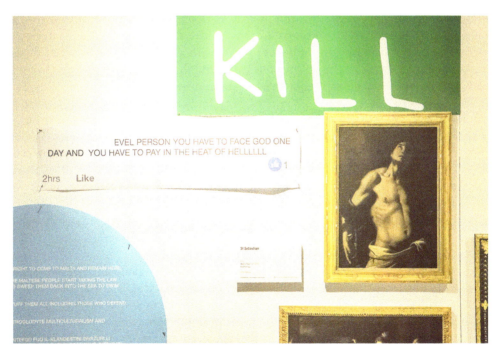

Figure 1.3: Hate speech in *Dehumaneation* beside a reproduction of *Saint Sebastian* (1694) by Mattia Preti and Bottega.

image of the Grand Master who led his knights to victory in that siege – a victory we still celebrate in Malta. Alternatively, the words "Shoot to Kill," lifted from an online comment about migrants arriving in Malta, hovered above a reproduction of a seventeenth-century painting of St. Sebastian pierced by arrows. This is how art investigates its own historical relationship with violence.

Yet, how could we shift this trans-historical examination of a profoundly distorted society beyond a public institution like a museum? This spirit of self-critique and institutional critique became a central topic of discussion. Institutional critique has been theorized as an ethical interrogation of the institution's power relations and its dealings with its public (Marstine, 2017). *Dehumaneation* was essentially about the need to resist the profoundly unethical and populist instrumentalization of love (of one's country, nation, people and so on) with a culture of hate that justifies itself on the basis of historical premises, constructed around notions of territory, faith and exclusion.

But another question crops up: What kind of ethics do we need to challenge the contemporary weaponization of nation that you speak of? This could not simply be an ethics founded on the same kind of moral wrath that led past artists to depict the brutal torture of a virgin martyr like St. Agatha. What separates our times from theirs is the way images, desire and hatred are communicated to audiences today, via the internet and the proliferation of social media. Our approach to ethics was informed by our knowledge that the hate speech we dragged into the exhibition is a by-product of our digital age and its distancing effect on people and their next-door neighbours. In this sense, our strategy was probably closer to Franco Berardi "Bifo's" ironic ethics (2011), resisting a mediated hatred by invading the audience's senses with a maximalist or Baroque design composed of different narratives, time zones, colours, shapes, thicknesses and textures. These non-verbal cues transmitted a call to action at the level of pure sensibility, not morality per se.

Shaun: These Old Master paintings formed a critical part on these walls bursting at the seams, which came together as a giant puzzle of the familiar–unfamiliar, known–unknown, the historical, the brutal contemporary – the move from "global colonialism" to the current period of "global coloniality" (Grosfoguel, 2011). Indeed, this exhibition was about lineages in Malta, the traceability of power and manifestations of hate over space and time, as well as resistance (textual, material, etc.). The latter was evident in the comments online by viewers, and a clear ideological positionality (mine and yours) without needing to spell things out, yet without resorting to abstraction. Importantly, we brought familiar and unfamiliar images and imagery into the field of significance because much of the very familiar (notably, religious imagery) within the Maltese field of vision may not be known (the story, that is) epistemologically. In *Dehumaneation*, we created effective linkages and juxtapositions to connect, explain and contest. For example, St. Agatha is carved into the stone entrance to the historical town of Mdina, but many may not have quite figured out that those are her own severed breasts on a platter, severed for refusing the sexual advances of the governor. Her crime was only that of being very attractive and refusing to oblige sexually when requested to do so, to be tamed and controlled in a way a woman was assumed to behave. We represented St. Agatha through a reproduction and also a painting of mine on the same wall, flanked by an online comment by a prolife man attacking a prochoice woman activist by resorting to mocking her breasts, stating that the least they (prochoice activists) could do was to possibly get a nicer "pair" as opposed to "this headless libtard." This renowned Maltese prochoice activist and academic existed only (it seems) through her body – meant to appease, to accommodate, to serve, to reproduce. Served on a platter of misogyny, she should be punished for refusing to obey, to be controlled and to be a good and "proper" woman.

In similar ways, the Maltese are accustomed to images of the darker invading Turks in the churches or in school textbooks, accompanied by the supposedly saving images of the not-so-dark Catholic Knights occupying main squares in the capital city. Yet what emerges very clearly is that the narrative continues to be spun in many respects – re-enacted, reshaped, yet the convenient motives remain. These include profound misogyny and oppression of women, the extraordinary racism articulated towards the collective category "Arab" rampant in Malta, and the incessant obsession with whitening ourselves to prove we are really European, where our history of mixture becomes a liability rather than a resource. The Knights, who historians attest did not treat the Maltese too kindly, to say the least, are celebrated and revered for liberating us from the darker bodies of the Turks. The figure of the colonizing Knight of St. John in shining armour came to represent a proud national identity, and for the far right, an icon of resistance towards those coming by boat: the "invaders." The George Cross awarded by the British Empire, too, is stripped of its colonial baggage of oppression. The "civilising" mission introduced racial Otherness as the ideological impetus for domination (see Quijano, 2008). Contemporary art has much to learn from the past, but also a lot of reckoning to do: to then educate about it, challenge it, dislocate it and reframe a present that is, at the very least, informed.

Raphael: The spinning of historical narratives is one of the critical junctures where education in resistance becomes not only relevant but necessary. We opted to include a number of corollary public events that asked questions we had encountered along the way; questions about an obsolete art world or obsolete institutions, about education as a platform for critique and redefinition of society, about the strange balance of ethics and aesthetics in a project like this. We organized online public debates, aired live on Facebook, as well as some exhibition tours with small groups followed by open discussions. Taking the discussion to Facebook was a deliberate provocation. It felt a bit like we were diving right back into the source of the hate speech. All the participants in these discussions – authors, academics, students, members of the general public and activists, including the prochoice activist you just spoke about – negotiated amongst themselves and with us their understanding of a gallery as a space of encounter, argumentation and learning. But this encounter extended itself beyond the museum's walls into the field of social media. We weren't targeted by anyone in particular, but perhaps what we really wanted was to render a safe institution unsafe. We know that art institutions often fail to engage seriously with migration, exclusions and discrimination. Chantal Mouffe (2013) has written of a more radical route for museums and cultural spaces, one that connects artistic ideas with localized political issues, multiplying public spaces and possibilities of debate in the process. Through a process of critical pedagogy (Giroux, 2011) in which civic society and artists examine struggles that straddle their fields of practice, museums can reconnect to the public realm and trace new strategies for social engagement.

Similarly, we approached these educational encounters in a spirit of debate that was intended to provoke further debate, deliberately mixing old and new, artistic and political questions. Nina Simon (2010) has written about "provocation through juxtaposition" (p. 158) in relation to exhibition design, referring to the placement of very different objects in close proximity to elicit new questions and responses from viewers. For us, this juxtaposition was not only carried out curatorially: with the inclusion of Old Master paintings, it was also an integral component of the exhibition's public programme in which we debated questions like – Does hate speech affect specific strata of Maltese society more than others? Is education efficient as a mitigation measure against hate speech?

But I'm also interested in your experience of these juxtapositions as an artist. Were the various talks we held an addendum to the "main event," or were they a process of interaction that the exhibition couldn't really do without?

Shaun: To be honest, I really do not know. As you explain, the reaction was far different from what we may have anticipated, not least because we most likely attracted people with very similar ideological beliefs, and importantly from the same cultural background, similar interests, with cultural capital: people, to use Bourdieu's (1977) words, occupying the same habitus. Wrestling for attention, too, online and offline is also something to contend with. Reflecting back, it feels like many of the components, including the talk, were necessary to us within the whole complex (yet incomplete) narrative we wanted to pedantically explore and put forward, and we only had to tell ourselves where and when we needed to stop. The issue was one of how to set up a well-researched piece. The debates streamed on Facebook attracted a substantial number of views, and there was some engagement through comments, but I feel that this, too, was a siloed effort. Our marginal contribution, I believe, was not so much in the debates that were generated. In fact, I think much of what we did was actually speaking to our own bubble. The contribution was in raising questions and pushing the boundaries of what is and should be permissible, if not expected, within an artistic space that may be depoliticized, and/or where talking politics may be not so common or even discouraged. One merit of *Dehumaneation* was that it highlighted how hate and dehumanization transcend class. The implication is that genuine and transformative resistance can only happen through an ontological approach that sees beyond borders, but which knows and is capable of navigating their complex crevices.

Raphael: Yes, I agree that this transformative resistance must be reflected in an activist stance in artmaking and exhibition-making. Otherwise, we run the risk of turning a display of hateful language and acts of oppression into a simplistic expression of "free speech." As you said, this would ultimately reflect a patronizing state of benevolence. By simply being "free" to express themselves, artists can unconsciously tick another box in the bureaucratic structures of cultural policy and inclusion. Ironically, their freedom becomes a kind of barrier that distances them from the root causes of injustice. As for the role of education in exhibitions and cultural spaces like this, it remains inadequate as long as it sees itself as a "neutral" discipline. If art cannot afford to be neutral, educators must think of themselves as artists. By doing so, they not only cultivate learning but renovate it.

References

Berardi, F. (2011). *Ironic ethics: 100 notes – 100 thoughts*. Hatje Cantz Verlag.

Betcher, S. (2004). Monstrosities, miracles, and mission: Religion and the politics of disablement. In C. Keller, M. Nausner, & M. Rivera (Eds.), *Postcolonial theologies: Divinity and empire* (pp. 79–99). Chalice.

Bourdieu, P. (1977). *Outline of a theory of practice*. Cambridge University Press.

Dworkin, R. (2006). A new map of censorship. *Index on Censorship, 35*(1), 130–133. https://www.indexoncensorship.org/2013/02/ronal-dworkin-free-speech-censorship/ (Original work published 1994)

Fanon, F. (1967). *The wretched of the earth*. Penguin.

Geertz, C. (1973). *The interpretation of cultures*. Basic Books.

Gerber, G. (2000). Doing Christianity and Europe: An inquiry into memory, boundary and truth practices in Malta. In B. Strath (Ed.), *Europe and the Other and Europe as the Other* (pp. 229–278). Peter Lang.

Giroux, H. A. (2011). *On critical pedagogy*. Continuum Books.

Grech, S. (2015). Decolonizing Eurocentric disability studies: Why colonialism matters in the disability and global South debate. *Social Identities: Journal for the Study of Race, Nation and Culture, 21*(1), 6–21. https://doi.org/10.1080/13504630.2014.995347

Grosfoguel, R. (2011). Decolonizing post-colonial studies and paradigms of political economy: Transmodernity, decolonial thinking, and global coloniality. *TRANSMODERNITY: Journal of Peripheral Cultural Production of the Luso-Hispanic World, 1*(1), 1–37.

Lemaire, L. (2019). The European dispositif of border control in Malta. Migrants' experiences of a securitized borderland. *Journal of Borderlands Studies, 34*(5), 717–732. https://doi.org/10.1080/08865655.2018.1457973

Marstine, J. (2017). *Critical practice: Artists, museums, ethics*. Routledge.

Mouffe, C. (2013). *Agonistics: Thinking the world politically*. Verso.

Osborne, P. (2013). *Anywhere or not at all: Philosophy of contemporary art*. Verso.
Pisani, M. (2012). Addressing the "citizenship assumption" in critical pedagogy: Exploring the case of rejected female sub-Saharan African asylum seekers in Malta. *Power and Education*, 4(2), 185-195. https://doi.org/10.2304/power.2012.4.2.185
Quijano, A. (2000). Coloniality of power, Eurocentrism, and Latin America. *Nepantla: Views from South, 1*(3), 533-580.
Quijano, A. (2008). Coloniality of power, Eurocentrism, and social classification. In M. Moraña, E. Dussel, & C. A. Jauregui (Eds.), *Coloniality at large: Latin America and the postcolonial debate* (pp. 181-224). Duke University Press.
Simon, N. (2010). *The participatory museum*. Museum 2.0.

Chapter 2

Museums as Intersectional Spaces for Artivist Solidarity

Riikka Haapalainen, Anniina Suominen, Tiina Pusa, Jasmin Järvinen and Melanie Orenius

This chapter responds to the themes of anticolonial museum work and pedagogical sensibilities by exploring two separate but intertwined art education projects (cases) carried out in collaboration with the Art Education Programme at Aalto University, the Finnish National Gallery's Ateneum Art Museum (later Ateneum), the Amos Rex art museum and individuals associated with local non-governmental organizations. This collaboration is founded on the university's societal role of collaborating with partner institutions from various cultural sectors with whom there is a shared interest to develop critical, impactful and research-based art education and museum pedagogies.

Moreover, the collaboration with museums and the university has created varied modes of working and thinking together as allyships (Ng et al., 2017) on issues in urgent need of critical rethinking that museums are unable to undertake alone. The cases presented here were seminars and a workshop series based upon the need for museum professionals to generate opportunities for further contemplation of complicated, complex, partially uncomfortable and uncertain, even unintentionally discriminatory and racist, contents and practices. All these are embedded in the museum collections, exhibition practices, communications with audiences and pedagogical work. The cases were: (1) *Queering/Reconceiving the Museum* (2019) and (2) *The Egypt of Glory exhibition* (2021).

Case 1: Queering/Reconceiving the Museum. This project and the consequent seminar, museum tours and workshops took place in 2019. The seminar was hosted by the Ateneum Art Museum, part of the Finnish National Gallery. The project's central aim was to support collective work to advance gender and sexual diversity and democratic cultures within the ethical, cultural and operational environment of the Finnish museum field. The project was implemented by faculty from Aalto University and professionals from the Ateneum Museum, in cooperation with the Culture for All Service and the Finnish Museums Association. As part of the seminar day, normative practices and attitudes as well as new openings were collectively and critically examined by museum professionals invited from all museum institutions in Finland. By identifying oppressive structures and sharing practices through which museum professionals are working actively against such structures, the aim was to draw attention to the power museums hold in creating and maintaining normative histories as well as striving to dismantle them. The *Queering/Reconceiving the Museum* project was a nominee for the national Pedaali Annual Award in Museum Pedagogy in 2020.

Case 2: The Egypt of Glory. This exhibition, which took place in the Amos Rex art museum (from October 2020 to March 2021), was the context for a workshop series wherein facilitators Melanie Orenius and Kataja Ekholm engaged art museum staff – including a curatorial team, a conservator, an Egyptologist, public programme personnel, technical staff and a communications team – in exploring the possibilities for new object relations (Ekholm & Orenius, 2021). *The Egypt of Glory* exhibition consisted of ancient Egyptian artefacts on loan from an Italian institution, Museo Egizio. Ekholm and Orenius engaged participants in discussions about anticolonialism within a museum by working with the objects acquired for Europe through colonial means and raising questions about violent colonial histories and the persistent continued logic of coloniality in exhibition spaces. The workshops focused on complex feelings and the possibility to initiate change by attending to those emotions, as well as by assuming responsibility and taking accountability. A significant emotion was grief, seen to be an essential element within a process of re-narrating a colonialist legacy as well as a thematic opening for exploring alternative relationships to the exhibited objects and their histories. Ekholm and Orenius (2021) studied these thematics further within their thesis, which was part of a larger *Shadow of Egypt* research and study project carried out in collaboration with Aalto University and Amos Rex. *The Shadow of Egypt* project won the national Pedaali Annual Award in Museum Pedagogy in 2021.

Both museums, Ateneum and Amos Rex, are located in the Helsinki city centre. Although the museums are almost neighbours, they are quite different in their collections, exhibition policies and audience profiles. Being the first public art museum in Finland and the first institution in Finland to employ a museum educator to mediate art, Ateneum has a long tradition and carries significant responsibilities nationally. Amos Rex is owned by a private association (https://konstsamfundet.fi/). It opened in late 2018 and has youth and children as its special target audience groups.

Both cases focus on different but intersecting aspects of equity and social justice (e.g. Nussbaum, 2012; Sen, 2012). They were built on antinormative, antioppressive, sensuous and sensible arts education pedagogies (Gershon, 2019; Kumashiro, 2002) and critical museum studies (Byrne et al., 2018; Janes & Sandell, 2019), which implies this approach is the antithesis of the ideologies that have built and maintained colonialist and discriminatory practices and enabled further oppression. Rather, this approach is sensitive to the complexity of the histories/herstories/theirstories; sensitive to the ethical and emotional issues involved; and further, founded on the understanding that all people's intentions, aims and participation are grounded in a holistic sense of being. Both cases are centred on caring pedagogies that address the underlying injustice and inequities as well as aiming to actively trouble and dismantle these, attending to the participants and co-learners holistically by aiming to generate spaces for solidarity.

In this chapter, we challenge the oppressive practices of museum institutions from an antinormative (queer) and anticolonial stance. *The Egypt of Glory* is only one typical example of a blockbuster exhibition that served its visitors with an ideologically safe and mainstreamed content, while its troubling colonialist foundations were concealed. We claim that the ethically troubling, colonizing content needs to be systematically scrutinized to change these practices (Procter, 2020). Similar examples can be identified from the Ateneum museum, which participates in Pride Week events but does not systematically question the national narratives that Ateneum and the Finnish National Gallery help to maintain, besides their harmful and oppressive implications for many. People identifying with broader sexual, gender or cultural diversity, other than the dominant majority, find it difficult if not even impossible to identify with the normative practices and rhetoric of the museums. Museums have established feminist and queer tours and support events that focus on dialogues about diversity. However, collectively, we need to work more systematically and much harder on our prevailing attitudes and practices until we reach more inclusive museum cultures and institutes that feel more welcoming to inherent diversity.

These cases and the consequent writing process challenge the prevailing binary divisions within museum knowledges and their inscribed hegemonic, hierarchical structures between people, objects and knowledges. For example, we note the separation between expert knowledge and so-called dilettante or amateur knowledge, or plain objects and objects of cultural heritage and value – even the divisions between museum staff and museum visitors. These challenges are not seen as external but primarily targeted at the authors themselves and their participation in the renewal and maintenance of these structures. We, the authors, strive to generate possibilities and opportunities for museum professionals and educators to collectively uncover and unlearn the discriminatory structures, politics and practices of museums and art institutions, to find ways to dismantle them and to formulate ways of articulating case-specific alternatives to them.

Universities have their societal role besides research and pedagogical tasks. This intersection is where we met as authors. The MA thesis projects of both museum cases provide a platform for wider discussions on critical museum practices. Advisors and students came together for a learning collective. During the writing process of this text, students became alumnae, and previous roles as advisors and students unravelled. Simultaneously, questions that were at first research questions in different MA theses became more shared and positioned as a wider societal challenge.

Working in collaboration to establish anticolonial and queerer museum practice

The presented cases reflect the current anticolonial struggle to rethink museums and museum work from within. They ask what is worth preserving in museum practices and what should be radically rethought. In our study, radical rethinking means a critical reading of all museum activities and knowledges through and with artistic, activist and antinormative pedagogies. From a theoretical perspective, anticolonial theory and queer pedagogy question what we perceived as socially normative or generally accepted, leading to a critical examination of social and institutional hegemonies and oppressive structures – and especially of our own privileges (Choi et al., 2018; Kumashiro, 2002). We suggest that acknowledgement of oppression and criticality towards museums' exhibitions and audience work is not sufficient to dismantle oppressive practices, as museums were founded upon these very same oppressive structures (Kumashiro, 2002; Smith, 2020). To instigate a systematic change, queering approaches are vital. The authors understand the term "queer" in its broader sense, meaning both the diversity of gender and sexuality and as non-normative feminist and activist aspirations of constantly questioning, looking beyond and troubling what we already know (Kumashiro, 2002; Suominen & Pusa, 2018).

The orientation in our cases, and within this study, is rooted in anticolonial studies, queer feminism, politics of solidarity, posthuman new materialism and intersectional feminism (Butler, 1990; Cameron, 2018; Kumashiro, 2002; Laitinen & Pessi, 2010; Rossi, 2015; Rousell et al., 2020). In both cases, our theoretical frames guided the planning, facilitation and realization from within. During the consequent writing and sharing process, rather than performing a systemic comparison or evaluation of the two cases, we used our dialogic writing space and our conversations to identify resonances, disconnects and conflicts that were previously unrecognized or suppressed to avoid acknowledgement of the uncomfortable, disruptive and discomforting. Through this, two perspectives emerged: (1) *Solidarity in speech: creating spaces for sharing* and (2) *Please, do not touch: Solidarity in object relations*. These perspectives are discussed more closely in the concluding sections of this chapter.

Solidarity in speech: Creating spaces for sharing

We understand that solidarity is a political strategy to recognize oppression and create spaces of resistance against structural oppression (Dai, 2016). When people with shared interests come together, new connections within thematic framings might emerge. According to Laitinen and Pessi (2010), solidarity both *appears* in acts and collaboration and *strengthens* through actions and collaborations. While conventional solidarity might take the shape of charity and volunteering or expressions of goodwill, for example by donating money or time (Lahusen & Grasso, 2018), we propose an alternative understanding of solidarity, which could mean "artivist" (Mouffe, 2013) solidarity.

Our projects aimed at creating spaces for professionals to reflect on their complex experiences, as well as offering support and openness to diverse perspectives without judgement or without relying on normative thinking. Being together and sharing experiences created room for a new understanding and a sense of togetherness to emerge. Acknowledging complex and often contradictory emotions and reactions played a crucial role in these processes.

One of the main goals for the *Queering/Reconceiving the Museum* seminar at Ateneum was to bring together professionals to share and to see if a sense of solidarity in the process of change could be created. The aim was to facilitate a seminar that would invite museum professionals and art educators to come up with a common vocabulary and understanding of queer pedagogy that could aid in creating more inclusive museum spaces and practices. In one of the workshops, participants were led to discuss their organizations' weaknesses in relation to diversity as well as in relation to the public's expectations. The group's shared consensus was that the desirable changes were slow and bureaucratic, and the budgets allocated to specific tasks could not meet the operational needs imposed by the ideologies. While they hoped for the museum to become more diverse and equal in practices and appeal, they acknowledged that the staff was predominantly homogenous, identifying as white and middle-aged. An organization's equity and equality strategy and implementation plan were seen as vital for the institutions to become allies for diverse voices and perspectives.

Post seminar, we (the project facilitators and three of the authors of this chapter) were left to ponder whether museums can truly diversify their practices and mission – if museum environments can be restructured so as to not further trigger minority stress, especially in those visitors who identify as belonging to several marginalized groups. Further troubling contemplation led us to ponder what inclusiveness and inclusivity really mean and whether this is even an achievable aim, considering the institutions' strong oppressive histories and continued practices. However, the activist and artistic potentiality of queer pedagogy was not fully actualized, as the "actions" occurred mainly in a speech and in articulations of queer orientations and pedagogies. Much was still lost, as the rich material and sensuous conditions and aspects of a museum work were not yet explored. Solidarity was manifested primarily in speech and initiated dialogues.

"Please Do Not Touch": Solidarity in object relations

In new materialist readings, people connect to and understand their surroundings through touch (Barad, 2015; Puig de la Bellacasa, 2017), yet touch and close physical proximity with the objects tends to be the primary prohibition in museum spaces. This prohibition is a direct act of power, as museums decide who gets to touch museum objects or even the casing protecting them. Some objects defined as less valuable can be touched by anyone, while other objects are not even to be seen by visitors; thousands of objects deemed irreplaceable are conserved in storage. As a result, it may be deemed that such practices disregard the power of objects in bringing people together (see Latour, 2005) and in creating communities of solidarity.

In the workshops organized by Ekholm and Orenius (2021), the participants and the makers of the *Egypt of Glory* exhibition were encouraged to consider the displayed objects as beings that contain all their own history/herstory/theirstory and also consider their creators, users, previous owners and robbers as well as the histories of their materials – possibly even their feelings. During the workshops, the notion of value became a question of historical value, which in turn raised questions about whose histories they were perceived to carry or communicate.

Besides the value and the stories associated with the objects, the participants examined the importance of touch in creating meaningful and emotional connections with the objects and with the fingers and hands that have previously touched them. Touch was defined as physical, emotional, social and political. Touches were also recognized as leaving marks.

When touch is prohibited, confined, structured or framed, sensuous being and relating with objects, people and histories/herstories/theirstories is restricted. In museum pedagogical practices, this indicates a denial of the importance of emotions and sensual presence in favour of the traditional gaze and cognition (e.g. the disembodied eye; Staniszewski, 1998). Not being able to touch and to be in touch with the museum content dismisses the diverse embodied experiences of museum audiences, and further, deprives exhibits of their material potentialities and agencies (Barad, 2015; Haapalainen, 2021).

Further, touch has often been understood narrowly as being limited to touching museum artefacts with the fingers or hands or accidentally bumping into an object or a display case, and with these assumptions come the associated prohibitions that claim to protect the artefact to be looked at or contemplated. However, being in touch with an object is a much broader notion, both multisensory and intersectional (resembling the forces of diffraction described by Barad, 2003). In one of the Amos Rex workshops, the museum professionals engaged in an exercise involving clay. During this exercise, they silently moulded clay in the presence of ancient objects. Afterwards, the participants shared their thoughts about their clay objects and about the experience of visiting the exhibition by touch. They were asked if they would want others to touch their object and in what way. The reactions and responses varied. This initiated discussions about the makers of the ancient artefacts: Were they meant to be preserved? Have they been misinterpreted? Who determines their value?

Conclusions

Above all, dismantling oppressive ideals and structures requires action. Therefore, antinormative and anticolonial museum work calls for the intersectional recognition of current privileges and the social, economic and cultural structures that maintain these privileges. In practice, this would mean troubling the traditions and actively unlearning processes (Choi et al., 2018; Kumashiro, 2002; Spivak, 2011). This eventually leads to disruptive and discomforting knowledges, interstices and, through these feelings, finally unlearning. Kumashiro (2002) describes disruptive feelings as a desirable part of antioppressive education, a way to change what we thought we already knew.

These approaches introduce non-verbal, embodied knowledge and sensuous epistemic orientation. They account for and enable embodied, emotional, sensuous relationality, being-with objects and others. They also actively question stagnant ideologies and normative practices that have created systems of oppression, marginalization and colonialism to continue and instigate further tragedies.

For example, in the *Egypt of Glory*-related workshops, the staff searched for ways to be in solidarity with objects and their colonial histories. Ekholm and Orenius designed the workshops to explore feelings regarding ancient Egyptian objects. Grief in particular became a central emotion and also a possible tool for anticolonial work. In this context, grief as an active and attentive process can change the ability to take on accountability, to be present with the emotions rather than inclined to flee or respond with defensiveness. Grief is not one sentiment but a constellation of many transitory emotions. Grief is a temporal process; to grieve is to create new relations and to bring new diversity into being with others and into personal and communal narrations. During a workshop, when discussing pain, grief and accountability, a member of the museum staff commented that apart from sorrow and shame, they found relief in the collective aspect of grieving.

For museum pedagogies, creating shared spaces for grieving introduces the notion of care (Puig de la Bellacasa, 2017). In practice, this means actualizing the gestures and actions of solidarity in the physical museum spaces, in the attitudes, rhythms, gazes, sentiments and ethical relations with and to others and the marginalized others or subalterns (see Spivak, 2011), bringing us to the need for artivist solidarity. Art educators are in key positions when it comes to audience engagement, but whether the contents of the museum are accessible or inclusive has to be found in the foundations of the museum: the curation, the texts, the choices of exhibitions and collaborators, recruitment and funding, to name but a few. However, to instigate true change, the conversation and scrutiny must permeate the institution as a whole. One must actively ponder even the most complex issues that may seem unresolvable and that do not readily submit to resolution. For example, within a museum context, what are the possible experiences of queer youth of immigrant backgrounds in relation to cultural heritage, and how might we overcome the forces of marginalization and repetitive discrimination?

Our cases urge us to understand museum practices and collaborations as intersectional, as a systemic whole where every decision and all minor details either work against or struggle towards a more antihegemonic, artivist and solidarity museum. Intersectionality can be seen as a transformative force to undermine the central operational logics of museum and exhibition institutions and create simultaneous, alternative, temporal and open centres. It enables those ghosts and gasps, vibes and vibrations that actively question and requestion the museum institution to foster active solidarity. Intersectionality entails understanding that queer and anticolonial approaches should not only permeate museums but be established as a foundational orientation, guiding all museum activities and agencies as well as collaborations among universities, non-governmental organizations and museum professionals. For solidarity to be actualized, we have to unbuild, unlearn and undo the oppressive and hegemonic structures and categories of histories, museums, languages, human–human and human–non-human relations. This process of un-doing with care, grief and artivist solidarity is what we suggest as a pivotal anticolonial and queering action in museum education.

References

Barad, K. (2003). Posthumanist performativity: Toward an understanding of how matter comes to matter. *Signs: Journal of Women in Culture and Society*, 28(3), 801–831.

Barad, K. (2015). On touching – The inhuman that therefore I am (v1.1). In S. Witzgall & K. Stakemeier (Eds.), *Power of material/politics of materiality* (pp. 153–164). Diaphanes.

Butler, J. (1990). *Gender trouble. Feminism, and the subversion of identity*. Routledge.

Byrne, J., Morgan, E., Paynter, N., Sánches de Serdio, A., & Železnik, A. (Eds.). (2018). *The constituent museum. Constellations of knowledge, politics and mediation. A generator of social change*. Valiz & L'Internationale.

Cameron, F. (2018). Posthuman museum practices. In R. Braidotti & M. Hlavajova (Eds.), *Posthuman glossary* (pp. 349–352). Bloomsbury Publishing.

Choi, B., Krauss, A., & van der Heide, Y. (Eds.). (2018). *Unlearning exercises: Art organizations as sites for unlearning*. Casco Art Institute: Working for the Commons & Valiz.

Dai, Y. (2016). Bridging the divide in feminism with transcultural feminist solidarity. In E. Chowdhury & L. Philipose (Eds.), *Dissident friendships: Feminism, imperialism, and transnational solidarity* (pp. 65–118). University of Illinois Press.

Ekholm, K., & Orenius, M. (2021). *A fish, a goddess, and a friend: How three ancient artefacts created a possibility for anticolonial understanding in the Amos Rex art museum* [Master's thesis, Aalto University]. https://aaltodoc2.org.aalto.fi/bitstream/handle/123456789/109808/master_Laukkanen_Roope_2021.pdf

Gershon, W. (Ed.). (2019). *Sensuous curriculum: Politics and the senses in education*. Information Age Publishing.

Haapalainen, R. (2021). Transsituational objects and things in participatory art. *Tahiti, 10*(4), 156–171. https://doi.org/10.23995/tht.103186

Janes, R., & Sandell, R. (Eds.). (2019). *Museum activism*. Routledge.

Järvinen, J. (2020). Queering/reconceiving the museum project and queer pedagogical practices in museums' audience work [Unpublished Master's thesis, Aalto University].

Kumashiro, K. (2002). *Troubling education. Queer activism and antioppressive pedagogy*. Routledge.

Lahusen, C., & Grasso, M. (2018). Solidarity in Europe–European solidarity: An introduction. In C. Lahusen & M. Grasso (Eds.), *Solidarity in Europe: Citizens' responses in times of crisis* (pp. 1–18). Palgrave Macmillan.

Laitinen, A., & Pessi, A. B. (2010). Vaatiiko solidaarisuus auttamaan? Solidaarisuus suomalaisten auttamisteoissa ja-asenteissa. *Janus, 18*(2), 355–373.

Latour, B. (2005). *Reassembling the social. An introduction to Actor-Network-Theory*. Oxford University Press.

Mouffe, C. (2013). Institutions as sites for agonistic intervention. In P. Gielen (Ed.), *Institutional attitudes: Instituting art in a flat world*. Valiz.

Ng, W., Ware, S. M., & Greenberg, A. (2017). Activating diversity and inclusion: A blueprint for museum educators as allies and change makers. *Journal of Museum Education, 42*, 142–154. https://doi.org/10.1080/10598650.2017.1306664

Nussbaum, M. C. (2012). Capabilities, entitlements, rights: Supplementation and critique. In T. Campbell (Ed.), *Justice and the capabilities approach* (pp. 173–188). Routledge.

Procter, A. (2020). *The whole picture. The colonial story of the art in our museums and why we need to talk about it*. Cassell.

Puig de la Bellacasa, M. (2017). *Matters of care. Speculative ethics in more than human worlds*. University of Minnesota Press.

Rossi, L.-M. (2015). *Muuttuva sukupuoli. Seksuaalisuuden, luokan ja värin politiikkaa*. Gaudeamus.

Rousell, D., Hohti, R., MacLure, M., & Chalk, H. L. (2020). Blots on the Anthropocene: Micropolitical interventions with young people in a university museum. *Cultural Studies – Critical Methodologies, 21*(1), 27–40. https://doi.org/10.1177/153270862095

Sen, A. (2012). Elements of a theory of human rights. In T. Campbell (Ed.), *Justice and the capabilities approach* (pp. 221–263). Routledge.

Smith, M. (Ed.). (2020). *Decolonizing: The curriculum, the museum, and the mind*. Vilnius Academy of Arts Press.

Spivak, G. C. (2011). *An aesthetic education in the era of globalization*. Harvard University Press.

Staniszewski, M. A. (1998). *The power of display. A history of exhibition installations at the Museum of Modern Art*. The MIT Press.

Suominen, A., & Pusa, T. (Eds.). (2018). *Feminism and queer in art education*. Aalto ARTS Books.

Chapter 3

Decolonizing Benjamin Franklin House Through Comics: Reflections and Potential

Kremena Dimitrova

How do the pressing contemporary challenges to morality and responsibility with regard to equality prompt us to rethink the prevalent colonial texts and representations in the museum and heritage sector? This chapter is an artful endeavour to chart new pathways to colonial knowledge as part of my ongoing interdisciplinary comics-based Ph.D. project exploring the use of the intuitive and reflective alongside the rational and analytical. In so doing, my research contributes to the growing body of artistic work concerned with revisiting and confronting the ways in which some people and events have been remembered and others disregarded in history (Godfrey, 2007).

My study serves as a revisionist exchange between an independent illustrator-as-historian and the question of what decolonial learning in a 21st-century biographical museum could entail. Using Benjamin Franklin House as a case study, I am exploring ways in which comics-based research methodologies can participate in representing and commemorating the intangible colonial traces in the museum by focusing on one of its marginalized 18th-century enslaved residents (Dimitrova, 2023). I recognize that looking across disciplinary boundaries can offer not only new ways of seeing the visible but also new ways of seeing the invisible in history. I argue that creative interventions as routes for research enquiry into the layered pasts of historic houses like Benjamin Franklin House can help decolonize and democratize them as important sites of learning about the colonial pasts.

Case study: Benjamin Franklin House and slavery

Hidden behind 36 Craven Street's small door is one of London's most treasured Georgian heritage gems. Dating back to 1730, Benjamin Franklin House became a biographical museum in 2006 and has since been enriching our knowledge about the statesman, inventor, scientist and one of the Founding Fathers of the United States of America, Benjamin Franklin (see Benjamin Franklin House, 2019). This prominent 18th-century historical figure was a lodger in the house from 1757 to 1775. I became involved with Benjamin Franklin House in 2015 when I was commissioned as an illustrator-in-residence to research and visually communicate Benjamin Franklin's affairs in London. I delivered creative workshops and developed educational projections and a children's sticker book to enhance the museum's historical offerings for younger audiences. Since then, my research has extended to exploring the house's lesser-known inhabitants.

Like many buildings, at first glance, Benjamin Franklin House seems unconnected to slavery: at least, not until one considers the historical period in question, the 18th century, or indeed the various roles Benjamin Franklin played as a diplomat in London whose wealth had accumulated on the back of slavery "as buyer, seller, and master of slaves" in Colonial America (Nash, 2006, p. 620). There is yet another even more direct link between the museum and slavery. During the nearly 16-year period, Benjamin Franklin lodged in the house, at different times he also shared the dwelling with other residents, including his son William and two enslaved persons called Peter and King. In that era, Peter was deemed to "belong" to Benjamin Franklin and King was William's "property." They were brought by the Franklins to 36 Craven Street in 1757 during one of Benjamin Franklin's voyages from the American Colonies (Nash, 2006; Newman, 2019). Soon enough, King, who favoured the name John King, "ABSENTED from his Master's Service." This notice appeared twice in *The Public Advertiser* newspaper on 16 February 1762 and 13 April 1762 as part of runaway advertisements published for the capture of the boy. The advertisements can be found in a digital database entitled *Runaway Slaves in Britain: Bondage, Freedom and Race in the Eighteenth Century*, compiled by researchers at the University of Glasgow.[1]

In a letter Benjamin Franklin wrote to his wife Deborah, he described John King as being "of little Use, and often in Mischief" (as cited in Newman, 2019, p. 1140). This could be one of the reasons why the Franklins did not go to all lengths to reclaim him even though they had discovered his whereabouts. In his poem *Benjamin Franklin, the lady and a runaway enslaved boy named King*, H. E. Ross creatively evidences the runaway's journeys in Suffolk (Noise of Art, 2020). John King lived with and served a woman who contributed to his education (Nash, 2006). Although there are very few existing historical traces about John King, they prove to be captivating. The runaway, however, does not appear in any of the histories Benjamin Franklin House communicates to the public. Taking equality and inclusivity into consideration, John King's omission is rather problematic, and my research serves as a means through which I can broaden the historical offering at the museum. Madge Dresser and Andrew Hann (2013) have stressed that there are wider societal implications of the judgements we make when deciding whose story to tell regarding a historic property, stating:

> The identification of particular individuals of colour associated with that property might well have a particular resonance for those members of the public for whom a visit to an historic property might afford not merely a day out but an encounter with heartfelt questions of family history, identity and belonging. And that personalised connection has an impact beyond those who count themselves among the descendants of the enslaved and the colonised to reach into our very notions of who 'belongs' to Britain.
>
> (p. 14)

Historians like Hayden White (1978) have similarly asserted that what we exclude from our narrative representations of the past carries greater significance than what we include in them. In her chapter of the book *Slavery and the British Country House*, Caroline Bressey (2013) calls for interventions that can acknowledge and represent colonial absences. I argue that where history has overlooked John King and the countless "absent" others like him, creative approaches can be employed as a means of filling the historical gaps. In so doing, I am reminded of how White (1988) understood art's usefulness not only for describing the past but also as a valuable method for analysing the past by stating that some things can only be conveyed visually. Peter Turchi (2004) has further highlighted art's potential not only to change what we see but also how we see. The different ways of seeing can lead to reflections, questioning and revision. When it comes down to slavery, revision can cause an imaginative return to the past to review and even modify the ways in which that same past is understood and remembered in the present. According to Karen Harvey (2016), "it is as a literary practice that the discipline of history becomes an act of representation; it is as a creative practice that the discipline of history becomes an imaginative way of knowing" (p. 14).

Why should we learn about John King, the rebellious runaway?

This research examines the combined effects of creative and historical ways of knowing and learning about slavery in Benjamin Franklin House. By focusing on re-presenting John King, I challenge the promotion and sustenance of white cultural hegemony in Benjamin Franklin House and as such respond to Tehmina Goskar's (2020) call for small museums to "spearhead [the] drive to decolonise museum practice" (n.p.). My research also responds to the public reckoning and interventions concerned with the rethinking of colonial histories and legacies in the United Kingdom that have proliferated in recent decades (Aldrich, 2010; Cubitt, 2012; Drayton, 2019; Dresser & Hann, 2013; Giblin et al., 2019). Movements such as Black Lives Matter and Rhodes Must Fall have prompted the museum and heritage sector to revisit its colonial links and to seek out effective and affective ways to communicate them through a process of decolonization to reflect the needs and expectations of contemporary and multi-cultural audiences. According to the Museum Association (2020), "Decolonization is not simply the relocation of a statue or an object" but an ongoing process (n.p.). A statue could be removed, relocated or destroyed, but when it comes down to a historic property such as Benjamin Franklin House, this would not be realistic nor sensible. Moreover, the removal or destruction of the tributes to colonizers not only keeps the attention firmly on the colonizers but also helps conceal or erase their actions. At the same time, the existence of the individuals they enslaved remains unchanged; they continue to be absent, hidden, unrepresented and ultimately forgotten.

With this research, I do not demand any forms of relocation or destruction but propose co-existence of memories in Benjamin Franklin House. Benjamin Franklin can continue to be commemorated within the museum's walls, while John King's commemoration can take place outside the museum to signify his escape to freedom. This ensures that both of these 18th-century residents are remembered as they both contributed to the historical narrative, albeit in different ways. History habitually remembers "great man" accounts of individuals like Benjamin Franklin, but John King's account is equally worthy of attention. Through their rebelliousness and resistance, runaways like John King "contributed to their own and others' eventual emancipation" in 18th-century Britain (see the University of Glasgow). In focusing on representing John King, my aim is to disseminate a version of slavery without falling back into yet another type of objectification and dehumanization of the enslaved as subjects in bondage on plantations. I argue that instead of decolonizing the enslaved, perpetuating bound portrayals of slavery in effect continuously recolonizes them as objects of study, as mere "subjected slaves," which subsequently underpins enduring systemic biases.

Peggy Brunache (as cited in Spread the Word, 2021) also reminds us that there is more to British colonial histories than the horrific and inhumane slave stories about Africans on far-away Caribbean plantations. Slavery took place in Britain too, where many bound people bravely challenged the slave system by running away in search of liberty. According to Brunache, "That Black history is British history. It belongs to all of us" (as cited in Spread the Word, 2021). Through her research collaboration with Simon Newman, Brunache has helped develop the project "Runaways," which creatively reimagines the stories of London's freedom-seeking men, women and children of the 17th and 18th centuries. Inspired by this much-needed and historically significant initiative, with the help of John King, my research similarly represents the less transmitted version of runaways' resistance, (self-)liberation and agency on British soil as a means of decolonizing the prevailing memory of enslavement. This is necessary because as Morayo Akandé has declared, "the runaways are the silent heroes who created opportunities for future generations of people of colour, and it is important that their existence is acknowledged and celebrated" (as cited in the University of Glasgow).

Decolonizing Benjamin Franklin House through practice

Rather than illustrating John King, I focus on representing and mapping his act of absenting himself from Benjamin Franklin House. In what follows, I outline how comics-based research approaches can be deployed to accomplish this. Amongst the many definitions of comics, Hillary Chute's (2008) is perhaps the most pertinent for the purposes of this inquiry as it relates to the enduring dichotomies and hierarchies within the historical field, such as time and space and presence and absence. According to Chute,

> Comics might be defined as a hybrid word-and-image form in which two narrative tracks, one verbal and one visual, register temporality spatially. Comics move forward in time through the space of the page, through its progressive counterpoint of presence and absence: packed panels (also called frames) alternating with gutters (empty space).
>
> (p. 452)

The empty space in comics that Chute alludes to, however, is not really empty. Scott McCloud (1993) explains that "despite its unceremonious title, the gutter [empty space] plays host to much of the magic and mystery that are at the very heart of comics" (p. 66). This is certainly true with regard to John King, who might be absent, marginal and marginalized in Benjamin Franklin House, but is otherwise at the very heart of the museum's history. I was similarly drawn to Chute's (2008) characterization of the page in comics as "a rich temporal map configured as much by what isn't drawn as by what is" (p. 455), which prompted the following question: What could absences teach us if only we noticed it, and how might comics in combination with maps be used to support active learning about absences in museums? As someone who specializes in comics and creative mapping practices and has been employed to visualize history in various museum and heritage contexts, I became particularly intrigued by the potentialities of their research encounter in an effort to re-present John King. In considering recent developments relating to comics-based research methodologies (Kuttner et al., 2020), I also reflected on the architectural characteristics (Bredehoft, 2006) and map-like topographies of comics (Moore, 2009; Peterle, 2021). There are various similarities and intersections between comics and maps, and there are significant operational synergies to be gained from their merger, especially in terms of audience engagement.

Giada Peterle (2021), for example, explains that the comics' pages invite authors and readers alike to engage in spatial choices and experiences regarding which pathways to take. Peterle (2019) highlights how this process parallels "carrying out a proper sequence of steps" (p. 2) which results in engagement that is emergent and performative with authors and readers undergoing "a truly mapping experience" (Peterle, 2017, p. 49). Our eyes partake in spatial drifting in non-linear and multiple directions, and Peterle (2019) compares this experience to the way we use maps, which similarly involves filling gaps and reconstructing narratives as a way of orienting ourselves. According to Peterle (2017), when examined "through their representational and non-representational, 'emergent' and processual features, comics show a temporary, mobile, contingent and unfinished nature that emerges in the performativity of their writing and reading practices" (p. 45). The acts of creating, reading and using maps can similarly be understood as having a temporary, mobile, contingent and unfinished nature. For instance, when making, reading or using a map, we can start, stop, restart, walk and navigate through it; we can depend on it for direction or not, expand the map by adding new features to it, and so on.

How and where should we learn about John King, the courageous runaway?

Following this, my propositions for museum education experiment with the idea of comics as maps or comics' cartographies. They complement the main museum experience offered at Benjamin Franklin House (2021), which involves theatrical performances in combination with audio and projections in its historic rooms. In my propositions, however, instead of passively receiving history, I invite audiences to engage with history in more dynamic ways by using the comics' cartographies as a means of re-enacting John King. Audiences can follow John King's steps and explore possible routes he might have taken beyond the boundaries of the museum, each time decolonizing the memory of his enslavement in time and space.

This proposed mapping experience promotes the idea of a dynamic museum without borders (Janes, 2016), and comics beyond the boundaries of their pages, that is, comics on the move, where colonial histories and knowledges can run free (Figure 3.1). My aim is to generate outcomes with heightened participatory mapping experiences that are accessible, inclusive and memorable and through which audiences can learn about, remember, reflect, read, see, narrate and run away with John King. This interactive approach encourages audiences to share ownership of the comics' cartographies by co-producing knowledges, meanings and interpretations, both mentally and physically depending on how they use the work as well as when, why and where. The purpose is to engage audiences in ways in which they can become active participants in the process of museum decolonization and decolonial commemoration. Each time we follow in John King's steps, we can learn something new that we previously ignored, fixing him in our minds as someone we must not forget – as an intangible heritage of enduring value.

Peterle (2019) highlights how emergent cartographic theory proposes "a creative engagement with maps as objects that are always in the process of mapping, as spatial practices that unfold in the hands of different users" (p. 2). Likewise, I envision my research project to result in an emergent anthology containing a series of experimental illustrative, diagrammatic, metaphorical and topographical comics' cartographies. The maps as comics and comics as maps represent anything from theories, concepts and emotions, to journeys, spaces and places relating to John King. Each time someone engages with the comics' cartographies, John King is brought to life in an unfolding process of mapping and becoming.

Perhaps this is what decolonization entails. Perhaps decolonization is an unfolding process demanding constant revisions, reconsiderations and novel conceptualizations. This idea for a multi-layered, interactive and performative museum audience approach corresponds to Jaume Aurell's (2015) view that "history is owned by those who experience or engage with it, not only by professional historians" (p. 149). Historians make history for historians; artists make history for everyone. Although historical representations in visual formats are not habitually used or understood by historians, they are certainly understood, sought after and even expected by contemporary publics. Surveying the rise in the number of artists working with archival material, Mark Godfrey in *The Artist as Historian* (2007) acknowledges that our artistic research methodologies result in outcomes that serve as invitations for audiences to reflect on and collectively remember the people and things of the past, "and to consider the ways in which the past is represented in the wider culture" (p. 143). This is why a symbiotic relationship between historical and artistic engagements with the past is a necessary step in the right direction.

Figure 3.1. Kremena Dimitrova, *Envisioning the invisible/mapping the unmappable*, 2021, digital collage. Copyright Kremena Dimitrova.

Conclusion

Creative interdisciplinary theory-practice research approaches can revitalize and expand the roles and social potential of museums, helping them in their mission to become more egalitarian and more inclusive sites of learning about the colonial absences concerning slavery. In contributing creative propositions for the decolonization of Benjamin Franklin House, I hope other museums will find insights helpful as a means of supporting the process of their own decolonization. Comics in combination with maps carry great interactive and meaning-making potential in terms of audience engagement and offer numerous unmapped terrains for reflective explorations, especially with regard to creative decolonial practices. While the propositions for museum education in this case are specific to John King and Benjamin Franklin House, they raise a set of broader interdisciplinary themes that could be relevant to artists, museum professionals, visual historians and historians more generally and could further strengthen the fruitful collaborations between museums and creative practitioners, now and in the future. Looking ahead, I hope this chapter, together with my ongoing Ph.D. research, will open new interdisciplinary avenues for comics-based research inquiry in museums and beyond, which will undoubtedly continue to expand as more previously hidden and marginalized histories become unearthed and demand attention, inclusion and representation.

Note

1. https://www.runaways.gla.ac.uk/

References

Aldrich, R. (2010). Colonial museums in a postcolonial Europe. In D. Thomas (Ed.), *Museums in a postcolonial Europe* (pp. 12–31). Routledge.
Aurell, J. (2015). Rethinking historical genres in the twenty-first century. *Rethinking History*, *19*(2), 145–157.
Benjamin Franklin House. (2019). *Franklin & the house*. https://benjaminfranklinhouse.org/the-house-benjamin-franklin/
Benjamin Franklin House. (2021). *The house today*. https://benjaminfranklinhouse.org/the-house-benjamin-franklin/the-house-today/
Bredehoft, T. A. (2006). Comics architecture, multidimensionality, and time: Chris Ware's Jimmy Corrigan: The smartest kid on earth. *MFS Modern Fiction Studies*, *52*(4), 869–890.
Bressey, C. (2013). Contesting the political legacy of slavery in England's country houses: A case study of Kenwood House and Osborne House. In M. Dresser & A. Hann (Eds.), *Slavery and the British country house* (pp. 114–122). English Heritage.

Chute, H. (2008). Comics as literature? Reading graphic narrative. *PMLA, 123*(2), 452–465.

Cubitt, G. (2012). Museums and slavery in Britain: The bicentenary of 1807. In A. L. Araujo (Ed.), *Politics of memory: Making slavery visible in the public space* (pp. 159–177). Routledge.

Dimitrova, K. (2023). Absented from his master's service: Benjamin Franklin House, slavery and comics. In R. Kauranen, O. Löytty, A. Nikkilä, & A. Vuorinne (Eds.), *Comics and migration: Practices and representation* (pp. 201–211). Routledge.

Drayton, R. (2019). Rhodes must not fall? Statues, postcolonial 'heritage' and temporality. *Third Text, 33*(4–5), 651–666.

Dresser, M., & Hann, A. (Eds.). (2013). *Slavery and the British country house* (pp. 13–16). English Heritage.

Giblin, J., Ramos, I., & Grout, N. (2019). Dismantling the master's house: Thoughts on representing empire and decolonizing museums and public spaces in practice. *Third Text, 33*(4–5), 471–486.

Godfrey, M. (2007). *The artist as historian* (Vol. 120, pp. 140–172). The MIT Press.

Goskar, T. (2020). *Small museums should spearhead drive to decolonise museum practice.* https://www.museumsassociation.org/museums-journal/opinion/2020/12/small-museums-should-spearhead-drive-to-decolonise-museum-practice/

Harvey, K. L. (2016). Envisioning the past: Art, historiography and public history. *Cultural and Social History, 12*(4), 1–27.

Janes, R. R. (2016). *Museums without borders: Selected writings of Robert R. Janes.* Routledge.

Kuttner, P. J., Weaver-Hightower, M. B., & Sousanis, N. (2020). Comics-based research: The affordances of comics for research across disciplines. *Qualitative Research, 21*(2), 195–214.

McCloud, S. (1993). *Understanding comics: The invisible art.* Harper.

Moore, A. (2009). *Maps as comics, comics as maps.* International Cartographic Association.

Museums Association. (2020). *Decolonizing museums.* https://www.museumsassociation.org/campaigns/decolonizing-museums/

Nash, G. B. (2006). Franklin and slavery. *Proceedings of the American Philosophical Society, 150*(4), 618–635.

Newman, S. (2019). Freedom-seeking slaves in England and Scotland, 1700–1780. *English Historical Review, CXXXIV, 570,* 1136–1168.

Noise of Art. (2020). *Benjamin Franklin, the lady and a runaway enslaved boy named King.* https://noiseofart.org/2020/10/27/poem-benjamin-franklin-the-lady-and-a-runaway-enslaved-boy-named-king-by-h-e-ross/

Peterle, G. (2017). Comic book cartographies: A cartocentred reading of City of Glass, the graphic novel. *Cultural Geographies, 24*(1), 43–68.

Peterle, G. (2019). *Comics and maps? A cartoGraphic essay.* http://livingmaps.review/journal/index.php/LMR/article/view/185/362

Peterle, G. (2021). *Comics as a research practice: Drawing narrative geographies beyond the frame.* Routledge.

Spread the Word. (2021). *Runaways announced: History, storytelling and escape from slavery in 17th and 18th Century London.* https://www.spreadtheword.org.uk/runaways-announced-history-storytelling-and-escape-from-slavery-in-17th-and-18th-century-london/

Turchi, P. (2004). *Maps of the imagination: The writer as cartographer*. Trinity UP.

University of Glasgow. (n.d). *Runaway slaves in Britain: Bondage, freedom and race in the eighteenth century*. https://www.runaways.gla.ac.uk/

White, H. (1978). *Tropics of discourse: Essays in cultural criticism*. Johns Hopkins University Press.

White, H. (1988). Historiography and historiophoty. *The American Historical Review, 93*(5), 1193–1199.

Chapter 4

Community Museums: Dialogical Spaces for Knowledge Creation, Mobilization and Income Generation for Marginalized Citizens in Brazil

Bruno de Oliveira Jayme

Worldwide, the arts have helped marginalized communities fight for social inclusion and community development because the arts have the potential to create and mobilize new knowledge, resist oppression and speak truth to power (Clover, 2015; Monk et al., 2019). Such power is achieved by engaging the viewer in a dialogue about social and political issues. When it comes to displaying artworks in museums, however, there is a problem. In many parts of the Western world, white male elitist standards, traditions and institutions have historically defined, displayed and imposed their artefacts, stories and world views upon the general public (Borg & Mayo, 2010). This perpetuates hegemonic oppression that "[has] legitimised prevailing structures of power through their own practices of colonialism, racism, sexism, classism, and ableism" (Clover, 2015, p. 303). In developing countries, this is problematic because traditional museums can perpetuate the European elitist status quo, which is disconnected from the reality of many countries such as my own, Brazil. As a counter-narrative for traditional and elitist museums, community museums have the potential to trouble colonialism, racism and classism (Bounia, 2017). Community museums can also share hidden narratives or even provide alternative narratives to share those marginalized stories.

This chapter invites the reader to journey to São Paulo, Brazil to explore the potentialities of community museums in (a) representing pedagogical sites where local knowledge is co-constructed and mobilized, and (b) providing income generation for socially excluded citizens. In the next sections, I discuss how 20 members of the National Recycling Social Movement (MNCR) produced artworks and curated a community museum that quickly garnered the attention of politicians, media and the general public. Arts-based research (ABR) framed participants' experiences during the artmaking process and curatorship while exploring the politics and learning that occur in community museums.

Community museums and ABR

By engaging the wider public in dialogue about social and political issues, community museums co-create and mobilize new knowledge while surfacing hidden or even forgotten stories of local communities. In social sciences, the role of community museums is to provide critical spaces to help marginalized citizens express their stories in their own voices, to fight for social justice and to become subjects of their own lives (Clover, 2015).

For Freire (1978), humans are subjects of history because we are immersed in myriads of social interactions and with our most immediate environment. These interactions mediate our inner capabilities of action, reaction and reflection on the ways we operate in the world while developing our critical thoughts and historical awareness. To be and become subjects of history, we must renounce a position of merely witnessing social phenomena, as passive receptors of history. On the contrary, we must be active subjects of history, taking ownership of our personal experiences and knowledge, our epistemic understandings, how we co-create and mobilize new knowledge in and through dialogical spaces and above all, how we understand how systems of oppression play out in our material world(s).

Community museums represent critical dialogical spaces and antioppressive tools for the co-construction of collective subjects, where communities – by curating their own stories – develop relationships with the self, the other and their environment. Community museums also mediate people's awareness about their own history, fostering reflection and critical understanding of their surroundings with the ultimate goal of transforming the collective future (Ocampo & Lersch, 2010). In a community museum, the subject is not the dominant culture but rather the collective local knowledge. Citizens who participate in the co-creation of a community museum evoke how life used to be, how life is now and how life can be in the future. It is up to the community to make such decisions, to choose how they want their stories to be told, which helps them define their own identities, replacing imposed and/or outsider's realities. From this perspective, community museums in general reject the hegemonic status quo of governmental policies, in the sense that these museums do not depend on the state or federal organizations to operate (Ocampo & Lersch, 2010). Community museums are grassroots and action-oriented spaces for learning, researching and understanding local knowledge.

Community museums are spaces for activating new forms of knowledge mobilization (KM) by opening opportunities for people to perceive their world(s) through different lenses in an effort to facilitate more conscious decisions on issues that affect their environment. For Cole and McIntyre (2003), community museums "initiate dialogue, evoke emotional, cultural, social, and political complexities" (p. 18). For them, community museums have a "unique and creative way of engaging the audience in meaning making and KM" (pp. 60–61). In this case, they go beyond the transfer of information. They construct and mobilize knowledge because they strive to initiate dialogue amongst visitors, sparking opportunities for critical thinking.

ABR helps us to explore learning in community museums, for as Clover (2011) states, the arts can "uncover or create new knowledge, highlight experience, pose questions, or tackle problems" (p. 13). The arts also generate trust, build community, and inspire individual and collective empowerment and emancipation. Artistic approaches to research mediate communication among participants because the arts bring together verbal, behavioural and visual modes of expression (Huss & Cwikel, 2005). Silverman (2000) claims that ABR draws from what people have to say, which may not be otherwise accessible in certain situations. Additionally, Clover et al. (2004) argue that these discourses introduce (and challenge) bias and show us "things that we might not want to see" (p. 282).

Research participants

Research participants in this case came from the sector of São Paulo–Brazil known as "recyclers." Recycling provides an important livelihood to many of the world's poor populations: this activity includes collecting, separating, classifying and selling materials for subsistence. Although recyclers contribute to overall environmental health, they remain socially and economically marginalized, facing harassment and disempowerment. In Brazil, approximately 60,000 recyclers are organized in cooperatives (Gutberlet, 2011) that provide employment, improve working conditions and increase environmental education (Gutberlet, 2008). These cooperatives are affiliated with the National Recycling Social Movement (MNCR), which helps recyclers with capacity building and networking with government and non-governmental sectors in an effort to create inclusive solutions to recycling management (Tremblay, 2013). The MNCR also plays an important role in KM and political advocacy for Brazilian recyclers and aims to improve their quality of life through recognition of this work and their strong political and leadership roles in this sector.

Art workshops

Once a week during the year 2016, I facilitated three art workshops with 20 recyclers affiliated with the MNCR. The goals of these workshops were twofold: (a) teach three art techniques to those interested in learning how to express themselves through an artistic form and (b) explore the potential of visual arts to help recyclers voice their stories under the theme "what it means to be a recycler." This theme aimed to create dialogue amongst recyclers and the general public and make visible the nature and importance of their work.

The first workshop was abstract painting. Incorporating an assemblage of materials, modelling paste and acrylic paint, recyclers created unique images that illustrated their experiences working in the cooperatives. Throughout the workshop, we continually asked – What does this object represent to you? Why did you decide to assemble those objects in that way? What do those images mean to you? These questions kept the conversation flowing and mediated recyclers' thinking about what they were creating. The final artworks embodied their stories of poverty and oppression but above all, stories of their fight for social inclusion.

The second workshop was dedicated to impressionism painting. For this workshop, participants brought photographs from magazines, newspapers or personal family photo albums to which they felt emotionally connected. These images were spread out on a table, and they chose one image as a reference for their artwork, explaining why they chose that specific image. Their image selection was intended to be an opening to visually voice their stories.

The third workshop featured mosaics. For this workshop, each recycler received one square of canvas and painted symbols or words that responded to the overall theme. Once painted, the squares were assembled to form a unified image. Later, during the art exhibits, the recyclers reproduced the mosaic technique with gallery visitors by asking attendees to paint their impressions about the displayed art.

The workshops described above were audio-visually recorded. Over 221 hours of video and sound material were produced, serving as my data corpus. Recorded sections that illustrated my claims were fully transcribed and translated verbatim. I used discourse analysis (Edwards & Potter, 1992) as an analytical tool for interpreting the transcripts. Additionally, over 100 paintings were created in this project. Participants chose one of their paintings to be part of a travelling community museum called *Recycling Stories*.

Recycling stories – What it means to be a recycler

The community museum travelled to seven different locations over six months: a public library, two city halls in two municipalities in São Paulo, a public square and a public elementary school, as well as one exhibit during the Rio+20 Conference in Rio de Janeiro and one exhibit during the MNCR Conference in the state of Paraná in the South of Brazil. At the exhibits, the paintings were hung on easels or carefully laid on the floor, enabling visitors to mingle amongst them. A mosaic station was set up on the side with paint and brushes, so visitors could visually express their impressions about the artworks. At least one recycler was present during the exhibit to engage visitors in conversation around the themes presented in their paintings. In total, seven mosaics were created, representing the seven locations visited by the community museum. Music, food and performers contributed to making *Recycling Stories* a lively space.

During the art shows, visitors were able to freely walk around the artworks and interact with the recyclers. Most of the conversation concerned the politics around the recyclers' work. From these dialogues, new recycling networks for cooperation were established, and many stories emerged.

Community museum sites of knowledge, co-creation and mobilization

The following two stories illustrate the power of community museums in mediating collective transformation and income generation for the recyclers. In the first episode, I introduce Luzia, a 55-year-old, one of the recyclers who participated in the workshops. This episode unfolded upon Luzia's return from Rio de Janeiro and Londrina in Brazil, where she participated at the Rio+20 Submit and the MNCR Conference, respectively. At these events, Luzia hosted *Recycling Stories* and facilitated mosaic workshops with visitors:

> Today, I perceive that there are different ways of seeing things. My views have expanded after we went to Rio+20 and to the South. It was cool. Now, let's create our mosaic, I said.

And then we called everybody to paint. So, we started to perceive that there are other universes that we can work together to help those who are trying to discover their own values. And that makes me feel with a more open mind.

Something has changed for Luzia that shifted the ways she operates in her environment. This is evident when she affirms that her views have expanded. She also explains that this shift was mediated by her participation in two events in which she participated (e.g. Rio+20 Summit and South America).

According to Mezirow (1997), transformative learning takes place when the individual expands their point of view. Such process is mediated through dialogue and reflection, in which a person becomes critical, able to recognize social, political and economic constraints and (re)act on these constraints. For Scott (2001), those who experience transformative learning may face a series of events so meaningful that old ways of thinking no longer apply. Luzia's engagement with gallery visitors was a tool for her self-transformation because such engagement mediated her critical reflection so greatly that her points of view changed. The energy exchange refers to her engagement with museum visitors through the artmaking process. The series of events that mediated her transformation, or what she poetically identifies as "perceive other universes," refers to her participation in those two events.

Luzia also affirms that her participation in those events was impressive ("it was cool"). She had never facilitated an art workshop before. This was a skill she gained through a previous mosaic workshop in which she participated. The fact that she facilitated the workshop on her own is evidence of her learning process about mosaic construction and how it can be used as a method to share people's stories since visitors' perceptions about the exhibit were illustrated in the mosaics. What happened cognitively with Luzia is what Brooks (2005), informed by Vygotsky (1962), identifies as visual thought: that is, the combination of meaning-making and artmaking processes. In other words, visual thought refers to the ways in which the individual makes sense of their surroundings through an artistic process (Brooks, 2003). The fact that Luzia was able to facilitate mosaic workshops serves as a confirmation of her visual thought construction, mediated during the workshops she participated in as a learner as well as a facilitator. Additionally, her visual thought offered entry to a membership that warrants her participation in future art shows. For Vygotsky (1962), such visual thought awakens a higher level of human consciousness, or what Freire (1978) calls *conscientização*, where people can reimagine alternative realities for themselves.

According to Luzia, producing the mosaic collaboratively with visitors helped them perceive other universes of possibilities to explore their own values. She does not articulate what those values are, but we gather that she refers to visitors' perceptions about the work recyclers perform since that was the theme of their artworks. Luzia concludes by stating that her experience of hosting *Recycling Stories* and facilitating mosaic workshops made her optimistic about herself and her opportunities, a reassurance of how this experience has helped her to perceive her surroundings differently.

Luzia's story is important because it highlights three potential benefits of community museums: (a) empowering participants to move out of their comfort zones by experiencing art in an authentic way; (b) establishing ownership of the stories recyclers wanted to tell and (c) mediating individual transformation.

Community museums – Alternative sites for income generation

In this section, I introduce Selma, a 56-year-old recycler and community leader in a low-income neighbourhood. In addition to working as a recycler, she is an active MNCR spokesperson. Her comments emerged during one of the exhibits in São Paulo:

> We didn't think about it. We just thought about sustainability. I will collect, separate and sell. So, this became such an absurd vicious cycle that we couldn't see other's horizons. We couldn't imagine that our mobile art gallery could be an event that would generate income for the recyclers.

When I designed this project collaboratively with recyclers, our intention was to explore the potential of visual arts for sharing their stories, with the ultimate goal of decreasing the prejudice they suffer. However, once the exhibition started to travel to different communities, visitors showed interest in the artworks and shared their desire to purchase some of the pieces. This was a remarkable moment for the recyclers because it added value to their work – not just as environmental agents but also as artists. When recyclers started receiving payment for their artworks, it sparked their confidence as artists in their own right. At the beginning of the project, they were unsure about producing art because they did not have previous formal art training. However, that lack of confidence shifted throughout the project; as one recycler said at the end, "I did not know I could do this." Most of the artworks were sold during the exhibits, and the price depended on negotiations between recyclers and their clients. Having monetary value added to their artworks empowered them to break through what Selma refers to as a "vicious cycle." That is, instead of just working in the recycling cooperative, their artmaking represented an alternative site for income generation.

Discussion

Historically in cases of extreme oppression, people have found ways of resisting dominant forces through community art (Milbrant, 2010), because the arts empower people to understand and commit to their own ideologies. Community museums highlight values and ideological messages that oppose hegemonic standpoints, crossing boundaries of age, gender, class and geography. A community museum is what Deleuze and Guattari (1980/1987) describe as a "minor" art form. For them, "minor" refers to arts created by minorities or marginalized people and is characterized by deterritorializations: that is, art that disrupts territories once taken by traditional art institutions. In this case, minor arts are political and collectively produced. When art exhibits take place within the community away from privileged areas, they indeed challenge socio-geographical spaces (Mandell, 2014).

Additionally, community museums break taboos when people's personal experiences bring forth the social identities of a community. This aspect of the art exhibitions was evident throughout this study because the *Recycling Stories* exhibition was created by the community for the community, and it challenged the confined walls of traditional art institutions. Moreover, our community museum generated dialogue amongst visitors and recyclers around environmental issues. The *Recycling Stories* exhibition indeed de-territorialized traditional art standpoints by challenging peoples' views of who can produce art and where art can be displayed. Such democracy of the arts welcomed ordinary people from different backgrounds to express themselves through artistic forms. Due to its mobility, *Recycling Stories* created alternative and affective spaces within everyday life. This was evident when the museum disrupted a public space in front of São Paulo City Hall, gaining the attention of politicians, media and the public. At that moment, in that public square, conventional public spaces were challenged, power questioned, alternative social dynamics established and a hopeful atmosphere was created.

As pedagogical sites, community museums should invite viewers to see their environment through different lenses by helping them to situate themselves within their own culture and history. Sandell and Nightingale (2012), for example, claim that art exhibits mediate individuals' *conscientização* because exhibits construct "new narratives that reflect demographic, social and cultural diversity, and represent a plurality of lived experiences, histories, and identities" (p. 121).

During one of our mobile exhibits, viewers expressed their opinions about *Recycling Stories*. According to one visitor, it is "something you don't see every day, everywhere." Another visitor said, "you always see traditional paintings," but because their community museum was innovative, this was an event that emerged out of their ordinary lives. Visitors' reviews about *Recycling Stories* add to the emerging counter-narrative about the current state of traditional museums.

One remarkable action-oriented result of *Recycling Stories* emerged after the exhibit at a public school, where Selma talked to the students and teachers about the importance of recycling. During her presentation, a few students felt connected with her story because they either knew or had a family member who worked as a recycler. Selma's story also got the attention of the principal, who decided starting that day to save recyclable materials from the school and donate them to Selma's cooperative. This partnership is ongoing.

Conclusion

Due to the playfulness of the arts-making environment, community museums were created where participants felt comfortable in sharing their deepest fears, frustrations and hopes for a different reality. This level of insight may not be possible with traditional ways of doing qualitative research, such as questionnaires. Even though the art workshops we presented did not require any previous art experience from participants, who became facilitators as well, these workshops moved people out of their comfort zones and helped them situate their journeys as recyclers into historical contexts, and perhaps most importantly, invited them to dream and fight for a different reality.

We hope that these stories can inspire art galleries to meet their potential by challenging the social injustice of current hegemonic social and political practices, and we invite social movement organizers to include art and art galleries as strategic spaces of contestation and empowerment.

References

Borg, C., & Mayo, P. (2010). Museums, adult education and cultural politics: Malta. *Education & Society, 18*(3), 77–97.

Bounia, A. (2017). Cultural societies and local community museums: A case study of a participative museum in Greece. *Zarządzanie w Kulturze, 18*, 29–40.

Brooks, M. L. (2003). *Drawing, thinking, meaning, TRACEY*. University of Loughborough.

Brooks, M. L. (2005). Drawing as unique mental development tool for young children: Interpersonal and intrapersonal dialogues. *Contemporary Issues in Early Childhood, 6*(1), 80–91.

Clover, D. E. (2011). Successes and challenges of feminist arts-based participatory methodologies with homeless/street-involved women in Victoria. *Action Research, 9*(1), 12–26.

Clover, D. E. (2015). Adult education for social and environmental change in contemporary public art galleries and museums in Canada, Scotland and England. *International Journal of Lifelong Education, 34*(3), 300–315.

Clover, D. E., Stalker, J., & McGauley, L. (2004). Feminist popular education and community leadership: The case for new directions. In *Adult education for democracy, social justice and a culture of peace: Proceedings of the International Gathering of the Canadian Association for the Study of Adult Education and the Adult Education Research Conference*. University of Victoria.

Cole, A. L., & McIntyre, M. (2003). Arts-informed research for public education: The Alzheimer's Project. *Proceedings of the Canadian Association for the Study of Adult Education (CASAE)*. Dalhousie University/University of King's College, Halifax, Nova Scotia.

Deleuze, G., & Guattari, F. (1987). *A thousand plateaus: Capitalism and schizophrenia*. University of Minnesota Press. (Original work published 1980)

Edwards, D., & Potter, J. (1992). *Discursive psychology*. Sage.

Freire, P. (1978). *The pedagogy of the oppressed*. Seabury.

Gutberlet, J. (2008). *Recovering resources – Recycling citizenship: Urban poverty reduction in Latin America*. Ashgate.

Gutberlet, J. (2011). Waste to energy, wasting resources and livelihoods. In S. Kumar (Ed.), *Integrated waste management* (pp. 110–113). InTech.

Huss, E., & Cwikel, J. (2005). Researching creations: Applying arts-based research to Bedouin women's drawings. *International Journal of Qualitative Methods, 4*(4), 44–62.

Mandell, J. (2014). They're not actors, but they're playing themselves. Undesirable elements turns 20. *TDF Stages: A Theatre Magazine.* http://wp.tdf.org/index.php/2012/10/theyre-not-actors-but-theyre-playing-themselves/

Mezirow, J. (1997). Transformative learning: Theory to practice. In P. Cranton (Ed.), *Transformative learning in action: Insights from practice* (pp. 5–12). Jossey-Bass.

Milbrant, M. K. (2010). Understanding the role of art in social movements and transformation. *Journal of Art for Life, 1*(1), 7–18.

Monk, D., de Oliveira Jayme, B., & Salvi, E. (2019). The heart of activism: Stories of community engagement. *Engaged Scholar Journal: Community-Engaged Research, Teaching, and Learning, 5*(2), 61–78.

Ocampo, C. C., & Lersch, T. M. (2010). The community museum: A space for the exercise of communal power. *Sociomuseuology, 38,* 135–152.

Sandell, R., & Nightingale, E. (2012). *Museums, equality and social justice.* Routledge.

Scott, S. M. (2001). Transformative learning. In T. B. Stein & M. Kompf (Eds.), *Craft of teaching adults* (pp. 152–160). Culture Concepts Books.

Silverman, D. (2000). *Doing qualitative research: A practical handbook.* Sage.

Tremblay, C. (2013). Towards inclusive waste management: Participatory video as a communication tool. *ICE Journal of Waste and Resource Management, 66*(4), 177–186.

Vygotsky, L. S. (1962). *Mind in society: The development of higher psychological processes.* Harvard University Press.

Chapter 5

"Becoming Ecological" for Nature Conservation: Insights From Two Museums in the Island State of lutruwita/Tasmania, Australia

Abbey MacDonald, Annalise Rees, Jan Hogan and
Benjamin J. Richardson

In response to global pandemics and catastrophic climate events, arts, culture and education institutions must begin to redefine existing boundaries and break with routine. Their preparedness and ability to forge new ways to reach, connect with and engage communities become critical for how artists and curators foster artful exchange between people and place.

This chapter attends to the interstitial spaces between artist/curator/audience to consider how conservation values are cultivated in cultural institution settings. Discussion examines how two exhibition case studies provide the means to encounter and foster conservation values through place-based educative and affective experiences. From this, we elicit an experiential meaning-making process of "becoming ecological" (Rousell, 2020) in museum settings.

Becoming ecological for conservation values: People, place, practice and process

In the context of COVID-19, artists and curators are grappling with myriad challenges in the current museum environment (Badham et al., 2021). Kerby et al. (2017) highlight the imperative for museums to create spaces of practice where artists and curators are sufficiently flexible to adjust to changing tastes, perceptions and priorities. Achieving this in museum settings is contingent upon a "slipperiness" (Deleuze & Guattari, 1980/1987) in mindset and practice that can anticipate shifting agendas for people and place. The sensibilities of artists and curators for this type of active responsiveness position them to leverage ecological perspectives and cultivate educative opportunities for their audience.

Research pertaining to affective experience in museum settings (Vallance, 2004) asks us to consider how relationality between people and place is kindled. This chapter ruminates on the implications that slipperiness may have for how we conceive and understand artist and curator relationality as a form of "becoming ecological" in museum settings. The authorship team employs a similar ecological approach by investigating how artists and curators transform practice *in* process to consider the potential for audience and community encounters. We liken this process of "becoming ecological" to an assemblage of people, place, practice and process, enabling a messy and fluid ecological network of meaning and making to unfold.

We share a discussion about two instances of our practice in place – institution and environment – and the subsequent interrelation of people and place made in and through artistic and curatorial practice. We draw out examples of becoming ecological and speculate on the potential to reach, influence and transform attitudes and behaviour towards developing different conservation values. In practising our own acts of curiosity, we are independently, collectively and collaboratively attuned to the affective dimensions of our own encounters in such settings.

The authorship team: Contexts, connections and curiosities

With the authorship team geographically dispersed across an island setting, we collectively arrive at and render our ecological relationality and becoming among place (museum/natural environment), people (artist/curator/audience), practice (artistic/curatorial) and values (aesthetic/conservation/pedagogic). The authorship team's assemblage represents a breadth of expertise across diverse contexts comprising environmental law, arts practice and education pedagogies. We draw on past and ongoing experiences of collaboration in research and environmental arts engagement initiatives, primarily in lutruwita/Tasmania, Australia. It is important to acknowledge that we reside on what European explorers previously named Van Diemen's Land in 1642, traditionally known as lutruwita, the *palawa kani* (Tasmanian Aborigines speak) name for Tasmania. The island has a complex postinvasion history; truths and stories of lutruwita/Tasmania continue to be recovered and rewritten in relation to/through/ from contemporary cultures of the island's First Nations peoples. In acknowledgement of the complex histories of place – particularly, the museum as a colonial institution – and diverse disciplinary settings from which our storylines emerge, we indicate *palawa kani* dual naming of place across the chapter. Further information with respect to First Nations place-naming process and practices in lutruwita/Tasmania are provided in our reference list (see Rimmer & Sainty, 2020; Tasmanian Aboriginal Centre, 2021). In turn, our context of inquiry includes two case study exhibitions from "an island state of paradox" (Hunter & MacDonald, 2017, p. 7) – lutruwita/Tasmania, off the southeast coast of the continental Australian mainland.

lutruwita/Tasmania remains home to delicate and unique environmental ecosystems and wilderness areas. This island is also notorious for its near genocide of the palawa people (Stone et al., 2017, p. 1). While more than 85 per cent of the island's old-growth forests have been decimated by deforestation, the island has also hosted some of the fiercest environmental activist movements in Australia's history (Richardson & Hogan, 2018). While lutruwita/Tasmania is now considered one of the most culturally vibrant creative communities in Australia, recent research suggests that it experiences some of the most challenging socio-economic issues in the country (Allen et al., 2018) and has amongst the lowest levels of educational attainment nationally (Rowan & Ramsay, 2018). These paradoxical circumstances create specific problems as well as potential drivers for re-imagining the more-than-human complexities of life in lutruwita/Tasmania.

The exhibitions: Practice and process/people and place

The Tasmanian Museum and Art Gallery (TMAG), along with its partner organization, Queen Victoria Museum and Art Gallery (QVMAG) in the North, are curating diverse, complex and multi-faceted storylines into an aesthetic of people and place. TMAG and QVMAG host the island's premier natural history and art collections (Foster et al., 2020; TMAG, 2021). TMAG (in nipaluna/Hobart) combines museum, art gallery and herbarium facilities for safeguarding the physical evidence of Tasmania's natural and cultural heritage and the cultural identity of Tasmanians (TMAG, 2021). Over the past 20 years, TMAG has "focussed on increasing Aboriginal voice within the collections and exhibitions" (Rimmer & Sainty, 2020, p. 33). QVMAG originally opened in 1891 and is situated on two land sites in the city of Launceston. For many years, the palawa people of lutruwita referred to this land as *palanwina lurini kanamaluka*, meaning "the town near river Tamar" (Riawunna Centre, 2021). As Australia's largest regional museum, QVMAG is a major cultural institution in its area, locally and nationally. The two sites include a dedicated art gallery, while the other houses natural sciences and history collections in a former nineteenth-century railway workshop (Lehman et al., 2020). In these spaces, intersections of natural-history displays and contemporary artworks are curated to interpolate complex narratives about people, practice and place. To explore this, we take a deep dive into two case study exhibitions from 2020 shown at QVMAG (Alastair Mooney's *Nest*) and TMAG (Lucienne Rickard's *Extinction Studies*) examining knowledge structures surrounding conservation.

(Be)coming home to roost: Alastair Mooney's *Nest*

Tasmanian interdisciplinary artist Alastair Mooney opened his first major solo exhibition, *Nest*, at QVMAG on 5 December 2020 (it closed on 21 November 2021). *Nest* highlights a series of works that reflect on the resilience and beauty of Tasmania's endemic birdlife in the face of human consumption and destruction (MutualArt, 2021). Mooney's practice draws influence from his early life in George Town on the northern coast of lutruwita/Tasmania. His experiences growing up and living in this coastal town fostered an enduring connection to and interest in the natural environment, with an acute awareness of the ecological interplay and tension between people and place.

Mooney's sensibility for grappling with this tension creates a threshold for slippage, allowing complex conservation narratives to emerge. While posthuman ecologies of the twenty-first century have the potential to produce ecological assemblages of value and concern, Rousell (2020) reminds us of the precarity of this threshold, where there is "equal potential for the emergence of toxic, cruel and divisive ecologies" (p. 1). The tenuousness of this sensibility is incisively articulated by *Nest* curator Ashleigh Whatling (2020), who suggests "it may be tempting to view *Nest* as a moralistic statement on the degradation of the environment [...] [however] the composition of the sculptures elicit a more nuanced reading" (p. 2).

While Whatling's critical essay situates *Nest's* roots in an anthropocentric framing, we crack open this discourse and locate a seedling of Rousell's posthuman "becoming ecological," sown into the rendering and reading of artistic and curatorial practice. The trouble with anthropocentrism is in its centring of humans, which by virtue [dishonourably] bestows on us the privilege of planetary dominance, resource extraction, mastery and stewardship (Braidotti, 2013). With artists and curators fast becoming ecological, we are being presented with exhibitions that invite us to recognize, examine and question how modes of more-than-human relations, in practice, process, place and person, become a matter of and for planetary survival (Bignall & Braidotti, 2018; Haraway, 2016).

When artistic and curatorial practice embraces the kind of symbiosis inherent to *Nest*, slippages of perception, experience and pathways between anthropocentrism and ecological becoming can occur. In visiting/revisiting Mooney's and our own encounters, an evocative space opens in which we can curate shifts and switches in perspective, relationality and meaning. *Nest* invites an encounter of conservation ecologies, through which multiple interpretations from the viewer are encouraged (Whatling, 2020).

The displacement of the rusting hulk of an actual car wreck from an abandoned quarry into the pristine museum setting, *Megahaliaeetus Dead Car* (2020) shifts subjectivities and situatedness of object, place, artist, curator and observer (Figure 5.1). Through Mooney's slippage between the playful, place-based encounters of art and nature of his earlier youth, a threshold of precarity alights – a moment for becoming ecological. The conservation value of "pristine" national parks becomes entwined with the discarded decaying detritus of human consumption. As Whatling (2020) describes, "While all of the other sculpted birds in this exhibition are life-size, the white-bellied sea eagle perched atop the rusted carcass of a small van has been rendered in colossal proportion" (p. 3). By looking into an apparent displacement that changes our point of view, this example compels us to consider the scale, weight and legacy of the human in the complexity of becoming ecological.

Through whispers of playful vernacular, Whatling's (2020) curatorial commentary into Mooney's practice gifts us "Easter eggs" for revisiting our own "stomping grounds" (p. 3). In another example, the juxtaposition of delicate Fairy Wrens perched atop crushed, discarded beer cans are rendered in butter-soft Huon Pine. The aluminium can, which Whatling (2020) reminds us is produced globally at a rate of 180 billion cans every year, is placed in "a stark contrast to the rare and measured growth of Huon Pine" (p. 8). The Huon Pine, between its exceedingly slow growth rate and being highly sought after by artisan sculptors, is itself emblematic of tension in the slippage between different moments of creative production (Lee, 2018). Mooney's sculpting of carefully and ethically salvaged Huon Pine not only "transforms an easily forgotten piece of rubbish into a thoughtful ode to camping trips long past" (Whatling, 2020, p. 8), but it confronts the ugliness and reality of our human practices of consumption and littering. In *Nest*, Mooney and Whatling set a breadcrumb trail attuned to the perils of becoming ecologies for toxicity, bitterness and apathy (Rousell, 2020).

Figure 5.1: Alastair Mooney, *Megahaliaeetus Dead Car*, 2020. Image courtesy of Queen Victoria Museum and Art Gallery. Photo by Rob Burnett.

Artists, curators and audiences become attuned to the breadth of tensions, possibilities and meaning in this museum setting. This premise of provocation for a becoming-ecological entanglement of place, person, practice and process underpins the manifestation of *Nest*. Duke (2010) reminds us that, in the context of museum encounters, the aim of artists and curators ought not to be to create specific lessons or directives but rather to provide context for unfolding learning encounters that are thoughtful and complex. These works are ideal examples of how artful exchange and encounters in museums can play a critical role in creating opportunities for people to communicate, engage, make meaning and socially relate in, from and for the cultivation of conservation values.

Lucienne Rickard's *Extinction Studies*

The artist Lucienne Rickard approached the TMAG in nipaluna/Hobart to host a public drawing performance to highlight the urgent issue of species biodiversity. The project, *Extinction Studies*, was commissioned by Hobart's Detached Cultural Organization, enabling Rickard to work in the gallery foyer five days a week for 16 months (Figure 5.2). While initially aiming for a sustainable platform to engage with the public, the space of the museum added

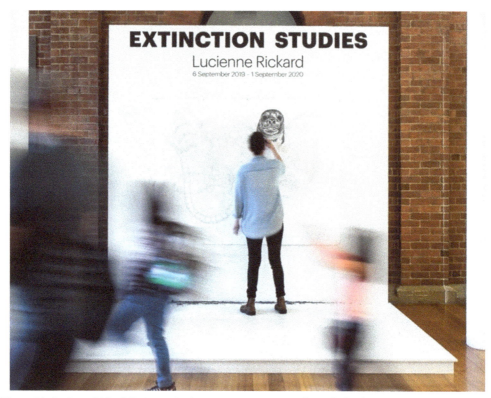

Figure 5.2: Lucienne Rickard, *Extinction Studies*, 2020. Image courtesy of Detached Cultural Organization. Photo by Jesse Hunniford.

another layer of complexity to the project by interweaving commentary about the project into the history of museums. As a practitioner actively responding to and performing in the museum setting, Rickard disturbs accepted hierarchical modes of knowledge production and presentation. Her reflexive process creates slippery movements for assemblage alluded to within Rousell's concept of "becoming ecological." Rickard's drawing process appears to inhabit the tradition of natural history aesthetics, where highly detailed and scientifically accurate renderings of specimens are isolated from distracting environmental data (Figure 5.3). She subverts this, however, by completing each drawing using one sheet of paper over the 16-month period. Each new species is drawn over the residue of the previous iteration: an evolving palimpsest of mark and time. One of Rickard's favourite aspects of the project was learning about evolutionary adaptations by species (Eslake, 2021). Rickard disturbed the categorization of scientific knowledge through drawing random species with no apparent links, apart from their recent inclusion in the International Union for Conservation of Nature (IUCN) Red List of Threatened Species (2021).

Figure 5.3: Lucienne Rickard, *Erasing Swift Parrot*, 2020. Image courtesy of Detached Cultural Organization. Photo by Jesse Hunniford.

To further trouble any association with the natural history tradition, Rickard erased each drawing after completing it. Artist and writer Maya Pindyck, in her practice-led research into frottage, interprets the writing of Deleuze and Guattari as a conceptual interpretation of aesthetic erasure, arguing that artists need to clear the ground of art creation from "pre-existing, pre-established clichés" (Pindyck, 2018). As Pindyck (2018) argues, "art, for Deleuze, is a matter of working sensation through material to rupture what already counts as knowledge" (p. 16). Cultural theorist Mieke Bal writes that an important part of engaging with a collection is to bring the past and the present together to allow affective and aesthetic moments of engagement.

Bal and Burke (2017) states, "curating is bringing works in one another's proximity, so that they can mutually speak to one another, thus modifying the sense and effect of each" (p. 31). Bal further argues that the politics of an exhibition intricately connects to its aesthetic strategies, which allow an affective space to emerge not only between the viewer and display elements but also between the elements themselves. Rickard in her performance successfully collides and disturbs traditions through the act of re-presentation and erasure.

The initial public response to Rickard's process was outrage; the erasure of art seemed more pressing than the eradication of entire species from the planet. The devotional practice of Rickard publicly creating intricate drawings inspired many followers and conversations. Drawing brings these objects to life, showing their exquisite glory; drawing becomes an act of remembrance, reverence and appreciation. As the drawings neared completion, crowds gathered around and became silent witnesses to Rickard's deletion, suggesting erasure in a museum context presents a paradox where the preservation of cultural content is foremost, and yet – then erased. The integration of Rickard's durational drawing performance at TMAG demonstrates the changing role of curation in natural history museums and art galleries. Rather than acting as repositories of artefacts and knowledge displayed in a metanarrative of progress and modernity, they become producers of affective stories that integrate with other disciplines and producers of culture (Witcomb, 2015). The collision of contemporary art practice with the field of natural history follows the call by critical theorist Andreas Huyssen (1995) for museums to provide "a terrain that can offer multiple narratives of meaning for people to hear and see the stories of others" (p. 34). Erasure in Rickard's work moves beyond the literal into affective territory. Drawing with scientific detail on the empty page fits comfortably within familiar and publicly accepted forms of knowledge production (Richardson & Hogan, 2018). However, witnessing erasure, particularly within the institutional setting, is a disruption of established hierarchical knowledge systems and challenges audiences to look again and question what they know. Rickard revealed that matter matters and that erasing data so painfully and thoroughly gained through acknowledged systems was affective and effective in transmitting the impact of a larger environmental issue: the erasure of biodiversity.

Reflections: Artful exchange for cultivating conservation values

Artists, curators and cultural institutions have a vital role in presenting content that explores human–environment relationships. Alastair Mooney's and Lucienne Rickard's exhibitions demonstrate the affective engagement potential of such collaborations. Institutional curating in museums such as QVMAG and TMAG offers multi-disciplinary knowledge exchange and critical engagement, thereby creating spaces for community participation and dialogue rather than mere passive appreciation. Recognizing how we can become ecological in our approach – where artists, curators and institutions work together to enable dialogic exchange – extends the possibility and potential for connecting people and place.

These case studies bring to the fore wider insights into the importance of environmental aesthetics, artists and institutional spaces for their curation and presentation. Aesthetics are a vital means through which people can encounter the natural world to nurture emotional affiliation and ethical commitment to other species and ecosystems. For many people, opportunities for direct aesthetic appreciation of nature may not extend beyond their urban neighbourhoods. The arts (liberal and creative) have a crucial role in enabling and mediating such experiences and aesthetic appreciation in general.

Although the arts engage widely with environmental themes, they do not always facilitate the necessary systematic attitudinal and behavioural changes for fostering conservation values. *Curating*, meaning the philosophies and techniques for framing aesthetic experiences, is key for influencing what one notices and the meanings ascribed to these experiences. Curation is typically associated with galleries and museums but can extend to many contexts, including cultural festivals, school curricula, government regulation and national park visitor facilities. With the philosophy of curating increasingly advocating a shift from didactic, "expert" presentation to the creation of active spaces inviting participant dialogue and interaction, curating can give considerable agency to the community in shaping our interpretation of artists' environmental aesthetics (Sachs, 2017, p. 16).

Assemblage-based approaches that adopt a "becoming ecological" mindset can actively engage audiences and facilitate conversations that bring to light the myriad ways we understand, interact with and ultimately value the environment. The opportunity to disrupt, expose, challenge and extend hierarchical knowledge structures and systems allows communities and individuals to re-examine thoughts, opinions and assumptions. This form of prompted self-reflection encourages and enables the re-imagining of ourselves and the environments with which we are intrinsically connected.

Conclusion

When engaging with/viewing curated artworks, we may experience dissonance. To resolve or accept the conflicts, slippage can provide a means for making sense of seemingly disparate pieces of sensory evidence. As discussed in this chapter, the narratives and conversations that emerge in response to this type of aesthetic curation have the capacity to alter perceptual understanding, with the potential for attitudinal and behavioural change. In the examples discussed, we have sought to consider the ways negative human environmental impacts can be attenuated, thereby providing a critical platform for discussions around ideas about conservation.

By exploring narratives and supporting conversations surrounding human/environment relationships, artists, curators and cultural institutions provoke inquiry into societal priorities. Examining priorities raises questions about notions of value and how such belief structures are shaped by the social, political, cultural and physical environments we inhabit. If we are to interact with each other and these environments and exercise ethically responsible behaviours, then we first need to be alerted to, aware of and sympathetic to the diverse ways people connect to place. Artists, curators and museums, in collaboration with audiences, collectively shed light on such connections, enabling a deeper understanding of the complex entanglements that bind people and place.

References

Allen, J. M., Wright, S., Cranston, N., Watson, J., Beswick, K., & Hay, I. (2018). Raising levels of school student engagement and retention in rural, regional and disadvantaged areas: Is it a lost cause? *International Journal of Inclusive Education, 22*(4), 409–425.

Badham, M., Wise, K., & MacDonald, A. (2021). Mona's 24 carrot gardens: Seeding an ecology of cultural value. In K. Lehman, I. Fillis, & M. Wickham (Eds.), *Exploring cultural value: Contemporary issues for theory and practice* (pp. 101–118). Emerald Publishing Limited.

Bal, M., & Burke, R. E. (2017). Sensing the present: "Conceptual art of the senses." *Text Matters: A Journal of Literature, Theory and Culture, 7*, 27–54. https://doi.org/10.1515/texmat-2017-0002

Bignall, S., & Braidotti, R. (2018). Posthuman systems. In R. Braidotti & S. Bignall (Eds.), *Posthuman ecologies: Complexity and process after Deleuze* (pp. 1–18). Rowman and Littlefield.

Braidotti, R. (2013). *The posthuman*. Polity Press.

Deleuze, G., & Guattari, F. (1987). *A thousand plateaus: Capitalism and schizophrenia*. Bloomsbury Publishing. (Original work published 1980)

Duke, L. (2010). The museum visit: It's an experience, not a lesson. *Curator: The Museum Journal, 53*(3), 271–279.

Eslake, S. (2021, January 21). "I almost cracked": 16-month artistic performance of mass extinction comes to a close. *The Guardian*. https://www.theguardian.com/artanddesign/2021/jan/25/i-almost-cracked-16-month-artistic-performance-of-mass-extinction-comes-to-a-close

Foster, S., Fillis, I., Lehman, K., & Wickham, M. (2020). Investigating the relationship between visitor location and motivations to attend a museum. *Cultural Trends, 29*(3), 213–233.

Haraway, D. J. (2016). *Staying with the trouble: Making kin in the Chthulucene*. Duke University Press.

Hunter, M. A., & MacDonald, A. (2017). Dark play: On an alternative politics of aspiration. In P. O'Connor & C. Gomez (Eds.), *Playing with possibilities* (pp. 16–23). Cambridge Scholars Publishing.

Huyssen, A. (1995). *Twilight memories: Marking time in a culture of amnesia*. Routledge.

Kerby, M., MacDonald, A., McDonald, J., & Baguley, M. (2017). The museum diorama: Caught between art and history. *Australian Art Education, 38*(2), 354–371.

Lee, E. K. J. (2018). *Redeeming "slippery" meaning from the gap between the present and past: Exploring visual art processes and visual representation* [Doctoral dissertation, University of Tasmania, Australia]. https://doi.org/10.25959/100.00030170

Lehman, K., Wickham, M., & Fillis, I. (2020). Visitor motivations in arts and cultural organizations: A regional context. In C. S. Ooi & A. Hardy (Eds.), *Tourism in Tasmania* (pp. 160–172). Forty South Publishing.

MutualArt. (2021). *Alastair Mooney: Artist biography*. https://www.mutualart.com/Artist/Alastair-Mooney/32E1338C057EDB70

Pindyck, M. (2018). Frottage as inquiry. *International Journal of Education Through Art, 14*(1), 13–25.

Riawunna Centre for Education. (2021). *Support for Aboriginal and Torres Strait Islander students*. University of Tasmania. https://www.utas.edu.au/riawunna/about-us

Richardson, B. J., & Hogan, J. (2018). The remarkable Tasmanian Devil: The aesthetics of persecution and protection. *Alternative Law Journal, 43*(4), 269–274.

Rimmer, Z., & Sainty, T. (2020). Palawa kani: Expressing the power of language in art and the museum context. *Artlink, 40*(2), 32–35.

Rousell, D. (2020). Cosmopolitical encounters in environmental education: Becoming-ecological in the intertidal zones of Bundjalung National Park. *The Journal of Environmental Education, 2*(2), 133–148.

Rowan, M., & Ramsay, E. (2018). Educational inequality in Tasmania: Evidence and explanations. *The Australian Educational Researcher, 45*(3), 277–295.

Sachs, A. (2017). Introduction. In C. Mörsch, A. Sachs, & T. Sieber (Eds.), *Contemporary curating and museum education* (pp. 15–18). Verlag.

Stone, A., Walter, M., & Peacock, H. (2017). Educational outcomes for aboriginal school students in Tasmania: Is the achievement gap closing? *Australian and International Journal of Rural Education, 27*(3), 90–110.

Tasmanian Aboriginal Centre. (2021). *Tasmanian Aboriginal place names.* http://tacinc.com.au/tasmanian-aboriginal-place-names/

Tasmanian Museum and Art Gallery. (2021). *TMAG – About us.* https://www.tmag.tas.gov.au/about_us

Vallance, E. (2004). Museum education as curriculum: Four models, leading to a fifth. *Studies in Art Education, 45*(4), 343–358.

Whatling. A. (2020). *NEST: Alastair Mooney* [Exhibition]. Queen Victoria Museum and Art Gallery, Launceston, Australia. https://www.qvmag.tas.gov.au/Exhibitions/Temporary-exhibitions/Nest-Alastair-Mooney

Witcomb, A. (2015). Toward a pedagogy of feeling: Understanding how museums create a space for cross-cultural encounters. In A. Witcomb & K. Message (Eds.), *The international handbooks of museum studies: Museum theory* (pp. 321–344). Wiley.

Chapter 6

On the Possibility of Reconstructing a Contested Past Through Memory Museums in Turkey

Esra Yildiz

Nation-states have a long history of violence and discrimination against minorities and ethnic groups (Butler, 2009; Laitin, 2007). Centralized control over the means of violence is one of the definitive characteristics of modern states (Giddens, 1985), and the state legitimizes its power through violence (Arendt, 1970) and its ideological apparatuses. As Ernest Renan (1882/1990) states, "forgetting [...] is a crucial factor in the creation of a nation" (p. 11). Thus, contested past and violent history are purposely forgotten, and I propose that memory museums can address this gap in the identity construction of a more multicultural nation-state dealing with the contested past. In Turkey, ethnic and religious groups such as Alevis, Kurds, Roma, Greeks or Armenians – and their histories and violence against them – are often excluded from official narratives as well as from public discourse. From the time of the Ottoman Empire to the foundation of the Turkish Republic and following this period, cultural diversity and multiculturalism have always been on the political agenda, yet the exclusion of minority rights and cultural diversity from the constitution represents how the state places minorities in political discourse.

In conjunction with the reconciliation between different ethnic and religious groups, the Justice and Development Party (AKP) – Turkey's ruling party since 2002 – initiated a Democratic Opening Process in 2009 with "Kurdish openings." In the later years, this included democratization of minority rights for the Alevis, Armenians, Greeks and Roma, and allegedly showed the democratic face of the current government. Within the framework of these democratization initiatives and in line with access to the European Union and harmonization with European law (Kaya, 2013), minority rights and the subject of multiculturalism were taken up by the AKP to solve Turkey's painful problems in the initial years of its governance. Until the authoritarian shift of governance after 2010, issues such as Kurdish-Turkish conflict were on the agenda of the AKP Government to consolidate its power. Confronting the difficult past of various ethnocultural and minority groups – in particular through testimony literature, witness documentaries and fictional films about controversial events – also increased during this period. But after the Gezi Park Protests in 2013 and the alleged military coup on 15 July 2016, the AKP changed its policy towards the democratization process and suspended reforms, including minority rights (Bilgiç, 2018). This also led minority groups to struggle more against the violations of human rights of the past and demand concrete steps be taken for the democratization of civil society. The lawsuits about controversial events that spanned many years were left unresolved or were proscribed, and perpetrators who were not prosecuted also created social unrest amongst people.

In this regard, memory sites, memory museums and counter monuments gained importance in confronting the past and urging reconciliation. Different from history, "memory takes root in concrete, in spaces, gestures, images, and objects" (Nora, 1989, p. 9). The performative aspect of memory binds us to the present and urges people to act for a more democratic society.

In this chapter, I discuss the possibility of reconstructing and remembering Turkey's controversial past through memory sites: in particular, memory museums. People's demands over decades for long-awaited justice are also reflected in keeping the remnants of the past through what Aby Warburg calls "image memory." The state does not acknowledge what happened in the past. Thus, the ongoing struggles of people and their demand for memory museums and memory sites are an important means for transforming public discourse about controversial historical facts and educating the wider public about contested pasts.

Reconstructing and visualizing the violent past through memory museums and counter narratives

Museums are one of the mnemonic institutions where people make memory themselves (Assmann, 2008) and in which cultural memory can be transmitted to the next generation. Sociologist Maurice Halbwachs (1992) has emphasized the social and collective aspects of individual memory. Individual memory is fragmented and functions within the collective memory. For collective remembrance and for confronting past traumas and conflicts in the last few decades – a time Pierre Nora calls a world-wide upsurge in memory – special emphasis was given to memory museums. As cultural institutions, memory museums emerged after the Second World War for remembering the Holocaust and confronting its traumatic past, then expanded to different countries that experienced similar historical upheavals. With the postmodern period, increasing interest in ethnic identity has also accelerated memory studies, including the impact of memory museums and counter monuments on society. In recent decades, coming to terms with the negative past such as genocides, wars and massacres all around the world accelerated the emergence of memory sites and memory museums for awakening people to the atrocities of violence.

Similar to the memory upsurge in the world since the 1990s, the survivors of certain traumatic events in Turkey as well as witnesses and victims' families have been struggling to make sure the contested past will not be forgotten. In addition to this decades-long search for justice, preserving the places where bloody events took place as memory sites and turning them into museums are among the main demands of the victims' families. Even though their demands are not acknowledged officially by the state, their struggles are helping to open up a new public space and form new counter movements (Ahıska, 2014) in Turkey. This can be considered an important attempt to inform and educate citizens and future generations about the nation's contested past.

While suppressing different historical narratives, the AKP brought different forms of remembering based on Sunni Islam heritage to the political and social agenda. The AKP Government glorified Ottoman history, Islamic culture and heritage with its museums such as The Museum of Islamic Science and Technology and the Panorama 1453 History Museum. After the 15 July 2016 coup attempt, a new memorialization process started (Solomonovich, 2021), and memory sites, monuments and public sculptures were created for the commemoration of that event. The government in turn attacked these efforts, regarding memory museums as a threat to the nation-state's identity based on Sunni Islam. Yet the demand for memory and human rights museums to memorialize war and genocides in the world (Nora, 2002; Young, 1993) has also impacted Turkey. The survivors and relatives of the people killed in violent events such as the Dersim Massacre (1938), the Maraş Massacre (1977) or the Sivas Massacre (1993) call on the state to construct museums and memorials to remember the traumatic past. However, constructing museums and memorial sites for these tragic events means the acceptance of contested histories at a state level; thus, the state refuses to build them. Acceptance of these sites apparently needs much more support from the wider public.

There is a strong opposition to the commemoration of certain political events and the preservation of the places in which these events took place as memory sites or memory museums. However, the AKP does not take responsibility for the violent political events that took place during its rule, such as people killed during the Gezi Park protests, the March 2016 Ankara bombing or the Roboski Massacre. Commemoration of some past events is also prohibited: for instance, International Workers' Day was celebrated again in Taksim Square decades later during the AKP rule but was banned in Taksim after 2013. It is not even permitted to commemorate the first of May near the monument in Taksim where 33 people died in 1977. Similarly, Gezi Park, an Armenian cemetery during the Ottoman Empire, where the AKP Government wants to build a shopping centre and the Topçu Barracks, is also closed to public gatherings and celebration of anniversaries. After the military coup attempt in 2016, the names of streets and bridges were changed to 15 July, and founding leaders of the Turkish Republic were removed from the venues, showing the AKP's desire to remember which period and how.

Suppression of memory usually works against the history of minorities and the left. For example, the Saturday Mothers' struggle is one of these histories. Galatasaray Square on İstiklal Street, one of the main streets of İstanbul, is known for the struggle of mothers for human rights. The Saturday Mothers, whose children "disappeared" from police custody in the 1990s during the Kurdish conflict, started in the mid 1990s to gather every Saturday in Galatasaray Square to make their voices heard by the wider public. In 2011, the Saturday Mothers were accepted at the state level, including one of the iconic leaders of the collective, the 103-year-old Berfo Mother. They were guests of the prime minister at the time, and it was promised that the conflict would be resolved. But in August 2018, they were banned from meeting in Galatasaray Square and subjected to police violence.

Construction of memory museums and collecting and disseminating the contested past through them means an acceptance of the nation-state's violent past. The memory museum proposals mentioned below, proposed by people who lost their families and relatives or who witnessed them or are survivors, are a call to the state and set up a confrontation with the past.

The possibility of memory museums

Madımak Shame Museum

The Alevis are the second largest religious and ethnic minority group in Turkey, after Sunni Muslims. They are not defined formally as a minority in the Turkish State, and their cultural, religious history and massacres targeted at them are not acknowledged. The Sivas Massacre is one of the important violent events for which Alevis are still seeking justice.

On 2 July 1993 during the Pir Sultan Abdal Festival, 37 people were killed in the Madımak Hotel, which was set on fire by right-wing Islamist extremists (Sivas Massacre, 2021). Thirty-three of the victims were intellectuals, mostly Alevis, visiting the city for the festival. Many years after the massacre, the Supreme Court of the Constitution has not been able to present a verdict to the victims' families. After its renovation, the Madımak Hotel was turned into the Sivas Science and Culture Center, and only a memory corner was left for the people who died there, including the perpetrators. The work of many non-governmental organizations and collectives to keep the memories of the killed intellectuals alive continues with efforts to build the "Madımak Shame Museum."

In the face of unwillingness to construct a memory museum, the families of victims created their own home memory sites by keeping the memories of their loved ones and their rooms intact, as if they are still alive. Yeter Sivri lost her two daughters, Yasemin and Asuman Sivri, during the violent event. Sivri shouts to the camera in the documentary film *Before Menekşe* (2012): "If you don't make this hotel a museum, your best day will be worse than mine." Her statement is a condemnation of the state for its refusal to establish a memory place, a museum for the commemoration of their loved ones. As did other victims' families, Sivri created her own home museum in the absence of real memory museum and sites.

Dersim Museum

In 1937 and 1938, during an uprising of Kurdish Alevis against the Turkish State, thousands of civilians were killed. This happened under the governance of The Republican People's Party and since then has been used to protest against the ideology of the Republicans. In 2011, the prime minister of the time, Recep Tayyip Erdoğan, apologized for the Dersim Massacre as one of the dark chapters of Turkey's history, but Alevis are still struggling for the recognition of their rights at the state level.

In the 2000s, the Dersim Barracks, used by Turkish military groups for the planning and organization of the massacre, was on the agenda of those who search for official sites that offer visibility of this violent past and who wished to turn it into a memory museum. In 2014, the prime minister said that the barracks would become a museum. In 2020, a museum was opened under the name Tunceli. People from different parts of civil society who previously participated in planning the museum were excluded at a certain point (Aslan, 2021), and the museum itself represents the ideology of the nation-state. Besides a memory museum, a counter monument similar to Peter Eisenman's "The Memorial to the Murdered Jews of Europe" in Berlin was also planned for construction. All these are attempts to preserve the political and social history and memory embodied in Dersim's past.

Prison Museums: Diyarbakır Prison Museum

Prison museums are important architectural remembrance spaces where citizens recall state confrontation with its past and push for further justice and human rights. One of the first of its kind in Turkey is the Ulucanlar Prison, turned into a museum in 2011 by the Altındağ Municipality in Ankara. But the Ulucanlar Museum excluded various parts of civil society and non-government organizations in its establishment process, and it also falls short of giving the overall proper history of the prison.

Diyarbakır Prison, another politically and historically important prison, was built in Diyarbakır (southeastern Turkey) after the military coup of 12 September 1980. It is considered "the hell of Diyarbakır" because it was a place of systematic torture for many years, particularly against Kurdish prisoners. For some ex-prisoners, "turning it into a museum would be an apology" from the state (as cited in Çakır, 2009), comparable to the transformation of Nazi concentration camps into museums. Even the prime minister of the period said in his speech in 2010 – "if the Diyarbakır Prison had the language, and if only it could speak" – as an acknowledgement of confrontation with the past and an acceptance that violence was perpetrated against prisoners. The people who survived, witnessed violence or whose relatives were killed there discussed turning it into a Human Rights museum or Shame museum. The very recent declaration about transforming it into a cultural institution "to eliminate bad memories" is an attempt to cover up what happened there.

The Truth and Justice Commission for the Diyarbakır Prison, founded by a group called "78's Initiative," organized an oral history project with the political prisoners, held symposiums in various cities and opened exhibitions consisting of artworks about the Diyarbakır Prison and its violent past. Preserving memories through art and museumification of the prison is considered important in dealing with the past. Gani Alkan, head of the association for the 78's Initiative, said that their aim is based on four pillars:

First, is to uncover everything that happened in the Diyarbakır Prison. Second, is to face it and convict the responsible. Third, is to reveal the aim and causes of systematic torture in the Diyarbakır Prison, to shed a light on why it was the cruellest in the Diyarbakır Prison. Last, is to establish a museum of memory.

(Museums of Confrontation, 2018)

To convey the prison's memory to a wider society, the aim is to open a museum after all the truth and facts about the Diyarbakır Prison are revealed, and after testimonies of ex-prisoners are collected and made public.

Roboski Museum

On 28 December 2011, 34 Kurdish people were killed by the Turkish Air Force on the Iraq–Turkey border because they were thought to be fighters of the Kurdistan Workers' Party, when in fact they were civilians being smuggled to Turkey. In their quest for justice, people from civil society and the Roboski villagers who lost their relatives established the Roboski Museum Initiative and the Roboski Museum Association to commemorate the event. On land donated by the Roboski villagers, a museum and a monument will be constructed on a collective-based approach with voluntary participation.

As reflected by the above-mentioned examples – the Madımak Shame Museum, the Dersim Museum, the Diyarbakır Prison Museum and the Roboski Museum – civil society has been struggling for decades to keep the sites of atrocious and violent events as memory sites and create museums of contested pasts in an effort to remember, towards a future that prevents the state from overwriting the histories of these places. This will help a nation to confront its past, take responsibility for what happened and enlighten future generations. This is part of the new role of museums in society today.

Since the 1990s, the role of museums and art and cultural institutions has been redefined by a new concept of institutionalism; within the framework of this concept, engagement with the public and making the public active participants in the creation of their various activities became much more apparent and important. Producing content about social, political and global issues shows attempts by museums and art and cultural institutions to apply methods of critical pedagogy and engage with the community. Memory museums have directly contributed to this new approach in the last few decades.

On the other hand, while the museums described above are yet to be constructed, the 23.5 Hrant Dink Site of Memory in İstanbul was opened in 2019 as the first one of its kind. In the former building of the Armenian newspaper, *Agos*, the site was designed to honour the memory of the founder of *Agos*, Hrant Dink, assassinated on 19 January 2007. Following his death, the Hrant Dink Foundation preserved the legacy of Hrant Dink and his vision for the reconciliation of Turkish and Armenian people (Hrant Dink Foundation, n.d.).

On the Possibility of Reconstructing a Contested Past Through Memory Museums in Turkey

The 23.5 Hrant Dink Site of Memory is one of the initiatives the Hrant Dink Foundation took to contribute to another future. This memory site was formed by observations and studies from different cities all around the world which had a similar past. With its various activities – from educational programmes to conferences and workshops – it aims to contribute towards the social transformation of society. As this chapter proposes, when that possibility comes true, the expression of an event that has not been acknowledged and that created an outrage in society plays a reconciliatory role within the memory museum over time.

Conclusion

In a personal interview, artist Fatoş İrwen, who was incarcerated in the Diyarbakır Prison for three years, said to me that she would like to donate artworks she produced during her imprisonment to the Diyarbakır Prison Museum if it opens one day (Figure 6.1). Her desire for exhibiting her artworks in a memory museum rather than a contemporary art museum

Figure 6.1: Fatoş Irwen, *Wall – Time records*, 2019–2020. Wall layers of Diyarbakır Prison No. 5.

shows that she sees the importance of memory museums and artworks, which are witnesses to the atrocities taking place there, as mediators for the reconciliation of conflict-affected societies.

Turkey has experienced multiple and diverse conflicts, the contentions of its past more pronounced since the decline of the Ottoman Empire and during the history of the Turkish Republic. In this respect, memory sites and memory museums can play an important role in defending human rights and democracy through initiating different conflict groups and different ethnic parts of society. Besides this, the violent and traumatic past that has scarred survivors and witnesses as well as the need for perpetrators to take responsibility should also be illuminated. The possibility of memory museums cannot be separated from political discussion because the subjects they represent are controversial, seen as a threat to the presence of nation-states. The presence of these museums is a statement against the atrocities of violence as they keep a collective past alive. These memory museums and sites are symbols for the concreteness of collective memory with all its controversies. As Huyssen (2011) puts it, "the continuing strength of memory politics remains essential for securing human rights in the future" (p. 621). Because "remembering is an ethical act" (Sontag, 2003), nation-states should take the responsibility of remembering by securing human rights and democracy through museums or other cultural institutions.

In the absence of memory sites and memory museums, people keep and reproduce their memories through home memory sites, documentary films and artworks. As in some cases, such as the Sivas Massacre, "leaving the burden of the issues that need to be faced only to those who have experienced the trauma, increases the burden of the trauma" (Çavdar, 2021, p. 262). Thus, the presence of memory museums is a necessary support from the public, for the public.

Achille Mbembe (2015) states that a museum, properly understood, is not a dumping place nor where we recycle historical "waste"; instead, it is foremost an "epistemic space." Mbembe's emphasis on the responsibility of museums to counter colonialist thought can also be considered for memory museums, which present contested pasts through new knowledge as epistemic spaces. Teaching different perspectives about the history of nation-states as a contribution to democracy, justice and reconciliation is one of the purposes of these museums. The possibility of their construction is critically important for Turkey.

Acknowledgements

The initial phase of this chapter was developed during my postdoctoral study at Humboldt-Universität zu Berlin with the International Postdoctoral Research Fellowship Program in 2014–2015. I would like to thank Professor Dr Christina von Braun and Professor Dr Claudia Bruns for inviting and hosting me in Berlin.

References

Ahıska, M. (2014). Counter-movement, space and politics: How the Saturday Mothers of Turkey make enforced disappearances visible. In E. Schindel & P. Colombo (Eds.), *Space and the memories of violence* (pp. 162–175). Palgrave Macmillan.

Arendt, H. (1970). *On violence*. Harcourt, Brace & World.

Aslan, Ş. (2021, March 13). Dersim Kışlası'ndan 'Tunceli Müzesi'ne: Bir mekânın toplumsal öyküsü. *Birgün*. https://www.birgun.net/haber/dersim-kislasi-ndan-tunceli-muzesi-ne-bir-mekanin-toplumsal-oykusu-330195

Assmann, J. (2008). Communicative and cultural memory. In A. Erill, A. Noenning, & S. Young (Eds.), *Cultural memory studies: An international and interdisciplinary handbook* (pp. 109–118). Walter de Gruyter GmbH.

Bilgiç, A. (2018). Reclaiming the national will: Resilience of Turkish authoritarian neoliberalism after Gezi. *South European Society and Politics, 23*(2), 259–280.

Butler, J. (2009). *Frames of war: When is life grievable?* Verso.

Çakır, B. (2009, August 25). Turn Diyarbakır Prison into a museum! *Bianet*. https://m.bianet.org/bianet/other/116637-turn-diyarbakir-prison-into-a-museum

Çavdar, O. (2021). *Sivas Katliamı, Yas ve Bellek*. İletişim Publications.

Giddens, A. (1985). *The nation-state and violence*. Polity Press.

Halbwachs, M. (1992). *On collective memory* (L. A. Coser, Trans.). University of Chicago Press.

Hrant Dink Foundation. (n.d.). *Story of 23.5 Hrant Dink site of memory*. Hrantdink.org. https://hrantdink.org/en/site-of-memory/about-23-5/story

Huyssen, A. (2011). International human rights and the politics of memory: Limits and challenges. *Criticism, 53*(4), 607–624.

Kaya, A. (2013). Multiculturalism and minorities in Turkey. In R. Taras (Ed.), *Challenging multiculturalism: European models of diversity* (pp. 297–316). Edinburgh University Press.

Laitin, D. (2007). *Nations, states and violence*. Oxford University Press.

Mbembe, A. (2015). *Decolonizing knowledge and the question of the archive*. Wits Institute for Social and Economic Research. http://wiser.wits.ac.za/content/achille-mbembe-decolonizing-knowledge-and-question-archive-12054

Nora, P. (1989). Between memory and history: Les lieux de mémoire. *Representations, 26*, 7–24. https://doi.org/10.2307/2928520

Nora, P. (2002). Reasons for the current upsurge in memory. *Eurozine*. https://www.eurozine.com/reasons-for-the-current-upsurge-in-memory/

Renan, E. (1990). What is a nation? In H. K. Bhabha (Ed.), *Nation and narration* (pp. 8–22). Routledge. (Original work published 1882)

Solomonovich, N. (2021). "Democracy and National Unity Day" in Turkey: The invention of a new national holiday. *New Perspectives on Turkey, 64*, 55–80.

Sontag, S. (2003). *Regarding the pain of others*. Picador.

Young, J. E. (1993). *The texture of memory: Holocaust memorials and meaning*. Yale University Press.

Part II

Museums of Purpose

Chapter 7

Disrupting Museum Education: Counter-Monument as a Pedagogical Space

Susana Vargas-Mejía

Museums, memorial centres, heritage institutions and other public forms of commemoration, such as counter-monuments, provide the public opportunities to address challenging issues, such as war and genocide, through artistic perspectives and through the public's own emotional capacity. The dimension of affect comes to the fore when approaching spaces such as counter-monuments, where tragedies and the violent past are being exhibited as a warning to the present – as is the case with *Fragmentos: Espacio de Arte y Memoria* by the Colombian artist Doris Salcedo.

Fragmentos is part of a national mandate to create commemorative monuments in Colombia. After almost six decades of armed conflict between the leftist group the Revolutionary Armed Forces (known by their Spanish initials FARC-EP) and the Colombian government, a peace agreement was signed in 2016. In this agreement, it was stated that three monuments would be constructed out of the weapons surrendered by the former guerrilla group FARC-EP. The first such work, made by the artist Doris Salcedo, was inaugurated in December 2018 in downtown Bogotá, under the name *Fragmentos: Espacio de Arte y Memoria*. The second piece, *Kusikawsay* by the artist Mario Opazo, was installed in the sculpture garden of the United Nations in New York on 23 August 2019. The third piece will be in Havana, Cuba, where the peace dialogues were held. This piece has not yet been built.

In the creation of *Fragmentos*, 37 tonnes of weapons handed over by the former Colombian guerrilla FARC-EP were used to create the floor, which occupies 800 square metres and is covered by 1300 metal sheets made of the FARC's melted weapons. Salcedo worked together with twenty female civilian victims of the Colombian conflict to build the installation to demonstrate how art contributes to a society that is embracing a post-conflict era. Although the intention of the government was to commemorate the victims through constructing a traditional monument, Salcedo opposed such a creation, arguing that it would glorify the war (Duzán, 2018). Instead, the artist wanted to take a different approach to the notion of commemorating violence and proposed a counter-monument that visitors can walk upon (Figure 7.1).

The manner in which *Fragmentos* operates stands in opposition to the traditional museum, where artworks are exhibited on walls and monuments are generally on plinths where an object is viewed, celebrated and contemplated. In these two examples, the works are not meant to be touched by the public. *Fragmentos* on the other hand offers a full immersion of our senses; we are stepping on melted guns and into a space focused on stories emerging from violence. In this way, the borders around museum education, art education and

Figure 7.1: Entrance to the installation. Photo by Juan Fernando Castro. Courtesy of *Fragmentos: Espacio de Arte y Memoria*.

monuments are shifting; as art educators, it is essential for us to take up these interruptions in our curriculum and instruction to move beyond simple categorization. In this chapter, I analyse the case of *Fragmentos* as a new pedagogical space where meaningful educational experiences are being addressed in the context of post-conflict Colombia.

Whereas traditional monuments are often highly visible, set apart from everyday spaces and difficult to access (Williams, 2007), counter-monuments rarely have these characteristics and instead create new spaces and impose innovative designs (Stevens et al., 2012). For Stevens et al. (2012), the notion of a counter-monument reshapes traditional ways of constructing monuments and often rejects and renegotiates the forms of public memorial art, "such as prominence and durability, figurative representation and the glorification of past deeds" (p. 952). Young (1992) was among the first scholars to discuss the notion of the counter-monument, analysing it from a German perspective. In addition to studying the state of collective memory, Young discusses the new generation of contemporary artists that emerged after the Second World War who were aesthetically sceptical of traditional memorials, but at the same time felt a responsibility to remember. They evoked critique by asking what conventional monuments tell us about, what must be remembered, and who decides what must be remembered and why.

Salcedo decided to intervene in this space by building a counter-monument and keeping the remains of the old construction as an allegory to the war: a constant reminder of the vestiges and "ruins" of the armed conflict left in Colombian society (Duzán, 2018). In a video interview, Duzán (2018) explained that constructing a monument was inappropriate given the circumstances and political conditions:

> A monument, as its name implies, tries to dwarf us with a unique look, a great truth from the past of a nation. The monument is vertical, therefore, hierarchical. The ideal right now is to build something much more democratic. A place where we can all stand equally and reflect on what happened to us. The monument is like an ode to the warlike triumphs and the counter-monument a parable that tells the pain of the victims.
>
> (6:58)

The artist did not want to glorify the war or the army. Salcedo clarified that this space does not support any political party or armed group. On the contrary, she aimed to build a space where reflection was possible for everyone interested. According to Salcedo (in an interview with Duzán, 2018), the monument is a form of forgetfulness: It leaves behind many voices that are not being represented. In other words, it has represented and prioritized a unique version of the story, which is the reason why she opted to create a counter-monument.

As Williams (2007) notes, memorials are often related to loss or mourning, whereas monuments honour greatness and valour. Monuments are frequently a physical indoor or outdoor representation of an event or a person that takes the form of sculptures or structures. In turn, counter-monuments emerge as a critical extension of the idea of traditional monuments. This idea was further developed in European countries beyond Germany: for example, the project *De/construction of Monument* in Bosnia and Herzegovina. Whereas monuments tend to honour a specific person or event, counter-monuments oppose this idea by providing the space to debate who should be remembered, as "the never-to-be-resolved debate over which kind of memory to preserve, how to do it, in whose name, and to what end" (Young, 1992, p. 119). To illustrate this, Herscher (2014) explains that memory, architecture and violence are correlated, and counter-monuments offer a space rather than a figurative representation of someone or something. Hence, the concept of a counter-monument is "nothing but the visitors themselves standing in remembrance, left to look inward for memory" (Young, 1992, p. 118, as cited in Herscher, 2014, p. 467), instead of commemorating a specific actor, which assumes the public understands and does not perpetuate the conflict (Herscher, 2014). The components of location, site, form and materiality compose the notion of monument and counter-monument, through which it is possible to recall values, moments, individuals and a specific event although "we often see measures of both in any single structure, making this distinction fuzzy" (Williams, 2007, p. 8). Young (1992) argues that monuments are a double-edged post-war legacy. A sceptical look at the memorial's traditional function, mass memory production and consumption were at the fore of Young's (1992) analysis:

> Like other forms of art, the monument is most benign when static: there when you face it, gone when you turn your back. But when it begins to come to life, to grow, shrink,

or change form, the monument may become threatening. No longer at the mercy of the viewer's will, it seems to have a will of its own, to beckon us at inopportune moments.

(p. 284)

Herscher (2014) and Sodaro (2018) suggest that monuments and more traditional forms of memory privilege a "unique truth" rather than facilitating discussions about challenging the past. Although *Fragmentos* creates a space for dialogues and openness, the artist has been critiqued by some viewers. Salcedo's work is intended to absorb the memories and experiences of those directly affected by the civil war and the politics fostering it. Salcedo is not explicitly affected by the memories and experiences herself, and this is considered by many as opportunism (Schneider, 2014, p. 26). However, the Colombian art critic Roca (2016) affirms that to categorize Salcedo as an opportunist is to ignore 40 years of continuous work. Moreover, such criticism demonstrates a misunderstanding of her purpose as an artist whose artworks are motivated by events that have marked us as a society. Salcedo turns these events into public acts, creating symbolic actions that might generate reflections around a specific topic.

In this sense, it is essential to locate *Fragmentos* as a work that generates tensions in different spheres, not only in socio-political terms (because half the population was against the peace agreements[1]) but also in the artistic dimension, given the polemic artworks and the criticism of Salcedo throughout the years (Bal, 2010; Malagón-Kurka, 2010; Rubiano, 2017; Schneider, 2014). This then raises the question: How can we use all these tensions and provocations to engage in meaningful learning processes related to peace in art education?

Fragmentos, empathy and learning

Uhrmacher and Tinkler (2008) examine the powerful impact of memorials and how they function as a mechanism to teach and develop empathy through understanding different forms of commemoration. They suggest that "educators should make monuments part of their curriculum" (p. 226), not only because of their power to bring past events into the present but also for the potential these spaces have to create memory "by turning time into space" (p. 226). In fact, memory is at the forefront when understanding a post-conflict society (Rocha, 2018). In *Fragmentos*, the potential of the space is that visitors are continuously stepping on the melted weapons used during the armed conflict, which is deeply evocative of lived experiences of war. To illustrate this, Thobo-Carlsen (2016) analyses the concept of "museum walkers" (p. 146) as agents that interpret the space in a multisensory and affective way. The experience visitors have at memorial museums, counter-monuments and spaces that commemorate war is not a passive walk-through. Generally, these spaces seek an emotional experience that facilitates engagement and learning (see Tamashiro & Furnari, 2015). In *Fragmentos*, the act of stepping on and walking on melted guns and experiencing the materiality of the space itself is extremely significant (Figure 7.2).

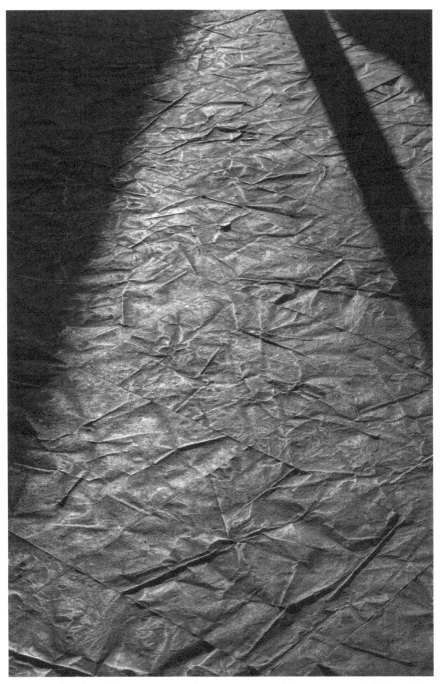

Figure 7.2: View of the floor. Photo by Juan Fernando Castro. Courtesy of *Fragmentos: Espacio de Arte y Memoria*.

Museum education and counter-monuments

Museums are sites that bring ideas and subjects to life in a way that school textbooks cannot, highlighting the excitement the experience provides (van den Dungen & Yamane, 2015). Although the authors do not emphasize counter-monuments, they do describe peace spaces that aim to celebrate reconciliation. This kind of commemoration as well as peace museums "are important instruments for educating a broad public about the need to move from a culture of war and violence to one characterised by peace and nonviolence" (p. 220). It is fair to question, then, what role *Fragmentos* has as a space with a wide range of opportunities to reflect on the Colombian armed conflict. That is why, at this point, museum education is an important framework to use to discuss the value of this space. It remains to be asked, with the characteristics of *Fragmentos* as a counter-monument – what role do museum education and peace education have in embracing the pedagogy embedded in such space? How can art education move in this direction?

The concept of *Fragmentos* is provocative. In addition to presenting a counter-monument to the Colombian armed conflict, it serves as a platform to display works by other artists. Thus, it is a space in constant motion; it is not static. Likewise, it is operated by the National Museum of Colombia as a venue opened to the public, and it is recognized as a counter-monument. In this regard, *Fragmentos* extends the parameters of spaces, affects, sensorial, ruptures, new contexts and pedagogical prompts that are significant for art educators to understand. As Williams (2007) argued, "traditional and formal distinctions between monuments, memorials, and museums are blurred, in intriguing ways" (p. 8). *Fragmentos* can be seen as a disruption within museum studies. Spaces such as *Fragmentos* shift away from the traditional model of art exhibition or museums in general, where the artefact and the objects displayed have inherited more interest than the site itself (Figure 7.3). How does *Fragmentos* become a different space when we, as spectators, walk through the space? The spatial effects in *Fragmentos* are relevant when appreciating them chiefly in terms of architecture, the melted weapons floor and the walk-through spaces and exhibitions.

Williams (2007) notes that spaces such as the Mostar Bridge in Bosnia, Poland's Wolfsschanze and Budapest's Statue Park are not established as museums, institutions or mourning places. Also, memorials such as Parque de la Memoria in Buenos Aires, Memorial to the Murdered Jews of Europe in Berlin and the World Trade Center Memorial in New York reinvent the space to bring historical commemoration into frequently visited outdoor public spaces, making them accessible to many people. Williams (2007) calls for more clarity and complexity "to enlarge standard concepts of the museological" (p. 181). Contemporary art responses to post-war scenarios are helpful in understanding and comprehending this growing body of counter-monuments worldwide, and in situating the importance of *Fragmentos* within post-conflict Colombia and beyond. For instance, the multidisciplinary project *De/construction of Monument*, held between 2004 and 2007 at the Sarajevo Center for Contemporary Arts in Bosnia and Herzegovina, explored the notion of counter-monument in post-Yugoslavia with the goal of recognizing and rejecting the violence of

Figure 7.3: Walking with *Fragmentos*. Photo by Juan Fernando Castro. Courtesy of *Fragmentos, Espacio de Arte y Memoria*.

the past. It represents the importance of creating spaces where the public can reflect on and discuss the history of violence. Likewise, the Arenberg Park flak towers in Vienna, Austria, originally Nazi bunkers, are currently used as art storage facilities and also a space for in situ art installations of the Mak Museum of Applied and Contemporary Art. Lachapelle (2011) discusses the significance of comprehending the historical context of some cultural objects such as the flak towers and, by extension, analyses the role of the viewer as an essential element to understand the significance of the space. As Lachapelle (2011) clarifies when explaining the space itself, "this necessarily means something different for each one of these viewers. Yet, all of these individual significations are correct: none of them can be rejected as somehow insignificant" (p. 20). Historical context and personal experience are two main concepts used to understand these places; they are, in fact, at the core of the concept of counter-monument. The memories and experiences each person has had throughout their lives have a vital role to play when experiencing memorials, monuments and counter-monuments. As with *Fragmentos*, post-war and post-conflict scenarios are being considered. In other words, turning facilities first conceived as war commemorations into art and cultural spaces, the importance of material culture and the opportunity to discuss the symbolism of these spaces are all essential to recall collectively what is at the core of *Fragmentos*: emotionality, life stories and historical context.

Learning through empathy and emotions: Experiencing *Fragmentos*

Fragmentos represents the reinvention of space to make it a possible social meeting place for reconciliation. This space can be a potential generator of experiences; it is heavily and profoundly laden with personal interpretations that are key to the visitor's experience (Lachapelle, 2011). In this way, memorial centres, museums and other heritage institutions use design tactics to evoke emotional responses from the visitors. For instance, Sodaro (2018) explains the importance of inspiring empathy and moral education at memorial museums to embrace and truly internalize the notion of "never again" (p. 173) by balancing the historical narratives with "affective-emotional experiences that will impact the visitor more fully" (p. 173). Similarly, Savenije and de Brujin (2017) bring to the conversation terms such as *historical empathy,* "in which interrelations of reason and emotion and the notion that emotional responses are shaped by people's cultural backgrounds have similarly been emphasised" (p. 833).

The emotional dimension is most prominent when visiting *Fragmentos*. Frois and White (2013) explain the aesthetic experience according to Jones's (1979) model, which consists of four elements: affective (emotional), extrinsic (instrumental), intrinsic (formal) and cognitive (intellectual) (p. 110). Each aesthetic experience can range across these categories, and as the authors suggest, "an ideal aesthetic experience would be one that acknowledges the four quadrants" (p. 111). Applying this to *Fragmentos*, the experience would be largely affective (emotional). For instance, Sodaro (2018) questions how museums can generate worthwhile educational processes through emotional encounters, attempting to enhance moral sensibility in the visitor's daily life and thus generate a possible change. The author points out that this is achieved primarily through the opportunity for visitors to identify with the victims. In other words, it is achieved through developing empathy by connecting the past to their own lived experiences. The video displayed at *Fragmentos* offers the testimony of twenty female civilian victims who narrate their life stories. Victims of sexual abuse during the armed conflict, these civilians' testimonies function as an emotional engagement. As explained by Savenije and de Brujin (2017), "narrating history through a singular perspective, such as that of an individual person, stimulates emotional engagement, allowing people to identify with the thoughts and feelings of historical actors" (p. 834). In summary, these perspectives provide a niche through which *Fragmentos* can be analysed from a critical art education viewpoint: There is a strong emotional engagement, which allows the visitor to engage with the history of violence from a self-reflective perspective.

The affective dimension is also examined through the vital lens of reconciliation. Zembylas (2007) argues that encouraging a curriculum that has empathy and reconciliation as pillars is key to reconstructing conflict-ridden societies where peace education is needed. *Fragmentos* achieves this by generating reflections on the experience of stepping on the melted weapons and by offering the testimonies of the female civilian victims, who worked together with the artist to create the floor. By recognizing the impact of war on their lives, visitors can connect "with that historical moment through the permanence of the physical object" (Uhrmacher & Tinkler, 2008, p. 226).

Given the challenging times Colombia is experiencing, it is valuable to highlight the benefits that art education can bring to a society that urgently needs change and innovation – to consider more fully how peace education, museums and other forms of commemorative practices could address these issues. Perhaps through art, it is possible to create conversations that help people rethink and reflect about peace in Colombia to promote healing. In this sense, I envision *Fragmentos* as a platform where peace education can generate meaningful reflections by leading discussions that make space for a variety of perspectives and a plurality of voices, rather than recognizing a singular truth – promoting critical thinking and an awareness of our recent and unforgettable history of violence.

Note

1. In 2012, former President Juan Manuel Santos began peace negotiations with the FARC-EP in Havana, Cuba. In October 2016, after four years of arduous negotiations, President Santos conducted a plebiscite as a way to endorse the agreements negotiated in Havana. Citizens were asked to vote on whether or not they approved of the peace agreements. The results showed that 50.21 per cent rejected the peace accord, while 49.78 per cent were in favour, with 37.43 per cent turning out to the polls (Rocha, 2018).

References

Bal, M. (2010). *Of what one cannot speak: Doris Salcedo's political art*. The University of Chicago Press.

Duzán, M. (2018, December 10). *Doris Salcedo en entrevista con María Jimena Duzán* [Video file]. YouTube. https://www.youtube.com/watch?v=MdNLzcx14uE

Frois, J. P., & White, B. (2013). Words for artworks: The aesthetics of meaning making. *The International Journal of Art & Design Education*, 32(1), 109–125.

Herscher, A. (2014). In ruins: Architecture, memory, countermemory. *Journal of the Society of Architectural Historians*, 73(4), 464–469.

Lachapelle, R. (2011). The landscape, the built environment, and the work of art: Three meaningful territories for art education and material culture studies. In P. Bolin & D. Blandy (Eds.), *Matter matters: Art education and material culture studies* (pp. 12–24). National Art Education Association.

Malagón-Kurka, M. (2010). *Arte como presencia indéxica: la obra de tres artistas colombianos en tiempo de violencia: Beatriz González, Oscar Muñoz y Doris Salcedo en la década de los noventa*. Edición Uniandes.

Roca, J. (2016, October 18). A la opinión pública, una carta abierta de José Roca. *Revista Arcadia*. https://www.revistaarcadia.com/agenda/articulo/defensa-a-sumando-ausencias-de-doris-salcedo/a57113

Rocha, M. (2018). Creating classroom materials: Efforts to open up a debate about Colombia's armed conflict. In B. Ramírez & M. Schulze (Eds.), *Transitional justice and education: Engaging young people in peacebuilding and reconciliation* (pp. 45–66). V&R Academic.

Rubiano, E. (2017). Victims, memory and mourning: Contemporary art in the post-accord scenario. *Análisis Político, 90*(1), 103–120.

Savenije, G., & de Bruijn, P. (2017). Historical empathy in a museum: Uniting contextualisation and emotional engagement. *International Journal of Heritage Studies, 23*(9), 832–845. https://doi.org/10.1080/13527258.2017.1339108

Schneider, M. (2014). *Material witness: Doris Salcedo's practice as an address on political violence through materiality* [Doctoral dissertation, Harvard University]. Harvard University Digital Archive. http://nrs.harvard.edu/urn-3:HUL.InstRepos:11746516

Sodaro, A. (2018). *Exhibiting atrocity: Memorial museums and the politics of past violence*. Rutgers University Press.

Stevens, Q., Franck, K. A., & Fazakerley, R. (2012). Counter-monuments: the anti-monumental and the dialogic. *The Journal of Architecture, 17*(6), 951–972. https://doi.org/10.1080/13602365.2012.746035

Tamashiro, R., & Furnari, E. (2015). Museums for peace: Agents and instruments of peace education. *Journal of Peace Education, 12*(3), 223–235. https://doi.org/10.1080/17400201.2015.1092712

Thobo-Carlsen, M. (2016). Walking the museum: Performing the museum. *The Senses and Society, 11*(2), 136–157. https://doi.org/10.1080/17458927.2016.1190067

Uhrmacher, B., & Tinkler, B. (2008). Engaging learners and the community through the study of monuments. *International Journal of Leadership in Education, 11*(3), 225–238. https://doi.org/10.1080/13603120801918772

van den Dungen, P., & Yamane, K. (2015). Peace education through peace museums. *Journal of Peace Education, 12*(3), 213–222. https://doi.org/10.1080/17400201.2015.1103393

Williams, P. (2007). *Memorial museums: The global rush to commemorate atrocities*. Berg.

Young, J. (1992). The counter-monument: Memory against itself in Germany today. *Critical Inquiry, 18*(2), 267–296.

Zembylas, M. (2007). The politics of trauma: Empathy, reconciliation, and peace education. *Journal of Peace Education, 4*(2), 207–224. https://doi.org/10.1080/17400200701523603

Chapter 8

Korundi Recreated: Participatory Experience Creates a Dialogue Between Past and Present

A Visual Essay

Anniina Koivurova and Tatiana Kravtsov

This visual essay approaches themes of heritage and memory through participatory art-based activities in a museum context. The focus is on a dialogue between past and present embedded in the history of Korundi House of Culture, located in Rovaniemi, Finnish Lapland (https://www.korundi.fi/en/Home).

Korundi House of Culture was originally an old post bus depot dating back to 1933 (Figure 8.1a) and one of the few buildings in Rovaniemi that survived the Second World War. After the war, the building was reconstructed using bricks from ruins of people's homes from all over the town. By preserving the memory and materials that survived the wartime, the building holds historical and emotional value on national and regional levels (Giebelhausen, 2006; Kuusikko & Ylimartimo, 2011).

Reshaped and expanded, the Korundi House of Culture opened in 2011 (Figure 8.1b). It is composed of elements from a former industrial building and new modern architecture, creating a dialogue between past and present, old and contemporary. The house accommodates the Lapland Chamber Orchestra and Rovaniemi Art Museum, which displays Finnish contemporary art and Northern art. Ever since its founding, Rovaniemi Art Museum has had a strong educational aim at museum pedagogy, especially through interactive workshops (Salo et al., 2016). In spring 2021, Anniina from Rovaniemi Art Museum and Tatiana from the Art-based Services for Tourism project (2019–21, University of Lapland) held a pilot workshop of creative activity in Korundi.

The aim of the workshop was to explore the potential of art-based participatory experiences to create a meeting point between the history and personal perception of the place and space. The brick wall was the basis of the storyline, which connects past and present and leads to a dialogue between history and contemporary art, existing side-by-side within the walls of the building.

Seven participants between 8 and 65 years of age – including locals, newcomers and international visitors – joined the open-invitation workshop. We started with an introduction from the Korundi lobby. Anniina gave a brief history to the present day, and Tatiana spoke about the qualities of clay, its transformation from mud to a solid brick and how clay as a material has a memory.

The participants were asked to approach the brick wall, choose a spot and explore the texture of bricks using multiple senses while thinking of the past and visualizing a story (Figure 8.2). A slow encounter with the heritage "surface" allowed the participants to contemplate and create a personal connection with the wall material.

(a)

(b)

Figure 8.1: *Then and now.* 1a (top): Post bus depot. Photo by Eino Maisonvaara, 1949. Archival image copyright: Rovaniemi Art Museum. 1b (bottom): Korundi House of Culture. Photo by Adam Piper, 2018. Archival image copyright: Rovaniemi Art Museum.

Each individual brick can be seen as a metaphor of memory, a smaller story within the larger narrative of the war and reconstruction. The first layer of the visual story was created with a sensorial frottage technique. Using graphite pencils and sticks, the participants rubbed the elements of the brick wall surface to transfer its texture onto the paper.

Visualization of the story continued in a workshop room, where the participants expressed emotion and feeling by adding a colourful layer on the top of their brick wall drawing using a photo transfer technique (Figure 8.3). From the archives of the Provincial Museum of Lapland, black and white images of the post-war ruins of Lapland – such as vehicles, street views and local people from the 1940s and 1950s – were offered to the participants. Cut and glued, the images created a layer with faces and elements symbolizing the past. While walls can be seen as a *collage* of bricks collected from the war ruins, this idea was reflected in the technique applied in the creative activity. Collage as a method allows us to layer various materials and elements, giving new meaning to them.

We ended the workshop with a feedback session that revealed personal dimensions of the process. Tuula Vanhatapio talked about her artwork, which represented her relative, an elderly woman who holds a secret (Figure 8.4). This opened a discussion about illegitimate children born during and after the Second World War in Finnish Lapland. These mothers and children were treated with contempt in local communities. We discussed that today in Finland, unspoken, sensitive and traumatic issues from that era can be reflected more openly.

The activity stimulated a multisensory experience and opened new perspectives for sensing the place by bringing an emotional narrative alive. The workshop fulfilled our aim

Figure 8.2: Exploring the bricks and making frottage. Photos by Tatiana Kravtsov.

Figure 8.3: *Collaging.* Photos by Anniina Koivurova & Tatiana Kravtsov.

to enhance personal awareness and sensitivity about the multiple layers of place, space and time. Art-based practice enabled the participants to make the dialogue between past and present alive and dynamic, adding new layers to it through personal expression and reflection shared with other participants (Figure 8.5).

The workshop will be developed further to facilitate cross-cultural and cross-generational encounters. The concept serves domestic and international visitors by offering a platform for creative multisensory activity on heritages and identities. We believe that such a workshop has the potential to enrich the way visitors experience an art exhibition situated in a particular place, making the museum visit more profound and personal.

Figure 8.4: Tuula Vanhatapio, artwork. Photo: Anniina Koivurova.

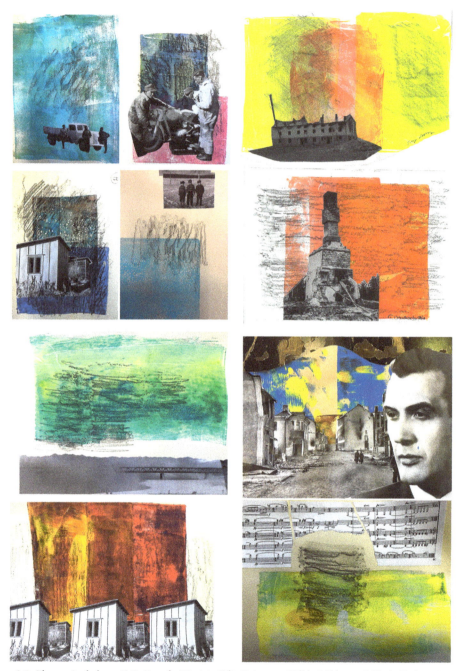

Figure 8.5: Zhanna Anshukova, Tuija Hautala-Hirvioja, Vilja Koivurova, Hilkka Liikkanen & Tuula Vanhatapio, artworks. Photos: Anniina Koivurova & Tatiana Kravtsov.

Acknowledgement

The University of Lapland supported the research.

References

Giebelhausen, M. (2006). The architecture *is* the museum. In J. Marstine (Ed.), *New museum theory and practice: An introduction* (pp. 41–59). Blackwell.

Kuusikko, R., & Ylimartimo, S. (Eds.). (2011). *Korundi. From a post bus depot into a house of culture* (L. Reinikainen, Trans.). LUP.

Salo, K., Koivurova, A., & Kähkönen, K. (2016). Where fragmentation and integration meet: Pedagogical challenges and opportunities for museums of contemporary art. *IMAG*, *3*(2), 55–63. https://doi.org/10.24981/2414-3332-3.2.2016.8

Chapter 9

Be the Nature: Enhancing Nature Connectedness Through Art Museum Pedagogy

Timo Jokela, Maria Huhmarniemi and Tanja Mäkitalo

This chapter presents the implementation and outcomes of a developing pedagogical art workshop for the art exhibition *With the Last Wolf* in the Särestöniemi Museum in Kittilä, Northern Finland. According to Mayer (2005), to learn how to teach, art museum educators have looked to sources in art history, which is why art history has played a determining role in the content of educational experiences for art museums. In this chapter, we move from museum pedagogy derived from discipline-centred art history to transformative experiences for visitors and co-knowing-centred pedagogy in a posthumanistic sense. We concentrate on the test bed in the Särestöniemi Museum to answer this research question: How can art museum pedagogy enhance nature connectedness? We also ponder the potential of new kinds of art education entrepreneurship related to the Northern ecoculture due to growing interest in the Arctic's creative economy (Jokela et al., 2022) and creative tourism (Huhmarniemi et al., 2021; Kugapi et al., 2020).

This case study was part of the Art-Based Services for Tourism (AST) research project, 2019–2021, funded by the European Regional Development Fund. The project supported art museum educators and artists in collaborating with tourism industry representatives to better mediate creative services for tourism agencies. The project included developing many art performances and workshops in Lapland for sharing cultural heritage with international travellers. In Lapland, when an art museum is in a remote location, most visitors are travellers visiting a museum alone or with a group, which is motivation to focus on tourists as a target group for art museum pedagogy.

Reidar Särestöniemi Art Museum

The Reidar Särestöniemi Museum presents the works of artist and professor Reidar Särestöniemi (1925–1981) and his living and working environment at the Ounas River, far away from other settlements. In addition to the gallery and atelier, the museum area includes Old Särestö, the Särestöniemi family farm dating from 1873, which represents the old architectural tradition in Lapland (Figure 9.1). The buildings on the small farm, the artist's childhood home, were restored in the early 2000s to reflect the way of life of the past and tell the story of the artist Reidar Särestöniemi and his family (Aikio & Aikio, 2005).

Reidar Särestöniemi is one of the most well-known Finnish artists and the most significant Lapland artist of his time (Hautala-Hirvioja, 2011; Polttila, 1985). His work reflects a range of influences, from European modernism to Russian art and prehistoric cave paintings.

Figure 9.1: Old Särestö buildings and view inside museum and the gallery. Photos courtesy of Reidar Särestöniemi Museum.

However, his main source of inspiration was Arctic nature and the Lapland people and their stories. In Särestöniemi's paintings, spring flowers bloom in a jagged way, the summer night sun glows red, frost birches shimmer in the winds of a winter day, bears and lynx embrace each other and seals in love rest on the shores of the Arctic Ocean. Särestöniemi examined nature, but he also looked deep inside himself (Hautala-Hirvioja, 2011; Hautala-Hirvioja et al., 2012; Ilvas, 2000). Often, he portrayed himself through his animal characters; through his art, he also conveyed threats to Lapland's natural environment caused by the utilization of natural resources (Hautala-Hirvioja et al., 2012; Polttila, 1985). On the one hand, Särestöniemi's colourful and nature-connected painting style has been criticized for exploiting the exotics of Lapland; on the other hand, some consider him an advocate of Northern nature.

Focus on the development work for the AST project included arts-based methods for meaningful and transformative tourism experiences and celebrating Northern nature and the diversity of local cultures and people. In this chapter, we describe the case study of art museum pedagogy in the Reidar Särestöniemi Museum for gaining transformative experiences that deepen participants' human–nature connectedness (Abson et al., 2017; Lumber et al., 2017; Mayer et al., 2009) and nature-based well-being (Capaldi et al., 2014; Simkin et al., 2020; Swami et al., 2016; Tyrväinen et al., 2014). We explore to what degree elements of Lapland's local ecoculture can be shared with visitors through art pedagogy in the Reidar Särestöniemi Museum. We also consider art museum pedagogy as a creative tourism service that can be beneficial for the growing creative economy in the Arctic.

Art museum pedagogy as creative tourism and enhancement of well-being

Much evidence exists supporting the museum setting as a unique space for art education and the value of museum collections and exhibitions as teaching resources (Ebitz, 2008; Mayer, 2005). It is common for art museums to use more resources for dialogical and pedagogical approaches to education (Dysthe, 2021; Riding et al., 2019). Museums can be part of a resilient, creative economy: building community bonds, reaching out to new generations and influencing the future of the museum's region (Buheji, 2019).

In this study, the Särestöniemi Museum's art and its artistic educational dimensions are approached from the perspective of new materialism and posthumanism, both as research methodology (Ulmer, 2017) and environmental art education (Ylirisku, 2021). A strong and interactive union of human and non-human nature is typical for Arctic communities, where ways of life can be considered an ecoculture. The "ecoculture" concept, which refers to interconnectedness and place-relations, is used to underscore the relationships among humans, their cultures and their ecologies (Parks, 2020). In the Arctic, traditional human–nature relationships emphasize the experience of nature's liveliness, will and agency. This so-called animistic worldview is typical of the belief traditions of the North and presented in the paintings by Särestöniemi.

In the AST research, as well as the connection with developing creative tourism, special attention is paid to pedagogical solutions, welfare and green care effects of activities in nature. Research has recognized the positive effects of being in nature (Abson et al., 2017; Capaldi et al., 2014; Lumber et al., 2017; Mayer et al., 2009; Swami et al., 2016; Tyrväinen et al., 2014). In Finland, forests, especially mature forests, have been identified as sources of renewal and stress release (Simkin et al., 2020). According to Lumber et al. (2017), feeling connected to nature is beneficial for well-being and pro-environmental behaviour. Contact, emotion, meaning, compassion and beauty are mapped as pathways for improving nature connectedness and as predictors of connections with nature, but knowledge-based activities grounded on sciences are not (Lumber et al., 2017).

The research process involved in the AST project included identifying the needs, challenges and expectations of art galleries and museums for creating tourist attractions for the summer season and for inviting tourists to visit the galleries. In the test bed for the Reidar Särestöniemi Museum, the Northern ecoculture and well-being impact of being connected to nature were in line with global concerns, such as loss of biodiversity and demands for empathy for non-human aspects of nature. Global environmental crises and local environmental conflicts underlined a need to transcend human-centredness. Pedagogical aims in the Särestöniemi test bed parallel environmental educators' efforts to develop pedagogical methods for enhancing human–nature connectedness and environmental awareness, as well as capacities and capabilities for taking action towards environmentalism. For example, in this case educators and scientists collaborate in developing educational methods for posthumanistic approach (Raatikainen et al., 2020).

Co-designing museum pedagogy as creative tourism

The methodological choice for the AST research project was art-based action research (ABAR). More of a research strategy than a research method, ABAR was developed by our team of art educators at the University of Lapland to combine artistic practices with regional development and community empowerment in the North (Jokela, 2019; Jokela et al., 2015, 2019). The goal was to develop professional methods and working approaches for art educators, community artists and artist-researchers through the cyclic ABAR process. The strategy shares some features with international arts-based research, artistic research, a/r/tography and action research. With these approaches, practical and theoretical research is conducted simultaneously, and interdisciplinary research topics are related to art as well as other fields of research such as education and regional development. ABAR is especially rooted in community arts and place-specific art forms: for example, environmental art and socially engaged art. These art forms served as the foundation for the Särestöniemi test bed.

The AST research began with co-design workshops, during which artists, art students and representatives of art galleries and museums brainstormed new services. These sessions were held at the galleries and museums and included an orientation to the art collections and surroundings of the museums, as well as information on future aims and customer analyses. A variety of ideas and preliminary concepts were envisioned during these workshops, some of which were chosen for further development and testing. Alternate ways of using photography as a tourism service were discussed in many of these brainstorming sessions, inspired by a growing interest in creative nature photography and the flow of self-portraits in social media.

Be the nature – Workshop realization

Art education student Tanja Mäkitalo collaborated with artist-researcher Maria Huhmarniemi to present an art workshop in the surroundings of the Särestöniemi Museum as a test bed for a tourism service. The aim was to gain practical ideas and potential strategies for developing the use of arts-based methods in creative tourism.

The workshop began with a tour of the exhibition and museum buildings. The Old Särestö farm provided a framework in which to situate works of art into a time of their own and to highlight connections among art, nature and the Northern ecoculture way of living. The Old Särestö farm also served as a framework to look at art in its original context and highlight the connections between Särestöniemi's art and the interdependence between nature and Northern people, who were largely self-sufficient and living with nature (Aikio & Aikio, 2005; Polttila, 1985). Livelihoods were obtained from many sources: domestic animal farming, small-scale barley and potato cultivation, reindeer husbandry, hunting, fishing and berry picking. The Ounasjoki, the main waterway, was a significant salmon river. Forestry, lumber floating and hauling brought in cash, and life was regulated by the annual cycle of nature (Polttila, 1985).

The workshop participants discussed the paintings presented in *The Last Wolf – An Emergency for Arctic Nature*. The exhibition included paintings that promote nature conservation as well as self-portraits in which Särestöniemi identifies himself with the forest, nature and animals. Mäkitalo and Huhmarniemi explained the historical and cultural background of painting themes in Lapland. Also, environmental conflicts in Lapland and artists' interventions to resolve them were introduced.

The schedule included time for participants to wander on their own around the surroundings of the museum environment. They were encouraged to search for a place that felt inviting and comfortable and were told to pick up materials from nature and to interact with them. On the second day of the workshop, the process continued. Mäkitalo and Huhmarniemi photographed each participant in the place they had selected, and themes that emerged from the participants' place-relation were discussed. The workshop closed with a joint reflection on the experience. Later, the participants wrote reflective essays based on journal entries on their experiences.

Photographs, recordings of discussions and essays written by participants served as research data for analysis of how the connection to nature was enhanced in the pedagogical experiment. Mäkitalo and Huhmarniemi selected a series of photos that illustrated the effects of being part of nature, and Mäkitalo (2021) analysed the essays to understand workshop experiences and estimate the level to which well-being was enhanced. The results were obtained by comparing how the participants describe their workshop experience in their reflective essays to nature-based well-being studies, which describe nature's abilities in enhancing well-being. The essays indicate both potential positive impacts as well as challenges when portrait photography workshops in nature are carried out as art museum pedagogy and as a creative tourism service.

Results and discussion

Analysis of the research data showed that the workshop had a positive impact on well-being, similar to what has previously been verified in studies on nature connectedness (Abson et al., 2017; Capaldi et al., 2014; Lumber et al., 2017; Mayer et al., 2009; Swami et al., 2016; Tyrväinen et al., 2014). Being in nature and interacting with elements of nature in the surroundings of the art museum provided recreation, relaxation, calmness, a sense of well-being and the reduction of anxiety and stress (Mäkitalo, 2021). Särestöniemi's paintings guided activities into playfulness in the forest and focused on reflection and representation of one's identity in nature. Capturing images with photographs encouraged participants to pay attention to the beauty of Northern nature, including the colours and materials of the place. Furthermore, employing all one's senses was essential to the experience. Some participants observed in their reflections that the workshop had clarified their self-images (Figure 9.2). The workshop can enable anyone to detach from everyday life, which may increase the possibility of transformative experiences.

Figure 9.2: A participant holding a stone in her arms. Photo by Maria Huhmarniemi, 2020.

Northern ecoculture and art education entrepreneurship

Getting to know Särestöniemi's art and its relationship to nature and animals opened discussions that highlighted posthumanism research and pedagogy (Ulmer, 2017). The idea of co-learning and co-knowing manifested in posthumanism offers new ways of observing, guided by the artist's personal expression (Figure 9.3). Experiences with Särestöniemi's art were two-fold in nature.

First, the participants' own sensory and physical work in nature – becoming familiar with the offerings of nature and the essence of the place – provided opportunities to understand Särestöniemi's art in a new way. Second, getting to know his art helped participants find connections in nature that would not have been achieved without familiarity with his works. Thus, the workshop was successful as an art pedagogy offering that magnified the interpretation of art.

Art historian Juha Ilvas (2000) assessed Reidar Särestöniemi's influence on contemporary art, stating that many of Särestöniemi's artistic solutions have become common only since his death: what was shocking at the time has been accepted today. In 2020, works by Särestöniemi are still topical, and posthumanistic philosophy – knowing with nature – offers a new focus for the interpretation of his art. Särestöniemi can be seen as a role

Figure 9.3: Two of the participants represented the forest industry in their portraits: one by identifying herself as a guardian of the forest and another using a field of cut forest as surroundings. Photos by Maria Huhmarniemi (2020) (left) and Tanja Mäkitalo (2020) (right).

model for artists who seek to promote the rights of Arctic nature through art. In addition to paintings, the Reidar Särestöniemi Museum offered an environment in which to discuss how nature formed the basis of the Northern ecoculture and to witness the relationship between humans and the rest of nature as equal. Northern cultures and communities such as the Sámi, but also the Finns in the region, have retained features in their ecocultures in which, for example, animals, lakes and rocks are considered to have spiritual and even personal characteristics. In one way, Särestöniemi's art and the Old Särestö site are remains of the old Northern animistic conception of the world that included interactions between animals and humans as well as a common destiny. Together, they open a window to the roots of the Northern ecoculture.

From this inquiry, we can also address an educational dimension through stories that transmit norms related to the balance between humans and nature. This is reflected and still appears in local ecocultures and stories of the North, and it is also reflected in Särestöniemi's art. The museum and its surroundings also support this approach.

An animistic conception of the world was represented in some of the workshop photographs captured during the test bed, such as when a participant held a stone like the way a child is held, or when branches grew from a human arm like a wing and a human face was covered by a bark mask (see Figures 9.2 and 9.3). In the process, the participants reached towards interactions between themselves and elements of non-human nature. Accompanied by discussions on global and local environmental conflicts and spirits of nature, the pedagogical approach engaged participants' own bodies, senses and cogitation. Evaluations of the piloted pedagogical workshop also indicate the potential for transformative creative tourism. The pedagogical approach can be further developed with an aim to present, share and revitalize elements of the Northern ecoculture. For example, encounters with animals did not take place during the workshop, and none of the participants identified themselves as an animal as Särestöniemi did in his paintings. Nonetheless, the Old Särestö, the courtyard and the collection of old items can inspire many

Mayer, F. S., Frantz, C. M., Bruehlman-Senecal, E., & Dolliver, K. (2009). Why is nature beneficial? The role of connectedness to nature. *Environment and Behavior*, *41*(5), 607–643. https://doi.org/10.1177/0013916508319745

Mayer, M. (2005). Bridging the theory-practice divide in contemporary art museum education. *Art Education*, *58*(2), 13–17.

Parks, M. M. (2020). Explicating ecoculture. *Nature and Culture*, *15*(1), 54–77. https://doi.org/10.3167/nc.2020.150104

Polttila, B. (1985). *Notes on the life of Reidar Särestöniemi*. Tammi.

Raatikainen, K. J., Juhola, K., Huhmarniemi, M., & Peña-Lagos, H. (2020). "Face the cow": Reconnecting to nature and increasing capacities for pro-environmental agency. *Ecosystems and People*, *16*(1), 273–289. https://doi.org/10.1080/26395916.2020.1817151

Riding, D., Talbot Landers, C., Grimshaw, N., & O'Keefe, H. (2019). Developing a not-knowing pedagogy in the public art museum. *The International Journal of the Inclusive Museum*, *12*(4), 13–22. https://doi.org/10.18848/1835-2014/CGP/v12i04/13-22

Simkin, J., Ojala, A., & Tyrväinen, L. (2020). Restorative effects of mature and young commercial forests, pristine old-growth forest and urban recreation forest: A field experiment. *Urban Forestry & Urban Greening*, *48*(2020), 126567. https://doi.org/10.1016/j.ufug.2019.126567

Swami, V., Barron, D., Weis, L., & Furnham, A. (2016). Bodies in nature: Associations between exposure to nature, connectedness to nature, and body image in U.S. adults. *Body Image*, *18*, 153–161. https://doi.org/10.1016/j.bodyim.2016.07.002

Tyrväinen, L., Ojala, A., Korpela, K., Lanki, T., Tsunetsugu, Y., & Kagawa, T. (2014). The influence of urban green environments on stress relief measures: A field experiment. *Journal of Environmental Psychology*, *38*, 1–9. https://doi.org/10.1016/j.jenvp.2013.12.005

Ulmer, J. (2017). Posthumanism as research methodology: Inquiry in the Anthropocene. *International Journal of Qualitative Studies in Education*, *30*(9), 832–848. https://doi.org/10.1080/09518398.2017.1336806

Ylirisku, H. (2021). *Reorienting environmental art education* [Doctoral dissertation, Aalto University]. Harald Herlin Learning Centre. http://urn.fi/URN:ISBN:978-952-64-0245-1

Chapter 10

Interpretation Design at a Crossroads With Museum Education

Richard Lachapelle

Museum interpretation designers share with museum educators many of the same interests regarding museum visitors and the quality of their experiences. Yet, the literature in interpretation design rarely mentions the educational aspects of museum design or museum educators as allies and colleagues. Likewise, there is a paucity of consideration for the educational role of interpretation design in the museum education literature. Using examples of exhibits from two different museums, I build a case that interpretation design is rooted in a multifaceted and multisensorial approach that contributes significantly to the learning potential of visitors' museum experience. I conclude that outstanding education-oriented interpretation design is the result of a close and mutually respectful collaboration among key museum professionals: the exhibition curator, the interpretation designer and the museum educator.

To fulfil its educational mandate, a museum implements a variety of established didactic programmes such as guided tours, workshops and web content. Museums also use other stratagems including extended labels, comparative displays and interpretation design. This chapter addresses the latter: the strategy of interpretation design that museums deploy within their exhibitions to encourage visitors to ponder and interpret museum exhibits.

What is interpretation design?

It is tempting to make the argument that all aspects of exhibition design bear some influence on learning in the museum. This is certainly true on a very basic level: Even a simple label provides visitors with a starting point for appreciation. However here, I argue that interpretation design is rooted in a multifaceted and multisensorial approach that does not depend solely on the use of text. Educationally oriented interpretation design is also visual and spatial and calls upon the use of additional materials – photographs, video and reconstructions – to better contextualize a museum object. A good interpretation design structure attends to a range of visitors' affective responses and cognitive abilities, as Roberts (2015) suggests:

> The distinguishing aspect of interpretation design is its intent to create engaging visitor experiences that contribute to learning and meaning-making while connecting visitors with a particular resource that may consist of a collection, story or site. Designers select

media and methods according to their suitability for a particular audience within a specific context.

(p. 380)

What are the objectives of educational interpretation design? What might such an approach achieve? First, educational interpretation design can encourage extended viewing and careful looking. Second, it can provide a viewing experience that is significant – perhaps even outstanding. Third, it can bring the visitor to meaningful interpretations by connecting artefact and design components. Finally, interpretation design can foster learning not only about the exhibit itself but also about museum and research practices (Lachapelle, 2019). Later, I will clarify this further.

Research into museum design and interpretation design

During the last decade, the focus of museum design has been changing. Tzortzi (2017) proposes that museums shift from "a functional to an expressive use of space" in their exhibition layouts to encourage more embodied forms of interactions with museum objects (p. 506). This assertion is based on research findings where exhibition spaces that contain and envelop visitors – as opposed to circulation spaces – "constitute spaces that must be occupied and 'inhabited,' rather than passed through quickly" (p. 506). A growing number of designers and museums now share this interest in "more embodied forms of interpretation, such as interactive 'hands-on' exhibits, along with text-based – and in-gallery – educational activities" (Hale & Back, 2018, p. 348). Gundersen and Back (2018) provide an interesting example of an innovative interpretation design produced with the intention of creating a more embodied experience for the visitor. The exhibit in question was part of an exhibition, *Imprints of War—Photography from 1864*, presented at the National Museum of Photography in Copenhagen, Denmark in 2014. The exhibit consisted of presenting a large photograph of the site where a particularly gruesome battle took place during the Danish-Prussian War in 1864:

> The image was staged as the centre of a dynamic installation that included filmic projection, light, sound and tactile physical objects, all contributing to a nine-minute course of shifting (and at some points moving) "tableaux." These were composed to offer different views of the image and point to a range of perspectives of relevance to its history.
>
> (Gundersen & Back, 2018, p. 306)

As early as 2008, the Steno Museum in Denmark adopted four principles to guide the design of its exhibitions: (i) arousing visitors' curiosity, (ii) challenging visitors with demanding content, (iii) using personal or expert narratives to facilitate insight and (iv) soliciting physical and/or dialogic participation from visitors. After conducting a review of this and other exhibition design paradigms, Skydsgaard et al. (2016) report that:

> The systematic use of [the Steno Museum] design principles has largely enabled a clear match between the aim of the exhibition and visitor outcomes. [...] These findings suggest that the use of the design principles is effective in informing exhibition design.
>
> (p. 65)

Other researchers agree. For Madsen and Jensen (2021), exploration is a key to learning in the museum and, therefore, exhibits need to be designed to encourage this process. Four criteria inform a design process that focuses on exploration: "user mind-set" (encouraging the attitude needed for engaging in exploration), "agency" (enabling the visitor's capacity to act and interact with the exhibit), "storification" [sic] (facilitating knowledge production through storytelling) and "narrative closure" (supporting reflection through the use of various forms of discussion) (pp. 154–171). Few publications exist in the museum literature on interpretation design, and this suggests a need for additional research.

Research method: Material culture studies, an investigative framework[1]

I have selected material culture studies as the research method for examining and analysing examples of museum exhibits where features exemplify the qualities of educational interpretation design. For the purposes of this inquiry, museum exhibits are regarded as human-constructed expressions deemed worthy of investigation because of the embedded knowledge they contain. Exhibits are also understood to be a significant component of the overall cultural production of museums, and as such can be considered as artefacts.

The sociosemiotics of material culture

To assist in my investigation of specific examples of exhibits as material culture, I call upon different sources from the literature in material culture studies. However, the work of Carl Knappett (2005) in particular has informed my method of analysis. He has proposed a research methodology in which signs are studied within networks of meanings. Knappett calls this approach the "sociosemiotics of material culture." In brief, the method consists first in identifying the affordances and constraints of artefacts. The term "affordance" was first proposed by psychologist James Gibson to describe the entire corpus of potential functions of an object, including the novel and unexpected purposes to which it may lend itself (as cited in Knappett, 2005). For example, a chair may be used for sitting, but it may also be used as an improvised bookcase. The term "constraint" originates with Donald Norman, who used it to describe the ways in which certain physical, logical, cultural and semantic features of an object serve to limit or constrain the range of possible functions (i.e. affordances) of that object (as cited in Knappett, 2005). For example, the specific shapes of puzzle pieces restrict the ways in which a two-dimensional puzzle can be assembled and thus, the ways in which its image can be recreated.

The second step in Knappett's methodology is mainly based on Piercian semiotics. It consists of evaluating the extended networks of objects based on semiotic relationships such as iconicity (i.e. relationships based on similarity, such as when a display item represents an entire class of objects); indexicality (i.e. relationships based on actual connections among objects, such as the image on a store sign); and symbolism (i.e. relationships based upon convention or upon a "parts to whole" connection, like a word in the English language) (Knappett, 2005, pp. 87–106). Finally, a basic tenet in the theoretical underpinning of Knappett's approach is that, instead of the traditional dualistic Cartesian separation of subjects and objects, there exists instead a symmetry between humans and non-humans (i.e. objects) and that both can be agents or artefacts. Knappett argues that, because of this symmetry, humans actually think through material culture.

Analysis of exemplars of educational interpretation design[2]

In this section, I present and discuss in detail two examples of museum exhibits[3,4] with those qualities of educational interpretation design that are the focus of this research. First, I describe each example, then before moving on to the next, I discuss each case in relation to the principles of the sociosemiotics of material culture and the objectives of educational interpretation design presented earlier in the introduction.

"Bringing the History of a Crossroads to Light"[5]

This first example of interpretation design is from a permanent installation in the Crossroads Montreal Exhibition at the Montreal Museum of Archaeology and History in Montreal, Quebec, Canada (www.pacmusee.qc.ca). This museum is more commonly referred to as Pointe-à-Callière Museum since it is situated on a point of land, Pointe-à-Callière, originally formed by the convergence of two rivers, La Petite Rivière Saint-Pierre and the St-Lawrence River. Over time, as the result of several civil engineering projects, the appearance of this area of land has changed considerably, and the Point itself is no longer identifiable at ground level. In 1832, La Petite Rivière Saint-Pierre disappeared from sight when it was converted to form a covered 375-metre-long stone masonry underground sewage collector. Nonetheless, the site of Pointe-à-Callière remains important since, for centuries, it was first a gathering place for several First Nations – the Algonquin, Huron and Iroquois; later, in 1642, it became the founding site for the first French settlement, Fort de Ville-Marie, in what is known today as the city of Montreal. As such, Pointe-à-Callière is now both a rich archaeological site bearing witness to over 1000 years of human activity and a museum, inaugurated in 1992, to protect the site's exceptional past and to educate visitors about the importance of this unique storied place.

In the museum, below ground level, evidence of archaeological investigations at the site of Pointe-à-Callière – conducted several years prior to the construction of the museum – remains and is well preserved. The excavations are now accessible for public viewing, thanks to the use of structural glass flooring that allows visitors to walk over, move through and visually explore the digs. Ancient foundations of buildings from different time periods have now been rendered visible, and artefacts found on site are displayed nearby within the same spaces. Several exhibits present and interpret the findings of the archaeological research. One of those is the *Bringing the History of a Crossroads to Light* exhibit, where a large display case groups artefacts found on site according to their respective time periods. The display case is designed in a manner that visually alludes to the layers of soil progressively excavated on site to uncover the artefacts presented in the case. Using individual shelves for each time period, the display case recreates five layers of soil, each associated with a specific period in which artefacts were found. The shelves correspond to the following periods, starting with the oldest on the lowest shelf and then moving up and forward in time: (i) *Before 1600: A Natural Meeting Place* (artefacts include a quartz arrowhead and scraper), (ii) *1600–1700: A French Settlement* (artefacts include French objects and an iron axe head), (iii) *1700–1800: a Merchant Town* (objects include a brass thimble and silver coins), (iv) *1800–1900: A Busy Metropolis* (artefacts include European porcelain and an iron padlock) and (v) *1900–2000 A Cosmopolitan City* (objects include a Coca-Cola bottle and an aluminium beer bottle cap). Furthermore (as described in the Montreal Museum of Archaeology and History exhibition text) since each shelf represents a different period (Figure 10.1), as a whole the stack of five shelves is also meant to symbolize the entire column of earth that had to be excavated from the site to uncover these objects in their respective time periods.

This exhibit is a good example of educational interpretation design in that it goes well beyond simply presenting a few artefacts. The design of this display case, while certainly effective in presenting these objects, also doubles as a symbolic representation of a fundamental principle of archaeology that posits how, over time, natural processes and human activities result in the accumulation of layers of soil and sediment one on top of the other. As a matter of course, these build-ups encapsulate fragments of all kinds of natural or human-made objects originating in the time during which the process of accretion occurs. In terms of affordances, the *Bringing the History of a Crossroads to Light* exhibit provides a framework for at least two simultaneous functions: the presentation of artefacts uncovered on location and the illustration of a scientific concept pertaining to the inscription of information in a material – in this case, soil – through an ongoing natural and human enacted process of accretion. From a sociosemiotic standpoint, this exhibit creates a network of relationships among the archaeological site, the artefacts and scientific concepts based on indexicality and symbolism (Knappett, 2005).

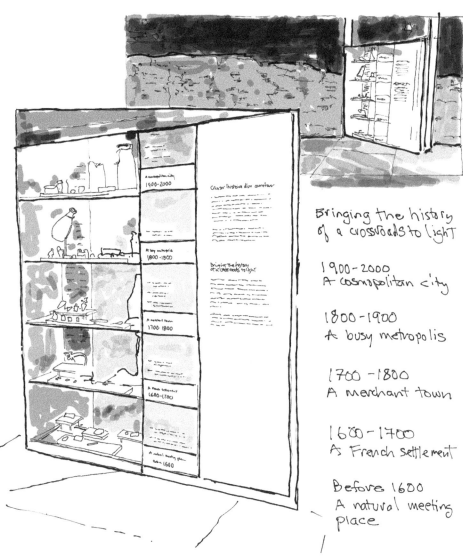

Figure 10.1: *"Bringing the History of a Crossroads to Light"* exhibit at the Montreal Museum of Archaeology and History. Inset above right shows the exhibit in its underground location amongst excavated foundation ruins. Original sketch by Richard Lachapelle, 2019/2023. Copyright: Richard Lachapelle.

In terms of the proposed objectives of interpretation design presented earlier in this chapter, the design of this display case promotes extended viewing by encouraging repeated looking to compare artefacts within the same time period for any similarities (looking left to right) and among different time periods for differences (looking up and down). Through an encounter with this exhibit, the visitor is provided with opportunities to learn by making meaningful connections among the artefacts, periods of origin, the site of origin and archaeological concepts. As a visit to an actual archaeological site, the Pointe-à-Callière's *Crossroads Montreal Exhibition* provides museumgoers with the very real prospect of a significant museum experience (Lachapelle, 2019).

"A Walk Through Time"

A second example of good interpretation design is taken from the American Museum of Natural History in New York City. In a series of displays grouped together in the Hall of Human Origins, the museum addresses the question of the origins of our species, Homo sapiens. One exhibit, *A Walk Through Time*, is the three-dimensional life-size presentation of a scene involving early hominids that took place millions of years ago and that likely unfolded almost as presented in this recreation. The restitution of the scene is not based on speculation; rather, it is an exercise of scientific inference based on actual evidence.

In 1978, at Laetoli in Tanzania, Eastern Africa, paleoanthropologists discovered two paths of footprints made 3.6 million years ago by two ancient hominids – probably members of the genus Australopithecus – as they walked across a plain covered in volcano ash. The ash had the consistency of wet cement since it had recently been soaked by rain. As a result, their passage through the area was recorded for posterity in two sets of travelling footprints that, over time, became fossilized. Scientists used topographic mapping of the preserved impressions to determine that the strides of the two walkers were similar to those of modern humans and, therefore, made by hominids. The two almost parallel series of footprints were found to match both in terms of pacing and separation. Scientists concluded that the two hominids making them were side-by-side as they walked together. The mapping of the footprints clearly revealed that one of the hominids was larger than the other and that their strides were so close together (about 30 centimetres apart) that their bodies were probably touching. Therefore, in the recreation of the scene, the museum has chosen to represent a male and a female walking together, although the museum admits that the couple might well have been a parent and child instead (see Figure 10.2). However, according to the American Museum of Natural History's exhibition text, the museum insists that this representation of an adult couple is consistent with the scientific evidence.

An encounter with this exhibit provides a rare opportunity to stand alongside ancient hominids and to experience first hand the ways in which we are both similar and different from these distant ancestors. The display case in which the models of the two hominids are presented as they walk is largely made of transparent glass and, unlike most display cases or sculpture podiums, stands at a ground level barely an inch or two above the museum floor. This allows for an easy comparison of self (as reflected in the glass) and the two hominids. A visitor first notices how much shorter they are, as these Australopithecus hominids stand at about chest height of an average modern human. Viewers notice other differences too,

Figure 10.2: *"A Walk Through Time"* exhibit at the American Museum of Natural History. Left inset: rear view of the exhibit where the foot tracks begin. Lower inset: side view showing a child about to step onto the reproduction of the Laetoli tracks. Original sketch: Richard Lachapelle, 2008/2023. Copyright: Richard Lachapelle.

such as the amount of body hair and other anatomical features. The hominids are clearly visible from several angles. Visible too, on the inside base surface of the display case, is the exact reproduction of the Laetoli footprint tracks – the original source of information on which the exhibit is based. The representation of the fossilized path walked millions of years ago actually begins well out of view behind the front part of the exhibit where the two hominids now stand. The front and back sections of the display are separated by a tall sheet of frosted glass and, unlike the front portion of the exhibit, the back part of the display is not enclosed in glass. At the back, a small sign invites visitors to step up onto the track and compare their feet with the footprints left behind by the two ancient pedestrians. This exhibit is made up of both classic museum display features meant to encourage careful looking and an interactive component intended to provide a more experiential exploration of the exhibit. As such, it probably appeals to both adults and children.

In relation to the principles of educational interpretation design, *A Walk Through Time* provides visitors with a meaningful experience: a multifaceted encounter with early hominids. It encourages sustained and attentive looking and, in doing so, nurtures the production of knowledge about human origins. Thanks to the prudent and restrained use of text, visitors can also acquire a better understanding of the scientific method as well as the practices of paleoanthropology. The success of this exhibit depends in large part on an imaginative use of affordances and constraints. This display was designed to serve both as a protective display case (the enclosed front part) and as a play structure (the interactive back part). When visitors step onto the rear platform of the exhibit, they establish a symmetry between the hominids and themselves as humans. In doing so, visitors assume the posture of both agents and artefacts; thus, they become part of the exhibit – often to the amusement and appreciation of the other onlookers. From a sociosemiotic perspective, the exhibit exploits principles of indexicality to point to connections between fossilized traces and ancient beings. It relies on principles of iconicity to reveal a complex network of relationships between modern visitors and these ancient hominids, between modern humans and all early predecessors and between prototypes of interpersonal relationships then and now.

At a crossroads with education

The exhibits examined in this chapter demonstrate how, in the very best of scenarios, good interpretation design can strengthen the impact of a museum display to the extent that an exhibit can take on an exceptional *educational* character. Rather than simply presenting an object, the exemplars discussed here succeeded in embarking visitors on a journey of discovery that is altogether sensorial, spatial, pleasurable and intellectually captivating. In both instances, these exhibits share similar features indicative of the interpretative, sociosemiotic and learning principles of educational interpretation design.

The powerful impact of education-oriented interpretation design operates on principles of Gestalt psychology. Wertheimer (1938) proposed "holism" and the "principle of totality" to explain how the perceptual effects of a system of components engaged in dynamic relationships are greater than the components themselves considered individually (p. 2). Interpretation design operates on this basis. In the case of the exhibits discussed here, if we were to isolate the artefacts from their associated exhibit design elements, the result would be a loss of meaning made possible only by the interaction of the design constituents with the museum object. Breaking these connections results in a subsequent shortfall in the educational potential of the exhibit.

In conclusion, it is noteworthy that good educational design can come only from a close and mutually respectful collaboration among three key museum professionals: the museum educator, the interpretation designer and the exhibition curator. It is clear that each brings their own expertise to the endeavour, which contributes equally to the success of these types of exhibits.

Acknowledgement

Funding for this research was provided by the Social Sciences and Humanities Research Council of Canada, Insight Grants Program – B. White, McGill University, Principal Investigator; R. Lachapelle & A. Sinner, Concordia University, Co-Investigators.

Notes

1. Parts of this discussion of material culture studies as a research method were previously published in – Lachapelle, R. (2011). The landscape, the built environment and the work of art. Three meaningful territories for art education and material culture studies. In P. Bolin & D. Blandy (Eds.), *Matter matters: Art education and material culture studies* (pp. 12–24). National Art Education Association.
2. I thank Malcolm MacPhail for his assistance with the figures for this chapter.
3. Examples from fine art museums are provided in R. Lachapelle (in press), *Educational interpretation design: Monkman, an exemplar from the fine arts*.
4. This section is based on documentation collected when I visited the museum in 2019.
5. This section is based on documentation collected when I visited the museum in 2008. The discovery of the Laetoli tracks was a significant advancement in the understanding of human origins and, therefore, it is represented in several different science museums worldwide.

References

Gundersen, M. G., & Back, C. (2018). Spatial meaning-making: Exhibition design and embodied experience. In S. MacLeod, T. Austin, J. Hale, & O. H. Hing-Kay (Eds.), *The future of museum and gallery design: Purpose, process, perception* (pp. 304–316). Routledge.

Hale, J., & Back, C. (2018). From body to body: Architecture, movement and meaning in the museum. In S. MacLeod, T. Austin, J. Hale, & O. H. Hing-Kay (Eds.), *The future of museum and gallery design: Purpose, process, perception* (pp. 340–351). Routledge.

Knappett, C. (2005). *Thinking through material culture: An interdisciplinary perspective*. University of Pennsylvania Press.

Lachapelle, R. (2019, September 1–7). *Can exhibition design play a role in the educational function of the museum?* [Paper presentation]. International Council of Museums, 25th General Conference, Kyoto, Japan.

Madsen, K. M., & Jensen, J. F. (2021). Learning through exploration at museum exhibitions. *Museum Management and Curatorship, 36*(2), 154–171. https://doi.org/10.1080/09647775.2020.1803115

Roberts, T. (2015). Factors affecting the role of designers in interpretation projects. *Museum Management and Curatorship, 30*(5), 379–393. https://doi.org/10.1080/09647775.2015.1055582

Skydsgaard, M. A., Andersen, H. M., & King, H. (2016). Designing museum exhibits that facilitate visitor reflection and discussion. *Museum Management and Curatorship, 31*(1), 48–68. https://doi.org/10.1080/09647775.2015.1117237

Tzortzi, K. (2017). Museum architectures for embodied experience. *Museum Management and Curatorship, 32*(5), 491–508. https://doi.org/10.1080/09647775.2017.1367258

Wertheimer, M. (1938). Gestalt theory. In W. D. Ellis (Ed.), *A source book of Gestalt psychology* (pp. 1–16). Routledge & Kegan Paul. (Original work published 1924)

Chapter 11

The Portuguese Contemporary Art Museum Today

João Pedro Fróis

Art museum pedagogies

> The museum has to function as an institution for the prevention and cure of "blindness" in order to make works work. And making works work is the museum's major mission.
>
> (Nelson Goodman, 1984, p. 179)

Art museums of the twenty-first century are experiencing a boom in visibility reinforced by the proliferation of new buildings, increased visitor numbers and a culturally globalized environment, suggesting that museums are becoming platforms for dialogue and experimentation, a democratic sharing of ideas – not just a repository of information about works of art. They are not, and never were, neutral in relation to the value and meanings attributed to the artefacts. Artefacts incorporate cultural, social and even personal aesthetic values, thereby offering opportunities and challenges for reflection on those values. In doing so, museums have the capacity to contribute greatly to individual self-definition.

As cultural entities, however, museums and their practices need to be continually questioned because our society is changing as well. For example, we witness the proliferation of marketing and other strategies designed to simplify public access to collections and increase engagement with the artworks. However, such strategies often fail to give full voice to the explicit and primary function of museums, which is education. Thus, further discussion about education is called for. For example, what is the role of education in art museums today? What are the relationships between curators and education specialists? What can we teach each other?

In this chapter, I offer two hypotheses as necessary frameworks for discussion about the function of art museums. The first focuses on our general relationship with the past, which is undergoing a profound change. An earlier worldview, with roots in ancient Greece, has been progressively replaced by a new chronotope (Bakhtin, 1937/1981). As Gumbrecht (2014) notes, "there is reason to believe that the chronotope of progress already imploded decades ago, even if our discourses, for purposes of communication and self-understanding, still perpetuate it" (p. 31). This chronotope frames our everyday awareness of time, history, change and agency, transforming the way we place ourselves in time as we relate to the past, present and future. It is characterized by a future we are anticipating and is approaching at an ever-increasing pace, with implications for public – either due to lack of human resources or the critical shortage of finances – Couto and Cabral believed that education, through the involvement of teachers and children of various ages, would be capable of forming new MNAA audiences. Like others in Europe and the United States, they understood that interactions with works of art had a pedagogical character and sought to expand these experiences between children and art as much as possible.

At the SMCA, the inspiring figure for educational action between 1999 and 2014 was Elvira Leite, who served as a consultant to the SMCA and worked with those responsible for coordinating the museum's Education Department. With a background in plastic arts and as a public school teacher, she was the personality who most influenced the educational outreach of this museum from the museum's formation. *Ab initio*, she adopted two founding principles as her motto: first, understanding the museum as a project and social instrument; and second, questioning the relation of the body in space and time and in communication with others. For her, individuals are always active protagonists and builders of their learning. Leite was inspired by the ideas of Arno Stern, Victor Lowenfeld, Herbert Read, Pierre Luquet, Paulo Freire, Bruno Munari and psychoanalyst Donald Winnicott, among others.

Leite was imbued with interventionist intentions soon after the April Revolution in Portugal in 1974. The revolution instilled in Leite a critical attitude towards sociocultural reality that informed her *compagnon de route*: the *project work* method (Carneiro et al., 1983; Leite & Malpique, 1986; Leite et al., 1989, 1990). She first worked with children from impoverished neighbourhoods in the city of Porto through visual arts creative expression activities, in schools and then at SMCA. She organized experimental laboratories that she designated as workshops for the study of the pedagogical relevance of the arts, aimed at the integral formation of the human being in the cognitive, affective and communicative dimensions (Leite & Victorino, 2006).

The methodology of project work was implemented in the various editions of the so-called "Project with Schools" of SMCA's Education Department. The project work methodology aims at solving problems (Guimarães & Leite, 2002; Leite & Victorino, 2008; Saraiva & Leite, 2012). This means that it starts with real issues and problems in situations that are felt to be important for the people involved – teachers, students and museum educators – who then occupy themselves with attempting to solve the problem. The search for answers requires planning and distribution of tasks and the collection of data and information carried out through communication and exchange of ideas within the group. Data collected individually or in small groups is debated and organized with feedback to the larger group. All work resulting from programme activities must result in an evaluated, socializable end-product – for example, an annual exhibition or a large collective installation, which in fact happened at the SMCA and participating schools alike. This product shows the enrichment of a group (e.g. school children) in terms of their involvement and, above all, in terms of understanding the problems and themes initially chosen by the parties involved (Figure 11.2).

Figure 11.2: View of the exhibition *Travel Narratives. A project with schools*. June/September 2004. Photo copyright: Catarina Providência. Photo courtesy of Serralves Museum of Contemporary Art, Porto, Portugal.

Projects with schools

1. *Travel Narratives (2002–2004)*. Between geography and literature (maps, reports and travel guides), the social and the cultural (the traveller and the tourist, the eyes of the artist, the photographer and the filmmaker), between reality and fiction, the journey is not just a theme. It is a genre from the landscapes of romantic painters to artists whose work evokes a nomadic condition; the journey continues to make your dream (Leite & Victorino, 2008, p. 29).

In this project, the educators selected specific areas to explore. They proposed journeys into the universe of the arts, science, literature, history and fiction and awakened the desire to tell and share stories.

2. *Portraits (2005–2006)*. In artistic developments of the 1960s, the self-portrait moved away from the traditional form of self-representation. Alongside happenings, performances and actions of all kinds, different artistic manifestations appeared in which the portrait was used as raw material, in an attitude of freedom from reality. These new forms of portraiture

include true/false portraits, simulacrum of situations, parodies, borrowed identities, distant memories or projections into the future (Leite & Victorino, 2008, p. 157).

The theme of the portraits focused on working with and raising questions around the construction of children's and adolescents' identities. In all thematic projects, attempts were made to awaken the ability to observe, interrogate and interpret, according to ages and contexts (Figure 11.3). The intention was to encourage dialogue between the SMCA and schools.

The projects took shape autonomously in programming thematic exhibitions, meetings with teachers, workshops in Serralves, seminars and training actions and cinema (conversation-projections) carried out by the Education Department. This programme, ideologically distanced from other more traditionally focused curatorships, today presents itself as the most coherent programme in the field of education among Portuguese museums. For example, workshops moved away from the strict organization of visual and plastic arts to educative purposes: "The workshops are spaces dedicated to creative activities: they explore concepts, technology and expressions with a view to carrying out works that reveal the imagination of each group" (Leite & Victorino, 2008, p. 17).

The practice of the SMCA and contemporary Portuguese art museums is guided by sophisticated artistic choices and discourses about social reality and people's lives, a

Figure 11.3: Workshop "My body has your face," part of the Educational Service programme *Portraits. A project with schools*, March 2006. Photo copyright: Ana Luandina. Photo courtesy SMCA, Porto, Portugal.

transforming vision of society conveyed by the exhibits shown. In the opinion of Leite and colleagues, action with groups (school children, youngsters or adults) should focus on the blurring of boundaries between the different modalities of artistic expression and on the erasing of boundaries between what art curators and educators propose for each exhibition. One essential commonality is that during the activities, references be made to artists whose works are related to the themes addressed as the artists provide new vistas in cultural education. By extension, Serralves Park has also always been understood as a significant learning space for the development of environmental and artistic education programmes.

The SMCA Education Department has thus focused on two main areas of work with the public: supporting visits to the various temporary exhibitions and focusing on its own programming and exhibitions. From the start, the Education Department felt it was urgent to establish a permanent team of monitors to moderate diversity, reinforced by the temporary and independent work of the collaborating museum educators. The idea was to maintain a small team responsible for coordinating and supervising the group of outsourced educators, which at one point consisted of 30 persons. This created a real difficulty as the museum needed to find a balance between the various demands of (temporary) educators of exhibitions and activities and the need to create continuity in goals and educational practice.

From the beginning, as a statutory mission of the museum itself, there was an interest in attracting groups from public schools. This interest corresponded with the administration's view to strengthening its hegemonic position among museums of this type in Portugal. In this sense, different types of programmes were designed for different groups. Workshops were also developed for groups of visitors with sensory and mental challenges and for people with hearing impairment. Serralves developed programmes that are regularly offered during all temporary exhibitions. It is interesting to note that the designation used in relation to people who interacted with the museum gradually changed from "visitors" to "the public" and finally to "participants," which indicates a changing view about the autonomy of the subject and an evolution of the role of the Serralves museum in relation to those who interact with it.

A study commissioned by the SMCA (2011/12) concluded that visitors were mostly people from the middle and upper classes of the city of Porto (68 per cent) and were between 26 and 35 years old, with a small number of visitors over 65 years old (7 per cent). About 80 per cent of the adult visitors have a university education and/or were working in education or the liberal professions. This is a prototypical stratification in museums of this kind in Portugal where visitors come from a class origin, educational background and age group similar to what Pierre Bourdieu and Alain Darbel had found in their *L'Amour del'Art: Les Musées d'Art et Leur Public* (1966). These data raise the *question*: Does a museum aim to cater to a specific audience or does its mission extend to other values?

Serralves Park had always been a huge attraction for visitors, and the annual event "Serralves em Festa" remains the most attended of all programme events. More than half of those interviewed state that the motivation for visiting Serralves is to experience the combined influence of both the Park and the Exhibitions. In the period of the "Serralves em

Festa," about 22 per cent of the visitors attended activities for children. The most frequented spaces in the city of Serralves were its Park (88 per cent) and the Exhibitions (80 per cent). For 74 per cent of the respondents, the factors that most attracted them to Serralves were what the survey organizers called "the architecture and beauty of the surrounding spaces."[3] In the case of the SMCA as in others, museum services must constantly consider data related to numbers of visitors because these bring financial resources and visibility. These are practical considerations, essential to the viability of the institution.

The Education Department's programmes were motivated by the need to reach a greater number of people, especially young people of school age, partly driven by the pressure exerted by guidelines from the Ministry of Education that recommended public schools take advantage of the cultural spaces supported by the State itself. The intention to involve the greatest number of people, communities of different origins and social strata – from the perspective of the most interventionist museum in the community – was reflected in programmes such as "the museum goes to school" and in interventions by guest artists with different groups. Some of these activities were marked by operational difficulties such as the lack of transport for groups from other cities close to Porto. Moving the museum's activities to the schools, training teachers or working closely with schools in the museum's adjacent neighbourhoods were less expensive solutions that worked out positively.

One of the criticisms accepted by those responsible for SMCA Education about their past experience has to do with the perception of the "crystallization" of ways of acting with the public. Emphasis is placed on the perception that not enough has been innovated at SMCA: in part due to the constant pressure felt from above to attract more public to the activities and thus increase the museum's visibility at the national level, and in part due to the precarious employment (labour status) of SMCA Education Department support teams.

The empowerment of the public appears as the leitmotif of educational practice and underlies the thought that shaped the educational actions in this museum. These actions entail meeting the public demand in relation to programming, connecting specific audiences with specific activities (always centred on the temporary exhibitions) and the actions of the Education Department itself. There is consensus about these ideas from the actors within the education service about the programmes they developed and the ideology that fuelled their action, yet this consensus is always accompanied by difficulties of dialogue across departments within the museum.

The instrumentalization of education for this purpose, and for competition among art museums for corporate support, permeates the directives of some of those responsible for SMCA education. But at the same time, in testimonies about the past, the educators realized it is necessary to deconstruct the idea of the museum as it stands today. In 2019, the SMCA administration acknowledged that the traditional model is exhausted and outdated but did not suggest alternatives. Former SMCA education leaders pointed to the urgent need for a greater distribution of powers in the context of the programming of artistic curatorial practices and education, with an emphasis on greater dialogue between the teams. Despite all the above-mentioned constraints, Sofia Victorino, a former head, thinks that the educational department is still to be considered a space of "freedom and subversion" within the institutional apparatus. For her, the sustainability and viability of these structures become an increasing challenge for museums today: "If the outsourcing model succeeds, how can the knowledge and experience transform the institution at a deeper level?"[4]

In fact, the *Project with Schools* was the bridge between the museum and schools in Porto – it is really the watermark of its programming, mediated by "relevant" thematic topics that attract teachers and students from primary and secondary schools. This type of interactive project, as well as the work developed with schools neighbouring the SMCA, enabled monitoring the impact of the sociocultural action of the museum in place, as exemplified in the annual themed exhibition organized by the Education Department.

The resulting programmes aimed to be convergent and interdisciplinary between museum curatorial practices and with groups of children and young people. The actions of the museum's Education Department could become platforms for debate and sites of sociocultural experimentation. The museum is then a space for questioning, promoting interactions with groups and communities and fostering perspectives of different experiences, as well as the contextualization and interpretation of artefacts. Education emerges as a way of enhancing encounters with art, including attention to artists' goals, aesthetic engagement and empathy. The artistic experience will always be a condensed experience, and education emerges as a possibility of "opening worlds" in a space of sharing. In the opinion of one coordinator, it is necessary to rescue words (and concepts) used in the past so that they regain some useful meaning today.[5] For example, it is necessary to remove the connotation sometimes associated with the word "education," often linked to something one does not like. The museum's task to reach more people and maintain the quality of what it offered is an ongoing challenge, a difficult task that challenges anyone who works in such cultural entities as art museums.

As in the case of the SMCA Educational Department, museums do not exist outside the political sphere of the socioeconomic context from which they originate and the cultural particularities of the country where they are developed. The challenge is to promote the exercise of democracy in museums and make them contemporary. Is building trust between community institutions and activating civil dialogue one of the ways to do this? I think the answer should be an unequivocal "yes." As we see in the model proposed by Serralves, reorganizing forms of participation of art museums in close dialogue with school institutions, and increasing participation, can be an important contribution to society. In this new chronotope, art museums will continue to develop new purposes and roles for tomorrow.

Notes

1. http://www.serralves.pt/en/foundation/the-museum/presentation
2. In 2019, as part of an academic presentation at the University of Coimbra, Cíntia Ferreira interviewed Elvira Leite, the consultant for education, as well as the four directors of the Serralves Educational Department (1999–2019). Some content from these interviews is used here.

3. In 2015, the total number of visitors to Serralves was 524,000, of which 97,000 were participants from the Department of Education. During this period, about 73 per cent of entries were free. https://assets.bondlayer.com/nsa343pdfl/_assets/nm7bmuvwcsn2c9mo0gpoj.pdf
4. Sofia Victorino, in an interview with Cíntia Ferreira. In *Museu de Serralves: 20 Anos de Serviço Educativo* [Serralves Museum: 20 Years of Educational Service], 2019, p. 159.
5. Liliana Coutinho, in an interview with Cíntia Ferreira. In *Museu de Serralves: 20 Anos de Serviço Educativo* [Serralves Museum: 20 Years of Educational Service], 2019, p. 161.

References

Bakhtin, M. M. (1981). Forms of time and of the chronotope in the novel: Notes toward a historical poetics. In M. Holquist (Ed.), *The dialogic imagination: Four essays* (C. Emerson & M. Holquist, Trans.) (pp. 84–258). University of Austin Press. (Original work published 1937)

Bourdieu, P., & Darbel, A. (1966). *L'amour de l'art: Les musées d'art et leur public*. Les Éditions de Minuit.

Carneiro, A., Leite, E., & Malpique, M. (1983). *O espaço pedagógico: A casa /o caminho casa-escola / a escola*. Afrontamento.

Cartwright, M. A. (1939). The place of the museum in adult education. *Museum News, 18*(8), 10–12.

Ferreira, C. (2019). *Museu de Serralves: 20 anos de serviço educativo* [Unpublished master's thesis]. Coimbra University, Coimbra.

Fróis, J. P. (2019). The emergence of museum education in Portugal: Madalena Cabral and the National Museum of Ancient Art. *Curator: The Museum Journal, 62*(4), 557–569.

Goodman, N. (1984). *Of mind and other matters*. Harvard University Press.

Guimarães, S., & Leite, E. (2002). *Habitares Serralves 2001 e 2002*. Fundação de Serralves.

Gumbrecht, H. U. (2014). *Our broad present: Time and contemporary culture*. Columbia University Press.

Leite, E., & Malpique, M. (1986). *Espaços de criatividade: A criança que fomos /a criança que somos através da expressão plástica*. Afrontamento.

Leite, E., Malpique, M., & Santos, M. (1989). *Trabalho de projeto: 1. Aprender por projetos centrados em problemas*. Edições Afrontamento.

Leite, E., Malpique, M., & Santos, M. (1990). *Trabalho de projeto: 2. Leituras comentadas*. Edições Afrontamento.

Leite, E., & Victorino, S. (2006). *Arte e paisagem*. Fundação de Serralves.

Leite, E., & Victorino, S. (2008). *Serralves: Projectos com escolas 2002-2007*. Fundação de Serralves.

Low, T. (1942). *The museum as a social instrument*. The Metropolitan Museum of Art.

Rectanus, M. W. (2020). Museums and the creative economy: Soft power, financialization, and activism. In *Museums inside out, artist collaborations and new exhibition ecologies* (pp. 171–213). University of Minnesota Press.

Saraiva, M., & Leite, E. (2012). *Quarto: Lugar de abrigo, identidade e evasão*. Fundação de Serralves.

Chapter 12

Museum-School Partnership: Synergizing Paradigmatic Engagements

Attwell Mamvuto

In my experience, access to museums as epicentres of art education in Zimbabwe has remained a preserve for elite schools, especially those offering art as a curriculum subject, thus catering to a minority proportion of the overall school population. Reasons for low participation rates vary from affordability to local cultural factors, different levels of appreciation and teachers' lack of appreciation of these critical resources. Teacher education programmes have not fully embraced museum education; hence low participation levels are also reflective of training. Despite these limitations, however, of late many primary and secondary schools in Zimbabwe are actively engaged in specific museum programmes that align with the curriculum, such as heritage education outreach that targets remote and marginalized schools and communities. Ongoing changes in curriculum, due to the introduction of the competence-based curriculum in 2015, have resulted in a more active symbiotic school–museum partnership than in the past. In fact, in each of the five administrative regions of Zimbabwe, each museum now has a full-fledged Heritage Education Department catering to the needs of schools to help build pedagogic bridges.

The purpose of this chapter is, therefore, an attempt to demystify accessibility of museums for the benefit of the general populace through a reconfiguration of the museum to include the concept of "community museum" (Brown & Mairesse, 2018, p. 3), thus redefining the nature of museum–school partnerships (Bobick & Hornby, 2013). I propose that paradigmatic shifts in relationships and activities between museums and schools as cultural and ideological institutions are critical for the future of learning. I also propose that it is possible to establish limitless relationships among institutions across the globe through a host of strategies: for example, facilitating museum education through online forums. Such shifts in Zimbabwe are aimed at facilitating equal access to the social capital and cultural knowledge imbedded within museums. I argue for the expansion of access through processes that have previously limited the audience to only a privileged few. This chapter is based on a review of available literature and experiences of the author, in addition to case examples that suggest practical directions for strengthening these emerging partnerships.

The museum and its shift in pedagogy

There is a shift from the past concept of a museum as "a building in which objects of historical, scientific, artistic, or cultural interest are stored and exhibited" to a space of engagement (Brown & Mairesse, 2018, p. 5). In this respect, democratization of museums is underway, blurring the boundaries between concepts such as "professional" and "public," which in turn leads to changes in values ascribed to museums – values such as social inclusion (Crooke, 2007). This is the case for The Mutare Museum of Transport and Antiquities in Zimbabwe (Figure 12.1), which has since transformed its role to include social research in addition to the traditional preservation of cultural artefacts. Through the Beit Trust programme, the museum has embraced the study of communities in the eastern highlands of the country, while the Natural History Museum of Zimbabwe and the Museum of Human Sciences in Bulawayo and Harare, respectively, have introduced programmes targeting full participation of stakeholders in museum affairs.

The local community is thus an active agent throughout all stages of the museum's development. Such a museum is socially sustainable as it draws its strength from the support networks established during its formation. The advantages of a community museum include people taking charge and responsibility for their own history and telling their own stories.

The Hwange rural community in the north-west of Zimbabwe, renowned for its pottery and wood sculpture, provides a good example of the potential for the future establishment of a community museum. Figure 12.2 demonstrates how cultural beliefs and values in the Hwange community can be depicted in wood sculptures – in this case by a local artist, Borniface Kamunjekete. Such sculptures provide opportunities for embodied learning about local values and are thus an essential part of museum education in that community.

To situate the shift to community in Zimbabwe museums today, I turn to Mayer (2005), who observed that museum education, which has had a pronounced impact on art education since

Figure 12.1: Mutare Museum of Transport and Antiquities, Zimbabwe. Photography courtesy of the National Museums and Monuments of Zimbabwe.

Figure 12.2: Borniface Kamunjekete, *Wood sculptures*, 2020.

the 1970s, remains significantly influenced by postmodern thought. Mayer concluded that the visitor's interpretation of art and artefacts in a museum reveals three major categories of literacies: visual literacy, museum literacy and interactivity. Extending this to the local context, the museum educators' focus has moved from the artwork, such as shown in Figure 12.2, as an object of appreciation (by experts) to the visitor's intellectual interrogation, which aligns more fully with the needs of the communities served. Prottas (2020) also observed a shift in the pedagogical role of the museum. With a gradual departure from expert-centred methodology to visitor engagement, such movement towards social methodology reflects the influences of educational psychology, psychology of vision and integration of interactive practices, and aims to develop acuity in reading objects from a perspective of personal value and relevance to the visitor. Perceptually, the interpretation of a visual object is often affected by the ideological position of those in authority, reinforcing the notion that for museums and museum education to take hold in Zimbabwe, communities must be at the heart of curatorial practices.

This brings the topic of interactivity to the conversation, as it relates to visitors' participation as a form of literacy (Mayer, 2005). Museum literacy aims to empower the visitor with a holistic experience of a museum. Rice (1995, as cited in Mayer, 2005) refers to museum pedagogy as a reciprocal and interpretive dialogue between the viewer and contexts. The role of the art museum is therefore to empower and enable visitors to have "personally significant experiences with museum objects" (Rice, 1995, as cited in Mayer, 2005, p. 365). To adequately cater to the needs of a new and diverse audience, Mayer (2005) suggests expanding the qualifications of museum educators to include art education, teaching qualification, museum education, museum studies and studio art, compared to the traditional art history and/or curatorial qualification. Thus, the visitor is guided by appropriately qualified personnel for a comprehensive visual experience. This is the case with the curatorial and other educational staff at the Natural History Museum of Zimbabwe, the Mutare Museum of Transport and Antiquities and the Museum of Human Sciences in Zimbabwe, who collectively hold varied professional qualifications for maximum curatorial guidance of museum visitors.

Museum–school partnerships

Going forward, Zimbabwe regards museum–school partnerships as a critical interface that promotes social cohesion and cultural sustenance. Building towards this goal presents some challenges. Borrowing from Bobick and Hornby (2013), who have explored museum partnerships with local universities in the United States (see also Brown & Mairesse, 2018; Foreman-Peck & Travers, 2013), the disconnect between museum educators and teachers as facilitators of learning suggests a fragile relationship that emanates from a number of factors, including

- prohibitive transport costs preventing schools from carrying out field trips;
- teachers tied to a school curriculum that emphasizes teaching skills for standardized assessments;
- challenges in aligning museum activities with the school curriculum;
- language barriers between teachers and museum educators;
- the perception that the role of museums is service provision, as opposed to true collaborative partners.

Similar issues have influenced museum education in Zimbabwe. In response, partnerships are forming on key cornerstones of practice; much as Brown and Mairesse (2018) suggest, three categories of relationships can be established between museums and schools that are constructive for the Zimbabwe experience. The first is *cooperation*, where an institution utilizes its resources and shares related information with its partner. The second is *coordination*, a formal and continued relationship in which each partner understands the organizational structure of the other partner and the planned efforts underway, as well as their constraints. The third is *collaboration*, where an institution offers its resources and reputation and accepts a new organizational structure and arrangement to reach a common goal with full commitment and responsibility. Thus, it is important for the school and museum to understand the nature of the relationships they are entering into before they start any joint programmes and projects.

Three facets of a successful partnership are programme management, teaching strategies and programme structure. Other considerations include establishing clear common goals, open communication, shared resources and realistic expectations by both parties, in addition to being patient and flexible in implementing the agreed priorities. To achieve a fruitful relationship, it is important that teachers are familiar with museum settings and methods of integrating such museums into their curricula. Teachers need to participate meaningfully in the relationship – for example, by engaging in methods of assessing children's learning in museums. They should coordinate instructional learning goals, activities and assessment modes that can be used to determine students' learning. The cooperating partners should be aware of the different modes of assessment that enhance students' performance. Fortunately, our association, National Museums and Monuments of Zimbabwe (NMMZ), participated in the review of the Competency-Based Curriculum (2015–2022), which resulted in the adoption of Heritage Studies as part of the curriculum. Therefore, when learners visit the different museums, they receive assistance from personnel who are fully conversant with school curriculum demands and expectations, including assessment requirements. Learners are therefore guided accordingly.

In our museums, students now interact with objects that provide tactile experiential learning and the generation of tacit knowledge. Because of full participation and hands-on involvement, students gain confidence in talking about the artefacts in a community context, inspired by the concrete objects. This is reminiscent of Downey et al. (2007), who found that museum–school partnership programmes contribute to increasing students' critical thinking skills, scientific thinking skills, communication skills, creativity and problem-solving abilities. To further develop these skills, learners should be engaged in activities that include leading panel discussions, conducting group projects and performing assignment tasks online.

For over 20 years, the NMMZ has run a number of programmes in conjunction with the Ministry of Primary and Secondary Education through the National Association of Primary Heads, including quizzes from cluster level up to the national level. In this regard, the NMMZ has been funding such activities, and it is also in partnership with Schools Development Committees for resource mobilization that can be a source for funding honoraria. Through mainstreaming some of the museum activities, schools have also been able to fund a number of museum and cultural activities, with the NMMZ playing a key oversight role. Funding would also allow participants in activities such as panel discussions, for example, to be paid a small honorarium for their efforts. Brown and Mairesse (2018) suggest the following

Propositions for Museum Education

Online learning as a critical pedagogical method offers possibilities for active learning through digital images, videos, audio content and games that are beyond the capacity of the physical spaces of the museum. Interactive virtual learning aims to extend opportunities for onsite experience; as Gaylord-Opalewski and O'Leary (2019) suggest, "[it is] a conduit for greater outreach and promotion to audiences that may never have the opportunity to visit the collections of a museum in person – due to budget, physical limitations, or distance" (p. 229). According to Din (2015), online learning directly accesses the learners, extending the utilization of under-utilized resources such as X-rays, maps, charts and diagrams, with possibilities for continually updating information, documenting learners' reflections and increasing communication. In turn, Mitchell et al. (2019) emphasized the need for self-directed and experiential teaching methods as part of twenty-first-century methodologies, thus embracing the blended teaching approach. In an example from Zimbabwe, Figure 12.3 illustrates an asynchronous platform at The Mutare Museum of Transport and Antiquities. The interactive platform enables students to access informational texts and visuals repackaged for effective self-directed learning. The online pedagogical paradigm expands the now already blurred physical boundaries between schools, communities and museums. Online platforms increase access to museums and local heritage, which is central to Zimbabwe's cultural contexts. Learners

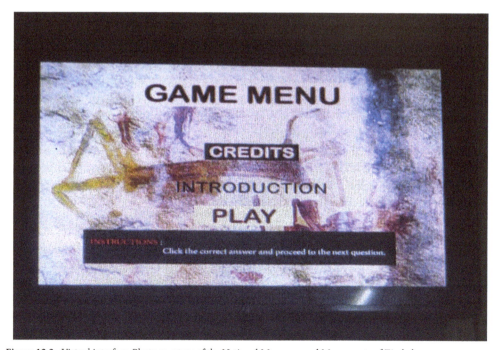

Figure 12.3: Virtual interface. Photo courtesy of the National Museums and Monuments of Zimbabwe.

can navigate through the various contents in an experimental and experiential manner, which offers a dynamic shift in museum education locally and nationally that is still to be fully articulated.

Concluding remarks

Museum–school partnerships are fast becoming critical for enhanced student learning in Zimbabwe. Although this synergistic potential is in its infancy, such partnerships are well established in some countries, while we may be described as still lagging. The barriers to museum–school engagement that resulted from geographical location are slowly shifting. Resources permitting, partnerships can now be established between and among institutions across the globe. This chapter has attempted to illustrate strategies that can be used to promote such relationships, with the assistance of interactive virtual learning technologies. Fundamental changes in the school curriculum towards museum education can be achieved if teachers and museum staff continue to collaborate towards a shared responsibility of educating the Zimbabwean learner.

References

Bobick, B., & Hornby, J. (2013). Practical partnerships: Strengthening the museum-school relationship. *Journal of Museum Education, 38*(1), 81–89.

Brown, K., & Mairesse, F. (2018). The definition of museum through its social role. *Curator: The Museum Journal, 61*(2), 525–539. https://doi.org/10.1111/cura.12276

Crooke, E. (2007). *Museums and community: Ideas, issues and challenges*. Routledge.

Din, H. (2015). Pedagogy and practice in museum online learning. *Journal of Museum Education, 40*(2), 102–109.

Downey, S., Delamatre, J., & Jones, J. (2007). Measuring the impact of museum-school programmes: Findings and implications for practice. *Journal of Museum Education, 32*(2), 175–187.

Foreman-Peck, L., & Travers, K. (2013). What is distinctive about museum pedagogy and how can museums best support learning in schools? An action research inquiry into the practice of three regional museums. *Educational Action Research, 21*(1), 28–41.

Gaylord-Opalewski, K., & O'Leary, L. (2019). Defining interactive virtual learning in museum education: A shared perspective. *Journal of Museum Education, 44*(3), 229–241.

Mayer, M. M. (2005). A postmodern puzzle: Rewriting the place of the visitor in art museum education. *Studies in Art Education, 46*(4), 356–368.

Mitchell, A., Linn, S., & Yoshida, H. (2019). A tale of technology and collaboration: Preparing for 21st century museum visitors. *Journal of Museum Education, 44*(3), 242–252.

Moore, C. (2015). Embracing change: Museum educators in the digital age. *Journal of Museum Education, 40*(2), 141–146.

Prottas, N. (2020). Beyond the cult of the author: The literary museum today. *Journal of Museum Education*, 45(3), 221–225.

Sanger, E., Silverman, S., & Kraybill, A. (2015). Developing a model for technology-based museum school partnerships. *Journal of Museum Education*, 40(2), 147–158.

Chapter 13

Every School Is a Museum: The Case of "Art for Learning Art" in Tegucigalpa, Honduras

Joaquín Roldán, Andrea Rubio-Fernández and Ángela Moreno-Córdoba

This study investigates the idea of creating contemporary art museums in schools located in contexts of social exclusion. From some actions of art teaching developed in Honduras, we use an arts-based educational approach (Marín-Viadel & Roldán, 2017, 2019) to characterize a school museum model that operates as the main promoter of arts education. We begin with a social constructionist perspective based on Berger and Luckmann (1968) and pedagogical constructionism (Papert & Harel, 1991), and consider studies of the educational function of the museum and contemporary approaches to art as an instrument of inclusion in Latin America (Rodrigues, 1980).

On the methodological use of images

This chapter follows a visual arts-based educational research methodology. We do not show isolated images but rather argue for some visual ideas through three visual essays built with several interconnected images (Figure 13.1). We structure the chapter by following aesthetic decisions to describe artistic and pedagogical processes, to present people and results and to emphasize methodological connections.

In our view, it would not make sense to explain this research in words alone. Visual connections between the images that compose a learning encounter help to interpret their meanings in the context of the research. Verbal explanations of visual content may make some meanings more concrete but at the same time reduce many others. As readers delve into the meaning of this project, they encounter images from aesthetics, symbols and poetry, as with any artistic image.

"Art for Learning Art" in Honduras

For the past five years, we have carried out a project based on the use of contemporary visual arts as a form of social integration and community development (Art for Learning Art in Honduras, http://arteparaaprender.org/honduras/). The schools where we work are in socially and economically depressed neighbourhoods, dominated by violence and poverty. In these three schools, art education activities were rarely present until our project began in 2015. In the course of the project, in these three schools more than 150 teachers and 8000 students, from kindergarten to baccalaureate, have been involved. Six professors and more

Figure 13.1: *Visual Abstract*, 2021. *10,000 Houses at two different museums:* Santa Clara School Museum in Honduras and Caja Granada Memory Museum in Granada. Top, *Mural*; bottom, *Drawing the mural*, Ricardo Marín-Viadel, 2017. Centre, *Exhibition set up*, Ángela Moreno, 2022.

than 70 postgraduate students from the University of Granada contributed to the project for one month or more.

Our main objective has been to promote artistic creation for social construction. Rodrigues (1980) points out that when the school is situated in a context of a risk of social exclusion, in addition to its usual functions the school needs to become a work of art for meaningful change to take place. When "social marginalisation corresponds in this context to artistic marginalisation" (Marín-Viadel & Roldán, 2020, p. 353), only collective cultural creation associated with a solid educational project can bring about long-term community change. The task of ACOES Honduras (Asociación Colaboración y Esfuerzo), the NGO with which we have worked over the years and the institution responsible for these schools, is to focus on achieving this collaborative local development. Yet, art was not present in the lives of students.

In this project, we began by conducting a teacher training programme for schools and designing a multitude of artistic activities with children of all grades. But after two years of the project, we concluded that this approach was not enough to create artistic culture because these activities and the results were not recognized and preserved for the entire school community: steps in an irreversible process of educational and cultural progress.

Every school is a museum

Luis Camnitzer's famous work "The Museum is a School" (2009) is an art installation where the artist wrote on the façade of several prominent museums in different countries: "The artist learns to communicate; the public learns to make connections." This artwork urges the institution that exhibits it to make a pedagogical commitment to its public (Camnitzer, 2009), and it demands from artists a different social attitude from that which had been proclaimed sufficient in the arts.

So, if the museum is to behave like a school, what should happen in a school museum?

In our project, the goal is to complement Camnitzer's incitement to museums. We try to provoke the notion of schools: If a school is also conceived as a museum, and a museum should be pedagogical, then a school must be a producer of artistic culture. Just as a museum cannot limit itself to being pedagogical by disseminating and exhibiting heritage, the act of pedagogy implies the participation of the public as learners. A school cannot dedicate itself only to transmitting culture but must also produce it, preserve it and recognize it. Its act of creation implies recognizing itself as a creative institution.

Extending the argument further, if the school becomes a museum, then it will be a space for observation and recognition of the aesthetic aspects of reality, and so the exercises and learning tasks become relevant objects that cannot be underestimated. They will not only be experiments but traces of findings, products of the thought and personal experiences – or put another way, collective cultural experiences. If the school is a museum, then its protagonists must act aesthetically, and the spaces and intellectual production created within it become a palpable culture, a shared poetics and recognized heritage, staging performance and spectacle. Learning is like creating; teaching is like exhibiting. Creation is the horizontal space to communicate exhibition and appreciation and learning and teaching because we all create, we all learn and teach, and we all appreciate and heal in the process.

Our intuition was that if we created a museum in the school, we would introduce a new key that could aesthetically permeate the educational community, taking a step beyond the conventional functions used in that specific context. In this way, the exhibitions have introduced something difficult to achieve in other ways: the idea of the value of culture. We believe this idea is central to human communities. It has no functional or practical purpose, but it is aesthetic, poetic and pleasing to human beings. Cerveny (2001), analysing Elliot Eisner's thinking on the aesthetic content of arts education, says:

> The notion that the value of the arts lies in their ability to help teach other subjects, is upside down. Instead, Eisner said, the rest of the core curriculum needs to make use of the teaching and learning approaches that address the same cognitive development that comes naturally and powerfully through a study of the arts. [...] Eisner believes that learning becomes a creative process and accomplishment in these other subjects then takes on the character of a work of art. (n.p.)

Museums, contemporary art, social exclusion and schools (MACES)

The concept of the art museum in critical museology has undergone drastic changes in the last 30 years (see Hooper-Greenhill, 2000; Santacana-Mestre & Hernández-Cardona, 2006 among others). Modernist conceptions of culture and art have moved to a more open conception where relational aesthetics (Iser, 1978), creative participation and cultural engagement are the main activities proposed to the public (see www.arteparaaprender.org and www.lainopia.es for two examples from Spain).

School has changed too. The idea of education and teaching methodology has evolved enormously with respect to the hegemonic pedagogical theories of the mid twentieth century, especially through critical, multicultural and postmodern pedagogical approaches. Therefore, the idea of creating a museum within a school cannot simply be built on outdated conceptions in which the identity of the museum is based on its paradigmatic architecture, nor on its powerful collection of works of art, nor focus exclusively on contemplative models where visitors only need to observe (Santacana-Mestre & Hernández-Cardona, 2006).

We use the acronym MACES, which we translate to mean in English either "mallet" or "hammer" (an instrument or a weapon) and "sceptre" (symbol of power) because in both Spanish and English it sums up all the terms we care to reveal here: museums, contemporary art and schools in a context of social exclusion. But we also consider it a fortunate metaphor for what we intend with these interventions: to turn these museums into instruments, to

Figure 13.2: Photo essay, 2021. Santa Teresa MACES 2019. Three photos by Joaquín Roldán, 2019. Left, *Drawing from Stones*; centre, *Exhibition*; right, *Looking at the final drawing*.

operate "artful weapons" that defend and symbolize the power of culture and education as a means of social integration.

A school is a museum with daily visitors, with works of art always evolving and growing. Museums in schools with a context of social risk, what we are calling MACES in this chapter, are neither buildings nor institutions other than the school where they are, nor a set of permanent works of art. A MACES is a collection of community art that grows artistically and culturally alongside the school and community where it is located (Figure 13.2). The model of contemporary art museum that we propose is a place where art can occur in terms of identity recognition, personal learning, social meaning and function, knowledge heritage and culture creation. It is a relevant place in the school, regularly visited by school audiences (students and teachers) to gain knowledge and aesthetic enjoyment, to be immersed in the sensorial or just to "hang out," enjoying time together. It is a place where contemporary art is practised and where the most exceptional objects we are capable of making and appreciating as a collective are collected and exhibited. These objects embody and symbolize visual ideas that matter to us as individuals and as a community.

The purpose is not to house expensive objects in market terms, nor that the works be recognized as valuable in traditional terms of authorship. The museum and each of its works are part of the educational community and the school institution; in this case, it took three years before the desires of those who organize and maintain the school would be expressed in its creation.

Artistic-based teaching in MACES

The museums created for schools in Honduras are conceived as spaces for artistic learning. The proposals are created from an a/r/tographic approach (Irwin & de Cosson, 2004), exploring the interconnection of art, research and teaching. More specifically, our

Figure 13.3: Photo-essay, 2021. Three photos by Andrea Rubio-Fernández, 2016, from Virgen de Suyapa MACES, 2016. Left, a collaborative installation by Anabel Arnaldos, 2016. Upper right, *Drawing with the soil of my house*; *Mixing the soil of my home with the soil of my school*. Lower right, *A little soil from every house in the neighbourhood around the school*.

proposals are situated within the a/r/tographic educational aspect of Artistic Teaching Methodologies (Roldán & Marín-Viadel, 2010; Roldán et al., 2021; Rubio-Fernández, 2018, 2021). These approaches shape acts of teaching and learning as acts of artistic creation.

In our methodology, we propose a set of games of collective art creation that allow the elaboration of large, collaborative artworks and a coherent final exhibition, during which the whole school participates at several points over a month or more of workshops. Our conception of the school museum of contemporary art for social construction implies a series of criteria for asking participants to intervene creatively on materials and elements in the exhibition:

- Collaborative drawings, installations or sculptures are designed through similar and multiple interventions by many people (hundreds or potentially even thousands).
- Materials and techniques should be simple and commonplace in the lives of learners.

- Individual interventions must be immediate with a unique, satisfactory and surprising visual result, while the collaborative installations created as the product of interventions and as a collective work of art must be visually extraordinary, rich, subtle and complex in their variations.
- Moreover, each collaborative installation and each particular intervention must be carefully considered for educators to produce relevant learning in visual, poetic or symbolic terms.
- The interventions requested of the learners should not require an expert technique, and they cannot be so rigid that they do not respect the development of the expression and creativity of each contributor.
- Educators must allow variations, but participants must respect the rules. These two efforts are necessary for a great collaborative artwork with aesthetic coherence, visual coherence and poetic eloquence. We search for variations without monotony.
- We always follow visual ideas deduced from other works of art to produce connections with other cultures, times and people. It is a methodology that moves "from the visual to the visual," which tries to avoid translations by emphasizing the development of new visual responses to known visual problems.

MACES artworks can be exchanged with other art museums to be exhibited, as is the case of the images shown in Figure 13.1. The drawing "Las casas" [The houses] was created at Santa Clara MACES in 2017 in Honduras, asking the participants to draw ten houses on large Fabriano paper measuring 500 × 140 centimetres. Materials were very simple: pieces of dried clay and graphite pencils. Some limits to the drawing action were added such as blue threads placed on the paper as horizontal guides to organize the drawing. Instructions to create were as follows: You have to draw at least ten different houses, no bigger than the space between blue threads, with red clay and grey graphite (more explanations on the process – in Spanish – are provided on the project's website: http://arteparaaprender.org/2017_h2/).

The following year, in March 2018, this drawing was displayed on the TATE Liverpool Exchange as part of the "From Mittens to Barbies" event. In addition, three months later in June 2018, the educational action continued in dialogue with this same enormous drawing at the Caja Granada Museum, within the "Arte para aprender arte" [Art for Learning Art] project in Granada, Spain (www.arteparaaprender.org). In this case, not only was the work exhibited but a collaborative creation proposal was designed based on it. Around 4500 visitors to the Museum in Granada were invited to participate. In 2022, the same mural was part of the exhibition *Art for Learning 2022* at the Caja Granada Museum, which commemorated the tenth anniversary of the project. This demonstrates that the quality of the works of art belonging to these local and educational initiatives – originally conceived as school and community devices for better artistic education – is recognized outside the educational and cultural context and is of interest to professional experts from contemporary art institutions.

MACES have to maintain their social and educational objectives without sacrificing the exhibition of exceptional works of art because, in order to produce aesthetic encounters, we need aesthetic values (Figure 13.3). The artistic content of these museums has been conceived as teaching/learning tools as well as active provocateurs of creative aesthetic experiences (Marín-Viadel & Roldán, 2020). All participants should consider them as authentic works of contemporary art, and consequently, they should be preserved and cared for after the end of each exhibition.

Collaborative creations and learning: Contributions from constructionism

Our a/r/tographic proposals have been collaboratively designed and created by a large team of art educators together with teachers and students in Honduras. The idea of collaborative creation throughout the process is crucial to the project because the artistic learning process we are pursuing is both a collective and a personal act, and the involvement of each individual must contribute to and respect the final collective product. In this sense, we rely in particular on the ideas proposed by constructionism (Rodríguez-Villamil, 2008).

The first concept is to consider works of art as "objects of / for thinking" (Papert & Harel, 1991). This means that "each creation is about an object that can be used by a subject to think about other things, using their own construction of that object" (Badilla & Chacón, 2004, p. 6). These objects are part of the learning process and the content learned. When it comes to creating meaning, Papert and Harel (1991) also differentiate between objects of experience and objects of thought. The first would be those we can manipulate in an accessible way; intuitively, both the object and the experience are taken for granted, but the latter allows us to inspect the world (Badilla & Chacón, 2004). They are artefacts or actions created to understand. The MACES proposals generate individual interventions that imply experiences of knowledge and collaboratively provide major creations that show evidence of shared visual thinking as artefacts for thought based on art. In those contexts, art learning is not limited to an experimentation with materials that we all know. These artworks exceed the act of individual experimentation as they are agreed on in a collective act that reaffirms them in community.

And here we find the second idea from Papert and Harel (1991): that of a "public entity," having to do with the construction of learning in community and with the collective construction of meaning created in shared and collaborative learning processes. We argue that such events do not occur in individual learning.

Conclusions

In this chapter, we present an educational project in visual arts in the context of social exclusion in Honduras. We have tried to show that there are enough epistemological and methodological foundations to propose a school museum model in these contexts. It is viable as long as the teaching methodology produces it as part of the teaching process. Also, it is necessary to recognize the products of the educational intervention as heritage. The exhibitions presented in this chapter have aroused the interest of our educational community in general, which expressed the desire in 2019 to make these exhibitions permanent. For us as promoters of the project, this has been the most important achievement.

Unfortunately, the fledgling museums have also suffered the crippling impact of COVID-19. The schools were closed by government order, so during 2020 and 2021, we were not able to continue the project. But community commitment to this art project has not changed. The project continues, and schools continue to preserve the works of art and promote new artistic productions.

We trust that we have been able to convey our understanding of the value of artistic productions made by children in unexpected circumstances in the developing world and that they have been presented here in ways consistent with the integrity of visual methodologies. These images constitute a visual argument about the importance and potential of MACES: relating visual processes, institutional spaces and creative action of the participants, together with the final objects exhibited in a respectful and conservation context.

References

Arte para Aprender [Art for learning art]. (2022). Universidad de Granada. www.arteparaaprender.org

Badilla, E., & Chacón, A. (2004). Construccionismo: Objetos para pensar, entidades públicas y micromundos. *Actualidades Investigativas en Educación, 4*(1–2), 6–10

Berger, P., & Luckmann, T. (1968). *The social construction of reality.* Amorrortu.

Camnitzer, L. (2009). *The museum is a school* [Installation]. Guggenheim, New York, United States. https://www.guggenheim.org/artwork/33533

Cerveny, K. (2001). Elliot W. Eisner, the role of the arts in educating the whole child: A Cleveland area presentation. *GIA Reader, 12*(3). https://www.giarts.org/article/elliot-w-eisner-role-arts-educating-whole-child

Hooper-Greenhill, E. (2000). *Museums and the interpretation of visual culture.* Routledge.

Irwin, R., & de Cosson, A. (2004). *A/r/tography: Rendering self through arts-based living inquiry.* Pacific Educational Press.

Iser, W. (1978). *The act of reading.* Johns Hopkins University Press.

Marín-Viadel, R., & Roldán, J. (Eds.). (2017). *Visual ideas: Arts-based research and artistic research.* Universidad de Granada.

Marín-Viadel, R., & Roldán, J. (2019). A/r/tografía e investigación educativa basada en artes visuales en el panorama de las metodologías de investigación en educación artística. *Arte, Individuo y Sociedad, 31*(4), 881–895. https://revistas.ucm.es/index.php/ARIS/article/view/63409

Marín-Viadel, R., & Roldán, J. (2020). Arts-based educational research and social transformation: A project of social a/r/tography. In P. L. Maaruis & A. G. Rud (Eds.), *Imagining Dewey: Artful works and dialogue about art as experience* (pp. 353–368). Brill.

Papert, S., & Harel, I. (1991). *Constructionism.* Ablex.

Rodrigues, A. (Ed.). (1980). *Escuelinha de arte do Brazil*. INEP.

Rodríguez-Villamil, H. (2008). Del constructivismoo al construccionismo. Implicaciones edcativas. *Revista Educación y Desarrollo Social*, 2(1), 72–89.

Roldán, J., & Marín-Viadel, R. (2010). Aprendizaje, innovación docente e investigación en educación artística basada en la fotografía. In J. Roldán & M. Hernández (Eds.), *El otro lado. Fotografía y pensamiento visual en las culturas universitarias* (pp. 36–63). Universidad de Granada, Universidad Autónoma de Aguascalientes.

Roldán, J., Marín-Viadel, R., & Rubio-Fernández, A. (2021). Metodologías artísticas de enseñanza de las artes visuales. In R. Marín-Viadel, J. Roldán, & L. Cálix (Eds.), *La enseñanza de las artes visuales en contextos de riesgo de exclusión social* (pp. 116–133). Editorial UNAH.

Rubio-Fernández, A. (2018). Cuatro estrategias didácticas basadas en arte contemporáneo: El proceso educativo como obra de arte a través de Metodologías Artísticas de Enseñanza-Aprendizaje. *Revista ANIAV*, 3, 67–79.

Rubio-Fernández, A. (2021). *Metodologías artísticas de enseñanza. Un modelo de enseñanza-aprendizaje basado en las artes visuales a través de la escultura* [Doctoral dissertation, Universidad de Granada]. https://investigacion.usc.es/documentos/615bc19bd9bf6a26275cd9a1

Santacana-Mestre, J., & Hernández-Cardona, F. X. (2006). *Museología Crítica*. Trea.

Part III

Pedagogic Pivots

Chapter 14

Not-Knowing: Creating Spaces for Co-curation

Deborah Riding

The pedagogical turn and move towards more participatory contexts in galleries have seen a growth in the co-curation of collections with audiences. This has become increasingly urgent as an institutional response to calls for decolonization and for these approaches to have a real impact on practice. I argue that they need to involve a significant shift in the epistemological position of those institutions. With reference to my own research, this chapter provides a theoretical and practical insight into a recent approach to co-curation at Tate Liverpool, highlighting the challenges and benefits of developing new knowledge and understanding of collections and their display by co-creating new knowledge together with audiences. During this time, I held the position of Programme Manager for Children and Young People in the learning department and worked closely with colleague Darren Pih, Exhibitions Curator.

This chapter explores how this epistemological position was fostered and explored through a curatorial project: *Ideas Depot*. The research I undertook explored the impact of institutional epistemology within the wider context of curatorial and education practice and developed a framework for the co-creation of knowledge between the gallery and its audiences. Four models of co-creation were constructed: the jigsaw, the reflective pool, the clash and the creative catalyst. All these models have the potential to build collaboratively generated knowledge about artworks, but the creative catalyst has the most potential for creating new knowledge between constituent groups. Associated with the creative catalyst is the development of a new institutional epistemology of not-knowing: one that embraces and cultivates uncertainty that is more equitable and fluid and retains a speculative space.

The context of institutional co-curation

In recent years, many galleries and museums have recognized the value of involving their audiences in exploring and responding to their collections. The resulting interactions have been developed through different models: supporting participants to learn "how" from existing curatorial practice, providing an authentic voice or developing a position of agency and empowerment. Through these various approaches, the knowledge contributed or generated is framed and perceived in different ways. However, a hierarchy between institutional and expert knowledge and other forms persists. For co-curation to be an equitable enterprise, all knowledge contributed and generated should be perceived and valued in the same way.

These models usually focus on inviting and supporting the audience's contribution and the impact on them themselves as individuals or as a constituency. Very rarely, if ever, do they focus on developing new knowledge about the artwork generated between the curator and the audience, including the learning of the curator. In museums, it has become established that a particular group or individual can provide a more authentic presentation of an artefact by bringing forward their situated knowledges, but in the case of the gallery of modern and contemporary art, certain knowledge still prevails as dominant, and that hierarchy is difficult to dismantle.

Current pedagogical and participatory curatorial models in favour of many museums of modern and contemporary art invite dialogical experiences and suggest a space for democratic knowledge exchange and shared learning (Obrist & Bovier, 2008; O'Neill, 2007; O'Neill & Wilson, 2010; Smith, 2012). The concept of integrated practice to support this has been introduced through curatorial and gallery education discourse, and structurally many art museums have adopted staffing and roles to adapt to this approach (Tallant, 2009). Integrated practice is problematic in this context, however. O'Neill (2012) distinguishes between the curatorial and the "paracuratorial," which offers potential, he argues, for "a terrain of praxis that both operates within the curatorial paradigm and retains a destabilising relationship with it" (p. 55). O'Neill describes the different ways in which some contemporary curators understand their practice as political, opening up multi-disciplinary spaces for exchange, but this still retains the authority of the curator and their associated knowledge. Tate Liverpool has explored these approaches for several years (Campolmi, 2016; Dall et al., 2016), but they are limited in their potential for learning-with.

Re-framing the gallery

While the artists' pedagogies prevalent in facilitated learning encounters prioritize the critical and reflective role of engagement, the conventional exhibition environment still upholds the authority of the institution and associated hierarchies of knowledge (Bennett, 2013). In recent years, the educational turn in curatorial theory has accommodated pedagogical and participatory art practice and created opportunities for a range of learning experiences to become more embedded into practice (Bishop, 2012; Cutler, 2010; Kester, 2004; Rogoff, 2008). However, whereas in the delivery of learning programmes in galleries, artists are presented as collaborators and co-learners who encourage dialogic experiences and multiple interpretations, this is not necessarily manifested in the self-led negotiation of a gallery space reliant on text-based, authoritative interpretation and traditional aesthetic experiences.

Sayers (2011) clearly articulates the tensions between the ideological position underpinning gallery education programmes that encourages the co-construction of knowledge, and the more authoritative and fixed position of the gallery, constructing the visitor as a learning subject. Accommodating this co-constructed knowledge within conventional exhibition processes is challenging, and Dewdney (2008) highlights the issues of museums acknowledging, making visible or distributing new knowledge. Exhibitions are often presented as texts or essays, researched and authored. However, their role within the gallery or museum can be to raise awareness of these constructed narratives, inviting critical engagement and debate (Lahav, 2000; Lord, 2006).

Constructed and enacted as a pedagogic space, however, galleries are still perceived as sites for knowledge banking. Knowledge is offered up for the visitor to *learn from* in the form of catalogues, written as "live" interpretation, with artist and curator talks and conferences, but in the context of gallery education, it is presented as knowledge to *engage with*. In developing the modern art museum as a space of reception, the viewer is separated from the development of knowledge presented through the exhibition. Although exhibitions can invite engagement with work on display, in general such engagement does not generate a dialogue. However, it is argued (Sayers, 2011) that the act of conversation inherent in facilitated gallery workshops can locate the audience at the site of knowledge production, which can be seen as a challenge to the exclusive authority of the museum.

Creating opportunities for those dialogues and voices within the exhibition process is key to dismantling these hierarchies. Bernstein (1999) identifies two key forms of discourse: vertical and horizontal. Here, associated knowledge is both binary and oppositional: "In the educational field, one form is sometimes referred to as school(ed) knowledge and the other as everyday common-sense knowledge, or 'official' and 'local' knowledge" (p. 163). Bernstein contrasts institutional pedagogy (vertical discourse) and segmental pedagogy (horizontal discourse) and aligns "hierarchical knowledge structures" and "horizontal knowledge structures" accordingly. Within a hierarchical structure, knowledge is gradually integrated towards a deeper and more "abstract" understanding (aligned in institutional contexts with scholarly and academic knowledge), whereas within a horizontal structure, knowledge is "accumulated" from a series of unrelated contexts and specialized languages. The horizontal structure, Bernstein suggests, offers the opportunity to introduce a "new language" to challenge assumed knowledge and empower the "speaker." These new voices can introduce different views and knowledge. Bernstein claims that it is often younger members within the horizontal structure who develop this new language, which presents issues for the more established voices in the structure:

> This new language can be used to challenge the hegemony and legitimacy of more senior speakers. The latter may be cut off from acquiring the new language because […] trained incapacity arising out of previous language acquisition, and a reduced incentive, arising out of the loss of their own position.
>
> (Bernstein, 1999, p. 163)

The purpose of the research study I undertook was to examine perceptions of knowledge and understanding of modern and contemporary artwork in a gallery learning context.

I explored a range of positions implicated in integrated learning and curatorial practices, including those of staff and audience and their experiences of co-creation. Participants took part in a gallery workshop, which involved group discussion, collaborative drawing and the connection of ideas across one of the gallery's collection displays. *Personal Meaning Maps* were also used to identify each participant's knowledge of a particular artwork before and after the workshop. Semi-structured interviews were undertaken and analysed thematically using a phenomenographic approach. The research presented co-creation of new knowledge as a model suited to learning together across the organization and between the gallery and its audiences: a "learning-with" that could have the potential for developing the more horizontal discourse Bernstein describes.

Exploring authenticity and rupture through the creative catalyst

Exploring the different ways that co-creation is experienced in terms of knowledge generation, I generated four models:

- **The jigsaw:** Different knowledge types are acknowledged and pieced together, providing a comprehensive knowledge base.
- **The reflective pool:** Different knowledge types are considered internally and temporally through processes of understanding.
- **The clash:** Different knowledge types test and challenge each other, retaining difference and tension.
- **The creative catalyst:** Different knowledge types interrupt and rupture existing knowledge to open up practice and epistemological positions to new directions.

The jigsaw, reflective pool and clash all create the conditions for different types of co-creation to be made visible and available for consideration; however, they are all limited by the authority of institutional knowledge. Within the model of the creative catalyst, knowledge is regarded as a rupture, experienced through interactions of different knowledges types. Interdisciplinary and intersubjective collaborations open possibilities to creatively explore unknown knowledge and practice. This seemed the model most closely aligned to a concept of co-creation. Within the creative catalyst, knowledge is seen as developed through, or following, interruption by introducing new ideas, concepts and experiences previously not considered and being open to them as valid contributions. The traditional and conventional norms of knowledge development in the gallery are thus challenged, as well as the knowledge proposed and its perceived value and status.

Gallery education has been articulated in recent years as an event, an intervention – interrupting and sometimes disrupting the gallery experience (Pringle & DeWitt, 2014). The concepts of unlearning/unknowing (Atkinson, 2012; Rogoff, 2008) are useful to help conceptualize this. Atkinson (2012) develops the concept of "real learning":

As a move into a new ontological state, real learning implies puncturing or modifying established patterns of understanding and assimilated configurations of knowledge on a local level. It is a process in which there is a firm challenge to see beyond current vistas of practice and formulate new ones.

(p. 9)

Atkinson conceives of these events within education as localized experiences that cannot be accommodated by conventional approaches and that demand a new pedagogy, or what he calls a "pedagogy against the state" (Atkinson, 2008). This pedagogy seeks to open practice to new possibilities and in particular, the "that-which-is-not-yet" (Atkinson, 2012). This move towards the unknown is destabilizing not only for the teacher but also for the learner, which Atkinson (2012) acknowledges:

The disruption of established ways of knowing, through learning events, means that learners need to be able to handle states of uncertainty as new knowledge and new competencies begin to emerge. This suggests a rather curious, almost contradictory, relation of learning to states of not-knowing.

(p. 10)

Like Bernstein's concept of horizontal discourse, Atkinson's "states of not-knowing" can also present a challenge for a model that supports "learning-with." The feminist application of diffraction to methodology and epistemology is perhaps helpful here (Barad, 2007). Rather than developing new knowledge within the same epistemic community and its conventions or indeed rejecting them, diffraction conceptualizes knowledge development as a process using existing and unfamiliar knowledge as lenses through which to envision something new. Diffraction suggests an awareness of other (whether that be the culturally constructed other or the unfamiliar) as part of the process of creating something new rather than repeating or ignoring knowledge that is encountered. Haraway (1987) refers to "patterns of difference," where perspectives, identities, practices and knowledge interact and are engaged with and through each other to provoke and catalyze new directions.

Interrupting and rupturing conventional epistemological positions enables us to open practice so that constructed subject positions with associated power relations, paradigms of knowledge and discourses can be more easily navigated. Within these spaces the "us and them" of the gallery/audience binary, curatorial/education divide and teacher/learner position can be destabilized. This is a familiar territory within gallery learning but not so within curatorial practice. The proposed model of "learning-with" considers all involved (staff and public) as learners, which has implications for well-established conventional relationships and authority. The aim of the creative catalyst is to develop conditions through which we can explore knowledge beyond conventional positions and paradigms. Knowledge in this conceptual space is unfamiliar and destabilizing as much for audience members as staff. However, it is essential to move beyond this discomfort and establish a new position for the institution in regard to its collections.

The not-knowing paradigm

Moving to a new paradigm of not-knowing presents an opportunity for the gallery to acknowledge and embrace this shift in epistemology, building resilience against the impulse to know. Strategies are required to support the visibility and acceptance of the uncertainty of the encounter and share the intellectual spaces for knowledge development about works and collections. This provides a genuine framework through which to generate new knowledge together, supporting co-curation in a more impactful and sustainable way, repositioning both expert and visitor and reframing engagement in the gallery as collaborative enquiry. Whereas not-knowing is perceived as a gap in cultural and educational discourse, for those concerned with artistic thinking, not-knowing presents an opportunity for more responsive, creative and speculative knowledge (Fortnum, 2013; Sheikh, 2006). For Jones (2013) fostering and retaining a sense of "wonder" resists the power dynamics inherent in models that seek to educate or emancipate the audience, instead proposing not-knowing and thinking together as a constant.

Curatorial transparency

"Learning-with" the research suggested that developing an approach that could reconfigure the exhibition format as research-in-progress might be helpful in creating spaces for productive and equitable "ruptures." Applying the notion of "learning-with" through co-creation of knowledge informed the development of a new collection display, co-curated with and for primary schools (students aged 4–11 years). The design of the conceptual and physical spaces for the display was informed by the theoretical framework I have described. I worked closely with the curator of an exhibition to translate the notion of a not-knowing paradigm into the project. Working with the curatorial conventions of an exhibition was the focus. We wanted to introduce new voices but without adopting a "learning how" approach. Rather than enculturating children into a curatorial community of practice, we aimed to establish conditions that would allow for a collaborative enquiry: "learning-with" the children involved. According to Adams and Owens (2015), a key issue with the community of practice model is "epistemological reproduction." In a community of practice, knowledge is passed on by the more accomplished member to the novice in an apprentice-like model. The knowledge that circulates is associated with the *practice* of the community. We tried to resist this model, balancing the exposure of the curatorial process to reveal its constructs, opening new ways of developing knowledge and understanding.

By revealing the constructed narrative, newly generated knowledge is able to puncture and disrupt. Creating the conditions for young children to understand the process – but feel confident interacting with it on their own terms rather than learning how curators usually do it – was important. A gallery resource, *Connecting Ideas*, was developed to support the children in exploring and considering which artworks they would put together and how they would be displayed and experienced. Gallery resources often support engagement with particular artworks and artists or exhibition themes but very rarely have the curatorial process itself as the focus. Co-curation of the new display was built into a parallel schools-in-residence research study (Riding et al., 2019) positioning children as equals offering a "diffracting" lens on the collection (Figure 14.1).

No matter how collaborative and integrated a programme is, learning and curatorial functions operate within separate domains as far as the exhibition process goes. In the main, research activity is undertaken behind the scenes and then presented. Learning departments then step in to activate engagement with an exhibition, and curatorial colleagues move on to the next piece of research. It was important for this project that we shifted this temporality: re-imagining the display as a repository of objects and knowledge that could be adapted, co-constructed and reassembled to create new knowledge and understanding. Rather than stepping back once the display was presented to the public, the exhibition curator continued

Figure 14.1: *Connecting Ideas*, 2021. School resource. Copyright: Tate. Photo by Deborah Riding.

to re-engage with the curatorial concept and artworks, constantly reinterpreting them with different groups of children both in the gallery and their classrooms.

Throughout this project, particular skill sets and expertise associated with learning and curating were evident and respected. Rather than working in parallel, they genuinely developed as a complementary but dual practice. Both skill sets were necessary simultaneously, and reflective practice supported each colleague as a critical friend. The challenge was to maintain a cycle of disruption rather than work towards an integrated model where "learning-with" could become redundant.

Ideas depot

The gallery space, as well as being suited to self-led school groups, needed to physically engage with the idea of mutability. A design was created that referenced gallery storage with a warehouse aesthetic that not only created a "behind the scenes" feel to the display but allowed for the easy "swapping" of works. Works were presented as individual objects with their usually unseen stretchers, raw canvas and conservation notes visible through the mesh supports (Figure 14.2).

Figure 14.2: *Ideas Depot*, 2021. Tate Liverpool. Copyright: Tate. Photo by Roger Sinek.

The temporary feel of their installation was reinforced by the display's title, *Ideas Depot*. The works themselves and the ideas and knowledge generated and circulating around them were framed as provisional and constantly in flux.

Focus was on processes of engagement and learning, with visitors encouraged to make their own connections with the works and each other's ideas, constantly co-constructing new knowledge about the works on display. In turn, a cyclical programme was developed to allow children from different schools to propose new works to be swapped in. These swaps continued to shift and change the dialogues between the works themselves, and the space evolved as a dynamic context through which to explore the creative catalyst model. Gallery interpretation was designed to be more propositional, engaging the audience through questions designed to relate their interactions with the works to their own observations or personal experience. As *Ideas Depot* develops, children involved in the co-curation process write labels for the works that are integrated with the gallery labels rather than distinguished as another voice.

This chapter has proposed a framework for co-curation through which to generate new knowledge together. Supporting this way of working in a more impactful and sustainable way repositions both expert and visitor and reframes both curating and engagement as collaborative enquiry. The implications of adopting new epistemological positions, I would argue, offer more genuine potential to co-create and "learn-with." Rather than presenting research with associated learning activities, the exhibition space itself becomes a learning and research context within which new perspectives, experiences and ideas inform the generation of new knowledge for the visitor, curator and institution.

References

Adams, J., & Owens, A. (2015). *Creativity and democracy in education: Practices and politics of learning through the arts*. Routledge.

Atkinson, D. (2008). Pedagogy against the state. *International Journal of Art & Design Education, 27*(3), 226–240.

Atkinson, D. (2012). Contemporary art and art in education: The new, emancipation and truth. *International Journal of Art & Design Education, 31*(1), 5–18.

Barad, K. (2007). *Meeting the universe halfway: Quantum physics and the entanglement of matter and meaning*. Duke University Press.

Bennett, T. (2013). *The birth of the museum: History, theory, politics*. Routledge.

Bernstein, B. (1999). Vertical and horizontal discourse: An essay. *British Journal of Sociology of Education, 20*(2), 157–173.

Bishop, C. (2012). *Artificial hells: Participatory art and the politics of spectatorship*. Verso Books.

Campolmi, I. (2016). Institutional engagement and the growing role of ethics in contemporary curatorial practice. *Museum International, 68*(3–4), 68–83. https://doi.org/10.1111/muse.12137

Cutler, A. (2010, Spring). What is to be done, Sandra? Learning in cultural institutions of the 21st century. *Tate Papers*. https://www.tate.org.uk/research/tate-papers/13/what-is-to-be-done-sandra-learning-in-cultural-institutions-of-the-twenty-first-century

Dall, A., Hyland, S., Leung, M., Riding, D., Straine, S., & Swan, M. (2016). We have your art gallery: Negotiations in co-creation. *Engage*, 37. https://engage.org/journals/engage-37/

Dewdney, A. (2008). Making audiences visible. *Tate [E]ncounters*, 2, 1–23.

Fortnum, R. (2013). Creative accounting: Not knowing in talking and making. In E. Fisher & R. Fortnum (Eds.), *On not knowing: How artists think* (pp. 70–88). Black Dog Publishing.

Haraway, D. (1987). A manifesto for cyborgs: Science, technology and socialist feminism. *Australian Feminist Studies*, 2(4), 1–42.

Jones, R. (2013). On the value of not knowing: Wonder, beginning again and letting be. In E. Fisher & R. Fortnum (Eds.), *On not knowing: How artists think* (pp. 16–32). Black Dog Publishing.

Kester, G. H. (2004). *Conversation pieces: Community and communication in modern art*. University of California Press.

Lahav, S. (2000). A special place, a learning space: Museums in the twenty-first century. *Art Book*, 7(4), 20–24.

Lord, B. (2006). Foucault's museum: Difference, representation, and genealogy. *Museum and Society*, 4(1), 1–14.

Obrist, H.-U., & Bovier, L. (2008). *A brief history of curating* (vol. 3). Jrp Ringier Kunstverlag Ag.

O'Neill, P. (2007). *Curating subjects*. Open Editions.

O'Neill, P. (2012). Curatorial constellation and the paracuratorial paradox. *The Exhibitionist*, 6, 55–60.

O'Neill, P., & Wilson, M. (2010). *Curating and the educational turn*. Open Editions and de Appel.

Pringle, E., & DeWitt, J. (2014, Autumn). Perceptions, processes and practices around learning in an art gallery. *Tate Papers*.

Riding, D., Grimshaw, N., Talbot-Landers, C., & O'Keeffe, H. (2019). Developing place-based pedagogies to challenge institutional authority. *International Journal for Art and Design Education*, 38(4), 927–942.

Riding, D., Talbot Landers, C., Grimshaw, N., & O'Keefe, H. (2019). Developing a not knowing pedagogy in the public art museum. *The International Journal of the Inclusive Museum*, 12(4), 13–22.

Rogoff, I. (2008). Turning. *E-flux Journal*, 00, 1–10.

Sayers, E. (2011). Investigating the impact of contrasting paradigms of knowledge on the emancipatory aims of gallery programmes for young people. *International Journal of Art & Design Education*, 30(3), 409–422.

Sheikh, S. (2006). Spaces for thinking. *Texte zur Kunst*, 62, 110–121.

Smith, T. E. (2012). *Thinking contemporary curating*. Independent Curators International.

Tallant, S. (2009). Experiments in integrated programming. *Tate Papers*, 11. https://www.tate.org.uk/research/tate-papers/11

Chapter 15

Children's Voices: Making Children's Perspectives Visible in Gallery Spaces

Lilly Blue and Sue Girak

The Botanical: Beauty and Peril makes me think of those unnecessary gardens

where we have the kind of lonely feelings that are beautiful.

(Elliott – 8 years old, 27 March 2019)

This chapter details a collaboration between the Art Gallery of Western Australia (AGWA) and City Beach Primary School (CBPS) through the pilot project *Children's Voices*. Recognizing children's contributions and "knowing" as valuable, artist/educators Lilly Blue and Sue Girak propose an interruption of conventional engagement approaches that tend to distinguish programming as exclusively "for" children, often diluting concepts and underestimating the capacity of young people to impact contemporary culture or engage with complex ideas. The project examines how the integration of artists' processes and classroom-based studio practices creates opportunities for higher-order thinking, aesthetic learning and multi-generational experience.

Children's Voices amplifies and makes visible their perspectives through the creation of labels exhibited as part of *The Botanical: Beauty and Peril* at AGWA from 6 July to 4 November 2019. The exhibition, co-curated by Melissa Harpley (AGWA) and Laetitia Wilson (Janet Holmes á Court Collection), contains over 200 works of art drawn from both collections that focus on Aboriginal and Torres Strait Islander, colonial and contemporary works from the past 200 years. This major exhibition explored the abundant and often romanticized beauty of the botanical world in contrast to the perilous threat of climate crisis.

The interpretive labels were created in response to twelve works of art in *The Botanical: Beauty and Peril*, amplifying children's perspectives as valued and making them visible to public audiences. The children were offered the opportunity to share their insights, questions and concerns in response to twelve reproductions of artworks to be exhibited, challenging the idea that a gallery space is exclusively the domain of curators. In this way, the children's labels serve to disrupt the singular curatorial voice and enable an expanded viewing of the work by all audiences. Drawing on methodologies used by the AGWA Learning Team and CBPS's higher-order thinking-through-art (HOT Art) programme, the development of the label content emerged from creative processes developed by Lilly Blue, head of Learning and Creativity Research at the gallery, and continued at school by Sue Girak, visual arts specialist.

"The 'difficulty with overpackaging the child as distinct and separate from adults [...] is an undercurrent of children being defined as a group of learners'" (Birch, 2018, p. 516). When we first met, we identified shared pedagogies that extend beyond didactic learning and could see the potential of testing new ways of working together. We expanded the impact of studio-based creative practice and arts learning pedagogies into the public domain by addressing the absence of children's voices in gallery spaces (Reid et al., 2016). Blue draws on her practice of locating studio environments within conventional learning settings, allowing for open-ended experimentation and non-linear material and iterative processes. Girak considers the art room as a laboratory to generate opportunities for non-hierarchical arts-led collaborations.

As arts practitioners, we explore the implications of aesthetic learning where opportunities are designed to "nurture appreciative, reflective, cultural and participatory engagement with the arts" (Greene, 2001, p. 6), engage critical awareness through self-reflective and explorative questions that arise through encounters with artworks (Dewey, 1934/1980) and embrace multi-sensory engagement in creative studio practice. As practitioners, we propose the notion of the child as "experiencer" (Birch, 2018), challenging the limitations of seeing the child solely as a "learner" with little to offer their peers, gallery staff or the public. In this way, the pilot was intended to test curator/educator/public responses to children's views and challenge singular narratives with multiple child voices. Disrupting the transactional model of predetermined single-visit school excursions led by AGWA Gallery guides and artists/educators, we instead aim to develop deeper engagement with a sequence of encounters and open-ended experiences harnessing children's tacit knowledge and, in doing so, support Greene's (1993) position: that the silenced should be heard to offer diverse perspectives.

The partnership: AGWA and CBPS

Children's Voices proposes new models of collaboration and sites of learning/experience, or what Banks et al. (2007) refer to as "life-long, life-wide, life-deep" learning (p. 12), expanding opportunities for children to have meaningful and impactful experiences outside their schools. AGWA is built on the lands of traditional owners, the Whadyuk Noongar people, and what was known as the Gooloogoolup swamp waterways, which once ran beneath the foundations of the architectural Brutalist building. The gallery was founded, and acquired its first work of art, in 1895 and now houses a collection of more than 18,000 works. As well as caring for the State Art Collection, AGWA develops multi-generational programming and projects together with artists, educators and communities. In 2020, AGWA released a five-year strategic plan with a commitment to become a laboratory for arts learning, academic inquiry, experimentation and creative research in partnership with the education sector, academic institutions, Aboriginal cultural authorities and multi-generational audiences.

This commitment grew alongside our recognition of the benefit and impact of the *Children's Voices* project. Each year, AGWA welcomes thousands of children from across Western Australia to participate in excursion-based guided tours, studio workshops and multi-generational participatory experiences. The AGWA Learning Team is responsible for education, children and families and for multi-generational programming, aligning curriculum links as well as drawing from multi-sensory and aesthetic pedagogies. Working with methodologies that are unfixed and open-ended allows for practice-led engagement beyond curriculum-aligned outcomes. This approach makes room for challenging questions about the wider role and impact of the arts in society – how gallery spaces can become accessible hubs of dynamic activity as well as places where diverse multi-generational views are visible and respected.

CBPS is a government primary school located in the Perth metropolitan area. The school's years 1–6 visual arts programme is based on the Western Australian Curriculum. It is a standalone subject run by the visual arts specialist teacher; children come to the art room for an hour a week. In addition to the regular art programme, the school introduced the HOT Art programme in 2019: a bespoke arts-led programme developed at CBPS and designed to enrich the curriculum through creativity. The overarching model used to frame HOT Art projects is based on the 4Cs of twenty-first-century learning – creativity, critical reflection, communication and collaboration – to help children develop competencies to navigate the complexities of this unpredictable century (Jefferson & Anderson, 2017). Within that framework, students are introduced to creative thinking by applying the five "Creative Habits of the Mind" to develop children's imagination and technical skills and their capacity for inquiry, collaboration and persistence (Lucas & Spencer, 2017) to engage with the curriculum beyond content learning. From CBPS's perspective, the AGWA and HOT Art collaboration positions young children as competent and discerning art viewers, making their voices heard in public spaces beyond the classroom.

The project: *Children's Voices*

Children's Voices saw the creation of twelve interpretative labels expressing children's views and exhibited them as part of *The Botanical: Beauty and Peril* at AGWA. The project sits within the development of new creative arts pedagogies at AGWA, focusing on learning strategies that extend beyond the curriculum and the potentially uneasy shift from the scaffolded experience of the child as a "learner" towards open-ended, non-linear opportunities for the child as an "embodied experiencer" (Birch, 2018). We make this shift alongside a commitment to value children's tacit knowledge and trust that their existing understandings and perspectives have value. We chose to further AGWA's multi-generational approach, inviting educators and parents to participate in the studio alongside children. Drawing on experimental and open-ended processes allows a personal approach to emerge for children, educators and parents, rather than working towards defined learning outcomes or a preconceived product. Aligned with an ongoing commitment to challenge single narratives with diverse multi-generational views, the project sits within a wider exploration of co-creating knowledge through collaborative and participatory processes where hierarchies are disrupted by the visibility and "significance of a child's contribution to contemporary culture" (Blue & Pollitt, 2021, para. 1).

a single view of any given artwork and emphasize an environment that has often not considered the children's experiences, let alone made visible their perspectives. In *Children's Voices*, all the children's responses to each artwork reproduction (collected over the term via written, verbal and recorded feedback) were collated into a Word document and edited by Blue without altering the children's sentence structure or meaning. She worked with a poetic process of distillation drawn from her studio practice to edit the children's responses into designed labels, which were then exhibited next to the original works alongside the conventional curatorial labels. To illustrate crossovers in perspectives and decentre a single child's voice, the decision was made to edit multiple child voices into a single statement. We are planning to develop the methodology further so that in future projects, children can participate in the editing process more collaboratively. The final labels saw traditional hierarchies disrupted by the presence and contribution of child voices in the exhibition space, impacting artists and viewers by offering unfamiliar and unexpected perspectives.

Label 2 in response to *Bushfire*, by Conor O'Brian

*Even though this artwork is about fire
which is very bright, there is so much darkness.
Something can be bright and dark at the
same time. It makes me feel like the world is
going to break.
It is missing houses, water, and the stars.*

Label 3 in response to [...] And meanwhile back on earth the blooms *continue to flourish*, by Brian Robinson

*The artist is reminding us that you can
make anything out of shapes, not just things
that look exactly like real life. The flowers could
be attacking the person, or maybe the
person is taking care of them.
There is no vase because flowers can be
everywhere and not just stuck in one place,
and then the rain can water them.*

Label 4 in response to *John*, by Siné Macpherson

*This artwork is beautiful, pretty and also sad
because it could have been a road accident.*

*It reminds me of my Uncle who was the first one
to ever die from a bull shark in the Swan river.
It is missing bright colours because the
artist wants you to feel sad, but also
remember that life is precious.*

Visiting *The Botanical Beauty and Peril*

When *The Botanical Beauty and Peril* was showing, Girak organized an excursion for the years 4 and 5 children who had worked on the labels at school. They participated in a one-hour workshop with Blue, a 45-minute guided tour of the permanent collection and unstructured time to view *The Botanical: Beauty and Peril* exhibition. Having free time in the gallery space was a deliberate decision to give the children the autonomy to engage with the works that resonated with them rather than spending time on a teacher-directed tour returning to the works examined months before. Many of the children recognized the artworks they studied in class. Some made connections between what they discussed in class and the *Children's Voices* labels, which gave them a sense of pride. What seemed to surprise the children more was the size of the original artworks that hung vertically on walls, compared to the A4 reproductions they worked with on the classroom floor. AGWA is working to make it possible for children to gain access to collection stores to see the original works before they are hung in the exhibition, with the understanding that a site-based opportunity to engage with original works of art will be different than responding to reproductions in a classroom setting. The artworks that seemed to captivate the children were previously unseen audiovisual works. The children spent most of their time wearing headphones, listening to artists' stories or watching the interplay of light and sound in installations. One artwork that particularly captured their attention was *Panoramic View of Albany (Kinjarling), The Place of Rain* by Sohan Ariel Hayes. This digital animation reimagines Robert Dale's coloured etching *Panoramic View of King George Sound* (1834). The children were so mesmerized as they watched the artist bring Dale's simple scene to life through movement and sound that it was a struggle to get them to leave the space to return to school. AGWA is looking to develop pedagogies and project structures that allow longer and more frequent on-site engagement with original works.

Curator Anecdote: Taking children's perspectives into consideration

Traditional art museum labels are too often didactic, telling visitors what to think, but these labels spoke of things that connected the hermetic world of the art museum to the real world which the children (and we) inhabit.

(Melissa Harpley)

Curator Melissa Harpley addressed the ten CBPS students during their second workshop at AGWA: explaining the concepts in *The Botanical: Beauty and Peril* exhibition, the background of particular works of art and her curatorial thinking. While some of the concepts were pitched at quite a high level, the seriousness of the encounter created the space for insightful and passionate responses from the young children, confident and enthusiastic about sharing their views on the impact of climate change, the role of art and the importance of the natural world.

In reflecting with Harpley after the session, she identified three unexpected learnings. First, it became clear that her choices of works for display – in all instances, not just this one – did not consider a younger audience. Second, her design choices for exhibitions did not really consider children, apart from once in what she described as a "perhaps somewhat tokenistic display of small objects at a low [kid-friendly] height" (M. Harpley, personal communication, 4 April 2019). Last, she recognized the wider implications of the few times she had worked on exhibitions that included children's labels: Adults had always written them. Harpley felt that with *Children's Voices* the exhibition was humanized and made more personal, allowing for a more emotional response.

Conclusion

Through *Children's Voices*, as artist/educators we propose that art galleries and schools can develop meaningful partnerships beyond transactional single excursion visits. This collaboration between AGWA and CBPS saw participatory engagements happening both at the gallery and at the school, interrupting a traditional didactic model and allowing for multi-dimensional learning experiences. The pilot project saw us develop a process of integrating aesthetic learning, child-led discourse and early year's imagination into wider gallery objectives. Through the installation of interpretive labels informed by children's responses, the singular curatorial voice was interrupted, and multiple child perspectives were made visible to public audiences. Valuing children's tacit knowledge and making their perspectives visible to wide public audiences had a positive impact on audiences, curatorial practice and gallery functioning. As curator, Harpley found that she had been unthinkingly conditioned to pitch her exhibitions to an adult audience and through the experience, recognized the value of a multigenerational approach.

References

Autry, L. T. S., & Mirawski, M. (2017). *Museums are not neutral*. https://www.museumsarenotneutral.com

Banks, J. A., Au, K. H., Ball, A. F., Bell, P., Gordon, E. W., Gutiérrez, K. D., Health, S. B., Lee, C. D., Lee, Y., Mahiri, J., Nasir, N. S., Valdés, G., & Zhou, M. (2007). *Learning in and out of school in diverse environments: Life-long, life-wide, life-deep*. LIFE Center.

Birch, J. (2018). Museum spaces and experiences for children – Ambiguity and uncertainty in defining space, the child and experience. *Children's Geographies, 16*(5), 516–528. https://doi.org/10.1080/14733285.2018.1447088

Blue, L., & Pollit, J. (2021). Child artist response project. *Big Kids Magazine.* http://bigkidsmagazine.com/about/child-artist-response-project

Dewey, J. (1980). *Art as experience.* Perigee. (Original work published 1934)

Greene, M. (1993). The passions of pluralism: Multiculturalism and the expanding community. *Educational Researcher, 22*(1), 13–18. https://doi.org/10.2307/7/1177301

Greene, M. (2001). *Variations on a blue guitar: The Lincoln Center Institute Lectures on aesthetic education.* Teachers College Press.

Jefferson, M., & Anderson, M. (2017). *Transforming schools: Creativity, critical reflection, communication and collaboration.* Bloomsbury.

Lucas, B., & Spencer, E. (2017). *Teaching creative thinking: Developing learners who generate ideas and can think critically.* Crown House.

Proctor, A. (2021). *The whole picture: The colonial story of the art in our museums and why we need to talk about it.* Cassell.

Reid, N. S., Cinequemani, S., & Farrar, C. (2016). "Kids know about art": Amplifying underrepresented voices in art museums through mentorship. *Visual Inquiry: Learning and Teaching Art, 5*(3), 379–392.

Simon, N. (2010). About. *The participatory museum.* http://www.participatorymuseum.org/

Chapter 16

The Art of Learning Art

A Visual Essay

Paloma Palau-Pellicer, Maria Avariento-Adsuara and Paola Ruiz-Moltó

This visual essay describes the ways in which a set of pedagogical actions and the artistic results of 1200 students created a body of work that operates as an institutionalized art collection. Our project is based on the artist and drawing teacher, Ferran Morell, born in Valencia, Spain, who in 1977 promoted an artistic teaching process of direct contact with artists and their artworks. In his methodology, he encourages artistic learning as a model of collective creation that encourages collaborative productions. This includes focusing on visual dialogues with the artworks and direct contact with contemporary artists like Fernando Zóbel, Antonio Saura, Manuel Mompó and Manolo Millares, among others. Over the years, the quality of pedagogical artworks from Morell's students has been recognized institutionally as a whole, resulting in a special collection currently held by the Enric Soler i Godes Foundation of the Jaume I University of Castellón. Inspired by this process, we engaged with students to apply this methodology (Figure 16.1).

The artistic structure can be immediately felt and, in this sense, it is aesthetic. Even more important is that this quality is not only a significant motive to undertake intellectual inquiry and to do it honestly, but that no intellectual activity is an integral event (an experience) unless this quality is present (Figure 16.2). Without such artistic honesty, thinking is not

Figure 16.1: Photo-essay: *Visual Abstract: Drawings 01*, 2021. Two photos by the authors: left, a fragment of a visual quotation (Equipo Crónica, 1973) with a child drawing; right, a child's composition, 2020.

Figure 16.2: Photo-essay: *Drawings 02*, 2021. Two photos by the authors: top, a fragment of a visual quotation (Equipo Crónica, 1969); bottom, children drawing, 2020.

conclusive and in turn, not pedagogic. In short, the aesthetic cannot be sharply separated from the intellectual experience, since it must bear an aesthetic mark to be complete (Dewey, 2008).

Morell's teaching proposals offer a way of proceeding in a very intuitive way, in part because Morell was not a specialist in art education. This approach is linked to current methodological models that redefine the relationship between artistic images and art students, such as teaching the visual arts expressed through contemporary critical museology projects that encourage visitors to participate through visual creation (see Marín-Viadel & Roldán, 2013–2020). Such artwork is first and foremost a visual artefact (Figure 16.3). Every work of art is an occasion for learning a visual concept, especially learning what the artist prioritizes in a particular work (Marín-Viadel et al., 2020).

Figure 16.3: Photo-essay: *Drawings 03*, 2021. Eight photos by the authors. Top, four fragments of a visual quotation (Renau, 1952, 1956, 1957a, 1957b); bottom, four fragments of children's drawings, 2020.

As a collection, the works produced have visual coherence and manifest the learning method that inspired them, and the collection can be used again as didactic resources for new generations. Following Roldán (2015), if it is possible to create artistic images useful for teaching art, then the most extraordinary visual results obtained by a group of students after a complete teaching-learning process can be considered valuable enough to constitute an artistic collection, and consequently, be recognized as an artistic legacy for the community.

Through our study, we investigate how an artistic learning product became part of an institutional collection (Figure 16.4). In this way, we create a symmetrical process in which we use our exhibition with the works of "Equipo Hoz" for artistic teaching.

First, we built on how the teaching-learning process is a didactic resource (Figure 16.5). We embrace the expansion of the idea of the museum as a generator of knowledge, as a social laboratory that allows students to investigate through artistic and aesthetic experiences. Creating a collection in this way means creating another form of inquiry with works developed from artistic practice, which generate and allow for continuity and further study. In each step of the process, we learn, evolve and modify parts of the suggestions made, much

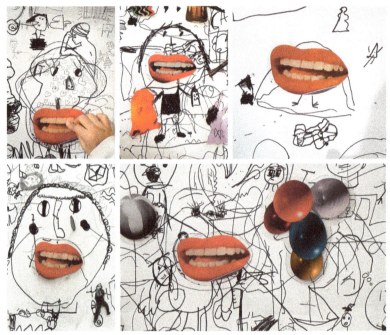

Figure 16.4: *Series: Mouths 01*, 2021. Five photos by the authors.

Figure 16.5: Photo-essay: *Stampings 01*, 2021. Four photos by the authors.

Figure 16.6: The collection of institutional art 01. Photo by the authors, 2021.

as Wojnar (1963) states, "To make people know, understand and experience all kinds of art and, if possible, to make them practice it" (p. 231).

In our historical, educational and heritage inquiry, we recognize these extraordinary artistic exercises as images of artistic value and interest that can be used as new visual references in new processes of teaching the arts, in ways yet to be imagined. The result of our inquiry was exhibited in the Cultural Center Menador at Jaume I of Castellon University (Figure 16.6).

References

Crónica, E. (1969). *The intruder* [Painting]. Valencia Provincial Council, Spain.
Crónica, E. (1973). *The pamphlet* [Painting]. Valencian Institute of Modern Art (IVAM).
Dewey, J. (2008). *Art as experience*. Paidós.
Marín-Viadel, R., & Roldán, J. (2013–2020). *Art for learning art project*. www.arteparaaprender.org
Marín-Viadel, R., Roldán, J., & Caeiro Rodríguez, M. (Eds.). (2020). *Learning to teach visual arts: An a/r/tographic approach*. Editorial Tirant Lo Blanch.
Renau, J. (1952). *The president speaks about peace* [Photomontage]. Valencian Institute of Modern Art (IVAM).
Renau, J. (1956). *A gift for hungry people* [Photomontage]. The American Way of Life Series, 43. Valencian Institute of Modern Art (IVAM).
Renau, J. (1957a). *Oh this wonderful war...! II* [Photomontage]. The American Way of Life Series, 34. Valencian Institute of Modern Art (IVAM).

Renau, J. (1957b). *The fascinating king of oil* [Photomontage]. Valencian Institute of Modern Art (IVAM).

Roldán, J. (2015). Visual arts-based teaching-learning methods. In S. Schonmann (Ed.), *International yearbook for research in arts education: The wisdom of the many. Key issues in arts education* (pp. 191–195). Waxmann.

Wojnar, I. (1963). *Aesthetics and pedagogy*. México: Fund of Economic Culture.

Chapter 17

Out of the Museum Into the Art

Lise Sattrup and Lars Emmerik Damgaard Knudsen

When teaching art, swapping the museum for a setting that allows experimentation enables art educators to practise an activist art museum pedagogy, where students learn by art through their engagement in the artistic process and its principles and places. This case study (Flyvbjerg, 2006) is based on participatory observations (Warming, 2011) of a ninth-grade class at KØS – Museum of Art in Public Spaces in Denmark (2021). The educators moved their lessons on a Gordon Matta-Clark exhibition out of the museum and into a public space – similar to the places/urban spaces Matta-Clark explored in his art. Through art-based research (Leavy, 2009), we examine how this approach supports an activist art museum pedagogy that helps students to understand art's critical potential and the relevance of such an approach for museum pedagogy at a more general level.

We are particularly interested in analysing the roles of the students, who were positioned as performing artists and as active participants instructed to follow and interpret Matta-Clark's artistic practice and principles in a setting like those in which he worked. From the perspective of "art pedagogical events" (Illeris, 2008), we explore the following questions: What happens when an art museum moves a lesson from the museum itself to a relevant place and instructs the students to use the artist's strategies? How does that affect the positioning of the students? How can it inspire an activist art museum pedagogy?

Activist art pedagogy today

Research on activist art pedagogy is currently flourishing, with the literature drawing attention to the potential to promote social justice and the possible impacts on participants and society in general. As an example of this approach, Sandlin and Milam (2008) study the phenomenon of culture jamming, finding that activist art pedagogy can connect learners with each other. Beyerbach and Davis (2011) find activist art pedagogy offers a feasible way of connecting both local and global issues to students' everyday lives. Dewhurst (2014) describes what happens when young people create activist art and how they can impact society, as well as how teachers can support their creative processes.

We apply an activist art museum pedagogy as articulated by Illeris (2017), who argues that education in art museums is dominated by cognitive approaches to learning and lacks an awareness of how art can be a medium for social critique and change. Indeed, many contemporary artists like Ai Weiwei and Jenny Holzer incorporate activism in their work by distorting images of conformity and drawing the public's attention to the shadowy, unspoken and unpolished parts of society and everyday life. Illeris suggests that a performative art pedagogy is more in line with these activist practices. To this end, she perceives museum education as an art pedagogical event consisting of different and changeable positions: that of audience, context, theme, object and performer. Illeris (2008) uses this notion of "positions" to challenge the fixed roles in museum education wherein students learn about art, pieces of art are reduced to something we look at and talk about (object position) and students are reduced to someone educators talk at (audience position). Illeris suggests that art museum educators can experiment with different positions that enable new ways of engaging with and understanding art. Aligned with performance theory, art is understood not just as a representation but also as a presentation, a doing (Jalving, 2017).

In this light, social criticism and change are not something students should learn about but something practised or inhabited as a change from within. Rogoff (2006) describes this embodied criticality:

> It reflects the search for a practice that goes beyond conjunctives such as those that bring together "art and politics," or "theory and practice," or "analysis and action." In such a practice, we aspire to experience the relations between the two as a form of embodiment, which cannot be separated into their independent components.
>
> (p. 1)

Similarly, we apply a notion of activist art pedagogy that aims to go beyond the conjunctives of art and activism, theory and practice, and analysis and action.

Outside the museum: The lesson

The lesson on Matta-Clark (KØS, 2021) was set in a large post-industrial area in Copenhagen called Refshaleøen. By using this setting for the lesson, the museum chose to focus on Matta-Clark's artistic practices and strategies rather than his works or biography. When the students arrived at the former industrial site, the educators gave a short introduction to the location and to central notions in Matta-Clark's strategies: gaps, voids, human-space and sky-space. All were explained in a handout, but without providing in-depth explanations or placing them in a historical context. On the contrary, the educators focused on letting the students explore the surroundings using only the camera lens on their phones and with their independent interpretations of the notions. These educational choices reflect central elements of the subject matter: Matta-Clark's interest in *terrain vague* (outlined later in this chapter), his preference for the camera as his artistic tool and, not least, his approach to art as activism, mirrored by the educators' explorative and performative approach to teaching art.

Gordon Matta-Clark

Matta-Clark explored what public spaces could be like and the differences art, architecture and activism can make. His art involved the performance of so-called building cuts – making holes in, rearranging, rematerializing and photographing abandoned buildings. These performances inspired his successors to understand art as intervention, co-creation and activism. He developed the notion of *anarchitecture* – a conflation of the words "anarchy" and "architecture" – and used it to explore possible uses for what was otherwise considered derelict and unusable plots of land in New York, purchasing them and documenting his alterations to the buildings through photographs and maps (Kastner et al., 2005). According to Solà-Morales Rubió (1995), Matta-Clark's interest in abandoned industrial areas is an expression of *terrain vague* aesthetics.

Terrain vague

The French term *terrain vague* has various meanings, such as wasteland: the intermediate stage between rural and urban or between industrial and residential areas. It is related to other terms like *herotopia*, which denotes a delimited but disruptive place contained within a larger space, like a cemetery in the city. As an aesthetic expression and as a notion, terrain vague has been used in films since the 1960s (Ursprung, 2016), but it was not until 1995, when the Spanish architect Rubió published the article *Terrain Vague*, that it became more widely known. Central to both Rubió's concept of terrain vague and Matta-Clark's anarchitecture is the importance of photography as a common way of describing and narrating the city because it triggers the spectator's imagination about what is outside the frame. In this way, says Solà-Morales Rubió (1995), we are actually able to see the building or the city through a photograph.

Studying an art pedagogical event

According to Flyvbjerg (2006), unusual cases (like the one presented here) reveal a great deal of information about a particular situation; as a case study, it enables an analysis of deeper understandings. Our fieldwork was designed as an anthropological, participatory observation study (Warming, 2011) with the aim of following the students, to mime what the students did and to bodily experience participation in the lesson ourselves (without claiming we had the same experiences as the students). After the lesson, the museum educator, Sofie Andreassen, assisted us in collecting the students' photographs and reflections – including fieldwork observations – during a workshop held at their school, where the students made collages using the photographs they had taken during the lesson at Rafshaleøen.

Multimodel poetization

We approached the project through an arts-based research framework (Leavy, 2009) to support a sensibility towards participants' experiences as well as situations we experienced ourselves. According to Leavy (2009), arts-based research is a valid and reliable approach that translates into authenticity and truthfulness, supported in this study by participatory observations.

We have produced four multimodal poetizations comprising photo collages and short dramatic scenes to present the themes found in the data material. By producing visual arts as a research strategy, we are able to grasp the subtleties of different situations, such as bodily experiences, when practising Matta-Clark's principles (Holm et al., 2018). The dramatic scenes are performances (Leavy, 2009) that voice students' participation in the lesson, their experiences in the post-industrial area and their camerawork. Together, the collages and scenes constitute a *poetization* of each theme in a multimodal way. A poem, according to Fairchild (2003), is "a verbal construction employing an array of rhetorical and prosodic devices of embodiment in order to achieve an ontological state, a mode of being, radically different from that of other forms of discourse" (p. 1). Similarly, being poetic and producing the poetizations give voice to the embodiment of an ontological state that the students enact. This is a different discourse from that which is commonly found in more conventional research papers, but the poetizations' multimedia form, as Finley (2018) remarks, can create a synergy. The poetizations bring text and images together and create a juxtaposition, which provides the spectator with an interpretational frame through the mutual evocation of text and images.

Poetization

The multimodal poetizations of the themes identified in the data are: (1) magic of the place, (2) exploring body, (3) artistic gaze and (4) handling works of art with care. We present each of these overlapping and interacting poetizations before analysing the art pedagogical events.

The magic of the place

We follow two students around the old wharf. As we turn a corner, an enormous building appears in front of us, and its gate is open (Figure 17.1).

> "Wow, it's crazy. Come, have a look," Peter shouts and steps towards the gate. "Isn't it just massive?"
> "Are we allowed to go in there?" Marie looks at Peter.

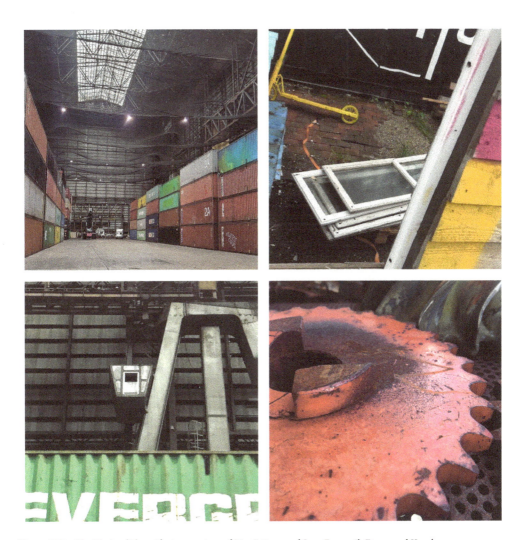

Figure 17.1: *The Magic of Place*. Photos courtesy of Lise Sattrup and Lars Emmerik Damgaard Knudsen.

After hesitating briefly, we all quietly step inside and look at the ceiling far above our heads. The building is packed with large containers, but still feels empty, and we all look at each other, silently wondering if this is off limits. Just below the ceiling, we see parts of a laddered path and sigh as we imagine ourselves climbing up there. Somehow, we are tempted to move further inside, curious about this mysterious place. Suddenly we hear a sound. Something is moving – like a creaky cogwheel starting to turn. We are not alone.

"Do you think that elevator is actually alive," Peter whispers.

Propositions for Museum Education

Marie laughs. "Yes, it probably got here riding on that yellow scooter!" Marie smiles at Peter and the fear of trespassing within a parallel universe seems to vanish as they continue to imagine and elaborate on other magical creatures and events.

"Hey you!" Suddenly a man's voice cuts through the air. "You are not allowed in here!"

An exploring body

Right in the middle of the street, between trucks and decaying buildings, the museum educators summon the students. The students gather around (Figure 17.2).

Figure 17.2: An exploring body. Photos courtesy of Marine Gastineau and Lise Sattrup.

"Now we want you to investigate human-space and sky-space using the cameras in your phones. Just as Matta-Clark would either limit a space or create propositions in a space by using his body, you too are to explore human-space. You can use yourself or each other. Moreover, Matta-Clark also photographed sky-space from different angles, and we want you to use your cameras to find out what a sky-space can be like. Be explorative and take your time."

"Exploring space with our phones. What does that mean?" says Sofie to Oscar.

"Wasn't it something about using different angles to capture the sky?"

"I'm not sure," Sofie responds. "Let's go that way." She points towards rusty containers left outside and starts climbing onto one of them. It is approximately 3 metres high and Oscar stares at Sofie with astonishment.

"Get up here!" Sofie laughs.

"No thank you! I think we were asked to use different angles, so I'm just going to take pictures from down here." Oscar moves to the gap between the containers, and when Sofie steps from one container to the other, he captures her movement.

An artistic gaze

For a second task, the museum educators ask the students to capture gaps and voids. Standing next to a group of students, we hear how they discuss the differences (Figure 17.3).

Emma is wondering what a void is and when it is just a gap. "Does it have to be completely empty to be a void or can it be a void even though it contains a small leaf?"

Anton does not reply.

We all continue to walk, scanning the space for what could be a completely empty void or a gap between things. Occasionally the students stop and take a photograph of both large spaces and tiny cracks in a concrete wall. We do the same and explore voids and gaps in multiple forms. Emma spots a pipe opening in a wall and puts her arm in it.

"What are you doing?" Anton sounds worried.

Emma laughs. "I'm trying to photograph this void."

"What does it look like?"

"I don't know. I can't see in there."

"Well, that doesn't make any sense." Anton looks away.

"It does, it does," Emma replies and lends him her phone. "Here it is. The void!"

"Wow, that's funny. I want to try too."

Emma backs up and turns her head. Other holes in the building suddenly appear. She sticks her arm and camera into them too to discover what is inside.

Propositions for Museum Education

Figure 17.3: *An artistic gaze.* Photos courtesy of Lars Emmerik Damgaard Knudsen and Lise Sattrup.

Handling works of art with care

After the lesson at Refshaleøen, the museum educators conducted a workshop at the school. The students were asked to review their photos and arrange them in collages in a way that produced new spaces.

> "To create new spaces means that you have to deconstruct the photos in front of you and create something that might look strange," says Sofie, the museum educator, scanning the students to see if they understand what she means.

Two of the boys, Peter and Jacob, sit quietly and look at each other with puzzled expressions.

"What now?" asked Jacob. "Do we actually cut up the photos?"

Peter shrugs and looks at the pile of photographs on the table. They do not talk much but start to move the images around, and after a while seem to discover something interesting. A number of the photos contain images of stacks of old chairs in a large stockroom. They begin to cut these up and rearrange the bits and scraps.

"Very interesting," Sofie comments, "but take a look at these empty areas. What can you do about that? Is it a void? Try to work on the empty spaces."

Peter and Jacob are eager to proceed, remaining in good spirits, and after a short while, they have created another collage. They proudly ask the museum educator to review their work. The class teacher seems surprised by their level of enthusiasm, and in a quiet moment tells Sofie how happy she is that the boys have completed an assignment for once. Peter and Jacob carefully put their artwork in a bag.

Analysis

The four poetizations illustrate how the museum educators support performative shifts. When moving the lesson out of the museum and into a setting like that which inspired the artist, the students engage with the place and the artist's strategies.

The Magic of the Place shows how public space is performatively positioned as the object the students have examined (Illeris, 2008). Terrain vague is characterized by an atmosphere of decay, desolation, catastrophe and defeat, but also by a sense of tentative hope, a potential for new narratives and for exploiting the empty spaces, resulting in a certain kind of tension as conveyed by Matta-Clark (Lee, 2001). A similar tension inspired the students' imagination, as shown in the poetization as they entered the large hall. By positioning the place as the object, the museum educators follow Matta-Clark's steps and performatively allow the place to have a voice and inspire our imagination. Through this shift in positions, we believe KØS actively supports the students' ability to sense the magic, wonders and surprises of Refshaløen as terrain vague.

The second poetization, *An Exploring Body*, illustrates how the students embody and perform exploration of the terrain vague. The lesson does not involve dematerializing the buildings in the sense of Matta-Clark's activist anarchitecture, but in contrast to conventional art museum education, the students were encouraged to climb, interact and engage with the materials. In line with Illeris (2008), students are not positioned as an audience but as performers when they search for human-space and sky-space. The poetization shows how Oscar takes photos of not just the old containers but also his classmates' interaction with the abandoned materials, illustrating how the place and new images come into being while the students bodily interact with the terrain vague. As in an installation that rejects a distant viewer position, the conventional demarcation of differences between place and observer dissolves. Similarly, the students become a part of events that are only visible from the inside, and all without any student injuries.

The Artistic Gaze shows how the museum educators instruct the students to investigate the terrain vague using Matta-Clark's notions of gaps, voids, human-space and sky-space. These notions support the students' interpretive processes and practices. During this process, students progress from being confused and disoriented to exploring and taking ownership of the project, such as when Emma uses her camera as an extended part of her body to photograph the unseen void within a pipe. While the museum educator provided only limited explanations of Matta-Clark's notions, Sofie supported the students in performing as artists and independently interpreted the notions as themes of their own. The students are not taught *a right way to see* (Illeris, 2008; Rogoff, 2006) but to understand art as curiosity, excitement and activism, just as Matta-Clark sought to do (Lee, 2001).[1]

The last poetization, *Handling Works of Art with Care*, illustrates how the students' learning process is characterized by frustration and struggle, but also experimentation and ownership. The museum educator positions herself as a teacher by asking the students to re-do their preliminary work – but rather than being seen as an audience, the students are positioned as artists whose work she acknowledges (Illeris, 2008). The educator uses the principles behind Matta-Clark's art to inspire the students to explore ideals of public space and reflect on what difference art, architecture and activism can make. At the end of the workshop, the students surprise their teacher – not only with their enthusiasm and by completing their assignment but also by showing their sense of ownership and care for their own artwork.

Across the four poetizations, the "betweenness" of artist, work of art, spectator, learning content and students translate into Rogoff's (2006) notion of dissolving the barriers between "art and politics," "theory and practice," or "analysis and action" (p. 1). Activist pedagogy demonstrates how museums generally benefit from approaches to art pedagogy at KØS. This approach could inspire future art pedagogy in new ways, just as Matta-Clark performed anarchitecture in post-industrial settings. If the setting changes beyond the museum, it is possible to engage the students in innovative artistic principles.

Discussing the methodology

For this study, we have applied a methodology comprising case study, arts-based research and participatory observation. As with case study in general (Flyvbjerg, 2006), our project risks missing relevant details and variations as the empirical data is limited to a lesson and a workshop in a single class. Furthermore, according to Leavy (2009), using arts-based research may lack academic legitimacy and hence miss being disseminated outside a dedicated network of scholars. Finally, Labaree (2002) argues that participatory observation faces the challenges of false representation, and participants might deny researchers' access. With these reservations, we have examined a lesson, a workshop, materials produced by students and our own photos to provide an in-depth view (Flyvbjerg, 2006) of what takes place when teaching is moved outside. Such an arts-based research approach supports truthfulness and authenticity (Leavy, 2009) by exploring and exhibiting students' artistic processes. By applying a participant observation strategy (Warming, 2011), we have been able to experience some aspects of what the students did and relate these experiences to the pedagogical framework without intervening in the process.

Conclusion

In this chapter, we have conducted a case study of KØS's lesson on Matta-Clark using participatory observation and an arts-based research methodology. We have constructed four poetizations, all of which were analysed using Illeris' (2008, 2017) theory of art pedagogical events. The analysis shows that, by moving the lesson out of the museum and into a relevant setting where students were tasked with applying the artist's principles, the museum educators positioned the students as performing artists. Moreover, the lesson motivated the students to interact with the place and materials at Refshaleøen, interpret Matta-Clark's principles for themselves and enthusiastically create photo collages. This chapter demonstrates that the pedagogical decision to move into a setting like that which inspired the artist, and applying the artist's principles, can inspire new ways of practising and understanding activist art museum pedagogy.

Note

1. The context of the KØS session is a Danish pedagogical culture in which children, since kindergarten and in schools, are encouraged to learn how to be outdoors. To explore new places in nature and in the community is seen as positive, and both parents and teachers accept that children can be at some risk of getting bruised (Williams-Siegfredsen, 2017).

References

Beyerbach, B., & Davis, R. D. (Eds.). (2011). *Activist art in social justice pedagogy: Engaging students in glocal issues through the arts*. Peter Lang.

Dewhurst, M. (2014). *Social justice art: A framework for activist art pedagogy*. Harvard Education Press.

Fairchild, B. H. (2003, June). *The motions of being: On intersections of lyric and narrative (a work in progress)* [Paper presentation]. West Chester University Poetry Conference on Form and Narrative, West Chester, PA.

Finley, S. (2018). Multimethod arts-based research. In P. Leavy (Ed.), *Handbook of arts-based research* (pp. 477–490). The Guilford Press.

Flyvbjerg, B. (2006). Five misunderstandings about case-study research. *Qualitative Inquiry*, *12*(2), 219–245.

Holm, G., Sahlström, F., & Zilliacus, H. (2018). Arts-based visual research. In P. Leavy (Ed.), *Handbook of arts-based research* (pp. 311–335). The Guilford Press.

Illeris, H. (2008). Det pædagogiske forhold som performance. In J. Krejsler, N. Kryger, & J. Milner (Eds.), *Pædagogisk antropologi – et fag i tilblivelse* (pp. 119–139). Danmarks pædagogiske universitetsforlag.

Illeris, H. (2017). Adult education in art galleries: Inhabiting social criticism and change through transformative artistic practices. In D. E. Clover, K. Sanford, L. Bell, & K. Johnson (Eds.), *Adult education, museums and art galleries animating social, cultural and institutional change* (pp. 229–243). Sense.

Jalving, C. (2017). Affect and the participatory event. *ARKEN Bulletin – The Art of Taking Part: Participation at the Museum*, *7*(2017), 115–131. https://www.arken.dk/wp-content/uploads/2017/04/bulletin-2017.pdf

Kastner, J., Najafi, S., & Richard, F. (Eds.). (2005). *Odd lots: Revisiting Gordon Matta-Clark's Fake Estates*. Cabinet Books.

KØS (2021). *Gordon Matta-Clark: Unravel the Unfound*. KØS – Museum of art in public spaces. https://www.koes.dk/en/udstillinger/tidligere-udstillinger/gordon-matta-clark-unravel-the-unfound

Labaree, R. V. (2002). The risk of "going observationalist": Negotiating the hidden dilemmas of being an insider participant observer. *Qualitative Research*, *1*(2), 97–122. https://doi.org/10.1177/1468794102002001641

Leavy, P. (2009). *Method meets art: Arts-based research practice*. The Guilford Press.

Lee, P. M. (2001). *Object to be destroyed: The work of Gordon Matta-Clark*. MIT Press.

Rogoff, I. (2006). *"Smuggling" – An embodied criticality*. European Institute for Progressive Cultural Policies. http://xenopraxis.net/readings/rogoff_smuggling.pdf

Sandlin, J. A., & Milam, J. L. (2008). "Mixing pop (culture) and politics": Cultural resistance, culture jamming, and anticonsumption activism as critical public pedagogy. *Curriculum Inquiry*, *38*(3), 323–350. https://doi.org/10.1111/j.1467-873X.2008.00411.x

Solà-Morales Rubió, I. (1995). Terrain vague. In C. Davidson (Ed.), *Anyplace* (pp. 118–123). MIT Press.

Ursprung, P. (2016). Eric Hattan and the crisis of representation. In A. Spira & L. Eitel (Eds.), *Eric Hattan, Works, 1979–2015* (pp. 57–62). Holzwarth.

Warming, H. (2011). Getting under their skins? Accessing young children's perspectives through ethnographic fieldwork. *Childhood*, *18*(1), 39–53. https://doi.org/10.1177/0907568210364666

Williams-Siegfredsen, J. (2017). *Understanding the Danish forest school approach: Early years education in practice*. Routledge.

Chapter 18

Thinking Ahead in Art Education...

Rolf Laven and Wolfgang Weinlich

Contemporary art education: From hierarchization towards actualization and renegotiation

In this chapter, we aim to reflect on the mission and concepts of current art education and present new guiding ideas for museums and art education concepts in Austria. Art, culture and their mediation are subject to constant change, which continually raises new questions. These questions seek new definitions of terms and concepts about things, created, designed and shaped by humans, which are reflected in culture and thus operate as aesthetic objects in museums. Museums as socially shaped institutions that cultivate art, cultural education and cultural offerings, with their function of collecting and preserving, could be cultivated more as a contact zone, as Nora Sternfeld (2016) suggests: "What if the museum was [...] defined by [...] the transgenerational transmission of knowledge around and with things and material? What if the museum were a 'memory site,' a 'contact zone,' or a 'third space' where history/s are shared?" (p. 200).[1]

In our view, this outlines emergent forms of learning that have an enlightening effect on widening educational perspectives. The museum today is about participation as Marion Ruth Gruber (2006) confirms: "Art and cultural mediation refers to all activities that make the artistic and cultural heritage in the context of the mediating institution understandably accessible to interested persons (recipients) and encourage participation" (p. 23).

For this reason, many art didacticians refer to more recent developments in contemporary art as issues of topicality and relevance (Krautz, 2013). This addresses subtle aspects of mediation, such as those between the past and present in society, and differences across time as it relates to the class structure in Austria (see Mörsch, 2016). By extension, the museum then should not only be defined by collecting, preserving, researching and mediating, but it should be understood as a place of participation, transgenerational transmission and a place that makes it possible to share ideas, along with questioning sedimented conflicts, histories and processes of negotiation, actualization and relocation (Sternfeld, 2016).

Reflections on didactics and its justifications

Analysing the essential reference points of art education, Jochen Krautz (2013) presents an anthropological orientation about the relations of self as co-human beings in a co-world, where past understandings of the subject are to be questioned. Thus, didactics align with art as art mediation, so art education is "the translation of new artistic 'strategies' into didactic settings" (p. 2). In our view, if one asks about the competencies of teaching art, the starting point is heterogeneous.

Hubert Sowa (2011) indicates that as an anthropological dimension of art education, our pictorial capacity is about the ability to represent, to perceive, to imagine and to communicate. In response, we build on Wolfgang Welsch, who enables us to acknowledge difference *differently*. The *ratio essendi* of art includes diversity: that is, "different works or types of works may require quite different modes of perception and criteria" (Welsch, 2017, p. 17). Our position is that in the future, it will be necessary to increase our search for ways to adequately address the diversity of criteria, paradigms, persons, works, perspectives and alternatives that operate as *offerings* for education and perception. It is important to open possibilities for subjective perception to discover the unknown for oneself and to reconcile potential trivializations of art in the process. These different modes of perception, illuminated by Wolfgang Welsch, require diverse and differentiated concepts of mediation going forward.

The qualities of art and pedagogy

According to Kristine Preuß and Fabian Hofmann (2019), aspects such as the sensual, surprise and irritation are important in museum spaces. Art education, they argue, should develop a fundamental understanding of the experience in ways that articulate concepts helpful for learning, such as pragmatism and phenomenology, where the focus is on experience. In this way, pedagogy is more related to the lifeworld. For such mediation, the museum experience is decisive, raising questions about the nature of experience, its availability and controllability, the role of the body and the social processes and power underway in museum spaces (Preuß & Hofmann, 2019).

Furthermore, Jerrold Levinson (2013) defines learning in terms of an aesthetic experience that emphasizes a pleasurable, novel perception. According to this, aesthetic experience is found in "the special": namely, aesthetic attention towards an object. Such an experience is unique and reflects an individual mode of attention and sensory perception, according to Martin Seel (2003). For Levinson (2013), aesthetic experiences can occur with any object. Nevertheless, works of art and artefacts hold distinct possibilities in this context, as they were created mainly for aesthetic experience. It may be argued too that aesthetics has become an everyday phenomenon and is thus no longer a special discipline for experts, suggesting the role of experts in museum education may be shifting towards different pedagogical priorities. For example, for the everyday world to be opened by means of perception, self-discovery must take place. Such an examination leads to a lively social awareness (not unlike fashion, festive design or even educational and media offerings) and by extension, museum visits. In art mediation, the distinction between high and pop culture, between creation and work, can be overcome. This is the idea that Krautz (2015) applies to art education.

As Jochen Krautz (2015) states, art education is at times unsure of its purpose: "Is the task art, and if so, which? Is it media and design? Or images in general? Perhaps also children's drawing? And what about creativity and aesthetic experience?" (p. 3). Asking about the big idea behind art education may also raise problematic questions about social relevance and cultural participation. Concepts such as involvement, active participation and empowerment can also be included in this conversation. The Latin-derived term "participation" is commonly understood as taking part, to be involved; in our view, that can mean a state of being as well as a process of becoming. Participation usually has a strong, positive pedagogic connotation, primarily associated with self-activity, empowerment and/or inclusion. In this way, the active recipient versus the cultural consumer is highlighted in the process (Laven, 2017).

Examples from the field

"KunsTraumSchool": A project description

On its fiftieth anniversary, the BÖKWE/ Berufsverband Österreichischer Kunst-und WerkerzieherInnen (Professional Association of Austrian Art and Crafts Educators), in collaboration with the participant students and their teachers, announced a school exhibition project in Vienna with the title *KunsTraumSchule* (ArtDream/RoomSchool, 2006/08), which was curated and designed by Rolf Laven. The focus was on the creative works of students. The aim was to show a current overview of creative activities across all types of schools through diversified teaching practices. Austrian schools, from elementary/primary education to general and vocational secondary schools, all had the opportunity to participate *in an anti-hierarchical positioning*. During information events leading up to the exhibition, the Viennese teachers were able to inform themselves fully about the project; as a result, this developed into an extensive joint project: 127 schools submitted around 2500 works by 2000 students. Of those submitted, 180 works and projects were selected and presented for exhibition. Two exhibitions took place in the exhibition hall Freiraum, in the Museumsquartier Vienna. In total, these exhibitions were visited by more than 130 school classes, and 3500 visitors were counted over two weeks.

Making visible what young people create

The exhibition of student works aimed to address issues beyond consumerism and the mainstream and to outline present realities and future expectations from the perspective of young people. This was implemented by students in the creative subjects of visual arts education, technical and textile crafts, and design during their academic school year.

Various facets of life were explored in the artworks, including images that surround us every day and related sources of historical knowledge. The theme of one's own identity was reworked to bring interdisciplinary and multidisciplinary perspectives to the fore. Other topics such as communication, social interaction, science and technology, sports and culture were also explored. More important than the choice of topics, however, was an individually motivated approach to subjective expression – be it with the help of experimental or playful methods. Another key theme concerned utopian images that conveyed an idea of possible

Figure 18.1: *KunsTraumSchule* exhibition. View with works of very heterogeneous participants – different school types, age groups, topics and interests. Copyright: Heinz Kovacic.

future realities. These expressions reflect images that children and young people have of the world we share and comment on what their tomorrow might bring.

The resulting exhibition was a selection of student works from all age groups and schools. From a curatorial perspective, the works were intentionally very different from each other. The focus was not on established art but on project-related initiatives and individual presentations of a wealth of projects and works realized in school life. Representational gestures were dispensed with, and the experimental field was brought to the foreground of the exhibition (Figure 18.1).

"SPEED" – An Endless Frieze

This art education project took place in the context of the museum exhibition *Kinetism – Vienna discovers the Avant-Garde*, from 25 May to 1 October 2006, in the Wien Museum Karlsplatz. These art-mediated actions were developed and implemented by Rolf Laven with school children between the ages of 10 and 18. Museum visitors of various ages were invited to participate.

Background and context

The point of reference for this mediation was a Kinetism exhibition curated by Monika Platzer and Ursula Storc (2006), which focused on shapes and colours in a rotating motion and rhythmic dynamics as an expression of a new sensibility for art. Viennese Kinetism served as the inspiration, referencing the first art movement in Austria in the 1920s with radically abstract approaches. It developed in secret, and the great significance of this movement became visible only in retrospect. In fact, it had emerged as a revolutionary pedagogical experiment at the School of Arts and Crafts (Laven, 2006). The charismatic teacher Franz Čižek named the movement as "activism pulsating with modern life" (Platzer, 2006, p. 17). Joy, sadness, anger, envy and longing were translated into dynamic formal play, just as much as coldness and glow (Rochowanski, 1922). What began expressionistically was refined with Cubism and Futurism as Kinetism, with notable artists Giovanna Klien, My Ullmann and Elisabeth Karlinsky.

Fifteen years ago, Vienna (re)discovered the Avant-Garde. With the estate of Franz Čižek, the Wien Museum (Platzer & Storch, 2006) owns the world's most important collection of kinetistic art as well as children's and youth art. Exhibits include practice sheets from Čižek's class and studio photographs. Kinetism originated in the laboratory atmosphere of Čižek's class at the Vienna School of Applied Arts. After more than 80 years, the most important Avant-Garde movement of the Viennese interwar period was finally recognized. In a "Speed Workshop" on the themes of movement-tempo-acceleration, Laven designed an "Endless Frieze" with groups of children and young people in honour of the movement (Figure 18.2). In total, more than 30 workshops, each three hours long, took place within four months in the summer of 2006.

After a dialogically guided tour through the exhibition, the participants were stimulated by a sound and rhythm backdrop. Participants could also bring their own sounds, and visitors mostly shared rock, heavy metal, rap and hip-hop. As intended, dynamic soundscapes were created, and the participants interpreted and creatively implemented their own approach to concepts such as movement, speed and noise. Painting was done on extra-long paper rolls, which were specially installed on an object stand and "endlessly" rotated.

Finally, a frieze with the programmatic title "Speed" was developed as a joint work of all participating groups. In this way, it was possible to comprehend what the Kinetism exhibition proclaimed: "New sensibility, new thinking, new seeing!" (Rochowanski, 1922, p. 8). The development of the frieze was processual: that is, it expanded lifeworld(s) (for more, see https://sammlung.wienmuseum.at/objekt/575945-331-sonderausstellung-des-wien-museums-kinetismus-wien-entdeckt-die-avantgarde-folder/).

Special features of this mediation

Past students and teachers were invited to share memories of their teacher Franz Čižek over coffee and cake after a guided tour of the exhibition. Part of the outreach programme was also a unique class reunion of former Čižek students at the Vienna (Wien) Museum. The

Figure 18.2: *Presentation*. "Endless Frieze" in the Wien Museum Karlsplatz. This is a joint work by a total of 30 participant groups. Copyright: Rolf Laven.

Figure 18.3: Participation: Creative workers celebrate their exhibition opening at the Wien Museum, Karlsplatz. Copyright: Rolf Laven.

conclusion of this art education project was the three-day presentation of works created in the workshops, exhibited in the open space of the museum's atrium (Figure 18.3).

Discussion

We presented a series of conceptual and practical possibilities for renewing the experiential space of the museum as part of mediating the encounter. The orientation towards anthropology presented by Sowa (2011) and Krautz (2013) served as a base to understand how specific ideas of the participants can be (rightly) addressed. In the projects outlined here, the participants can be described as highly heterogeneous. Their ongoing exchange with art developed from their respective capacity for visual, perceptual, imaginative and communicative actions and attitudes (Sowa, 2011).

Furthermore, addressing different modes of perception (Welsch, 2017), telling stories (Sternfeld, 2016) and bringing forward life-world connections by offering experiences of the body were shared as social processes to clarify and explore attitudes and actions. We believe experiencing surprises, irritations or sensuality as suggested by Preuß and Hofmann (2019) – along with Sowa's (2011) intended exploration of each individual's pictorial capacity for perceiving and sharing – offers a basis for experimenting in new ways within the museum space. The exploration of sound worlds involved risk-taking by individuals sharing their own sounds with their group, then sharing in joint creative processes, followed by sharing their experiences with others. They made biographical aspects visible: namely, being a contemporary witness of Kinetism as in the children's art class. This was all part of the experimentation that took place in our projects.

In the dynamics of the art mediation process, collaborative working groups formed alongside individuals, and together they took account of each other and their artmaking. The *offering* to create more, and the subsequent reunion of former students and teachers at the exhibition, brought together broader audiences of different people, languages and generations. The dynamics of Viennese Kinetism could be traced in an interactive, bodily and sensual way at this moment. The holistic, diversely enriching educational claims of our students (in this case) became accessible and comprehensible for the audience. The active participation of young people in questioning social issues, as realized by the creative themes and mediums they employed, resulted in more social awareness through the exhibitions. The fact that the contributions of young people were shown meant a number of social values and beliefs were brought into question. Hierarchies can be questioned in this way, and viewing habits can be expanded: last but not least, young people's views of the images and the world become an active part of our societal conversations. This also has *anti-hierarchical potential* in the Avant-Garde tradition, since images have become the supporting elements of communication and enculturalization processes in our societies.

In turn, the school as an institution and as a museum was also given the opportunity to open to broader audiences. Students as artists experienced extracurricular forms of thinking, and they were encouraged to make their own contributions clear to the outside world. This kind of active reception leaves behind passive consumer culture and instead, as Sternfeld (2016) suggests, generates possibilities for creating spaces for sharing history/ies.

In different ways, the projects "Endless Frieze" and *KunsTraumSchule* tried to break up museum expectations by making the spaces and events accessible to people of all ages. Sensory-bodily mediation concepts were initiated, through which it is possible to encounter a wide variety of works and address specific forms of perception. By creating conditions for participants to express themselves creatively on an extra-long frieze, we arguably set in motion social processes and dialogues. With the emphasis on dialogue and experience, space was created for self-location and self-actualization of one's creative actions in exchange with others. Learning with a sense of experience and condensing lifeworld references, as Preuß and Hofmann (2019) call for, becomes possible. Relocating the self as well as co-writing history/ies becomes conceivable. But curiosity and excitement also emerged. This was especially apparent when meeting older former students as contemporary witnesses and when the young people visited the exhibition of their own works.

The self-experienced *mediation offerings* described here suggest the person who experiences and acts on site forms their narrative in relation to the event, artwork and space. Such an understanding of learning brings dialogue and perception to the heart of museum education in vital ways. The participants, who were very different from each other, actively received *and* participated in works of art. So it is not the culturally significant contents that are adapted; rather, the respective sensual-aesthetic person determines their own access via the mode of perception that they feel. Built on new understandings and enabling co-design and reflection, projects developed into contact zones (see Sternfeld, 2016) and achieved visibility and participation in the process. In our case, such understanding of learning encouraged numerous sensual, surprising or even irritating experiences to emerge (Preuß & Hofmann, 2019).

Conclusion

Aspects of future-oriented teaching

If we follow anthropological justifications of mediation and its didactics, a change of perspective is possible in the future. Art mediation itself carries this out in the form of a change of attitude. The sole purpose of collecting, preserving and researching is transcended with engagement and application. A redefinition of mediation and its didactics is made possible through the offerings of dialogue and experience. Such anthropological conceptions explore the human towards art, not art towards the human (see Sowa, 2011).

The forms of learning presented in these cases, which enable self-determined enlightenment, imply the following:

- Sowa (2011) as well as Krautz (2013) justify an anthropological orientation: The visual capacity, the individual abilities for imagination, perception and communicative

capacity of the respective participating persons are seen as central contents of mediation and its didactics.
- Understanding learning as an aesthetic experience (Levinson, 2013): Various occasions are given to develop pleasurable, novel, questioning perceptions of an object. In this way, a special mode of attention and sensory perception (Seel, 2003) is targeted by the attitude of the facilitator as well as by the actions offered.
- Diversity is important: Different mediation concepts are needed to address different modes of perception because multiple creations, types of works and paradigms require multifaceted approaches (Welsch, 2017).
- Increased life-world reference places experience centrally: Sensual, surprising, joyful or irritating experiences as well as physical-bodily and social experiences should become possible (Preuß & Hofmann, 2019).
- Comprehensibility with which artistic and cultural heritage is made accessible to interested persons stimulates greater participation (Gruber, 2006).
- Sharing history/ies is made possible (Sternfeld, 2016).

We propose that in the future, we strive to deepen questions about the tasks and attitudes of art education and its didactics, leading to greater attention and refinement of perception for both participants and providers of exhibitions. The development of contents becomes clear throughout as an individual perceptual event, which – much as our examples demonstrate – is possible only from a respective starting point of a specific situation. In this way, anthropologically oriented, art-mediating offerings could bring about a realization of the self, with more comprehensive and ever-deepening art participation (Sowa, 2011). The pursuit of such diversity requires crossing museum "borders" with aesthetic perception. This is the comprehensive task of art education and its didactics.

Note

1. The translation of quotations from German into English was done by the authors.

References

Gruber, M. R. (2006). *E-Learning im Museum und Archiv – Vermittlung von Kunst und Kultur im Informationszeitalter.* https://www.academia.edu/817176/E_Learning_im_Museum_und_Archiv_Vermittlug_von_Kunst_und_Kultur_im_Informationszeitalter

Krautz, J. (2013, April). Ich, Wir, Welt: Zur Systematik und Didaktik einer personalen Kunstpädagogik. *Forum Fachdidaktische Forschung, 8.* https://www.uni-hildesheim.de/media/forschung/fff/Schriftenreihe/KRAUTZ_Schriftenreihe_01.pdf

Krautz, J. (2015). Auf dem Weg zu einer Systematik und Didaktik der Kunstpädagogik auf anthropologischer Grundlage. Ein Arbeitsbericht zuhanden der Allgemeinen Pädagogik. *Vierteljahrsschrift für wissenschaftliche Pädagogik, 1*(2015), 87–120.

Laven, R. (2006). *Franz Čižek und die Wiener Jugendkunst*. Schriften der Akademie der bildenden Künste: Vol. 2. Schlebrügge Editor.

Laven, R. (2017). Empowerment im inklusiven ästhetisch-künstlerischen Werkstattunterricht: Aktive Gestaltung statt passiver Teilnahme. In M. Blohm, A. Brenne, & S. Hornäk (Eds.), *Irgendwie anders – Inklusionsaspekte den künstlerischen Fächern und der ästhetischen Bildung* (pp. 113–118). Fabrico.

Levinson, J. (2013). Unterwegs zu einer nichtminimalistischen Konzeption ästhetischer Erfahrung. In S. Deines, J. Liptow, & M. Seel (Eds.), *Kunst und Erfahrung. Beiträge zu einer politischen Kontroverse* (pp. 38–60). Suhrkamp.

Mörsch, C. (2016). *Urteilen Sie selbst: Vom Öffnen und Schließen von Welten*. https://www.kiwit.org/kultur-oeffnet-welten/positionen/position_2944.html

Platzer, M., & Storch, U. (2006). Kinetismus: *Wien entdeckt die Avantgarde* [Wien Museum - 25. Mai bis 1. Oktober 2006]. Hatje Cantz.

Preuß, K., & Hofmann, F. (2019). *Der Erfahrung Raum geben: Vorschläge zur Theoriebildung in der Kunstvermittlung und Museumspädagogik*. https://www.kubi-online.de/artikel/erfahrung-raum-geben-vorschlaege-zur-theoriebildung-kunstvermittlung-museumspaedagogik

Rochowanski, L. W. (1922). *Formwille der Zeit*. Burgverlag.

Seel, M. (2003). *Ästhetik des Erscheinens*. Suhrkamp.

Sowa, H. (2011). *Grundlagen der Kunstpädagogik – anthropologisch und hermeneutisch*. Favorite – Schriften zur Kunstpädagogik. Bd. 5. PH Ludwigsburg.

Sternfeld, N. (2016). *Das Museum deprovinzialisieren*. https://www.academia.edu/30313563/Das_Museum_deprovinzialisieren

Welsch, W. (2017). *Wie Kunst uns die Augen öffnet. BÖKWE Fachblatt des Berufsverbandes österreichischer Kunst- und WerkerzieherInnen*. Vienna.

Chapter 19

Social Functions of Museum Education in Double Peripheries: Between Museology and Sociology

Dominik Porczyński

There are at least three ways in which museums may be linked to knowledge (Jordanova, 1989): (1) by looking at an object, one may learn not only about the thing itself but also about broader context, (2) ways of exhibiting contribute to the construction of meaning and (3) museums offer different kinds of knowledge, yet some objects are not easily classified and maintain connections to different disciplines. This means that knowledge exists not by itself but as a product of social practices.

Interpretation (Alexander & Alexander, 2008) and communication (Weil, 1990) are among the most important museum tasks. Traditionally, interpretation was the sole responsibility of the museum; however, that is a contested notion today as visitors are encouraged to exercise their own views. The number of publications covering the topic supports this directive (e.g. Crooke, 2007; Hein, 1995; Hooper-Greenhill, 2007; Ziębińska-Witek, 2020). The term "museum education" is also very broad, crossing borders between disciplines and evading precise definitions (Gajda, 2019). Another problem is the inconsistent use of terms. Different authors understand museum education as "responsibilities" (Weil, 1990), "aims" (Szeląg et al., 2014), "roles" (Hooper-Greenhill, 1999) or "functions" (Pater, 2016). This is a result of positioning pedagogy at the border of two spheres: practice and science. Empirical research in the field of pedagogy can be applied to museum teaching processes, yet many papers are written by educators with ad hoc practical purposes, without the need of locating pedagogy within a broader conceptual framework. Such a situation is counterproductive from the perspective of museology. Following that, my aim is to (1) provide a theoretical background to study museum education as a social practice located in the broader context of academic discourse and (2) describe functions of museum education in peripheral Poland.

As Hooper-Greenhill (1999) suggests, studying the educational role of the museum needs to be supplemented by sociological and philosophical theory. But their terminology may also be murky. As Merton (1968) argues, the notion of "function" is often equated with terms such as use, purpose, motive, intention, aim and consequence. This makes the discourse confusing. Because of the empirical nature of my research, I use "function" to mean the study of what museums *actually* do in the field of education.

My understanding of function comes from Znaniecki (1965) and is connected to his broader theoretical framework. He encourages empirical research of social action to understand society and its culture. On this basis, Znaniecki developed group and institutional theory. According to this theory, an institution is a formal group in which individuals perform formal (institutionalized) roles, cooperating for the achievement of a common purpose (Znaniecki, 1945). Groups may be researched in the same way as roles.

They have their social circles (audience), rights and functions, which may be investigated by collecting data on group member performances since the group is a creative synthesis of personal roles (Znaniecki, 1954). Thus, the study of the educational role of museums is based on observing the practices of those staff members who are more or less involved in the construction and transfer of symbolic patterns: educators, curators and managers.

The weakness of Znaniecki's theory is the lack of appropriate attention to the material sphere of the environment in which collective practices take place. This can be overcome by introducing elements linked to the sociology of objects (e.g. Gell, 1998; Krajewski, 2013; Latour, 2005). According to this orientation, artefacts are not only products of human action but also agents that somehow shape behaviour. Put another way, it is difficult to understand nineteenth-century peasants without learning about the conditions they lived in, the clothes they wore or the tools they used in their trades. So in the museum context, without accepting the agency of artefacts, any study of educational role would be incomplete.

Double peripheries

Peripheralization derives from inequalities existing on several levels: global, state, regional or local. It concerns various spheres of existence: economic, geographical, social, cultural and so forth. The notion of double peripheries means being a peripheral region of a peripheral state. States can be divided into ones that are more or less powerful, but this notion also relates to regions and communities within particular countries (Broszkiewicz, 2010).

The cultural version of this globalization theory not only maintains the inequalities but also puts the stress on the discursive form of the process. Local actors can introduce global patterns, and at the same time, they can also modify or even reject them (Roudometof, 2016). Museums are strongly connected to this type of globalization (while still being the subject of the economy). The spreading of museums across the world in the nineteenth century is an example of the process (Prösler, 1996), yet those institutions helped to popularize particular symbolic systems, such as nationalism (Anderson, 2006; Bennett, 1995) or scientism (Hudson, 2014). International networks such as the International Council of Museums allow cultural elements to be spread between institutions. In this case, it is difficult to clearly distinguish this core-peripheral mechanism, but the most influential ideas such as new museology (Vergo, 2006) or constructivist approaches to museum education (Hein, 1998) appeared in the West and then spread across the museum world.

Poland is defined as either a semi-peripheral or peripheral country. The region that is under scrutiny – *województwo podkarpackie* (Subcarpathian Region) – is located in southeastern Poland; thus it is the state's periphery geographically (far from the capital and eastern European Union border), economically (one of the poorest regions in Poland and the European Union) and culturally (one of the most conservative regions). Of course, the whole region has also more or less excluded areas; the regional capital, Rzeszów, stands out from the rest of the voivodeship. The region is mostly rural, except for Rzeszów's airport and one completed highway (A4), which is not very well connected with the rest of the country with its poorly developed railroads and the expressway S19 under construction. Its importance relates to its transitional character – on the border with Ukraine – and growing interest as a tourist destination as part of the Carpathian Mountains – Bieszczady.

However, this peripherality does not make museums of the region peripheral. While there are museums resembling a nineteenth-century model, most of them have adopted ideas of new museology. Due to social networking and participation in state-level dialogues as well as in international museums and educational organizations, local staff are open to new patterns in cultural pedagogy. Some of them, as in the Regional Museum in Stalowa Wola, function as local authorities on the education of visitors with special needs. Education is therefore important. A recent study (Porczyński & Vargová, 2020) shows that institutions of the region mix core and local patterns. So while they offer various educational programmes and try to cover all possible audiences, most of the educational practices are conducted by curators (many units do not employ people in educational positions), and they mostly apply a didactic, expository model, although a constructivist one appears more often in the case of an adult audience. The lack of separate educational units and positions is the result of insufficient funding, yet the slightly lower status of educators in comparison to curators reflects a pattern that developed during the communist period (Szeląg, 2012).

With this introduction to museums in Poland, my study is based on two research projects conducted in the Subcarpathian Region in 2015–2016 and 2018. Data, collected in 52 museums in the area, included 170 quantitative surveys and 62 in-depth interviews carried out with employees. In this chapter, I use qualitative data.

Educational practice

Educational functions

The museum cannot perform its educational role without its social circle – people who positively evaluate the museum. I focus on one particular partner of this cooperation, schools. In peripheries, organized school groups make up the largest audience.

The topics of museum educational practices come out of the struggle between what a museum may offer based on its collection and what Ministry of Education experts assume students should learn at every stage of education: curricula. Three educational functions may be distinguished: providing additional knowledge paths, supporting curriculum and substituting for school in certain fields.

Some parts of museum educational programmes are based on collections and do not refer to curricula. They come closest to the idea of supra-formal education, carried out in the institutional context yet outside of schools and providing additional knowledge. At the time of my study, teachers rarely reported interest in *additional knowledge paths*: "There's a firefighting museum for example, yes? […] And why can't there be a lesson in the museum? After all, in any school, no one learns about firefighting" [Curator 1].

The list of possible topics often exceeds the school's needs. These may include areas that curators prioritize but are not always inclusive of the conditions under which teachers work. Museums have their own agendas, and their fields of expertise cover only partially those of schools. Therefore, museums do not need to limit themselves by preparing only such topics that are interesting to schoolteachers.

Museums function as *school support* by touching on knowledge connected to curricula that the school for some reason cannot provide. It may be because of teachers' lack of knowledge on a topic or lack of conviction that museums can broaden those perspectives:

> Such a museum [type] as ours is very important. Why? Simply because curricula in schools […] skip completely this history of our region, of Subcarpathia, and here is […] where historians come in; they learn about many things, they learn from us.
>
> (Manager 2)

Since the museum possesses artefacts directly connected with certain historical events, it arguably provides a better learning opportunity than the school. Some educators, however, express a conviction that in certain ways, museums began to *substitute for schools*:

> The curriculum completely simplified our knowledge about the past, about the culture, and maybe even our ordinary ability to interpret. The school doesn't provide the possibility to interpret. That is the key. And the kids visit [us] after first, second, third, at the beginning of the fourth stage [of education] so nearly before matura exam[1] and suddenly it turns out that this year for matura they have a task to look at a painting and to say what do they see. Wow, but where's the key? […] It didn't **say what they should see** but to **say what do they see**.
>
> (Educator 1)

The interlocutor addresses two issues here. The school convinces students that there is only one valid interpretation of the artwork – an inflexible model of teaching that ignores the findings of constructivist pedagogy. Students are not allowed to draw their own conclusions but follow the key that guides their analysis. The educator also criticizes their lack of general knowledge. Young participants in museum educational programmes are not able to interpret artworks without assistance. Even if they manage to analyse the painting, their reading is regarded as simplified and unimaginative.

Pedagogical functions

Museum pedagogical functions are more about certain social skills, about particular forms of participation in society and/or about demonstrating a certain kind of attachment to the nation, a region or a local community. On a most general level, pedagogical functions concern *proper behaviour and respect for other people*. They may also relate to the phenomenon of a private homeland – the space where we grew up and feel attached to (Ossowski, 1984). This is close to a soft version of local patriotism. Addressing an important event – from a national or international perspective – curators and educators emphasize the contribution of local actors in historical processes. In such cases, a function of museum education is *the development of the sense of regional pride and identity*:

> We [...] act locally, so if there is an exhibition about the Second World War [...] we show citizens of Jasło, citizens of county at Monte Cassino or [...] in the First Division of Polish Army. We don't show [...] General Berling who might be found in every encyclopaedia or other generals – right – we show citizens of Jasło who fought there. We've got Jasło pilots, so if there is a uniform of Battle of Britain' pilot, our Jasło pilots appear who took part in it.
>
> (Curator 3)

The interviewee treats historical events as important elements in the struggle with Nazi Germany and shows how local community contributions can be a source of pride.

Thus, the pedagogical function of the museum has much to do with providing role models. Working with historical material, educators may recall war heroes, scientists, politicians and others. They can speak about certain codes of conduct that they find appropriate. In Poland, conservative museum representatives favour historical events because of their systems of values. In such cases, the pedagogical function relates to *developing patriotic attitudes*:

> We want to speak about culture, about tradition, about past, about patriotism [...] about the love for the homeland, love for culture, about good manners, about appropriateness, about righteousness, about all these traits which today are not trendy, not sexy, and not cool at all.
>
> (Manager 1)

The interlocutor shows the past system of values as superior to the modern one, which he finds lacking in important elements related to tradition and patriotism. Important here is that the manager represents a view strongly connected to the pre-war elite, so this role model is based on a specific symbolic system treated as a universal one. This does not mean such an approach exists in all Subcarpathian museums, even if the region is more conservative than the other parts of Poland. It shows that the discussion of modern civic education in the country involves social actors with different views – conservative and liberal – and museums may likely participate in this discourse.

Bourdieu's and Darbel's (1991) study on museum audiences contained a conclusion concerning the possible involvement of museums and schools in cultural change. For instance, social class can impact access and interest in visiting cultural institutions. It is therefore educational institutions' role to create conditions allowing the younger generation to improve cultural capital. Thus, trips to museums organized by schools are perceived as *preparation for cultural participation*. They allow children and youth to see places they probably would not visit in other circumstances:

> To learn, this young generation needs to interact exactly with a museum. It may be often seen when someone walks into the museum for the first time, they feel something like disconcerted. It seems for me it should be in a high school, at least – I don't know – in the curriculum during three years of high school, there should be a visit to a museum, to a philharmonic or to a theatre.
>
> (Manager 3)

The problem of cultural participation is, however, complex. Without cooperation among institutions, schools and families, young people's cultural preparation is unlikely to improve. My interviewees also shared opinions about the low quality of cultural and art education in schools. According to them, museums play an important role in *developing aesthetic sensitivity and interest in arts*, culture, history and more:

> I think, even such little ones may learn something. Activities are conducted so even kindergarten children come and open their mouths, hearing all that is spoken about. Through such activities, it seems for me, art may be loved, even by the smallest participant of social life.
>
> (Educator 2)

Empowerment

Finally, people from the past can be treated as role models: Zdzisław Beksiński, a world-renowned artist; Ignacy Łukasiewicz, inventor of the first modern kerosene lamp and an oil industry pioneer; Fred Zinnemann, the Hollywood director; or Helene Deutsch, a psychoanalyst. All play important roles in Polish and world history. Educators can draw on their achievements, skills and moral traits as examples for younger generations. There is, however, another possibility for positive influence which can be used in educational practices: *empowerment*.

> It is not only about transferring knowledge. The point is to make these young people – in all these small communities – lose their inhibitions. […] Beksiński's phenomenon is an excellent issue because, suddenly, a bloke from a hole of a town far worse than it is today (because this interwar or after-war 'hole of a town' was a real hole, right?) becomes a well-known person, becomes a person whose works are used in films, in Hollywood and beyond, about whom movies are made, right?
>
> (Manager 4)

Since the region is peripheral and underdeveloped in a Polish context, showing that one can overcome obstacles and be successful despite negative circumstances might be especially important in local educational enterprises.

Problems with curricula

Museums are subjects of various regulations introduced at local, regional, national and supra-national levels. I will focus on educational policy, which my interlocutors often address as the largest source of problems in developing an effective model of cooperation.

Over the last quarter of a century, Poland has experienced three major reforms of the educational system, not to mention several changes in curricula. Before 1999, the organization of school education was based on the eight-year primary school. After graduating, a student is selected from a three-year vocational school, a four-year lyceum or a five-year technical school. After the 1999 reform, a new system was introduced: six-year primary school, three-year secondary school and three or four-year high school. However, a 2017 reform returned to the previous model. None of the reforms addressed the problem discussed by both schoolteachers and educators: School programmes are overloaded, and teachers experience difficulties with achieving goals set by curricula. This is the source of one problem in the organization of museum trips, especially at the high school level. To organize an excursion, teachers need to convince a school principal that the museum lesson will cover topics contained in the curriculum. Usually, one school hour is not enough to get to the museum and back, so they need to involve other teachers and classes.

To help teachers, some museums adjust their educational programmes to curricula. They prepare topics that cover certain elements of the school programme, hoping that this convinces teachers and administrators that a visit to the museum will not be a waste of time. Despite this, it is difficult to visit a museum, not only because of the overloaded programming in schools but because current curricula have decreased the number of hours related to arts, culture and history.

My interlocutors with the most work experience trace the source of the problem to the 1999 reform:

So, earlier the role of the museum within the educational system was different?
It was complementary [...] There was a solid knowledge base, drilling down on particular topics, and the illustration being the museum.

(Educator 1)

Before educators can proceed to the main topic of the museum lesson, they need to fill the gaps in students' knowledge; this needs time, which usually is limited. Art education in Poland was always of poor quality, but after 1999 the number of hours dedicated to the topic significantly decreased. It was not treated seriously either by schools or students and was often taught by people without a background in the field.

The other problem hampering cooperation between the museum and the school results from double or even triple peripherality of certain municipalities:

> [T]eachers have curricula, they have to prepare for exams [...] and it's difficult for them to find time... I think that in large cities they find it more easily [...] It is much worse here in this regard.
>
> (Manager 2)

For schools located far from cultural centres, it is difficult to organize an excursion. In addition to negotiations with principals and colleagues, teachers need to organize a means of transport (public transport in peripheral Poland is not the best), and the distance increases the time needed for a trip. In comparison to their large-city peers, students living in the periphery have fewer opportunities for cultural participation. Some museums in the region try to prevent this exclusion by visiting schools with lectures or workshops, but due to the lack of personnel, this is very difficult.

Conclusion

This study demonstrates how the educational function of a museum exceeds the simple transfer of knowledge. Visitors can learn more about the past of the region but also find some role models in present times. The peripheral context, connected to the problem of exclusion, makes the function of empowerment especially important. Although this chapter does not cover all topics, it offers a starting point for further comparison with more-or-less peripheral regions and more details concerning educational functions, such as whether they apply to other locations.

The findings of this study demonstrate there are critically important problems in school education in Poland, especially in the matter of humanities. I advocate for a serious discussion about the content of school curricula and rethinking the museum–school relationship. The cultural education in schools should be either improved or completely ceded to museums (often, they do it anyway). Museum visits should become a compulsory component of an organized system of education on every level.

Note

1. A high school leaving exam in Poland.

References

Alexander, E. P., & Alexander, M. (2008). *Museums in motion: An introduction to the history and functions of museums* (2nd ed.). AltaMira Press.

Anderson, B. R. O. (2006). *Imagined communities: Reflections on the origin and spread of nationalism* (rev. ed.). Verso.

Bennett, T. (1995). *The birth of the museum: History, theory, politics*. Routledge.

Bourdieu, P., & Darbel, A. (1991). *The love of art: European art museums and their public*. Polity Press.

Broszkiewicz, W. (2010). *Kapitał kulturowy młodego pokolenia Polski współczesnej: Studium na przykładzie wybranych społeczności Podkarpacia* (Wyd. 1). Wydawn. Uniwersytetu Rzeszowskiego.

Crooke, E. (2007). *Museums and community: Ideas, issues and challenges*. Routledge.

Gajda, K. (2019). *Edukacyjna rola muzeum*. Nomos.

Gell, A. (1998). *Art and agency: An anthropological theory*. Clarendon Press.

Hein, G. E. (1995). The constructivist museum. *Journal for Education in Museums, 16*, 21–23.

Hein, G. E. (1998). *Learning in the museum*. Routledge.

Hooper-Greenhill, E. (Ed.). (1999). *The educational role of the museum* (2nd ed.). Routledge.

Hooper-Greenhill, E. (2007). *Museums and education: Purpose, pedagogy, performance*. Routledge.

Hudson, K. (2014). *Social history of museums: What the visitors thought*. Palgrave Macmillan.

Jordanova, L. J. (1989). Objects of knowledge: A historical perspective on museums. In P. Vergo (Ed.), *The new museology* (pp. 22–40). Reaktion Books.

Krajewski, M. (2013). *Są w życiu rzeczy: Szkice z socjologii przedmiotów*. Fundacja Bęc Zmiana.

Latour, B. (2005). *Reassembling the social: An introduction to actor-network-theory*. Oxford University Press.

Merton, R. K. (1968). *Social theory and social structure*. The Free Press.

Ossowski, S. (1984). *O ojczyźnie i narodzie*. Państwowe Wydawnictwo Naukowe.

Pater, R. (2016). *Edukacja muzealna: Muzea dla dzieci i młodzieży*. Wydawnictwo Uniwersytetu Jagiellońskiego.

Porczyński, D., & Vargová, L. (2020). Museum education in semi-peripheries: Social, cultural and economic aspects of the globalisation of Polish and Slovak heritage institutions. *Muzeológia a Kultúrne Dedičstvo, 8*(2), 31–54. https://doi.org/10.46284/mkd.2020.8.2.3

Prösler, M. (1996). Museums and globalization. In S. Macdonald & G. Fyfe (Eds.), *Theorizing museums: Representing identity and diversity in a changing world* (pp. 21–44). Blackwell.

Roudometof, V. (2016). *Glocalization: A critical introduction*. Routledge.

Szeląg, M., Towarzystwo Autorów i Wydawców Prac Naukowych 'Universitas', & Muzeum Pałac w Wilanowie. (2014). *Raport o stanie edukacji muzealnej: Suplement. Cz. 2 Cz. 2*. Towarzystwo Autorów i Wydawców Prac Naukowych UNIVERSITAS; Muzeum Pałacu Króla Jana III w Wilanowie.

Szeląg, P. (2012). Wprowadzenie do historii edukacji muzealnej w Polsce. In M. Szeląg (Ed.), *Edukacja muzealna w Polsce. Sytuacja, kontekst, perspektywy rozwoju. Raport o stanie edukacji muzealnej w Polsce*. Narodowy Instytut Muzealnictwa i Ochrony Zbiorów, Muzeum Pałac w Wilanowie.

Vergo, P. (2006). Introduction. In P. Vergo (Ed.), *The new museology* (pp. 1–5). Reaktion Books.

Weil, S. E. (1990). Rethinking the museum. *Museum News, 69*(2), 56–61.

Ziębińska-Witek, A. (2020). Musealisation of communism, or how to create national identity in historical museums. *Muzeológia a Kultúrne Dedičstvo, 8*(4), 59–72. https://doi.org/10.46284/mkd.2020.8.4.5

Znaniecki, F. (1945). Social organization and institutions. In G. Gurvich & W. E. Moore (Eds.), *Twentieth century sociology* (pp. 172–217). The Philosophical Library.

Znaniecki, F. (1954). Social groups in the modern world. In M. Berger, T. Abel, & C. H. Page (Eds.), *Freedom and control in modern society* (pp. 125–140). D. van Nostrand Company.

Znaniecki, F. (1965). *Social relations and social roles: The unfinished systematic sociology*. Chandler Publishing.

Chapter 20

The Role of the University Museum in Museum Education: The Example of the University of Tartu Museum

Jaanika Anderson

This chapter explores the educational role of the University of Tartu Museum (UTM) in the context of the national education system of Estonia, a small country (1.33 million citizens, area 45,339 square kilometres) in Northern Europe with Estonian as its official language.[1] The educational activities of the UTM date from the early nineteenth century, when the first steps were taken to support the teaching process visually. Today, the museum has evolved into the basis for a systematic educational activity that supports the school curriculum, acts as an internship base for students and offers various leisure activities of an educational nature. The mission of the UTM is to offer high-quality interdisciplinary museum education to comprehensive schools, support students via an internship, maintain national self-awareness through the history of Estonia and contribute to the development of a science-based Estonia. Focusing on the role of the UTM in Estonian museum education, this chapter analyses public documents and development plans as a prerequisite for the educational work of the UTM. Different educational activities are observed as case studies to map the focus and effectiveness of the UTM's activities as well as problematic areas that may deviate from its objectives.

Education in Estonia

University museums have great potential to support the educational activities of comprehensive schools and achieve the learning objectives in an interdisciplinary way while strengthening the national identity of this small country in a globalizing world.

The history of formal education in Estonia dates from the thirteenth and fourteenth centuries, when monastic and cathedral schools were founded for educating the clergy. In 1632, the university was opened in Tartu by the Swedish King Gustav II Adolf (*Academia Gustaviana*) but was closed because of the Northern War in 1710. The Enlightenment did not leave the Estonian territory untouched, however, and the university's re-opening (*Kaiserliche Universität zu Dorpat*) occurred under Tsar Alexander I in 1802. The University of Tartu (UT) became a national university in 1919, teaching in Estonian after Estonia gained its independence (Siilivask, 1985).

The Estonian education system is currently divided into general, vocational and non-formal education. The levels of formal education comprise pre-school, basic, upper secondary and higher education.[2] The national curricula establish the standards for basic education. According to the Education Act, the aim of education is to create favourable conditions for personal development in the context of the world economy and culture, shape people who respect and obey the law and provide the prerequisites of lifelong learning for everyone (Statistikaamet, 2021).

The Estonian national curriculum states that modern and diverse teaching methods and tools should be used in planning and implementing studies, including museum education; studies may be organized outside the school premises, including in museums (*Riigi Teataja*, 2011a, 2011b). This is a prerequisite for schools to teach with a non-formal learning process characterized by learner-centredness, flexibility, accessibility and balance between individual and social learning (Statistikaamet, 2021). While informal learning means learning from a family member, friend, colleague or independently visiting museums and libraries in one's free time (Statistikaamet, 2021), non-formal education is a much more organized and targeted activity aimed at conscious development in different environments.

Estonian schools stand for the preservation and development of the Estonian nation, language and culture (*Riigi Teataja*, 2011a, 2011b). UT is defined as a promoter of the Estonian language and culture in the context of continuing globalization (University of Tartu, 2020).

Development of museums and museum education in Estonia

For centuries, the main purpose of museums was to conserve and interpret objects considered the artistic, cultural and natural treasures of the world and to use the collections to distribute knowledge (Hooper-Greenhill, 1992). Many people see museums as a place that preserves and displays artefacts, but museums are much more complex institutions that fulfil different roles. Talboys (2011) has said our concern as humans is that we pass on the understanding of ideas and actions we have inherited from our forebears to our children so that they might have a better chance of personal and social growth, and museums are specifically designed for exploring and interpreting our material culture.

The growth of universities and museums in Estonia since regaining its independence from the Soviet Union in 1991 has been explosive. This is largely related to the transition from the command economy to the market economy and gaining freedom in all areas (e.g. expression, thought, action). According to Statistics Estonia, the country has the most museums per 100,000 inhabitants among European countries – 175 museums and 225 museum sites in 2020.[3] In the 1990s, changes took place in the activities and organization of Estonian museums, with a great leap in all areas of museums over the last 30 years. The restoration of Estonia's independence brought access to the world and development opportunities. Exhibition activities were modernized, which means attention was paid to contemporary museology: exhibitions changed from being object-oriented to visitor-centred, and target groups and various inclusive activities were considered.[4] The focus moved to educational activities, and schools became an important target group for museums.

The position of museum educator has a short history in Estonia, coming into focus only in the late 1990s. The transmission of information was no longer limited to uninterrupted monologues by a tour guide, but keywords like inclusion, interdisciplinarity, discovery and active learning emerged. On the one hand, intense competition began in the field of non-formal education; on the other hand, museums started to offer very diverse specialist programmes.

Today, Estonian teachers visit museums and can order diverse educational programmes for students. The situation creates excellent preconditions for educational cooperation between the school and the museum. However, not many classes attend museum programmes for various reasons:

- School programmes are tight, proper museums are far away, the visit takes the whole school day and it takes extra time for the teacher to find the finances and plan the time for museum trips.
- Museums offer more programmes related to history or the environment and not so many science programmes; teachers value museum education but prefer natural environments, nature houses, farms, theatres and other institutions that provide non-formal educational activities.
- Not all teachers value museum education if the subject can be taught in the traditional way at school.

Museums and museum education are not free of charge for pupils in Estonia. Sometimes such study visits are financed by the local government, or support is sought from project funding or collected from parents. It is easier to fund science and environmental programmes than history and art programmes held outside school because the Environmental Investment Centre provides many grants.[5]

Some municipalities have found effective solutions for schools. To develop general and specialist competencies, schools in Tartu can participate in extracurricular active learning programmes through a procurement centrally organized by the City of Tartu (practised since 2013). Teachers can choose programmes for different school levels from the list of museums. Programmes usually take place in museums in groups of 24 students, and the length of one contact hour is 45 minutes.

Museum education does not have to replace school lessons but rather enrich school learning, and therefore the aim should not be to use the same methodology as in schools. Most teachers tend to combine the museum trip with preparatory and follow-up activities at school. In some cases, museum visits are useful for different subjects, especially at lower school levels. Effective museum visits require more collaboration and planning from teachers, but there are also benefits.

Role and importance of academic museums

It is well known that universities have libraries, but there is less knowledge about museums. University museums can support teaching, research, learning and disseminating the results of science, as well as provide community relations, programmes for schools, and cultural events and serve as wonderful places for special events. The university museum is distinguished by the wide range of people it can attract in addition to students and academics (Kelly, 2001).

University museums have generally evolved from commemorative, ceremonial, decorative and teaching collections gathered from various sources during the history of a university. In some instances, external benefactors have donated their private collections to a university or have their roots in the collections of learned societies (Kelly, 2001). University museums usually continue collecting and acquiring new items in the course of institutional renewal, and their art collections usually grow due to different institutional and national anniversaries.

Museums, including university museums, have also experienced a transformation in recent decades. The focus has moved from objects to people, and a visitor-centred approach creates more positive experiences. To strengthen the contemporary role of university collections, it is important to know our collections and be aware of the practical needs of schools, as well as the crucial role school curricula play in research, community engagement and economic development (Vakharia, 2017). An important keyword is availability – university collections should be digitally accessible (Weber & Sticker, 2017). In Estonia, there is a national effort to digitize heritage so that it can be used by schoolchildren, researchers and those interested.[6]

Although the university museum is part of the university, learning in the university museum is not necessarily formal or academic; it can also be non-formal or informal and distinguished from academic courses (Lord, 2007). Born out of eighteenth-century enthusiasm for an enlightened citizenry, art museums have provided educational programmes almost from the time they were established (Newsom & Silver, 1978). University museums are repositories of visual and physical evidence dedicated to knowledge generation and transmission. Today many university museums, particularly art museums, engage in cross-disciplinary programming with both exhibitions and events. Exhibition projects constructed specifically to cross the boundaries of disciplines often evoke new perspectives and insights. Purposive exhibitions that are grounded in cross-disciplinary contexts can generate debate, critique and conversation (Simpson, 2019).

Clearly, the university museum is not just a classroom in and of itself but an extension of the academic experience as a whole (Simpson, 2019). Academic heritage should be made available to as many people as possible through exhibitions that are visited independently, and likewise through planned educational activities for different generations. University collections are an important part of the cultural landscapes of nations and form cultural landscapes themselves (Weber & Sticker, 2017). UT, as the national university, has a strong connection with the national identity of Estonians.

Formation of the UTM and its growth as an educational institution

From the nineteenth century, teaching in many subjects such as geology, archaeology and natural history was, more often than not, done in the university museum itself; the idea of the object lesson or teaching through close contact with artefacts and specimens was firmly embedded in the higher education experience (Stomberg, 2012). Many layers of language, culture and history have overlapped over four centuries at the UT. The university's history, with its collections and art museum, started vigorously in 1803 when the statutes of the re-opened university provided for a cabinet of natural sciences, a collection of physics instruments, a laboratory of chemistry, a collection of anatomical preparations, a cabinet of pathologies, a collection of technology, military models, an observatory, a botanical garden and an art museum (Figure 20.1; Grenzius, 1803). The UT Art Museum became important for providing visuals for lectures in art history, classical archaeology, aesthetics and numismatics from the moment of its establishment in 1803 (Anderson, 2019).

The University's art museum became the first museum in Estonia to deal with education and complement educational activities (Anderson, 2015). The museum's first director, Johann Karl Simon Morgenstern (1770–1852), was influenced by the ideology of the Enlightenment; he believed in the paramount importance of education and valued self-education, relying on noble models, literature and art. He especially placed his hope in the study of the ancient world, classical literature and art, and laid the foundation for the art collection that is still used today (Anderson, 2019). The UT Art Museum is now located in the university's main building as a branch of the UTM; the other parts include the observatory (established 1820) and the museum of the history of the university and science (established 1976), located in the cathedral.[7] This collection of buildings has developed into an educational centre at the UTM in recent decades. Similar developments have occurred throughout Estonia's museums.

Figure 20.1: University of Tartu Art Museum. Photo by Angelina Pjatkovskaja.

The overall goal of the *Estonian Lifelong Learning Strategy 2020* is to create learning opportunities for all Estonian people that meet their needs and abilities throughout their lives. Different educational activities in the UTM support the strategy through thematic diversity. UTM provides informal learning, such as family visits and children's camps rooted in entertainment and leisure, and non-formal learning. This supports the aims of the national curriculum by exposing pupils to educational programmes in the museum environment. The University's historical campus, including the UTM, has been awarded the European Heritage Label,[8] and therefore every building has a story to tell about the development of Estonian higher education, science and the formation of the Estonian Republic – a place where every Estonian can be proud of their language and nationality and find support for their national identity.

The UTM has played an important role in the development of modern museum education in Estonia by preserving and mediating the University's heritage and communicating science via exhibitions and educational programmes. In its activities, the UTM proceeds from the statutes and development plan of the UTM and UT to meet the needs of schools and the museum's collections, buildings and location. The UTM statutes present it as the central museum for the history of science in Estonia; it researches, preserves, mediates and disseminates history, scientific history, art and the history of the UT through both the educational history and ancient culture found in the museum's collections (Tartu Ülikooli Muuseum, 2018).

The UTM welcomed over 15,000 school visitors in 2019 (6000 in 2020 due to COVID-19) from across the science and humanities curricula. Schools visiting the university museum discuss the fact that they are also at the Estonian national university. Although we have the Estonian National Museum, Estonian History Museum and Estonian Art Museum deeply connecting the identity and history of Estonians, the national university in Tartu plays an important role in preserving the Estonian language, culture and identity and in developing a science-based Estonia. Likewise, a cluster of museums can be found in every country, performing the role of national museums and participating in the nation-building process (Aronsson & Elgenius, 2015).

Educational activities of the UTM

Museum visitors have different needs and expectations: museums can often fulfil many but not all of them. UTM focuses on visitors with educational needs, although it also wants to attract tourists by providing experiences and discoveries in different historical buildings.

The diversity of themes housed in the different historical buildings of the UTM presents an opportunity as well as a challenge. Educators with differing professional expertise (astronomy, art history, history) have been employed to deliver educational programmes. We consider it important that museum educators work together with other museum professionals to avoid becoming distanced from the collections. Talboys (2011) has written that if curators, conservators, designers, educators and all other staff understand each other and work together, their needs can be satisfied to the fullest extent – the museum is strengthened and visitors receive the best possible experience.

The UTM delivers diverse educational activities for the national curriculum as well as for leisure and entertainment. Examples of these activities are described below. They are sustainable in the sense that the museum has practised these activities for years but constantly monitors and updates them to suit current needs and issues in the education system and society.

Educational programmes in situ

The UTM has a wide range of educational programmes for all school levels and even for kindergarten children at all three venues (Figure 20.2). The programmes are divided into permanent and temporary exhibition programmes and special programmes. The art museum has a collection of plaster casts made after classical sculptures and an exhibition

Figure 20.2: Educational programme. Photo by Angelina Pjatkovskaja.

of Egyptian mummies, which are the basis for art, history and mythology programmes. The observatory provides programmes in astronomy, space and geography. A wide range of educational programmes is provided in the cathedral building, based on the permanent exhibition about the history of the university and the church in which the museum is located, including science programmes (chemistry, physics, biology and maths), and history programmes about mediaeval Estonia.

Online educational programmes

In 2020–2021, the UTM developed several successful online programmes[9] for schools forced to use distance learning due to COVID-19. The teachers explored programmes on different themes based on key collections in the art museum, the observatory and the cathedral. The students could visit each location virtually, listen to explanations by the museum educator, look at objects, ask questions and solve tasks. These diversified learning processes and teaching opportunities provided significant support for schools. We developed these programmes with the knowledge that they will continue to be useful, and there is no fear that online programmes will rob the museum of its visitors. Study trips to the museum still occur, but the new learning solutions will motivate teachers to integrate more museum lessons into their classes because ordering such material is quick and flexible. Museum education has been made more accessible to all groups with educational needs.

Activities with the Crazy Scientist

The UTM has a special character, the Crazy Scientist, who is curious and helps children discover different aspects of the world (Figure 20.3). Crazy Scientist day camps are most popular among small groups of fifteen children aged 7–12. The goal is to take care of children during the holidays when their parents are at work while offering entertaining educational activities with peers. These became particularly important in 2020 and 2021 when everyone had to be isolated because of COVID-19.

Every year, the Crazy Scientist holds a conference for children in grades 1–3 (aged 7–10 years). There is a special topic each year: for example, Save Electricity! Be Healthy! Go to the Forest! The Soil Is Gold! The Crazy Scientist instructs teachers and students on how to conduct research, and then the children carry out the research and make a presentation with the help of their teacher. This is how children get their first major research and performance experience. In 2020 and 2021, the parents also made a significant contribution to the research because schools had distance learning in the spring. Feedback shows that this provided enjoyment for the whole family.

Figure 20.3: Crazy Scientist with children in the cathedral building. Photo by Angelina Pjatkovskaja.

Internships for students

Internships play an increasingly important role in modern higher education, providing the opportunity for acquiring social and professional skills that can help university students find a job. The UTM is a highly professional institution with departments for collections, communication and education. This allows the museum to offer a wide range of internships that deal with exhibitions, educational activities and collections, as well as translation and communication internships. The UTM is flexible and based on the students' needs, making it a valuable internship opportunity. The UTM employs 38 people in 28 full-time positions, but because there are many part-time positions, 30 to 40 interns – undertaking activities like collection descriptions and database entries, creating social media content, teaching and delivering art activities, translating and editing exhibition materials – can work here each year. Internships also help the museum cooperate with institutes and faculties, keeping the museum close to the activities of the university.

Conclusion

The UTM, the cradle of museum education in Estonia, plays an important role in comprehensive schools, although originally it was established as an art museum for university students. Educational programmes take place in the observatory, art museum and cathedral, covering the whole school curriculum. In addition to knowledge, programmes also support the development of general competencies and help to maintain national self-awareness through focusing on Estonian history. Programmes also contribute to the development of a science-based Estonia, which is important for a small nation in a globalizing world. The Crazy Scientist character introduces scientific achievements to children and popularizes the work of researchers.

While museums must attract different target groups, more and more Estonian teachers understand that museums are highly professional institutions with experienced museum educators, where it is possible to access complementary material on specific themes in an enjoyable format. The pandemic provided impetus to improve accessibility to museum education; online programmes were launched, which became popular immediately and can be accessed in the future at any time.

Museum internships are valuable for students who can work during their studies, gaining experience of working in a museum and improving their employment prospects. This opportunity also introduces the importance of the museum as a custodian and mediator of academic heritage. Through internships, the museum has closer contact with the university, which creates preconditions for cooperation and meeting each other's needs. These initiatives and programmes demonstrate the important role the UTM plays in Estonian society and educational life.

Notes

1. Of Estonia's population, 68.4 per cent are Estonian, 24.7 per cent are Russian and 6.9 per cent are others (2020). The number of persons with higher education is about 373,800. In 2020, there were 521 comprehensive education schools, with 155,000 pupils in studies.
2. Ministry of Education and Research: https://www.hm.ee/en
3. Statistics Estonia: http://www.stat.ee
4. Since the 1990s, several buildings for local museums and national museums have been renovated (the Estonian History Museum in 2018 and Estonian Maritime Museum in 2012) and new ones constructed (the Estonian National Museum in 2016 and the Art Museum of Estonia, or KUMU, in 2006).
5. Environmental Investment Centre: https://www.kik.ee/en
6. Republic of Estonia Ministry of Culture. *Action Plan for Digitisation of Cultural Heritage*: https://www.kul.ee/en/node/41
7. The cathedral was rebuilt as the university library in 1809 and since 1982 has accommodated the UTM.
8. European Commission. *Culture and Creativity: Cultural heritage*. https://ec.europa.eu/culture/cultural-heritage/initiatives-and-success-stories/european-heritage-label-sites
9. One of the programmes, Ancient Greek culture, is available to the general public at https://sites.google.com/view/vana-kreekakultuur/avaleht

References

Anderson, J. (2015). *Reception of ancient art: The Cast Collections of the University of Tartu Art Museum in historical, ideological and academic context* [Dissertationes Studiorum Graecorum et Latinorum universitatis Tartuensis 7]. University of Tartu Press.

Anderson, J. (2019). The use of the University of Tartu Art Museum collection in teaching between 1803 and 1918. *History of Education, 48*(5), 575–590. https://doi.org/10.1080/0046760X.2019.1615560

Aronsson, P., & Elgenius, G. (Eds.). (2015). *National museums and nation-building in Europe 1750–2010*. Routledge.

Grenzius, M. G. (1803). *Statuten der kaiserlichen Universität zu Dorpat*. Kaiserliche Universität Dorpat.

Hooper-Greenhill, E. (1992). *Museums and the shaping of knowledge*. Routledge.

Kelly, M. (2001). *Managing university museums*. Organization for Economic Co-operation and Development (OECD).

Lord, B. (2007). *Manual of museum learning*. Altamira Press.

Newsom, B. Y., & Silver, A. Z. (Eds.). (1978). *The art museum as educator: A collection of studies as guides to practice and police*. University of California.

Riigi Teataja. (2011a). *National curriculum for basic schools*. https://www.riigiteataja.ee/en/eli/524092014014/consolide

Riigi Teataja. (2011b). *National curriculum for upper secondary schools*. https://www.riigiteataja.ee/en/eli/524092014009/consolide

Siilivask, K. (1985). *History of Tartu University 1632–1982*. Perioodika.

Simpson, A. (2019). Why academic museums matter: Four frameworks for considering their value. *University Museums and Collections Journal, 11*(2), 196–201.

Statiskikaamet. (2021). Handbook of Educational Statistics.

Stomberg, J. R. (2012). Transforming the university museum: The Manchester experience. In S. S. Jandl & M. S. Gold (Eds.), *A handbook for academic museums: Beyond exhibitions and education* (pp. 20–35). Museums Etc.

Talboys, G. K. (2011). *Museum educator's handbook*. Ashgate.

Tartu University Museum. (2018). *Statute of the Museum of the University of Tartu*.

University of Tartu. (2020). *University of Tartu Strategic Plan for 2021–2025*. https://www.ut.ee/sites/default/files/www_ut/ulikoolist/university_of_tartu_strategic_plan_2025.pdf

Vakharia, N. (2017). Mapping the museum universe. In Y. Jung & R. Love (Eds.), *Systems thinking in museums* (pp. 17–26). Rowman & Littlefield.

Weber, C., & Sticker, M. (2017). University collections: An important part of the German cultural landscape. *University Museum and Collections Journal, 9*, 24–30.

Part IV

Sites of Sensorial Practice

Chapter 21

"You Have to Form Your Mediators. It's a Series":
On Mediation, Encounters and Deleuze in the
Art Museum

Marie-France Berard

Vancouver Art Gallery. Notepad in hand, I attempt to keep up with a flow of thoughts, observations and impressions as "fieldnotes" for my doctoral research (Berard, 2017). As a long-time art museum educator, I still wonder about encounters with art, not to define them and pin them down in terms of what they are but to think what they might produce. And I still wonder about my role among the moving assemblage of bodies, artworks, knowledge, being in tune with current socio-political issues and recognizing the complex history of the Western art museum – rooted in elite private or national collections that derived benefits from imperialism (Bennett, 1995; Duncan, 1995; McClellan, 2008).

Something grabs my attention; I hear a friendly voice talking to me. I lift my nose from my notebook. With a nod, they ask about my focused writing. A term paper? Yes, this is field work for my dissertation. I briefly explain my topic and hand out an oral consent form. They are happy to chat.

"On the art encounter? How interesting." They love encountering artworks but feel that sometimes things happen after, that ideas linger and then come back much later.

"I like to come and visit on my own, it's easier that way to interact with other visitors. And I love to share my enthusiasm. My name is E."

We are both fascinated by the works in the exhibition, Unscrolled: Reframing Tradition in Contemporary Chinese Art (2014–2015, and see Zhang, 2015).

"Especially Sun Xun's film and painting installation Shan Shui – Cosmos. I just love it!" says E.

So do I. Superlatives, words of appreciation and some "did you notice" form the basis of our dialogue for a moment. And the birds [...] I ask, "What do think of those beautiful animated birds in flight? They are exquisitely drawn."

"Yes, but did you notice the background?" I cannot resist to add. Always the gallery educator, I wonder why this overwhelming desire to make sure I point out key information.

"What do you mean?" E asked.

My suspended question prompted something, a movement [...] they make a move towards Sun Xun's gallery space. I follow and we step into the installation Shan Shui-Cosmos. Inside, the white cube of the gallery is transformed. We step into another world. It is a world of deep muffled sounds – perhaps water curling at the bottom of a waterfall or the roaring of a powerful river, and on every wall large fluid brushstrokes of black, green and some red evoke the topography of Southern China with curvy mountains and steep valleys. But when I step closer to the wall paintings, they seem so abstract, more like graffiti marks of paint freely dripping, the brushstroke fluid and energetic. The gallery space is now a magical world of the moving *image with three different projections: some of a fighting sea serpent, abstract dots evolving into constellations and fantastic creatures, exotic colourful birds flying into a traditional black ink landscape painting.*

Sun Xun plays with the overlapping of modes of representation. *The large-scale animated films are projected directly onto the painted landscape, and there is a third layer of hanging reproductions of landscape or paintings of exquisite birds, dating back from the Song Dynasty, or his own ink drawings of a monstrous water serpent fighting a giant turtle. My senses are overwhelmed. There is the impossibility of grasping the entirety of an ever-changing visual spectacle, the presence of the deep roaring sounds of rumbling waves. Spontaneously, E. and I engage and start playing with the work. In turn we point out and notice the quality and the manifest skill of the artist's brushstrokes. From afar, the paint work evokes a vague mountainous landscape but from close up, the signs are purely abstract, fluid, gestural strokes, but E. recognizes the quality and acknowledges Sun Xun's deep training and skills in traditional Chinese calligraphy. We exchange some more about the artist's grandfather, who experienced sustained hardships during the Cultural Revolution, and the artist's layered conversations with China's political and artistic history.*

I thought I knew the installation well with repeated visits and extensive study due to my work as gallery educator. To my delight, E. points out through a hand gesture, with exclamation, details in Sun Xun's complex imagery which I had overlooked. In his desire to take into account the body of the viewer and the entire space of the wall, there is a magical moment when the traditional ink landscape with animated majestic birds in flight perfectly overlap with the hand-painted mural of mountains and valleys in the museum space. For a brief moment, a transformation. The layering is a fleeting effect, yet the formal strategy invites a new narrative, the conversation in-between two artistic and historical realities that flow, connect and dialogue in and through the work of art. How did I miss that?

"But what did you mean, when you asked if I had noticed the background?" says E.

We had been playing with the work, discussing how the copies of old scroll paintings suspended in the installation were perhaps the historical source for the motifs of the colourful birds flying in the digital animation. Sun Xun plunges the viewer into the maelstrom of his mind; the apparent confusion, juxtaposition, layering of images, historical and contemporary references provoke thinking. It is a wonderful metaphor of an artistic process.

"I invite you to pay attention to the small garden scene and the waterfall behind the birds […] now look around the space," I said. *My body turns and points to the reproduction of a landscape from the period of the Song dynasty that was suspended on the opposite wall, visible yet also partially covered by the projected film animation showing the fighting water serpent. We move closer.*

E. gasps, "Yes, I have seen this, but I did not make the connection!" *There in full view, yet easy to overlook, is the view Sun Xun reproduced for the background of his birds in flight. E. is fascinated, partly because they had seen the reproduction during an earlier visit yet without actually noticing the similarities and connection to this ink painting from the Song Dynasty. E. and I became aware that Sun Xun had set up an invitation. We accepted this invitation, and our renewed encounter as a playful conversation with the work made us participate in some of the ways the multimedia installation thinks and makes manifest.*

On mediation: Mediating in the art gallery space

While the informal pedagogical artistic encounter described in the narrative happened a few years ago, it is one I often return to as I try to think differently about certain aspects in the role of museum educator – a generic term. More specifically, I am interested in the art gallery educator in relation to mediation in the art museum or art gallery. (I use both terms interchangeably in this chapter.) According to museologists Desvallées and Mairesse (2010), in the context of museums, mediation is a term found mostly in France and French-speaking institutions since the 1980s, at times in tandem with or instead of the term "interpretation," perceived as a more formal educational function. In the later 2000s, the term "cultural mediation" emerges in the Anglophone museum literature. Taken to be less focused on transmission and the construction of knowledge than the role of "educator," the cultural mediator aims to be an agent of societal change by seeking to bring public and cultural institutions into socially, politically and aesthetically relevant conversation and relations. This encompasses various modalities of socio-cultural interventions and negotiations outside of formal educational systems and is grounded in a commitment to critically examine the societal role and relevance of museums (see Dufresne-Tassé, 2018; Kaitavuori et al., 2013; Mörsch & Chrusciel, 2012; Paquin, 2015; Paquin & Lemay-Perreault, 2016). Desvallées and Mairesse (2010) define mediation as

> an action aimed as reconciling parties or bringing them to agreement. In the context of the museum, it is the mediation between the museum public and what the museum gives its public to see. […] museum or cultural mediation refers to a wide range of activities carried out in order to build bridges between that which is exhibited (seeing) and the meanings that these objects and sites may carry (knowledge).
>
> (pp. 46–47)

This metaphor of the mediator/museum educator as an intermediary, as a bridge providing means and opportunities to facilitate connections in-between visitors and artworks, is a powerful metaphor which has fuelled my work for many years. Nonetheless, when thinking of the fluxes, movements and the complex educational space E. and I created, another concept seemed necessary. The image of the bridge suggests a stable territory as beginning and arrival. Granted, there was intentionality when I first opened up about certain aspects of Sun Xun's elaborate video installation: the disciplinary reflex of an art historian and museum educator wanting to make sure that E. would see, notice and "know." And yet this first bridge soon began to move, distort and morph into a more rhizomatic series of dynamic connections and flows from one idea, comment, affect, image, embodied experience and previous knowledge to another.

It was quite by chance that I stumbled upon French philosopher Gilles Deleuze's concept of mediators, or *intercesseurs* as it is known in the French original text. A chapter title in *Negotiations* (1990/1995) caught my attention, although I soon realized the concept was not developed along the lines of the bridge metaphor or as a defined role with characteristics since, for Deleuze, we have to *form* our mediators. In a text engaging with topics loosely covering the interplay among philosophy, art, science and the act of creation, Deleuze (1995) asserted

> Mediators are fundamental. Creation's all about mediators. Without them nothing happens. They can be people – for a philosopher, artists, scientists; for a scientist, philosophers or artists – but things too, even plants or animals, as in Castaneda. Whether they're real or imaginary, animate or inanimate, you have to form your mediators. It's a series. If you're not in some series, even a completely imaginary one, you're lost. I need my mediators to express myself, and they'd never express themselves without me: you're always working in a group, even when you seem to be on your own. And still more when it's apparent: Félix Guattari and I are one and another's mediators.
>
> (p. 125)

As the focus of this chapter, working with the Deleuzian concept of mediators is inviting me to shift away from the metaphor of the bridge towards perceiving the museum itself, the art world, socio-political forces, historical discourse, the exhibition space and my role – however privileged – as offering "milieus" and sites of experiences where visitors can form their own assemblages with artworks, knowledge, ideas, other beings and place. I am reminded of Kaustuv Roy (2003), who so aptly wrote, "The use of Deleuzian concepts is to help pry open reified boundaries that exists not just in thought, but as affective investments that secure those territorialities" (p. 13). Without the desire to suggest a set of practices or a template to follow, I wonder how I can complicate the role of gallery education by studying how the concept of "mediator" functions. I aim to "gain insight into what it can do" (Bal, 2009, p. 17), to tease out how the use of the term can be generative to expand and think differently, even as a way to live. According to Deleuze (1995), creation is all about mediators; without them nothing happens, and thus I entertain potential avenues of practice and possibly a different perception of the role of art museum education.

Creation and the concept of mediators or *Intercesseurs*

Although Deleuze did not elaborate extensively on the concept of mediators in his writings, mediators formed through friendship or visits to art galleries were essential to his work and the creation of thought (see Colebrook, 2002a; Deleuze & Parnet, 1996). "Mediators" in plural form – not a fixed role, not an identity nor a set of practices or a professional description, not the mediator as an intermediary in a negotiation. Instead, mediators are necessary for creation; as argued in Deleuze's major opus *Difference and Repetition* (1994), thinking is a creative act: "To think is to create–there is no other creation–but to create is first of all to engender 'thinking' in thought" (p. 147). Engendering genuine "thinking" does not happen *ex nihilo*; to produce and create – whether new ideas, visual forms, musical lines or anything – we need to form our mediators: that is, become part, create or embark in a series – however small, temporary, unstable and imaginary is the assemblage.

Extensively developed by Deleuze and Guattari (1980/1987), the concept of assemblage refers to a complex set of relations and connections of bodies, objects and modes of expressions coming together over different periods of time and space. For instance, the notion of "museum" is in itself a complex and indefinite assemblage: not simply the juxtaposition or bringing together of artworks, modes of display, disciplinary discourses, catalogues and staff, but the ever-moving interconnections of smaller series such as an exhibition, with the pressures and flows of disciplinary practices, managerial decisions, architectural spaces impacting bodies, colonial systems of power, discursive practices and relations with the culture and politics of place. Series can be understood as smaller parts of assemblages. As Colebrook (2002b) explains, a series is not a sequence with a specific or proper order, "it is a connection with no ground or reason outside itself […] nor could there be a closed series […] One more element could always be added" (p. 170). And thus a crucial point for using the concept of assemblage is that, while the assemblage does not have a predominant centre or a specific temporality, it produces "a new reality, by making numerous, often unexpected, connections" (Livesey, 2010, p. 19).

Instead of the image of the tree imposing, as Deleuze and Guattari (1980/1987) write, the verb "to be" (p. 25) and the focus identities, they prefer the horizontality and type of connectivity of the rhizome whose "fabric […] is the conjunction, and…and…and…" (p. 25). Therefore, to produce thinking not as a mode of tracing the known but as thinking otherwise, one has to enter a series. And it is important to underline that, as I cited earlier, one has to *form* one's mediators. Mediators can be people, ideas, things, memories, non-human, imaginary characters or situations. They are encountered and are not assigned "out there," awaiting to transmit, share and communicate a pre-existing idea. In other words, suggests poet and philosopher Jean-Philippe Cazier (2015), if creating cannot happen without mediators *(intercesseurs)*, what defines our relation to the mediator is not only in what they are, it is about the movement from one to the other, in-between them both. Creative thought is that movement. Our relation to mediators is not about linking two distinct and abstract terms as in a juxtaposition; it implies a movement, a becoming – no matter how subtle. Thus thinking – any creation – requires the coming together of an assemblage in which we are caught in a dynamic relation with our real or imaginary mediators.

Entertaining possibilities

Deleuze appreciated visiting art galleries for the opportunities of chance encounters and being pushed to thought (Sauvagnargues, 2013). Instead of the usual definition of encounter as the simple act of "coming against," for Deleuze (1994) a genuine encounter happens when one meets something, someone, an idea, a concept, anything that is not an object of recognition, and this "something in the world forces us to think" (p. 139). Although he did not elaborate on museums specifically, my own encounter with the concept of mediators was generative, if not provocative, for thinking otherwise about the important role of gallery education. Ideas explored in this chapter in no way underestimate or disregard the important work done in critical, feminist, decolonial and dialogical approaches to art gallery education (see Mörsch, 2009), for thinking-with Deleuze is not just a pedagogical approach, a curriculum strategy, technique or programme – it is a way of being in the world. Lastly, it could be argued that my engagement with E. was not representative of the standard practices of art gallery educators such as gallery tours, artist talks or hands-on workshops, and thus less relevant to support my thinking. I selected the narrative with E. and the installation *Shan Shui-Cosmos* because I lived it as an artistic encounter and an educational event, which precisely opens up and moves beyond the standard image and perception of what gallery education is or should be.

As I revisit this experience, I realize that we temporarily created a series; we became each other's mediators and expanded the series by forming inanimate and animate mediators. We strolled into Sun Xun's video installation, responding to the materiality of the work, which called for our bodies to move closer, step back, notice a detail and bring up previous knowledge such as E.'s embodied expertise in Chinese calligraphy and ink painting and "bounce off" ideas with each other, touching on history, politics and art history. Forming our mediators and entering a series enabled, or should I say created, the movement of thought and thus further enriched the temporary assemblage with the artwork. Forming our mediators prompted new knowledge about the multimedia installation, contemporary artistic practice, new ideas about my doctoral work and still today, thinking otherwise about practice as a museum educator.

And while gallery educators will never know what mediators people create, what series they become part of, what assemblages have been formed or what thinking otherwise might create a line of flight or a new idea in a day, a week or a year's time, I see this as a key role which is aligned, and yet other than, facilitating, communicating, sharing or critically examining. Following Deleuze's (1994) philosophy is an invitation to the gallery educator to the creation of thought by enacting thinking and telling "do with me" rather than "do as I do" (p. 23). For me, this is the ethical dimension of being and experimenting with and through the arts.

Lingering thoughts

To close, I wish to bring forward again the connections between life as formed by virtualities (not possibilities because that term implies a goal outside of) through/in experiences and experimentations or encounters, or when one actualizes something – yet one can never tell in advance what the body will do. Deleuze (2007) condenses all these ideas in the last text written shortly before his death in 1995:

> We will say of pure immanence that it is A LIFE, and nothing more. It is not immanent to life, but the immanence that is in nothing else is itself a life. [...] A life contains only virtuals. It is composed of virtualities, event, singularities. What I am calling virtual is not something that lacks reality. Rather, the virtual becomes engaged in a process of actualisation as it follows the place which gives it its proper reality. The immanent event is actualised in a state of things and in a state of lived experience.
>
> (pp. 391–392)

This quote could become a motto for art museum educators. It is important to consider and value the art experience, simply to live an experience of encountering, for one never knows what it can produce in terms of ideas and connections or what virtual potentialities will be actualized. Indeed, that will depend on each person's political, social, cultural or personal assemblage – and more on the mediators individuals have created and what series they are part of.

As outlined by Marks (2010), Deleuze is strongly committed to ethics, which asks how to live in this world. For Deleuze, ethics is related to becoming – as the very dynamism of change moving towards no specific goal. Becoming is not about changing from one state of being towards another; becoming is always in the middle because there is no arrival point, no destination. What does this imply? This is how it should be done, according to Deleuze and Guattari (1987):

> Lodge yourself on a stratum, experiment with the opportunities it offers, find an advantageous place on it, find potential movements of deterritorialisation, possible lines of flight, experience them, produce flow conjunctions here and there, try out continuums of intensities segment by segment, have a small plot of new land at all times. [...] Connect, conjugate, continue: a whole "diagram" as opposed to still signifying and subjective programmes.
>
> (p. 161)

Becoming, therefore, is not about moving towards transcendent values, such as hoping or moving towards becoming a view of the self. For Deleuze, this view of becoming prevents us from actualizing the potentials that are already in life. So how do we actualize those potentials? Through experimentation, because only in experimentation can we have encounters, and through various encounters large or small to create one's mediators and engender thinking within thought. Is this not precisely the type of invitation and opportunities that we can set up in gallery education? In this chapter, I have entertained the thought of the gallery educator as Deleuzian mediator: not simply a bridge connecting people to content, meaning or negotiating sense and interpretation but rather creating, through the various pedagogical situations and events, privileged milieus of encounter with and through the arts. Creative thought is that movement.

References

Bal, M. (2009). Working with concepts. *European Journal of English Studies*, *13*(1), 13–23.

Bennett, T. (1995). *The birth of the museum: History, theory, politics*. Routledge.

Berard, M.-F. (2017). *On the experience of encountering art in museum spaces: An inquiry with Gilles Deleuze's concepts of desire and assemblage* [Doctoral dissertation, The University of British Columbia]. CiRcle. https://dx.doi.org/10.14288/1.0361128

Cazier, J.-P. (2015, February 4). Gilles Deleuze: Logique de la création. *Mediapart*. https://blogs.mediapart.fr/edition/gilles-deleuze-aujourdhui/article/040215/gilles-deleuze-une-logique-de-la-creation

Colebrook, C. (2002a). *Gilles Deleuze*. Routledge.

Colebrook, C. (2002b). *Understanding Deleuze*. Allen & Unwin.

Deleuze, G. (1994). *Difference & repetition* (P. Patton, Trans.). Columbia University Press.

Deleuze, G. (1995). *Negotiations: 1972–1990* (M. Joughin, Trans.). Columbia University Press. (Original work published 1990)

Deleuze, G. (2007). *Two regimes of madness* (D. Lapoujade, Ed., A. Hodges & M. Taormina, Trans.). Semiotext(e).

Deleuze, G., & Guattari, F. (1987). *A thousand plateaus: Capitalism and schizophrenia* (B. Massumi, Trans.). University of Minnesota Press.

Deleuze, G., & Parnet, C. (1996). *Dialogues*. Flammarion. (Original work published 1980)

Desvallées, A., & Mairesse, F. (2010). *Key concepts of museology* (S. Nash, Trans.). Armand Collin & ICOM – International Council of Museums. http://icom.museum/fileadmin/user_upload/pdf/Key_Concepts_of_Museology/Museologie_Anglais_BD.pdf

Dufresne-Tassé, C. (2018). Éducation, action culturelle, médiation. Trois concepts, trois groupes d'acteurs, trois silos dans le paysage québécois. In S. Wintzerith (Ed.), *Cultural action. Action culturelle. Acción cultural* (Vol. 28, pp. 109–128). ICOM-CECA: Smithsonian Center for Learning and Digital Access.

Duncan, C. (1995). *Civilizing rituals: Inside public art museums*. Routledge.

Kaitavuori, K., Kokkonen, L., & Sternfeld, N. (Eds.). (2013). *It's all mediating. Outlining and incorporating the roles of curating and education in the exhibition context* (Vol. 3). Cambridge Scholars Publishing. http://www.pedaali.fi

Livesey, G. (2010). Assemblage. In A. Parr (Ed.), *The Deleuze dictionary* (rev. ed., pp. 18–19). Edinburgh University Press.

Marks, J. (2010). Ethics. In A. Parr (Ed.), *The Deleuze dictionary* (rev. ed., pp. 87–89). Edinburgh University Press.

McClellan, A. (2008). *The art museum from Boullée to Bilbao*. University of California Press.

Mörsch, C. (Ed.). (2009). *Documenta 12. Education II. Between critical practice and visitor services*. Diaphanes.

Mörsch, C., & Chrusciel, A. (Eds.). (2012). *Time for cultural mediation*. Institute for Art Education of Zurich University of the Arts (ZHDK). https://www.kultur-vermittlung.ch/zeit-fuer-vermittlung/v1/?m=10&m2=8&lang=e

Paquin, M. (2015). Médiation culturelle au musée: Essai de théorisation d'un champ d'intervention professionnelle en pleine émergence. *Animation, Territoires et Pratiques Socioculturelles*, *8*, 103–115. https://edition.uqam.ca/atps/article/view/493/146

Paquin, M., & Lemay-Perreault, R. (2016). Typologie des médiations muséales: Des logiques d'intervention au registre d'actions culturelles. *Muséologies, 8*(2), 121–139.

Roy, K. (2003). *Teachers in nomadic spaces: Deleuze and curriculum*. Peter Lang.

Sauvagnargues, A. (2013). *Deleuze and art* (S. Bankston, Trans.). Bloomsbury.

Vancouver Art Gallery. (2014–2015). *Unscrolled: Reframing tradition in contemporary Chinese Art* [Exhibition]. Vancouver, Canada. https://www.vanartgallery.bc.ca/exhibitions/unscrolled-reframing-tradition-in-chinese-contemporary-art

Zhang, T. (2015). Unscrolled: Reframing tradition in Chinese contemporary art. *Yishu, 14*(5), 104–110.

Chapter 22

Learning Changes the Museum

Ricardo Marín-Viadel and Joaquín Roldán

Inquiry questions and description of the research problem

When someone learns something in a museum, that person changes, but the museum changes too. The assertion that works of art have the power to uniquely activate learning and emotion in museum visitors is akin to being axiomatic for art education and museum education research (Hudson Hill, 2020). We are not going to contradict such a statement; rather, our inquiry aims to reverse the direction between cause and effect. Instead of asking how museum artworks provoke learning in their visitors, we are asking – How does the learning of museum visitors provoke changes in the artworks exhibited in the museum?

What traces does learning leave on the works of art? How is it possible for the artworks to remain unchanged in the presence of the profound emotional and cognitive experience of their viewers? How can we visualize, through a collaborative artistic intervention, that our learning has transformed the museum's works of art? If we are changed due to our interaction with an artwork, we cannot then un-see, so in this way, the work has changed: that is, the artwork-as-experienced has changed.

This arts-based educational research project was developed as a collaboration between the Museum Casa de los Tiros in Granada and the University of Granada, Spain, to produce a collaborative intervention carried out jointly by university students, university professors and artists of the city in dialogue with the museum's director and conservation department on the theme "Art Education and Museum."

Beyond a foundation in academic literature, the idea of reversing the terms of the question about what changes when learning happens in the museum comes from literary works, especially from the short stories and tales of the Argentine writer Julio Cortazar (2001). The general atmosphere of the characters and events created by Cortazar intermingles insignificant real circumstances with a delightful fiction. A paradigmatic example of Cortazar's aesthetic-literary game was his inversion of the title of Jules Verne's 1872 novel *Around the World in Eighty Days*, which – in his book of short stories published in 1967 – Cortazar turned into *Around the Day in Eighty Worlds* (Cortazar, J. [1967]. *End of the game and other stories*). With this game of transpositions, he demonstrated that the sentence still made sense despite having exchanged the subject for the predicate and that this inversion provoked the appearance of a new parallel universe, which was intimate, candid and fascinating.

Of course, visitors-in-relation change the artworks that museums display. However, much of the concern of this relationality focuses on the security and conservation departments of art museums to prevent visitors from touching or breaking, either intentionally or next visit was face-to-face in medium-sized groups (according to museum regulations), with explanations, suggestions and subsequent discussion with museum professionals. This second face-to-face visit also had to be documented photographically by each student. As a synthesis of the three visits to the museum – the initial personal visit, the personal virtual visit and the guided group visit – a photographic report was organized, highlighting the work of art on which the intervention would be designed.

3. The third phase focused on the ideation, development and selection of the visual ideas proposed by each student. The students worked individually and in small groups in the university classroom for three two-hour sessions. Based on the notes and photographs obtained in the previous phase, the first ideas and visual sketches on the theme began to develop. Each individual project of intervention in the museum was elaborated and refined to reach its maximum expressiveness.

4. In making an initial selection of the intervention projects with museum pieces, students applied three criteria: (a) the artistic-educational quality of each intervention proposal, (b) its suitability to the conservation conditions and requirements of the artwork that would be intervened or modified and (c) a balanced distribution of interventions in each of the twelve rooms of the museum in addition to the hallway, the central courtyard, the main staircase and a room called the Cuadra Dorada, dedicated to lectures and poetry readings. In total, we had sixteen areas available for potential interventions. In agreement with those responsible for the museum, we negotiated a maximum of two interventions in each of the areas so as not to drastically change the usual atmosphere of the museum and make it unrecognizable. The interventions were to be sufficiently subtle so that the slight modifications could be noticed without difficulty, but at the same time always maintain the general appearance of each room and each work of art. The reaction to the final result depended on the subtlety of the interventions. If the modification was too noticeable and became the focal point of the room, then the goal of the proposal would disappear.

5. Students elaborated, refined and prepared the final design and production of the visual works. During this phase, the Granada artist Julio Juste participated due to his profound knowledge of the museum, as did Aurora Mateos, head of conservation, to definitively outline the suitability and feasibility of each intervention.

6. For the exhibition, all the students participated in the layout, labelling, signage and lighting of each intervention. The official opening ceremony and press conference followed the usual procedures of any other temporary exhibition in the museum.

7. The seventh and last phase corresponded with monitoring the exhibition and analysing how the public interacted with the intervened pieces.

Participants

This project involved 75 students from the Faculty of Education, 40 students from Fine Arts, 15 students from the master's programme in Visual Arts and Education and three professors from the Schools of Education and Fine Arts. Each person had to focus on a critical understanding of how the museum represented them, imagining how they would inhabit it and how their gaze transformed the works of art on display. As a result of their analysis, each person had to propose transformations of the artworks that represented their learning in the museum. Artistic interventions (photographs, performances and installations) would be exhibited alongside the artworks, delicately or abruptly transforming the museum.

Results

Interventions produced by students articulate the notion of transposition and suggest pedagogic potential in how the museum changes in relation to visitors. Student interventions were notably creative and extended the artworks in ways that embodied responsiveness.

For example, Nicolasa Navarrete devised and sewed a quilt of four square metres, with scraps of different printed fabrics over which she superimposed old photographs of her relatives transferred to acetate paper. This quilt was spread on the floor of the Cuadra Dorada room, where the coffered ceiling consists of carved and polychrome wood with the biography of several kings and queens of Spain, and with the mottos of the Granada-Venegas noble family, who constructed the building currently used by the museum. She established parallelism between the main characters of the history of her country, represented on the ceiling of the room, with the characters of her closest family ancestors. This comparison between stories (macro and micro stories) was an idea that guided many of the interventions.

Javier Navarro-Romero imagined that one of the queens, whose portraits hung on the walls of the main staircase, had forgotten her ruff on the sofa on the landing (Figure 22.1). He creates a charming ruff with white cloth laces, pigeon feathers and paper.

Another example of a critical intervention was created by Noemí Genaro-García in the room dedicated to romantic travellers, where she appropriated the furniture of a nineteenth-century bedroom, turning it into her own room and occupying it with her personal objects and clothes. During the exhibition, it was curious to observe the reaction of the public visiting the museum, who on more than one occasion cautiously backed away from entering the room, believing that they had inadvertently entered a person's private room. The museum building was an old family house, not exactly a palace, and the dimensions of the rooms correspond approximately to a large room. This domestic size facilitated the confusion between a public space and a private space.

In Figure 22.2, the student started with a photograph by José García-Ayola, part of a substantial collection of portraits of popular characters, streets and scenes of the Alhambra. She sought to introduce herself in the photograph by posing alongside the melancholic gypsy. Working with a digital copy of the original photograph, she took a self-portrait with her usual hairstyle, glasses and university dress. She kept the general greyish intonation of the albumen paper positives and very aptly positioned herself to the left of the gypsy woman. Because she positioned herself on her right, she did not destroy all the charm of

Figure 22.1: Ricardo Marín-Viadel and Joaquín Roldán, *The queen's ruffs*, 2021. Left, photo-essay composed of three photos: (1) top left corner, *Paper and metal*, 2009, (2) top left centre, Noemí Genaro, *Javier observes his piece from above*, 2009, (3) bottom left, Javier Navarro-Romero, *Coat of arms, portraits and ruffs*, 2009. Right, *Funerary crowns*. Installation with two sculptural pieces made of different types of paper, 60 cm in diameter approximately, on the second red sofa of the main staircase of the Museum Casa de los Tiros, which includes an indirect visual quotation (Anonymous, c.1601–1700).

Figure 22.2: *Old and contemporary photographs*, 2021. Photo-essay. Left, Ricardo Marín-Viadel and Joaquín Roldán, *Wall with old photographs of gypsies from Granada*, 2009. Right, Ana María Díaz-Rodríguez, *Gypsy and me*, 2009. Digital image composed of a self-portrait by the author and a visual quotation (García-Ayola, c. second half of the nineteenth century). Room 7, The Spanish Costumbrismo.

the character's gaze in the original photograph. The new photograph, unframed, was placed next to the ones that cover the walls of this room of the museum.

Inspired by a clay sculpture of a gypsy woman by Luis Molina-de-Haro, made in the first half of the twentieth century, primary teacher-training student Rocío Sánchez-Cano devised a sound photo-installation composed of three interventions (Figure 22.3). The

Figure 22.3: *Two thoughtful female figures*, 2021. Photo essay. Left, Rocío Sánchez-Cano and Joaquín Roldán, *Thoughts*, 2009: sound photo installation with one photograph, a printed acetate paper strip and an audio with the buzzing of a fly, which includes an indirect visual quotation (Molina-de-Haro, c.1901–1950). Right, Rocío Sánchez-Cano and Joaquín Roldán, *Student and sculpture* 2010: photomontage. Room 7 The Spanish Costumbrismo.

first was a photographic self-portrait, carefully studying the size, the general chromatic intonation and posture. This photograph was incorporated into the metal base on which the sculpture is exhibited. The second intervention consisted of printing a swarm of flies on a narrow strip of transparent acetate paper and placing it on top of the display case in which the sculpture was exhibited. The lighting in the room cast the flies' shadows on the forehead of the clay bust. Third, a small music player, hidden behind the glass case, filled the room with the faint but persistent buzzing of a fly. In Spanish, there is a sentence referring to a person who is self-absorbed or distracted by their own thoughts: *estar pensando en las moscas*, literally "be thinking about the flies," which could be equivalent in English to the expressions daydreaming or absent-minded.

Interventions also extended to religious iconography: for example, Lorena Raya-Rubia mixed her photographic self-portrait with the photograph she had taken of the carved wooden high relief of Our Lady of Sorrows. She simply placed her photograph on top of the antique piece of furniture next to another polychrome clay carving. The chromatic equivalence and the analogy between her wavy blonde hair and the fabrics surrounding the Virgin's head served to connect one image with the other. In another example, Nieves Tormo-Villareal devised their intervention by placing a small paper umbrella, like those commonly used in mixed drinks, in the hands of the figurine of a small naked child representing the Infant Jesus, lying on a very colourful carpet. The museum's display case exhibits several eighteenth and nineteenth-century polychrome clay devotional figures of the archangel Saint Gabriel and the Virgin Mary. The paper umbrella distorted the atmosphere of religious figures, transforming the scene in ways that harkened to a tourist beach, further enhanced by the figurine's carpet which, woven in horizontal stripes of bright colours, reds, blues and yellows and decorated with geometric figures, corresponds to the typical designs of the Alpujarra (mountainous area of Granada) from the sixteenth to the nineteenth centuries. These carpets were of varying colours because they were woven with scraps and rags of fabrics and used clothes. The similarity of the decorative style of these traditional carpets with the current fabrics and towels for sunbathing on the beach served to distort the general sense of the group of sculptures in that display case at the museum.

Discussion

As the artistic interventions by students were subtly integrated with the museum's original pieces, during the month-long exhibition the museum alerted visitors with a discreet sign at the entrance door:

> These interventions, which are all marked with a yellow label, have been made based on the ideas or emotions or memories that the artworks have aroused in their viewers. Some interventions are ironic, others are critical, but in all of them we have tried to unite the stories told by the museum with the personal experiences of its current visitors.

In the seven examples we have selected from among the 35 interventions that took place in the museum, it is clear that one of the main strategies for devising the interventions was to incorporate a self-portrait alongside the people represented in the museum's artworks. The quality of the results depended on how each person was able to understand in depth the formal, semantic, ideological and contextual qualities of each work of art in order to establish a visual dialogue with that piece of heritage from the present, producing a new and disturbing image for visitors to consider.

Acknowledgements

This publication has been possible thanks to the R+D+i project of the Ministry of Science and Innovation, Spanish Government, code PID2019-109990RB-I00, entitled "Methodologies of Social Intervention based on Visual Arts: Cultural Creation, Education, Inclusion and Heritage."

References

Anonymous. (*c*.1601–1700). *Retrato de la emperatriz Isabel* [Portrait]. Oil on canvas, 120 × 93 cm. Museum Casa de los Tiros, Granada. http://ceres.mcu.es/pages/Viewer?accion=4&AMuseo=MCTGR&Ninv=CE00821

Cortazar, J. (1967). *End of the game and other stories*. Pantheon Books.

Cortazar, J. (2001). *Cuentos completos, vol. 1* [Complete short stories, vol. 1 by Julio Cortazar]. (Spanish and English Edition). Alfaguara.

Diego, E. de. (2007). *Thomas Struth: Making time*. Museo del Prado.

France, P. E. (2019). *Reclaiming personalized learning: A pedagogy for restoring equity and humanity in our classrooms*. Crowin.

García-Ayola, J. (*c.* late 19th century). *Gitana* [Photograph]. Albumen hard copy, 21 × 15 cm. Museum Casa de los Tiros, Granada.

González-de-la-Oliva, F., & Hermoso-Romero, F. (2005). *Museo Casa de los Tiros de Granada: guía oficial*. Consejería de Cultura de la Junta de Andalucía.

Hudson Hill, S. (2020). A terrible beauty: Art and learning in the anthropocene. *Journal of Museum Education, 45*(1), 74–90. https://doi.org/10.1080/10598650.2020.1723357

Iser, W. (1978). *The act of reading: A theory of aesthetic response*. Johns Hopkins University Press.

Jasinski, I., & Lewis, T. E. (2016). The educational community as in-tentional community. *Studies in Philosophy and Education, 35*, 371–383. https://doi.org/10.1007/s11217-015-9480-5

Junta de Andalucía. (2018). *Museo Casa de los Tiros*. http://www.museosdeandalucia.es/web/museocasadelostirosdegranada/inicio

Kletchka, D. C. (2018). Toward post-critical museologies in U.S. Art Museums. *Studies in Art Education: A Journal of Issues and Research in Art Education, 59*(4), 297–310.

Krauss, R. E. (1985). *The originality of the avant-garde and other modernist myths*. MIT Press.

Malinin, L. H. (2016). Creative practices embodied, embedded, and enacted in architectural settings: Toward an ecological model of creativity. *Frontiers in Psychology*, 6. https://doi.org/10.3389/fpsyg.2015.01978

Marín-Viadel, R., & Roldán, J. (2019). A/r/tografía e investigación educativa basada en artes visuales en el panorama de las metodologías de investigación en educación. *Arte, Individuo y Sociedad, 31*(4), 881–895. https://doi.org/10.5209/aris.63409

Marín-Viadel, R., Roldán, J., & Caeiro-Rodríguez, M. (Eds.). (2020). *Learning to teach visual arts: An a/r/tographic approach*. Tirant.

Molina-de-Haro, L. (c.1901–1950). *Gitana* [Sculpture]. Clay, 42.50 × 22 × 25 cm. Museum Casa de los Tiros, Granada. http://ceres.mcu.es/pages/Viewer?accion=4&AMuseo=MCTGR&Ninv=CE00531

Sánchez-López, I., Pérez-Rodríguez, A., & Fandos-Igado, M. (2019). Com-educational platforms: Creativity and community for learning. *Journal of New Approaches in Educational Research, 8*(2), 214–226. https://doi.org/10.7821/naer.2019.7.437

Sinner, A., Irwin, R. L., & Jokela, T. (Eds.). (2018). *Visually provoking: Dissertations in art education*. Lapland University Press.

Chapter 23

Encounters on the Fringe of a Museum Tour: *Trailing Behind* as a Site of Affective Intensities

Keven Lee, Melissa Park and Marilyn Lajeunesse

The Montreal Museum of Fine Arts in Canada created the programme *Sharing the Museum* in 1999, in which visitors who are "not-your-typical museum-goer" (CBC News, 2019) are invited for free guided tours and workshops. Such initiatives have shifted the perception of museums as empty repositories for the elite towards considering them as places for learning, social engagement and wellness for everyone (Camic et al., 2014). The Museum of Modern Art in New York started *Meet Me at MoMA* in 2006 for persons living with Alzheimer's disease and related disorders. This led to a proliferation of such programmes, with subsequent research documenting increases in socialization and improved mood for those with the disease and their carers (Belver et al., 2018; Rosenberg, 2009; Smiraglia, 2016).

In 2009, Marilyn Lajeunesse, the Adults and Community Groups programme officer at the Montreal Museum of Fine Arts, created *Art Links* in collaboration with the Alzheimer's Society of Montréal. *Art Links* is specifically designed for caregivers and persons living with Alzheimer's to take a break from their daily schedule and get together to talk, laugh and create. The thematic tour of three to five artworks is followed by a gathering in an art workshop for refreshments and an activity in which participants can explore elements of the preceding experience. Like other programmes, *Art Links* is designed to create a welcoming environment, promote wellness and counter isolation as well as stigmatization, and research shows that visits are experienced as a space of belonging (Fortune, 2021). In this chapter, we focus on what happens at the margins of the tour, what we are calling *trailing behind* and what it can provide.

Trailing behind as a perplexing particular

To understand what might be at stake at the margins of the tour, we use critical phenomenology 2.0 (Mattingly, 2019) and focus on the *perplexing particulars* that emerged during *Art Links* tours. Drawing upon Hannah Arendt's work on defrosting concepts, Mattingly defines this as "an experience-near process of concept destabilisation" (p. 416) to highlight the critical potential of phenomenology to unsettle the concepts attached to phenomena under investigation. She proposes that anthropology's attention to descriptive details makes it a discipline well-suited for concept destabilization. While Arendt's defrosting method involves raising questions, Mattingly's critical phenomenology attends to surprising, yet concrete encounters that question taken-for-granted concepts and "guards against their ossification" (p. 432). What makes a "particular" perplexing is when its concreteness and singularity cannot be reduced to a general concept or contained by a general category, thus both revealing and opening their limits. We focus on two *Art Links* tours from an ethnography of persons living with Alzheimer's and their carers to closely examine what happens when *trailing behind* at the margins of the museum tour. Drawing from Keven's fieldnotes (in italics) of his participant observations of Alfred and his friend Claire,[1] we illustrate how surprising encounters, as perplexing particulars, ask us to reconsider concepts that we take for granted.

"I Feel so Calm"

Fifteen minutes before the tour starts, Keven meets Claire and Alfred.

> Claire is about 5 feet tall with shoulder-length blond hair. When she talks, her voice is steady and calm, her body remaining quite still. In contrast, Alfred's height of 5 foot 10 inches, his fuzzy greyish hair that stands on end, and his personality give the impression that he towers over her. Rhythm and changes in tonality punctuate his speech, and his rapid gestures accentuate the sense of him being in perpetual movement. He calls himself "motor mouth," explaining that "when you have a motor it just keeps going, and going, and going, and going. That's me. I drive people crazy!" As a retired teacher, he proudly boasts how well-suited he was for this job, saying, "I was getting paid to do what I love best. Talk to people."

It is 2 p.m., and the tour starts. Alfred and Claire go with the first group in the elevator, already nearing capacity. Keven boards the second elevator.

> Catching up with the first group, I see Alfred alone, standing still on the interior bridge connecting two museum pavilions. Claire has already crossed the bridge and is in the adjacent gallery. Beyond her, the first half of the group is already headed towards the next gallery. Alfred is looking at something that is out of my sight.

Keven makes his way onto the bridge.

> Close to the edge of the bridge, there is a 6-foot-tall oval sculpture made from black material. The sculpture is backlit by the natural light coming through the windows all around. I walk by Alfred, who is looking at it. His stillness compels me to stop and face him.

About ten seconds of silence pass:

ALFRED: "How beautiful… I feel so calm."

> Intrigued by his statement, I turn my whole body towards the sculpture, to be oriented in the same direction. At first, the sculpture remains as a tall, uniform black oval shape.

After a few seconds, my eyes get accustomed to the light. We are silent. A minute passes. Distinct features of a delicate and elongated face of a person, of a woman, slowly emerge. Soft lines appear and delineate the contours of the nose and gently closed eyes and lips, with no apparent sense of muscle tension.

The black material absorbs the diffused light, camouflaging the topography of the face. The sign indicates that the sculpture is Jaume Plensa's *Chloé in Barcelona* (2014).

ALFRED: "I feel so calm."

KEVEN: "What is it that makes you feel calm?"

ALFRED: "I am not quite sure…"

I am unsure what he says next, but I recall also feeling calm at that moment.

Alfred's stillness, separation from the group, and quietness are surprising. The shifts from non-stop punctuated talking to silence, from constant movement to calmness and from being in the centre of a group to being alone are perplexing particulars.

Fostering ambiguity

According to Mattingly (2019), the perplexing particular "eludes explanation" (p. 427), raising questions about the taken-for-granted. In the case of tours like *Art Links*, objectives like "countering isolation" underscore assumptions about persons living with Alzheimer's and related disorders being alone. In addition, "wandering" stresses the potential danger of their being alone when not with the group (Solomon & Lawlor, 2018). Yet, Alfred's repetition of "calm" and engagement with the artwork represent what one expects of a gallery tour. He is also not alone. If, at first, *trailing behind* can evoke an image of being left behind, close attention to concrete particulars shows how Alfred is actually *central* to a museum tour. By drawing Keven into close observations of an artwork, Alfred enacts his role as a teacher, perhaps even an arts educator who gets Keven to notice details and have an experience of calmness. The singularity of this moment questions categorical assumptions about what a museum tour for persons with Alzheimer's ought to attain as well as about the category of "Alzheimer's" itself.

In *Art Links*, Claire is always in-between Alfred and the group, keeping an eye on both to make sure he stays within its proximity. Yet, close attention to this phenomenon as it emerges in other contexts of Alfred's life also shows how Claire contributes to *trailing behind* by being *slightly ahead*, by a few steps, which helps Alfred know which direction to go. She has learned the hard way to not pressure him when he stops to talk to passers-by or comment on the things he sees. Whenever she does pressure him to keep going, Alfred gets angry and then needs time to calm down. To avoid these disagreements, Claire always makes sure to add an hour to their commute time. One time, to catch his attention, she even stepped out of the bus while Alfred was still inside talking to strangers. He then got off at the next stop. Actual life outside the museum does not allow her to always stay with Alfred, especially if they are late for an appointment or he needs to make his way home. Recently, she started to organize for adapted transport to take him to *Art Links* and other events when she cannot go with him. These concrete particulars raise other questions about *trailing behind*, especially in relation to Alfred.

> Over time, Claire asks if I will participate in Art Links with Alfred. Florence, the art therapist, also asks me, explaining that Alfred is "not an easy participant." He is always talking and often behind the group. This sets an expectation for me to help him stay with the tour, creating tension within me. Do I push him to join the tour or trail behind it with him?

If a critical phenomenological lens helped identify *trailing behind* as a perplexing particular in the museum, we turn to affect theory to explore the embodied tension Keven experiences when asked to be Alfred's companion several *Art Links* later.

Trailing behind as a site of affective intensity

Gregg and Seigworth (2009) claim no one thing can be called affect theory since "affect and its theorisation [...] will exceed, always exceed the context of their emergence" (p. 5). To understand the implications of Keven's experience of tension and Alfred's attentiveness, we first draw upon "stickiness" and "orientation" (Ahmed, 2010, 2014a, 2014b) to underline the place of the body in how we move towards or away from our surroundings. We then turn to Massumi's (2002) concept of "resonance" to underscore how the multiplicity of relations in-between objects – both living and non-living – that, even if easily missed, are experienced as intensity.

"That is much better for me!"

Ahmed (2010, 2014a) speaks of affect as "sticky" in two ways. First, affect binds objects together, engaging or sustaining relations. Affect also sticks to objects through histories of contact. Through sustained relations and "stickiness," objects become affective. Taking happiness as a starting point, Ahmed (2010) suggests that certain objects even hold the promise of affecting us in "the best way" (p. 22). The tendency to pursue an object or not is what she refers to as an "orientation," and a "good" orientation would be to "be oriented in the right way towards the right objects" (p. 34).

> It is almost 2 p.m. The tour is about to begin, still no signs of Alfred. I finally find him and Lisa, another participant, at the museum café two levels up from where we usually gather. Alfred

greets me, then tells me how "upset" he is at the adapted transportation, which dropped them off "way too early," in comparison to the usual. It is now 2:10 p.m. I tell them that the group is waiting for us. Lisa announces she has to go to the washroom. So does Alfred. I wonder, what is the quickest way to the group, since both Alfred and Lisa use walking aids.

The more direct way out of the café requires taking a staircase, while another route involves walking through the restaurant to a set of elevators.

As we walk through the restaurant, we come across a friend of mine. Lisa, slightly ahead of me, stops and turns her head as I introduce them, adding, "We're here for an organized tour of the Calder exhibit, to which we are already late." Alfred starts telling his story about how hard it's been living with Alzheimer's, "In a year, no sport, no more girlfriend, no more motorcycle!" I am caught in-between Lisa, who wants to join the group, and Alfred, who wants to stay and talk.

Alfred is stuck to the conversation in the way that Ahmed speaks of affect as being sticky, as what binds together.

KEVEN: "The group is waiting on us to begin the tour, so is Lisa."

ALFRED: "That is much better for me! (pointing towards my friend and her companion). I'm always alone at home. Meeting new people is good for me."

Alfred is stuck.

I remember Alfred saying, in an earlier interview, "My best therapy is if I can make people smile." I tell Alfred that I will take Lisa to the group. On my way back to him, I come across the art therapist, Florence, who had found him in the interim, and she tells me that Alfred does not want to go on the tour. As I arrive back, I see Alfred, my friend, and her companion talking and smiling.

This moment creates tension within Keven between competing orientations or "goods," between the promise of a tour designed to decrease isolation and the promise of what can happen when *trailing behind*. Yet at this moment, Alfred is no longer "alone at home." He is oriented to what he considers his "best" therapy, making others smile. Affect theory helps illuminate that which might affect us "in the best way" (Ahmed, 2010, p. 22), and by what may be hidden in the first place. If the *Art Links* tour promises the enjoyment of being with others, Alfred finds this very object by *trailing behind* it. "After my friends depart, I text Florence to locate the group, taking Alfred to meet them in a room of Alexander Calder's brightly coloured metal sculptures and mobiles."

In the next section, we turn to examine this tension between competing orientations as the affective intensity of resonance.

"They are all moving!"

Massumi (2002) says that resonance is what gives substance to the space between objects. Resonance is not linear; the relation between an object and itself complicates the relation between that object and other objects. Likewise, feeling comes with having a feeling, with having a feeling. It is continually complicating itself. This is what Massumi would refer to as resonance, in which "sensation is never simple. It is always doubled by the feeling of having a feeling. It is self-referential" (p. 13). The exhibit of Calder's sculptures provides the ideal context to trace how stillness can also be felt as intensity of resonance.

> We find the group in a large, white-walled room. Calder's sculptures and mobiles are lit so that they project shadows all around. I walk around by myself, getting immersed. After a moment, I look around to notice that Alfred is sitting in a corner of the room, looking in front of him at a fish mobile made from metal and wires that is hanging from the ceiling. I walk over to him. He doesn't turn, but points to the wall, saying:

ALFRED: "The fishes are amazing ... How is that even possible?"

Only one fish is suspended from the ceiling. However, the use of the plural form of the word, fishes, directs attention to the shadows projected on the walls.

KEVEN: "Did you know that museum lighting is an art in itself?" (pointing at the moveable lights and the tracking system).

ALFRED: "How incredible!" (still looking at the wall).

Alfred's insistence – "amazing," "incredible" – alludes to the intensity that Massumi (2002) relates to resonance as the back-and-forth movement in-between the surfaces of objects that, like an echo, reverberate in-between surfaces into an intensity that is felt:

> An echo, for example, cannot occur without a distance between surfaces for the sounds to bounce from. But the resonation is not on the wall. It is in the emptiness between them. […] With the body, the "walls" are the sensory surfaces. The intensity is experience.
> (Massumi, 2002, p. 14)

This rising intensity points our attention to what is happening between the sensory surfaces of his body, the fish and the shadows.

KEVEN: "What about the *fishes*?"

ALFRED: "How incredible they are. They are all moving." Yet the shadows are not moving.
    Sylvie, a caregiver, overhears the exchange.

Sylvie: "This is truly beautiful. At 2:45 p.m., they usually make the sculptures spin, and the shadows are all moving."

Alfred: "Why didn't we come for that?!"

Alfred's query suggests the opposite of his earlier claim that the shadows "are all moving."

Keven: "The lights are all moveable."

Alfred: (*interrupting*) "How incredible the fishes are!"

The repetition of "incredible" and heightened tonality of his voice underscores the intensity felt by Alfred. For Ahmed (2014a), emotion presses upon our bodies and involves "affective forms of reorientation" (p. 8). Alfred's emotionality presses upon and reorients Keven's attention away from the lights:

Keven: "Tell me about the fishes."

Alfred: "They are all moving."

In what appears to be stillness, the allusion to movement stresses that resonance is not only occurring between Alfred and the shadows but also extends to what is happening in-between the shadows themselves.

> A single suspended fish projects three shadows onto two different walls. They each have a different size and direction. From left to right, the first shadow is almost horizontal and parallel to the floor, as if heading towards the other two. The following shadow is slightly lower, with its head pointing downward, as if plunging into waters' depths. The last shadow overlaps across two walls: its body on the left wall, while its head is on the right. This fish's body points downward while its head points upward, as if about to jump out of the water.

The echoes rebound in-between all the surfaces – the surfaces of the suspended fish, the shadow of each of the three fish, the wall itself, Alfred and Keven. This reverberation is a movement that, according to Massumi (2002), *is* intensity, converting the distance between surfaces into a sense of immediacy: "Resonation […] is a qualitative transformation of distance into an immediacy of self-relation" (p. 14). As the distance between Alfred and this sculpture is reduced, he is immersed in the immediacy of the relations in which he finds himself. These qualitative transformations, the resonance that links him to what is before and around him, also illustrate how the simple act of turning one's body towards another's orientation gives Keven an entry into an experience of intensity. In this qualitative transformation *with* another, *trailing behind* opens a window onto a world of relations in which Alfred is no longer behind but at its very centre.

Coda: Trailing behind *With*

We began with a surprising encounter: Alfred standing alone in the middle of an interior bridge. Although the group kept going, he felt calm even if uncertain about what held him in place. Yet, Alfred's "I feel so calm" embodies a break from the push of a daily schedule, while his "incredible" signifies the enjoyment that *Art Links* is designed to achieve. Critical phenomenology helped illuminate these moments as perplexing particulars that unsettle expectations of where and when moments that lead to "a break, to talk, laugh, and create together" occur. For Alfred, such moments often occurred when *trailing behind*. To understand the intensity of experience in those moments demanded another kind of attention.

Affect theory highlighted the world of relations that kept Alfred in place; those relations which are in-between objects can go unnoticed at first glance. The concepts of stickiness and orientation delineated how it might be the "promise" of an object (e.g. putting smiles on people's faces) that contributes to Alfred's *trailing behind*. Even when he is behind the group, he is "never alone" (Massumi, 2015, p. 6). He is in a world of relations with everything the museum has to offer, such as artworks, other passers-by, shadows and many other surfaces. The intensity of the experience – articulated in Alfred's repetitions of "amazing," "incredible" and "they are all moving!" – gives him a place to inhabit where he is simultaneously orienting and oriented: "What moves us, what makes us feel, is also that which holds us in place, or gives us a dwelling place" (Ahmed, 2014a, p. 11). In contrast with his relatively recent challenging experience of "no sports, no girlfriend, no motorcycle!" and having to take adaptive transportation that he associates with Alzheimer's, his "I feel so calm" and experiences of wonder give him that dwelling place.

When Keven pauses or lingers near him, he invites Alfred's initial reflections on the calm he felt with Chloe and the wonder he experienced with the fishes. Yet, it is Alfred's insistence that awakens something in Keven, compelling him to turn his whole body to align with Alfred's own, orienting to what was there right in front of him. For Ahmed (2014b), orientation is not just how we tend towards or away from certain objects; it is also "how we begin, how we proceed from 'here'" (p. 95). A shift in bodily orientation could result in ways of proceeding from here. Instead of feeling the pull of *what is the right thing to do* or trying to explain the craft of illuminating art, Keven is now *with* Alfred. Together, they witness the beauty of still, yet moving, shadows on the walls. The "right" orientation may be less about the tour or trailing behind, and more about how cultivating the museum as a place of dwelling *with* others attends to such moments of affective intensity.

Let us propose *trailing behind-with* as not merely tagging along but an experience in which we turn our bodies towards what is at stake for one another, towards what is already actually there. In those moments of affective intensity, Alfred is no longer *trailing behind*. He is at the very centre, supported by the underlying values of "fluidity" and "organicity" of *Art Links*, which welcomes the unexpected instances of spontaneity that happen inside or outside the written scenario. Allowing such moments to emerge in-between objects and others allows for a shift in Alfred's position: from someone who is "not easy" and who used to be admired by his students to one who puts smiles on the faces of others and points out hidden and complex worlds of movement and relations. So how do we proceed from here? What if museums could be thought of as spaces in which bodies – living or non-living – are appreciated as *affecting* as much as they are affected?

Note

1. Ethical approval was received by McGill's Faculty of Medicine IRB. We have given pseudonyms to participants, other than our co-author Keven.

References

Ahmed, S. (2010). *The promise of happiness*. Duke University Press.

Ahmed, S. (2014a). *The cultural politics of emotion* (2nd ed.). Edinburgh University Press.

Ahmed, S. (2014b). Mixed orientations. *Subjectivity*, 7(1), 92–109.

Belver, M. H., Ullán, A. M., Avila, N., Moreno, C., & Hernández, C. (2018). Art museums as a source of well-being for people with dementia: An experience in the Prado Museum. *Arts & Health*, 10(3), 213–226.

Camic, P. M., Tischler, V., & Pearman, C. H. (2014). Viewing and making art together: A multi-session art-gallery-based intervention for people with dementia and their carers. *Aging & Mental Health*, 18(2), 161–168. https://doi.org/https://doi.org/10.1080/13607863.2013.818101

CBC News. (2019, September 24). *How Montreal's Museum of Fine Arts has attracted a broader visitor base*. https://www.cbc.ca/news/canada/montreal/sharing-montreal-museum-of-fine-arts-in-20th-year-1.5294688

Fortune, D. (2021). Envisioning museums as welcoming spaces for belonging. In T. D. Glover & E. K. Sharpe (Eds.), *Leisure communities: Rethinking mutuality, collective identity and belonging in the new century* (pp. 181–191). Routledge.

Gregg, M., & Seigworth, G. J. (2009). An inventory of shimmers. In M. Gregg & G. J. Seigworth (Eds.), *The affect theory reader* (pp. 1–25). Duke University Press.

Massumi, B. (2002). *Parables for the virtual: Movement, affect, sensation*. Duke University Press.

Massumi, B. (2015). *Politics of affect*. Polity Press.

Mattingly, C. (2019). Defrosting concepts, destabilising doxa: Critical phenomenology and the perplexing particular. *Anthropological Theory*, 19(4), 415–439. https://doi.org/https://doi.org/10.1177/1463499619828568

Plensa, J. (2014). *Chloe in Barcelona*. Montreal Museum of Fine Arts.

Rosenberg, F. (2009). The MoMA Alzheimer's Project: Programming and resources for making art accessible to people with Alzheimer's disease and their caregivers. *Arts & Health, 1*(1), 93–97.

Smiraglia, C. (2016). Targeted museum programs for older adults: A research and program review. *Curator: A Quarterly Publication of the American Museum of Natural History, 59*(1), 39–54.

Solomon, O., & Lawlor, M. C. (2018). Beyond V40. 31: Narrative phenomenology of wandering in autism and dementia. *Culture, Medicine and Psychiatry, 42*(2), 206–243.

Chapter 24

The Educational Turn and A/r/tography: An Interplay Between Curating, Education and Artmaking

A Visual Essay

Jaime Mena and Guadalupe Pérez-Cuesta

This visual essay addresses how audiences and educators assume an active role in the definition of curatorial discourses in the a/r/tographic exhibition *Art for Learning Art*,[1] held annually at the Museo Memoria de Andalucía, Granada, Spain, since 2013 (Figure 24.1). The exhibition is developed as part of research projects that aim to present novel encounters between arts and pedagogy. Primary and secondary students participate, as do university students, families and adults who attend the exhibition.

In terms of form, this visual essay is organized by means of photographic pairs. The dialogue established between the internal elements of each image creates a specific narrative that leads to the exploration and argumentation of ideas (Marín-Viadel et al., 2017). The images are not illustrations of the text, nor does the text explain the images. In a/r/tographic research, visual creation and writing are two interconnected forms of enquiring that generate meaning together (Irwin, 2013).

Figure 24.1: J. Mena & G. Pérez-Cuesta, *Building the exhibition*, 2021. Left, G. Pérez-Cuesta, *Cortés and the audience*, 2017. Right, G. Pérez-Cuesta, *Art-cards*, 2017.

Propositions for Museum Education

The a/r/tographic exhibition as a response to the educational turn

In 2008, the researcher and curator Irit Rogoff defined the educational turn as a curating trend that is seeking more participatory exhibition formats. According to Rogoff, curators face the challenge of rethinking the significance of their main attributes (collect, preserve, show, visualize, discuss, contextualize, criticize, advertise and showcase) to blur the gaps between art, exhibition displays and people (Figure 24.2). The aim is to redefine museums and art centres as platforms for experimentation and learning based on an interdisciplinary, flexible approach that integrates curatorial research, artistic intervention, pedagogy and audience participation (Tallant, 2010). The traditional idea of a spectator is replaced by an empowered audience that acts by means of enquiring, interpreting and making within an interdisciplinary exhibition space conceived as a cultural ecosystem (Rogoff, 2008; Tišliar, 2017).

Although educational events are gaining presence in museums and art centres, curators keep conceptualizing exhibitions and events so that they are the ones who establish the role of the audience and educators in the cultural project (Christensen-Scheel, 2018; Graham et al., 2016). In order to bring curators, educators and visitors closer, a/r/tographic practice conceives of events not only as spaces for exchange between the institution and the audience but also as actions that promote equivalences between the artistic creation and educational process, giving rise to horizontal relationships among the artworks, the exhibition discourse and the audience and educators (Irwin, 2013; Roldán & Marín-Viadel, 2014). In this sense,

Figure 24.2: J. Mena & G. Pérez-Cuesta, *Concept*, 2021. Photos: Left, G. Pérez-Cuesta, *Taking Part*, 2017; right: *Making*, 2017.

Figure 24.3: J. Mena & G. Pérez-Cuesta, *Action*, 2021. Photos: Left: G. Pérez-Cuesta, *Gaze*, 2017. Right: G. Pérez-Cuesta, *Picasso's transparency*, 2017.

our a/r/tographic exhibition is organized by means of micro-events. The micro-event is a short-term meeting for small groups that promotes a dialogue by means of artmaking. The museum educator offers the audience some specific materials (e.g. vinyl letters or decks of cards) through which they encourage an artistic way of encountering artworks. Each micro-event has its own autonomy, but when it is added to other micro-events of the exhibition, each acquires a more complex dimension as it is enriched by the rest of the proposals. The result of these micro-events is a creation that integrates as one the artwork, the audience's artistic reading and the exhibit design (Figure 24.3).

Final considerations

The exhibition not only represents a framework for developing pedagogical artworks through which school and high school students, as well as families and adults, may approach art education by means of metaphorical and aesthetic positions (Roldán & Marín-Viadel, 2014), but also makes it possible to reflect on curatorial strategies and participatory formats and strategies. If

Figure 24.4: *Making the Exhibition*, J. Mena, J. & G. Pérez-Cuesta, 2021. Photos: Top, G. Pérez-Cuesta, 2017, *On-going*. Bottom: G. Pérez-Cuesta, 2017, *Layout*.

the educational turn asks about the capacity of artistic and curatorial practices to place people at the core of the curatorial project, a/r/tography consolidates the centralization of people in the museum experience (Figure 24.4). The balance of the exhibition moves forward from the object to people, placing events as fundamental processes that call on audiences, educators and curators to take part in the exhibition as researchers, artists, learners and teachers. The exhibition is disclosed as a form of living inquiry, of which only its beginning is known because its end is determined by the inquisitiveness and activity of visitors, educators and curators.

Note

1. http://www.arteparaaprender.org

References

Christensen-Scheel, B. (2018). An art museum in the interest of publicness: A discussion of educational strategies at Tate Exchange. *International Journal of Lifelong Education*, *37*(1), 103–119. https://doi.org/10.1080/02601370.2017.1406544

Graham, J., Graziano, V., & Kelly, S. (2016). The educational turn in art. *Performance Research*, *21*(6), 29–35. https://doi.org/10.1080/13528165.2016.1239912

Irwin, R. L. (2013). Becoming a/r/tography. *Studies in Art Education*, *54*(3), 198–215. https://doi.org/10.1080/00393541.2013.11518894

Marín-Viadel, R., Roldán, J., & Genet, R. (2017). Photo pairs in arts-based research and artistic research. In R. Marín-Viadel & J. Roldán (Eds.), *Visual ideas: Arts based research and artistic research* (pp. 70–85). Editorial Universidad de Granada.

Rogoff, I. (2008, November). Turning. *E-Flux Journal*, *00*. https://www.e-flux.com/journal/00/68470/turning/

Roldán, J., & Marín-Viadel, R. (2014). Visual a/r/tography in art museums. *Visual Inquiry*, *3*(2), 172–188. https://doi.org/10.1386/vi.3.2.172_1

Tallant, S. (2010). Experiments in integrated programming. In P. O'Neill & M. Wilson (Eds.), *Curating and the educational turn* (pp. 186–194). Open Editions/De Appel.

Tišliar, P. (2017). The development of informal learning and museum pedagogy in museums. *European Journal of Contemporary Education*, *6*(3), 586–592. https://doi.org/10.13187/ejced.2017.3.586

Chapter 25

Redescribing Territories: Inhabiting the Continuum of Art Production and Education

Lene Crone Jensen and Hilde Østergaard

In recent decades, the relation between young people and art institutions has progressively developed in line with the emphasis on creating a culture of participation and diversity, thereby strengthening the institutions' legitimacy as democratic and inclusive formation spaces. For most art institutions, however, the involvement of young people is primarily associated with classical educational activities that complement the curriculum, affirming knowledge and values associated with current exhibitions in the institution and privileged, often academically based statement positions. Only to a lesser extent have initiatives and co-creation with young people – based on their lives, competencies and world views – been integrated into exhibitions or events with an authority and legitimacy that signals the activity and content could be relevant to a larger audience. In other words, Eileen Hooper-Greenhill's

Figure 25.1: E. B. Itso, *Black Square*, 2020. Collaboration with students from FGU Copenhagen. *Down to Earth*, Photographic Center. Photo by E. B. Itso, 2020. Copyright: E. B. Itso.

From a curatorial point of view, our aspiration to create new territories is also an attempt to form a new community of practice as formulated by the Swiss learning theorist Etienne Wenger (1998). And it is our goal to create a base for making sense within this new community, to use the American organizational theorist Karl E. Weick's (1995) concept of sensemaking. In the following, we analyse our methods using their theories as a backdrop, with KUNST:form's project *Down to Earth* as an example.

Down to Earth

Down to Earth was created in collaboration with Danish artist E. B. Itso, Fotografisk Center and a group of students from FGU Copenhagen: a preparatory, craft-based school for young people aged 16–25. The students all have social, personal or curricular challenges that have delayed a direct path in standardized education, and instead, they take extra time to explore future possibilities through basic academic subjects as well as craft-based teaching – for instance, in visual art.

The purpose of the project was to make an exhibition at Fotografisk Center in line with KUNST:form's methods of production. The exhibition was conceptualized by E. B. Itso and consisted of artworks created through a collaboration between the artist and the students. Students also took part in tasks involving communication and education. The project thus embraced both formats: Commissioned Works and Behind the Scenes.

The title of the exhibition was inspired by the French philosopher and anthropologist, Bruno Latour's (2017) book of the same name, *Où atterrir?* (English title: *Down to Earth*). Latour argues that to understand who we are and where we are going, we must think of social challenges along with questions of ecology, land and territories. In his geopolitical theory, Latour shows how the current climate and socio-economic crises highlight the link among territories, power and privilege of the ruling and increasingly wealthy classes; at the same time, he points out the need to draw a map of new positions for the earthly, where all concerned can live together. For KUNST:form, this way of thinking includes territories within the art world: to act wisely and care for the earth, it is imperative for young people, as well as other underrepresented citizens, to have a bigger influence. Our positions need to be rethought.

With these ideas as a backdrop, the participants in *Down to Earth* became engaged in what Etienne Wenger (1998) defines as a community of practice, or a space and a model for the development of knowledge, identity and meaning. Such communities are characterized by three conditions. They are all based on mutual engagement, "in actions whose meanings they negotiate with one another" (Wenger, 1998, p. 73). They involve a joint enterprise, "defined by the participants in the very process of pursuing it" (p. 77). And finally, the community of practice consists of a shared repertoire that "reflects a history of mutual engagement," and which "remains inherently ambiguous" (p. 83). By virtue of their points of departure, be they professional and/or areas of responsibility, the process involved students and artists and curators gradually redefining and adjusting roles for the execution of the project (the joint enterprise), as well as the meanings, procedures, techniques, methods and language that were built up throughout the project (shared repertoire).

Ownership and co-creation: Commissioned work as a format

While the curatorial framework was set by KUNST:form, the artistic framework was defined by E. B. Itso. A recurring feature of his work is an investigation of the city and how people adapt to and use public space. In our case, this involved a series of twelve workshops taking place over three months before the exhibition. As part of these workshops, E. B. Itso organized site-specific performative interventions in which the young people participated as protagonists. The interventions took place in an area close to the school once known as "the Black Quadrangle" in Copenhagen, which in the 1980s was a centre of the "BZ movement" house occupations.

The series of interventions was based on the movement's alternative urban strategies, historical events, situations from everyday life and the struggle for affordable housing. The students were instructed to perform specific, simple actions, using a new main material for each intervention that symbolically restaged an incident, gesture or place that was meaningful to the squatter movement. For example, E. B. Itso and the young people from FGU set up a huge black piece of cloth across a street (Figure 25.1) that blocked off all traffic around the spot where, in 1983, a group of squatters escaped from an occupied house through a tunnel they had dug under the street while an estimated 1000 police were preparing to clear the house. It was a spectacular event that won the admiration of many people and the media, and today there are still marks from the tunnel in the asphalt. The interventions, or re-enactments, were documented by E. B. Itso, and with the students' interventions were turned into photographic works, videos and installations. The final works were influenced by their collaboration and the unpredictable process that took shape and made sense along the way.

The fact that the young people knew very little about this era and the stories that, for older generations, have passed into Copenhagen mythology was an aspect that challenged the process of what Karl E. Weick has called "sensemaking" in this new community of practice. Sensemaking, according to Weick (1995), involves the process of creating a strong narrative that can contribute to uniting an otherwise loosely organized group of people and reducing the uncertainty and ambiguity that might arise in the group. Weick (1995) does not provide a recipe or any fixed method but reminds us that sensemaking is an ongoing project that must be continually adjusted.

In the context of *Down to Earth*, it was the role of KUNST:form to fill in the gaps in communication and identify how student involvement could be developed – and in turn, to think of actions supporting E. B Itso's artistic ideas in the best ways possible. This we did by continuously combining the workshops with presentations, evaluations and dialogue about relevant topics, as well as more improvised actions that identified priorities in the process.

To begin with, the artistic project was abstract and a little difficult for the students. But for each performative act, E. B. Itso's intentions were embodied and made into something personal. Besides participating in the interventions, the workshops required the students' active involvement in finding materials or formulating content more visibly. Defining a word that for them signified an important value today is one example. They came up with the expression LIGE NU with the double meaning right now, equality now (Figure 25.2a). The expression was used in a play with letters on wooden boards placed along a façade in a busy street, close to what was once a bank and a target for the squatters' protests against capitalism. But even a simple intervention with the students walking around with cardboard boxes on their heads, which E. B. Itso had been inspired to perform through different historic material, became an embodiment of various individual, existential thoughts (Figure 25.2b).

In the later workshops, students' commitment increased and ownership of the actions belonged more to the community. Eventually, the students themselves formed a performative intervention and created a work for the exhibition (Figure 25.3). Here, the focal point became what they had evolved in conversations and from input on the interventions: today's lack of care between people and lack of interest in each other in a public space. Although it was an independent work, the link to interventions conceptualized by E. B. Itso was obvious. The cardboard boxes, for instance, reappeared but in a new storyline. The sensemaking and shared repertoire that reflected the mutual commitments of the students, E. B. Itso, KUNST:form and FGU in this new community of practice was taking form.

In other words, with each workshop, the five factors that Karl E. Weick has described as a prerequisite for sensemaking became more pronounced: *effectuation* (it must happen in practice, show, don't tell), *triangulation* (we must be able to understand it in several ways), *affiliation* (more people must contribute or join the processes of sensemaking), *deliberation* (it requires plenty of time for consideration) and finally *consolidation* (we create a common context about the meaning) (Weick, 2001). Triangulation and affiliation had a particular focus for KUNST:form because these qualities relate to a recognition of the group's differences, ability to see things from more perspectives and the fact that work requires everyone to contribute before it makes sense. Repeated dialogue and evaluation, where we could get a sense of both the students and the artist, were seminal.

Not unexpectedly, one issue discussed by the students was the extent to which they were just "extras" in E. B. Itso's project or had real influence. It was also a question the young people did not agree on. In 1992, the child-rights academic and sociologist Roger Hart (1992) described participation as a continuum between tokenism and citizenship – depending on the degree of real influence, not only on fixed content but on the rules and structures behind it. From our ongoing dialogue and evaluation with the young people in *Down to Earth*, it became apparent that they experienced being at both ends of this continuum, but gradually came to see their contribution as more and more influential, even when disagreeing. They

Figure 25.2: (Above) E. B. Itso, *LIGE NU/RIGHT NOW*, 2020. Photo by E. B. Itso, 2020. Copyright: E. B. Itso. **(Below)** E. B. Itso, *Untitled*, 2020. Photo/video by E. B. Itso, 2020. Copyright: E. B. Itso. Both in collaboration with students from FGU Copenhagen. *Down to Earth*, Photographic Center, 2020.

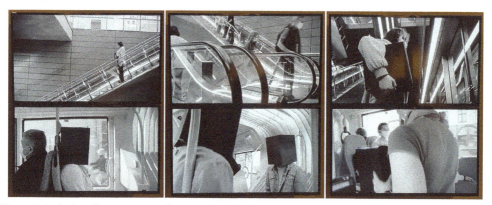

Figure 25.3: Students from FGU. Copenhagen, *Metro/Bus*, 2020. Video still by students. *Down to Earth*, Photographic Center, 2020. Copyright: FGU.

gained new perspectives on how to work together and how to apply tools to unfold their own ideas and methods.

A crucial element was that the workshops were to culminate in the professional exhibition at Fotografisk Center. This fact strengthened the young people's belief that what they had to say was relevant to others. Although consolidated as a joint enterprise at this point, this was also a consolidation of activities with new positions, originating in individual situations and expectations. This diversity, or friction, was necessary in the efforts to redescribe territories.

The development of a shared repertoire: Behind the scenes

A recurring discussion in connection with participatory processes and social artworks revolves around the consequences of artistic and social values. Art historian and critic Claire Bishop's (2006) landmark contribution to this debate represents a general scepticism. She perceives social artworks as naïve and the artists lacking the necessary awareness of the sometimes vulnerable fields in which they operate. Comparatively, and with a strong ethical orientation at the expense of aesthetic quality, curator, educator and museum director Sally Tallant (2010) is more concerned with finding ways to create integrated programming as a union of curation and education.

Fotografisk Center placed themselves more in line with Tallant, with an awareness that the outcome could not be anticipated but possessed its own qualities. They had previously participated in KUNST:form's pilot programme IMAGINARIUM, and knew about the principles behind *Down to Earth*. The key difference was that for this intervention, they went in with the whole organization and all the exhibition space. The commitment and challenge of the institutional framework were significantly bigger in *Down to Earth*.

The interaction between students and the Fotografisk Center crystallized later in the process through the students' involvement in the education programme and marketing initiatives. It was also these initiatives that emblematically made visible the challenging mechanisms in the effectuation and affiliation processes because they included external parties (audiences, media) who were not involved in the joint enterprise and the shared repertoire. An example was the press release, which had to be considered carefully in terms of the format. Two students contributed with text made in workshops with KUNST:form and the art centre. Yet, despite the visibility of the students' contributions, the criteria for the press release in terms of targeting the media and art critics remained rooted in an existing repertoire of language use and information requirements. In relation to activities aimed at visiting schools, the students' imprint was significantly stronger. Their ideas for and design of the learning activities and material were carried out in dialogue with KUNST:form and the Fotografisk Center.

Fotografisk Center is a small, agile organization experienced in incorporating temporary workers. It seemed organizationally straightforward to involve the students. Despite great openness, the students' work with communication and education also challenged the institutional framework, as the art centre does not really have the resources to handle the more extended focus on education activities. The combination of the procedural nature of the project and the institutional framework for communication with deadlines, specific formats and related activities created minor friction points – an aspect that, like several other situations, points to the need for time, repetition and *deliberation* (time for consideration) to develop a common repertoire and redescribe territories.

In sum, to take form as a new terrain that mixes the territories of art with that of pedagogy, a joint enterprise like *Down to Earth* must be repeated. A shared repertoire must be established, negotiated, randomly pursued and built upon before new roles, hierarchies, meanings and artistic possibilities become manifest. This requires openness and extra time from all participants along with resources for coordinating content and carrying out joint work in new ways within the organization of the institutions.

If one area were to be pointed out that could have taken *Down to Earth* a step further, besides consolidating the sensemaking and the narrative of the joint enterprise, it would have been to include the students in the curation and technical work with the installation of works. Unfortunately, this was not possible due to lack of resources and time as well as the necessity to change the formal or micro-political relationship between the art institution and the students/school, not least in terms of administration, safety regulations and insurance.

The murky sides of encounters

From a curatorial and organizational perspective, working strategically to create new territories among young people, artists, art and educational institutions is, in our view, the same as insisting on conflicts, dilemmas, frustrations and difficulties as both artistic and pedagogical potentials. It is undoubtedly easier to curate and produce professional art exhibitions with young people simply visiting their schools after the completion of the exhibitions.

But is there a new relevance and a different quality we all need from this convergence of the territories of production and education? Not just for the sake of art and pedagogy, but to find a foothold and create grounding and empathy in a divided world? *Down to Earth* was an experiment that – despite occasional discomfort, scepticism and frustration among ourselves as curators, the artist, the young people, their teachers and the art gallery staff – was seen predominantly as positive and brave and met with enthusiasm for the process. It was received and embraced as a product in the same manner by its audience and the press. This may be because E. B. Itso and the students' joint and wry message on urban life concerns us all.

Weick's concept of sensemaking and Wenger's communities of practice can make visible the organizational micro-actions that shape the continuum between conviviality and manipulation between the institution and those outside – to recall the definition of the radical diplomat. By using their methods, we may become better at taking precautions around organizations in advance, taking initiatives further, ensuring repetition and the realization of a joint enterprise through mutual engagement and a shared repertoire, which then affects all parties, including external interests. With young people as co-creators of artistic content and the institutional frameworks, this continuum and micro-actions can be shaken up. The prerequisite is that the curator will act as a radical diplomat, entering the stage with a suitable reverence and a strongly convergent attitude that deliberately messes up the territories to "occupy the murky sides of their encounter" (Graham et al., 2008, p. 100).

References

Bishop, C. (2006). The social turn: Collaboration and its discontents. *Artforum International*, 44(6), 178–183.

Graham, J., Graziano, V., & Kelly, S. (2008). Radical diplomacy. In A. Kanngeiser, P. Rojo, & M. Zechner (Eds.), *Vocabulaboratories*. LISA. https://www.researchgate.net/publication/335244107_Radical_Diplomacy

Hart, R. (1992). *Children's participation: From tokenism to citizenship*. UNICEF Innocenti. https://www.unicef-irc.org/publications/100-childrens-participation-from-tokenism-to-citizenship.html

Hooper-Greenhill, E. (2000). *Museums and the interpretation of visual culture*. Routledge.

Latour, B. (2017). *Où atterrir? Comment s'orienter en politique*. La Découverte.

O'Neill, P., & Wilson, M. (Eds.). (2010). *Curating and the educational turn*. Open Editions.

Sheikh, S. (2010). Letter to Jane (Investigation of a function). In P. O'Neill & M. Wilson (Eds.), *Curating and the educational turn* (pp. 61–75). Open Editions.

Tallant, S. (2010). Experiments in integrated programming. In P. O'Neill & M. Wilson (Eds.), *Curating and the educational turn* (pp. 186–194). Open Editions.

Weick, K. (1995). *Sensemaking in organization*. Sage Publications.

Weick, K. (2001). *Making sense of the organization*. Blackwell.

Wenger, E. (1998). *Communities of practice: Learning, meaning and identity*. Cambridge University Press.

Chapter 26

Senses and Sensibility: Finding the Balance in Sensory Museum Education

Emilie Sitzia

Museums have the potential to be territories of educational experimentation as they are not bound to target age groups or to specific cognitive outputs (Sitzia, 2018). Yet as Classen (2007) and Classen and Howes (2006) argued over a decade ago, the privileged position of the "museum of sight" needs to be re-evaluated if we are to increase museums' impact on learning. The importance of multisensory learning and its general benefits and impacts have been widely studied over the years (Gardner & Hatch, 1989; Shams & Seitz, 2008). However, the implications of this knowledge and its application to museums as educational spaces are still rather marginal, despite the fact that more and more museums are attempting to stage multisensory exhibitions. This gap between theory and actual exhibition outcomes also means that less attention has been given to multisensory exhibitions' negative side effects and to efficient implementation strategies. In this chapter, I ask – can there be too much of a good thing?

The importance of the senses in learning processes has been acknowledged in a large body of educational literature: ranging from the positive impact of senses on learners' capacity to build connections between various bodies of knowledge and to memorize better (Craik & Lockhart, 1972), to the reinforcement of learning through sensorial preferences and contextualization (Gardner, 1985; Harris, 2020; Petty, 2004), to the constructivist educational approach asserting the importance of (physical) experience on learning processes (Dewey, 1899; Kolb, 1984; Piaget, 1929), and to the application of experiential learning to museum learning (Hein, 1998). Similarly, the importance of multisensory learning and its benefits and impacts in both formal and informal education settings have been widely studied over the years (Gardner & Hatch, 1989; Matthews, 1998; Shams & Seitz, 2008).

This chapter investigates multisensory museum learning along with its darker counterpart, visitors' sensory overload, and proposes strategies for the efficient use of the senses in museum learning. I begin with a literature review to establish the (expected) benefits for the institution and the impact of multisensory installations in museums on learners/audiences. I address key questions: How is learning reinforced? What is the senses' impact on memorization? (How) does it trigger emotional learning? (How) does it contribute to the narrative capacity of the museum? I explore the impact of sensory overload on visitors and the associated risks of cognitive disjunction and distraction. A specific exhibition example from the Museum of Civilizations of Europe and the Mediterranean (MuCEM) in Marseille, France, is analysed to illustrate the argument. Finally, I address strategies for curators, exhibition designers and museum educators to use multisensory education efficiently in the museum, focusing on aspects of scale, balance and coherence, and personalization and intimacy.

Multisensory learning in the museum

To clarify what is meant by learning in the museum, I align my definition with the widely accepted one proposed by Falk and Dierking (2000), who define learning in museums as a combination of cognitive learning (i.e. the learning of cognitive information such as artists' names, artistic periods and movements, etc.), affective learning (i.e. learning to love or value a particular type of art or learning empathy) and psychomotor learning (learning to move in a limited space – for example, within prescribed distances). To this learning triad, it is necessary to add social learning – even if it overlaps to some degree with the other three, just as the other three somewhat overlap with each other.

As I have argued elsewhere, learning in museums is not limited to a static acquired body of knowledge but encompasses an active and self-generating dimension so that alongside the learning of content, specific skills are developed (Sitzia, 2018).[1] In all these various aspects of learning in the museum, the senses play a key role. I focus on three aspects of the impact of sensory education that seem essential: experiential learning and holistic approaches in the museum; sensory congruence, divergence, and learner engagement; and sensory experiences, narratives, and learning.

Experiential learning and holistic approaches in the museum

Embodied education (or somatic learning) – learning that involves a variety of senses – has long been recognized as valuable to the learning process (Matthews, 1998). Matthews (1998) has argued for a holistic form of education and acknowledged the neglect of the senses in current educational structures. Museums are potentially a space where embodied education could be once again brought to the fore (Classen & Howes, 2006). Indeed, museums are not solely places of knowledge but are also widely acknowledged as spaces of experience.

As early as the nineteenth century, Dewey (1899) had highlighted the importance of learning through experience. While experience and embodied ways of knowing are seen as broadly beneficial to learning and to adult learners in general, multisensory learning is still mostly used in educational institutions for young learners. Piaget (1929), one of the founders of the constructivist approach to education, asserted that the acquisition of knowledge and the process of meaning-making are generated by the interaction between experiences and ideas in the mind of the learner. In philosophical and experimental psychology, sensorial experience is acknowledged as the key to a constructivist approach to learning. Building on Dewey's and Piaget's work, Kolb (1984) asserted the importance of active experimentation and concrete experience in his experiential learning cycle. Later, Hein (1998) applied experiential learning to museums and showed that they can adapt to create accessible constructivist learning environments.

The stimulation of various senses through experiential learning therefore makes the museum a potential space for a holistic approach to learning. This potential is linked to the networked nature of memorization. Craik and Lockhart (1972) outlined the positive impact of the senses on learners' capacity to build connections between various bodies of knowledge and to memorize better. Ward (2014) further clarifies how memory formation is linked to feature binding: During the memorization process we connect features, including sensory ones. He also argues that a richer sensory experience allows us to retrieve the whole from its parts in a more efficient way as a sensory-part retrieval allows for full memory retrieval. Thus, theoretically, the richer the sensory experience in the museum, the more efficient the learning process and the longer-lasting the memorization.

Sensory congruence, divergence and learner engagement

Ward (2014) issues a warning about the importance of meaningful sensory associations, arguing that semantic congruency plays an essential role in multisensory memory. Put simply, we remember better through pre-existing learned multisensory association; if a new association is created, the link needs to be meaningful or otherwise it is counter-productive to memorization (Ward, 2014).

However, while sensory divergence can hamper learning, it can also help generate new ideas and stimulate learning. As Jarvis (2009) explains, transformational learning happens when a person takes what he calls the "lifeworld" for granted and has a sensation/disjuncture that leads them to give meaning to this sensation and attempt to resolve the disjuncture. From this experience, individuals attempt to practise resolution and once again take their lifeworld for granted. Jarvis (2009) shows that learning happens in the gap, in the constructive friction between the lifeworld as it is perceived and the disjuncture/sensation provided by the experience (in our case, a divergent sensory stimulus), which then creates a new alternative meaning/interpretation. This is potentially relevant when tackling dissonant or contested heritage. A balance needs to be found between reinforcing existing connections and using sensory congruence to reinforce memorization and create new (less expected) connections.

This goal is particularly important for the relationship between sensorial experience and engagement. Although studies aim to understand the visitor experience during museum visits (Csikszentmihalyi & Hermanson, 1995; Doering & Pekarik, 1996; Falk et al., 1998), a more targeted investigation is necessary into the impact of sensory convergence and disjunction on museum visitors' experiences. Csikszentmihalyi's concept of "flow" and Falk and Dierking's concept of "minds-on" both point in the same direction; that is, multisensory experience, engagement, and learning are closely connected.

Sensory experiences, narratives and learning

As Roberts (2014) highlights, "at their most basic, museums communicate. In communicating, they ignite memories, activate emotions, and spark interchange. What visitors do with these possible responses is part of the narrative they craft" (p. 137). Roberts continues by recognizing the unpredictability of visitors' narratives, yet a visitor's ability to generate a narrative is enhanced within multisensory installations. Indeed, having a broader range of stimuli encourages visitors to connect sensory experience to existing memories and knowledge and to engage with the content emotionally and physically.

While reinforcing learning and allowing for sensorial preferences and contextualization (Gardner, 1985; Harris, 2020; Petty, 2004), multisensory installations shift the role of the museum learner from a passive recipient to an active participant able to connect closely with their intimate sensory experiences. This means that what happens in the museum happens (physically) to them as individuals. It modifies who they are, their self-narrative and their biographical storytelling, and it also promotes emotional learning. As an example, when students are asked about their best memory of a cultural education event, it is rarely a passive experience they remember (Falk & Dierking, 1995). Instead, they remember, usually with great sensory detail, "doing something" in the museum that shifted the way they thought about museums or their content. The museum sensory experience has entered their autobiography, their self-narrative.

Bruner (1986) distinguishes between two paradigms: logic/scientific and narrative. The narrative paradigm does not promote the creation of truth as does the logic/scientific paradigm, but rather its focus is meaning. Such utilization of the narrative paradigm in the constructive learning process leads to enduring knowledge as opposed to fleeting knowledge because knowledge created with sensory anchors is situated in the biography of the learner. Knowledge created through interwoven cognitive and emotional learning is thus potentially longer-lasting.

The literature clearly establishes, then, the benefits of a multisensory approach to learning in the museum. These expected benefits range from a more holistic and experience-based practice of learning, increased engagement and longer-lasting memory to deeper understanding, with a greater ownership of the knowledge created through stronger narratives and greater connections between cognitive and emotional learning. Being more than the "eyes-only space" benefits the visitor's learning experience (Classen & Howes, 2014, p. 19).

Sensory overload, cognitive disjunction and distraction

But as I asked above, can there be too much of a good thing? Can the multiplication of sensory stimuli in exhibition spaces become counter-productive to learning? To answer this, I consider the negative elements of sensory overload, cognitive disjunction and distraction, and then look at the possibility to weave the senses together.

Cognitive and sensory overload is a well-known problem for museums (Maxwell & Evans, 2002). So-called "museum fatigue" is often identified as one of the main barriers to museum visitors engaging in learning processes. Visitors simply cannot engage deeply with museum content when they are fatigued (Allen, 2007). This fatigue can be caused by a broad range of issues, such as the repetition of technical information, passive delivery or sensory overload.

Yet it is important to specify that sensory overload is not determined by the number of senses mobilized. Ward (2014) highlights that "the actual amount of information is of less importance and the brain is quite capable of avoiding 'sensory overload,' provided the sensory information is not conflicting" (p. 281). Therefore, conflicting or at least misaligned sensory (and cognitive) stimuli create issues. This is often described as cognitive disjunction: that is, a visitor's incapacity to connect the cognitive pieces of information provided by the museum with each other and with the sensory stimuli.

Maxwell and Evans (2002) go beyond museum fatigue and disjunction to identify distraction, which they define as a combination of issues to do with circulation paths, high visual exposure and noisy and crowded spaces, all of which become especially problematic "when attention must be shared among multiple, competing signals" (p. 5). They also connect the impression of control on the part of visitors to their motivation and ability to learn. This sense of control often expresses itself in "perceptual clarity" (p. 5) or lack thereof, which links back to the problems of sensorial and cognitive congruency discussed above.

Maxwell and Evans (2002) also argue that sensorial experience in the museum is tightly connected to emotional affect. They suggest that negative emotional affect can be triggered if the museum space is too bare or, inversely, if it is too distracting or highly complex in terms of sensory stimulation. This can lead to disorientation and feelings of anxiety in visitors, all of which have a negative impact on learning.

Clearly, museum fatigue, cognitive disjunction and distraction are all real risks that can impact learning outcomes. If not woven together meaningfully and in a balanced manner, the senses can interrupt a holistic learning experience and even trigger a negative experience rather than aiding memorization or enhancing visitors' experiences.

L'Orient Sonore: A case study

The MuCEM in Marseille (France) is well known for experimenting with alternative forms of engagement and multimodal content. An ambitious exhibition in this regard was *L'Orient Sonore: Musiques oubliées, musiques vivantes* (July 2020–January 2021). Focusing on endangered Arab musical traditions from the early twentieth century to the 1930s, it addressed matters of conservation and the celebration of Arab sound heritage. The topic's complexity was compounded by objects that were difficult to exhibit (LPs, field recordings, video installations, dance, documentary, etc.), and it was complemented by a digital component.[2]

Tiina Roppola (2012) proposes a framework through which to analyse exhibitions from the point of view of designing for visitor impact. This framework is particularly applicable to the MuCEM example in terms of how it considered the impact of space and senses on visitors. I have therefore operationalized Roppola's framework to allow for a detailed analysis suggests that by networking with existing memories, reinforcing emotional and cognitive connections and entering the biographical narrative of the visitor, sensory museum education can have a strong impact on learning. Weaving the senses with the content of the exhibition and generating a tight connection with visitors' existing sensory palettes is important. To create this personal experience and ensure respect for individual levels of sensitivity, signage to warn visitors of the sensory intensity of the exhibition experience would be useful.

Conclusion

This chapter demonstrates that the benefits of sensory museum education are many, but as with all things, it is a question of balance. Museums should take steps to avoid sensory overload, cognitive disjunction and distraction. To do so, strategies such as the three suggested above should be employed at the institutional level in the use of sensory education. Furthermore, applying these strategies necessitates close collaboration of curators, educators, audience departments and exhibition designers. If these conditions can be met, then the "museum of sight" can be re-evaluated, and museums can in turn increase their impact on learning, fulfilling their potential role as places of educational experimentation.

Notes

1. With this definition of learning, I align myself firmly with constructivist learning theorists. In the constructivist model, learners are active in producing knowledge and are themselves the measure of that knowledge: the knowledge created needs to "make sense" in the reality of the learner rather than adhere to a standard "truth" (Hein, 1998, p. 34).
2. https://orientsonore.fr/a-propos/. I will not consider the exhibitions' digital component; instead, my focus is on the sensory experience of visitors in the space without any complementary tools.
3. I have chosen to leave out broadening here as in this exhibition, broadening was mostly delivered through traditional textual formats and online material rather than sensory experience. It is important to note that content-wise, this exhibition was extremely rich.

References

Allen, S. (2007). Exhibit design in science museums: Dealing with a constructivist dilemma. In J. H. Falk, L. D. Dierking, & S. Foutz (Eds.), *In principle, in practice: Museums as learning institutions* (pp. 43–56). Alta Mira Press.

Bruner, J. (1986). *Actual minds, possible worlds*. Harvard University Press.
Classen, C. (2007). Museum manners: The sensory life of the early museum. *Journal of Social History, 40*(4), 895–914.
Classen, C., & Howes, D. (2006). The sensescape of the museum: Western sensibilities and Indigenous artifacts. In E. Edwards, C. Gosden, & R. Philips (Eds.), *Sensible objects: Colonialism, museums and material culture* (pp. 199–222). Berg Publishers.
Classen, C., & Howes, D. (2014). *Ways of sensing: Understanding the senses in society*. Routledge.
Craik, F., & Lockhart, R. (1972). Levels of processing: A framework for memory research. *Journal of Verbal Learning and Verbal Behaviour, 11*, 671–684.
Csikszentmihalyi, M., & Hermanson, K. (1995). Intrinsic motivation in museums: Why does one want to learn? In J. H. Falk & L. D. Dierking (Eds.), *Public institutions for personal learning* (pp. 67–77). American Association of Museums.
Dewey, J. (1899). *School and society*. Chicago University Press.
Doering, Z. D., & Pekarik, A. J. (1996). Questioning the entrance narrative. *Journal of Museum Education, 21*(3), 20–23.
Falk, J., & Dierking, L. D. (1995). Recalling the museum experience. *The Journal of Museum Education, 20*(2), 10–13.
Falk, J., & Dierking, L. D. (2000). *Learning from Museums: Visitor Experiences and the Making of Meaning*. Rowman & Littlefield.
Falk, J., Moussouri, T., & Coulson, D. (1998). The effect of visitors' agendas on museum learning. *Curator: The Museum Journal, 41*(2), 107–120.
Gardner, H., & Hatch, T. (1989). Educational implications of the theory of multiple intelligences. *Educational Reader, 8*(8), 4–10.
Gardner, R. C. (1985). *Social psychology and second language learning: The role of attitude and motivation*. Edward Arnold.
Harris, A. (2020). *A sensory education*. Routledge.
Hein, G. (1998). *Learning in the museum*. Routledge.
Jarvis, P. (2009). Learning to be a person in society. In K. Illeris (Ed.), *Contemporary theories of learning* (pp. 21–34). Routledge.
Kolb, D. A. (1984). *Experiential learning: Experience as the source of learning and development*. Prentice Hall.
Matthews, J. C. (1998). Somatic knowing and education. *Educational Forum, 62*(3), 236–242.
Maxwell, L. E., & Evans, G. W. (2002). Museums as learning settings. *Journal of Museum Education, 27*(1), 3–7.
Petty, G. (2004). *Teaching today*. Nelson Thornes.
Piaget, J. (1929). *The child's conception of the world*. Routledge & Kegan Paul.
Roberts, L. (2014). *From knowledge to narrative: Educators and the changing museum*. Random House.
Roppola, T. (2012). *Designing for the museum visitor experience*. Routledge.
Shams, L., & Seitz, A. R. (2008). Benefits of multisensory learning. *Trends in Cognitive Sciences, 60*, 411–417.

Sitzia, E. (2018). The ignorant art museum: Beyond meaning-making. *International Journal of Lifelong Education*, *37*(1), 73–87.

Ward, J. (2014). Multisensory memories: How richer experiences facilitate remembering. In N. Sobol Levent, A. Pascual-Leone, & S. Lacey (Eds.), *The multisensory museum: Cross-disciplinary perspectives on touch, sound, smell, memory, and space* (pp. 273–284). Rowman & Littlefield.

Chapter 27

Towards a More Human-Centred Museum: A Narrative of an Imagined Visit to a Trauma-Aware Art Museum

Jackie Armstrong, Laura Evans, Stephen Legari,
Ronna Tulgan Ostheimer, Andrew Palamara
and Emily Wiskera[1]

Alex had never visited their local art museum in person, but during the pandemic, they participated in a series of virtual museum programmes focused on well-being. Throughout that difficult time, Alex formed a connection to the museum through interactions with staff and other participants, which eventually encouraged them to set foot inside.

Alex had felt a bit overwhelmed when first arriving at the museum, but their virtual experience and curiosity helped them cross the threshold. After the visit, Alex felt elated, a result of feeling inspired, seen and welcomed throughout their time at the museum. On the way home, Alex retraced the visit in their mind and tried to remember all the little things that had come together to make them feel a sense of belonging. They pulled out their cell phone and began texting a friend, eager to share their experience with someone else.

Given the current collective trauma of not only an international pandemic but also the heightened spotlight on injustice, violence and strife over the past years, our museums *must* become more purposefully trauma-aware and responsive if we are to be relevant to our visitors' needs. The awareness that our visitors are likely suffering varying degrees of psychic pain makes this a necessary moment for educators and their museums to embrace trauma-aware practices. In response to this unprecedented moment, we – a group of museum educators, an art therapist and an academic – came together to ask, "What might it look and feel like for a visitor to move through an idealized trauma-aware museum?" In answer to this, we imagine Alex's (to whom we deliberately do not assign a trauma background or a gender by using they/them pronouns) visit to an imaginary art museum, where their experience is shaped by trauma-aware principles and practices. We use an approach we have named "Trauma-Aware Art Museum Education" (T-AAME) and apply it to Alex's museum visit through six principles: (1) safety; (2) empowerment, voice and choice; (3) collaboration and mutuality; (4) trustworthiness and transparency; (5) peer support and (6) cultural, historical and gender issues (SAMHSA, 2014).

As with universal design, we believe that trauma-aware practices can benefit all museum visitors, not just those who identify as having experienced trauma. Though we have shared examples of what T-AAME constitutes in our own work at our home institutions (Armstrong et al., 2021; Evans et al., 2020), we are writing this chapter as a proposition for what museum education can be – and more than that, what the museum as a more human-centred and education-focused institution can become. To be effective, trauma-aware practices cannot be relegated to one default department – education – but need to be embraced and embodied by every single department in the museum. Though we have focused only on Alex's experience as a visitor, we also advocate that these trauma-aware practices can be used behind the scenes amongst museum colleagues.

As a group, we have gravitated towards a definition of trauma that is inclusive of physical, psychological, emotional and social trauma. We recognize that trauma is multi-layered and is both objective and subjective; what one person experiences as traumatic another person might not. We are using narrative to detail Alex's museum trip because we believe narrative is a more humanistic mode of writing. Narrative writing has long been used in trauma recovery (Feldman, 2014; Frank, 1997); with its emphasis on connection and authenticity, we advocate for narrative as a trauma-aware mode of writing. Alex's reflections are notated by the italicized script. In between Alex's narrative, we write about trauma-aware theory as it applies to proposed practice.

Six principles of trauma-aware practice

Safety

When Alex arrived at the museum, they were warmly greeted and the online ticket they had pre-purchased was quickly scanned by an attendant. A large screen showed a floor-by-floor guide to the museum with images offering glimpses into what Alex might expect to see there. A staff person standing nearby approached Alex, noticing that they looked a little puzzled. They helped Alex determine where to start based on Alex's interests.

As Alex moved through the galleries, they realized all the security officers were wearing regular clothes rather than uniforms or formal suits like they had seen in other institutions and in movies. When Alex looked closer, they noticed each security officer's lanyard was personalized with descriptions such as "Ask me about photography," "I'm an artist educator," and "My three favourite artworks here are..." Alex noticed that the security officers seemed relaxed as well and genuinely appeared to enjoy engaging with visitors.

Feeling safe is a privilege that not everyone experiences. Trauma survivors often report feeling unsafe in their bodies and experience a range of symptoms that indicate an overwhelmed nervous system. If people do not feel safe, they cannot think of anything else because the need for safety overrides everything (Weinberg, 2020). Van der Kolk, a world-renowned trauma specialist, stressed that "the single most important issue for traumatised people is to find a sense of safety in their own bodies" (as cited in Interlandi, 2014, para. 15). There are differing degrees of safety people can experience, and a museum can take steps to help people have "safe enough" experiences by considering safety as a multi-layered concept that includes physical, psychological and interpersonal safety, among others (Treisman, 2021). When people experience physical, emotional and psychological safety, they are able to think, collaborate, innovate, create, explore, connect and empathize.

Another helpful way for museums to think about safety has been attributed to trauma specialist Dr Gabor Maté, who stresses that safety is about connection, not eliminating all threats (Moore, 2020). Throughout their visit, Alex experienced a sense of safety in multiple ways that emphasized connection: They felt welcomed and invited into the museum, they experienced agency and autonomy during their visit, they were sufficiently oriented to the museum, they had respectful interactions with staff, they perceived that staff felt content in their roles and they were able to meet their physical and emotional needs as they arose. With this sense of safety and stability, Alex was able to go forward and more fully experience the museum.

Empowerment, voice and choice

Alex had expected to passively learn facts about art. Instead, a facilitator enroute began by explaining that each participant's interpretations and experiences were significant, and everyone was encouraged to share their perspectives. The facilitator also validated that some may prefer to participate by listening. The conversations were rooted in the art but were about real life. Alex had a sense that they mattered in the group.

As they passed through the exhibits, Alex saw a rack of materials with a sign on it reading, "Take me if you want. Or...wander!" The materials included drawing pads and pencils, a guidebook called "Pause and Reflect: Engaging with Art for Introspection," and other self-guides available in hard-copy and digital formats. There were also several free programmes offered that day: an orientation tour, a discussion about Afro-Futurism in front of a new acquisition and an improv game. Alex was surprised by how many choices there were. In the galleries, Alex saw that many of the paintings had a space for visitors to share their interpretations or responses to questions. A guard even asked Alex what they thought of a sculpture, and they chatted for several minutes, listening to each other's interpretations. There was a station asking for ideas about an upcoming exhibition. Alex felt respected and valued by the museum because of all the ways they were invited to contribute, participate and respond. It was different from other museums, and Alex felt like they mattered.

A sense of empowerment involves feeling that one's experiences, wisdom and knowledge have value, and that one's opinions, needs and desires matter to others (SAMHSA, 2014). Empowerment in a museum setting involves policies and operations that help each visitor feel in control of their own visit – with choices to make, a voice to be heard and support available as needed. The idea of empowerment is not new in museum education; it has been an intentional best practice for many years, though it is often understood simply as including the visitors' interpretation and meaning of objects in gallery programmes (Roberts, 1999). A trauma-aware framework adds a new dimension to empowerment beyond giving visitors a voice in their experiences with art. A museum based on trauma-aware principles cares about the whole person and the impact of their entire experience at the museum on their sense of well-being. A trauma-aware focus on empowerment, then, is museum-wide and can be felt by the visitor at every step of their experience through interactions with museum staff, the tone and content of museum signage and materials and the kinds of activities visible throughout the museum. Through wanderings, Alex saw and felt evidence of the museum's emphasis on giving visitors a voice and a choice, making them feel empowered by knowing both of these things mattered to the museum.

Collaboration and mutuality

Heading towards what they thought was the gallery for contemporary art, Alex found themselves in a part of the museum that seemed to be alive with a whole different energy. Through a studio window, they saw a small group of art makers busy at work with a hands-on activity. Alex happily recognized the educator as the same one who had facilitated their well-being workshops online. Next, a line of school-aged children filed past them.

Alex then wandered into a space that had art on exhibit. The text on the wall explained that the exhibition was a collaboration between seniors and adolescents who had been brought together virtually during the pandemic and were now showing the fruits of that exchange in art form. The work brightened Alex's already good mood, and they wondered about getting involved in these kinds of projects as a volunteer. Alex moved onto a warmly lit space that seemed to block out most of the ambient sounds of the museum. Alex took in the scene all at once. A mother and child sat on a low, plush seat, the mother speaking quietly to the child. There were two screens discreetly installed showing digital art that swirled and danced fluidly. Alex felt a sense of calm. Upon leaving the room, they noticed large, clear text on the wall that explained how the museum had consulted with a community committee for neurodiversity in order to create the space.

Meaningful collaborations in museums engage in relationship building and mutuality that balances power and allows for shared decision-making (SAMHSA, 2014). Community collaborations in museum programming have long been the domain of education teams, but there is both a call and a need for collaborations to be transversal across museum departments, including curatorial, front-of-house, research and security. These collaborations should be founded on a reciprocation of shared authority and privilege and on a plurality of perspectives of contemporary museum public (Ferguson & Renner, 2019). These collaborations then influence the culture of mutuality between staff and visitors, among visitors and between visitors and the collections. The increasing body of research validating the well-being benefits of museums is invariably founded on common themes of connection, inclusion, stimulation and longevity (Fancourt & Finn, 2019). These findings are borne out by the evolution of museum-based programmes that privilege the institution's relationships with stakeholders, be they members of the visiting public, healthcare professionals, academics or activists at every stage of development. Alex saw meaningful evidence of collaboration during their visit, from the neurodiversity activities to the project between seniors and adolescents.

Many museum programmes do not, or have not yet, developed a model of collaboration founded on mutuality, risk-creating programmes, exhibitions and content *for* their public by working *with* their public. In doing so, they risk perpetuating dynamics of colonialism, marginalization and classicism and find themselves spending more time doing damage control for oversights rather than carefully developing collaborations that may ultimately lead to more meaningful experiences for all. A trauma-aware approach to collaboration ensures that the authority and lived experience of community partners is woven through the fabric of the entire museum and benefits the visitor, group and employee alike.

Trustworthiness and transparency

In anticipation of their in-person visit, Alex explored the museum's website to learn more about the institution itself. They were encouraged to see the museum's mission statement, which emphasized the museum's dedication to being a community-centred organization. On their visit to the museum, Alex noted examples of this community focus in the collaborations.

At the museum, Alex turned a corner and saw a room with floor-to-ceiling panes of glass on two sides. A couple of big skylights let natural light into the room. Inside, a woman worked on an old, cracked painting, held tightly in place on an easel. Around her were tiny paintbrushes, magnifying glasses and a lot of other scientific and art equipment. Alex read on a sign that this was the museum's art conservation studio, which they compared to an art hospital. The museum had chosen to make the conservator's work visible to visitors so that the public could better understand how art is made, cared for and preserved for the future. Alex spent a long time watching the conservationist meticulously clean the painting. Finally, Alex moved on with a better awareness of how much work it takes for the museum to care for its collections.

It can be challenging for institutions to gain the trust of trauma survivors (Tolley, 2020). Traumatic responses can destabilize a person's ability to trust other people and institutions. Museum visitors who have had traumatic experiences can struggle to find solace in a public space that feels intimidating or unsupportive of their needs. When institutions like museums can align their beliefs, values and words with their public actions, visitors with trauma can better recognize and accept the museum's reliability and credibility. Transparency in a museum invites visitors behind the curtain and reveals things about the museum that might normally remain opaque. A museum's willingness to be transparent can lead to greater intimacy with visitors. Trustworthiness and transparency are deliberate actions that museums can take to foster a sense of caring among staff, patrons and community partners that are sustainable and equitable (SAMSHA, 2014). For museums, this requires first and foremost a shift from being the sole, authoritative voice of culture to a more variegated and collective approach to making decisions with the public (Ferguson & Renner, 2019).

During their visit, Alex experienced transparency from the museum, and it made them trust the museum more. Alex saw a distinct connection between the museum's community-focused mission statement and how they included their community in museum projects. Alex saw their identities and perspectives represented in the contributions of the community committees, which led them to think they actually belonged at the museum, whereas they previously questioned whether or not the museum cared about people like them. Alex's observations at the conservation studio made them feel that the museum trusted them to see into operations that might normally have remained hidden.

Peer support

Thinking it might be nice to sit down for a few minutes, Alex decided to step into a gallery that looked and sounded like it might be a place to watch a film. As Alex approached, they noticed a large label placed next to the room's entry. The wall label warned visitors of potential emotional activation caused by the subject matter of the film and listed the contact information for related organizations offering free assistance should visitors need extra support. Despite Alex's own experience with this topic, they felt comfortable entering the space and watching the film because of this warning. As Alex emerged from the film room, they noticed a wall outside the room where other visitors had been invited to share their reactions to the film. Taking a moment to read over the written and illustrated responses, Alex was surprised to see how many others shared similar lived experiences, which filled Alex with a sense of connection and acceptance.

Alex's validation of lived experience embodies the principle of peer support. Interactions between people who share similar experiences are critical connection points that help with "establishing safety and hope, building trust, enhancing collaboration, and utilising their stories and lived experience to promote recovery and healing" (SAMSHA, 2014, p. 11). The practice of peer support recognizes that people who share common experiences are best able to understand and empathize with each other while offering the benefit of what they have learned. Peers come in many forms within museums, from museum staff to other visitors, and support can come through a variety of interactions.

Alex experienced multiple layers of peer support, even when not directly interacting with others at the museum. An invisible peer to Alex was the museum's interpretation specialist, who created the sign Alex encountered at the entrance to the film room. Due to his knowledge of trauma-informed practice and his own personal history of trauma, the interpretation specialist knew that others like him might have an emotional response to this work of art. He acted as an unseen peer to Alex, reassuring them that their potential response was normal and valid. The interpretation specialist took this peer support a step further by offering additional resources for professional help to support Alex beyond their visit, if needed. Alex also found support and acceptance in the form of the response wall, which encouraged visitors to process, externalize and share their thoughts and feelings with others. Even though Alex and other museum visitors were not physically together, Alex experienced a sense of dialogue and community with them by reading their responses and finding mutual understanding therein.

Cultural, historical and gender issues

Alex noticed that the museum had "all gender" restrooms in addition to ones marked for women, men and family. Alex was pleased to see this. What impressed them more was the inclusion of pronouns on most of the staff's lanyards. They noticed a few people did not have their pronouns but instead had something like "Hi! Please call me _____." Alex felt comforted to know that staff had agency over what to share or not share, and they saw a diverse representation of pronouns that left them with a sense of belonging and acceptance. Alex overheard a tour guide explaining that the museum had recently returned several Navajo ceremonial objects after engaging in dialogue with a delegation of Navajo Nation members. The museum had found three objects with dubious provenance and chose to return the objects to living ancestors of those items. Alex felt relieved to know the museum was engaging in these challenging issues.

Alex paused on a comfortable bench and listened to some of the museum's free audio on their phone. Alex heard a diversity of voices and perspectives represented, including conservators, architects, scientists, art therapists, psychologists, graphic designers, musicians, educators, researchers, poets, visitors and more. There were also verbal descriptions for people with low to no vision and playlists for children. Alex found the audio to be inclusive, accessible and culturally humble.

Cultural, historical and gender issues are often interwoven with other trauma-aware principles. When an institution focuses on cultural, historical and gender issues, they acknowledge and address historical trauma, eschew cultural stereotypes and actively interrogate bias and provide responsive support to those with differing gender, racial, ethnic and cultural needs (SAMSHA, 2014). Museums and historical trauma are inextricably intertwined because historically, museums have separated objects from their cultures, often without the consent of the source community, and put them on display (Besterman, 2016). This history of the museum is a colonialist one, and there have been urgent and vocal calls for museums to decolonize by diversifying their objects, peoples and perspectives. For these historical and contemporary reasons and for many others, museums can be challenging spaces for many visitors, and every effort should be made by museums to make the spaces more accessible and inclusive. Alex saw the museum's efforts through the representation of diverse staff voices, respect for visitors' individuality and culture and their examination of collections to determine if they had been ethically acquired. Though Alex was impressed by the museum's handling of gender, cultural and historical issues, in our view no museum should ever feel complete in these areas and should always be striving to listen and reflect more on how they can improve and adapt, based on visitor and staff feedback.

Conclusion

In this chapter, we felt it was important to focus not only on what educators can do to be more trauma-aware but also on what the museum as an educational institution can do and what it can be. Alex's experiences throughout the museum demonstrated how the entire museum can be trauma-aware through the six principles of safety: (1) empowerment, (2) voice and choice, (3) collaboration and mutuality, (4) trustworthiness and transparency, (5) peer support and (6) cultural, historical and gender issues (SAMHSA, 2014). Though we took care to show that trauma awareness should be spread throughout the museum, we do believe that, as we have seen with other important and necessary changes in museums, educators are the ones leading the charge for museums to be trauma-aware (Acuff & Evans, 2014). For many years, museum educators have recognized that our practice has a therapeutic dimension, though we have typically considered emotional labour a tacit part of our work. If a trauma-aware framework expands the parameters of what it means to be a museum educator, it also requires an evolution of how we think about the museum as an institution and its role in communities and society. We need to remember that a visitor's relationship with a museum includes the entirety of their experience, not just their participation in an education programme, and that as institutions, museums have the potential to create moments of joy, connection, calm and healing. Without everyone on board, our efforts could be for naught and can even cause harm. Therefore, T-AAME involves educating all museum stakeholders about the implications of the framework, including the operational implications for all departments, not just the education department. This will add still another new, well-deserved and long-time-coming dimension to the responsibilities of museum educators and their leadership role in shaping the culture of the whole museum.

Note

1. Author names are listed in alphabetical order.

References

Acuff, J. B., & Evans, L. (2014). *Multiculturalism in art museums today*. Rowman & Littlefield Publishers.

Armstrong, J., Evans, L., Legari, S., Palamara, A., Tulgan Ostheimer, R., & Wiskera, E. (2021). Weaving trauma awareness into museum education. *Journal of Museum Education*, 46(4), 454–466. https://www.tandfonline.com/doi/full/10.1080/10598650.2021.1981045?utm_medium=email&utm_source=EmailStudio&utm_campaign=JOE09646_4170723

Besterman, T. (2016). Crossing the line: Restitution and cultural equity. In L. Tythacott & K. Arvanitis (Eds.), *Museums and restitution: New practices, new approaches* (pp. 19–36). Routledge.

Evans, L., Palamara, A., Legari, S., Tulgan Ostheimer, R., & Wiskera, E. (2020, June 29). Trauma-aware art museum education: Principles and practices. *Art Museum Teaching: A Forum for Reflecting on Practice*. https://artmuseumteaching.com/2020/06/29/trauma-aware-art-museum-education-principles-practices

Fancourt, D., & Finn, S. (2019). *What is the evidence on the role of the arts in improving health and well-being? A scoping review.* WHO Regional Office for Europe.

Feldman, D. B. (2014, June 6). Writing wrongs: Writing about trauma leads to better endings. *Psychology Today.* https://www.psychologytoday.com/us/blog/supersurvivors/201406/writing-wrongs-writing-about-trauma-leads-better-endings

Ferguson, M., & Renner, K. (2019). A museum without walls: Community collaboration in exhibition development. *Museum Scholar, 2.* https://articles.themuseumscholar.org/2019/05/01/tp_vol2fergusonrenner/

Frank, A. W. (1997). *The wounded storyteller: Body, illness, and ethics.* University of Chicago Press.

Interlandi, J. (2014, May 22). *A revolutionary approach to treating PTSD.* The New York Times. https://www.nytimes.com/2014/05/25/magazine/a-revolutionary-approach-to-treating-ptsd.html

Moore, D. S. (2020, May 3). Healing from addiction. *The Compassionate Doctor.* https://www.drsarahmoore.com/post/healing-from-addiction

Roberts, L. C. (1999). *From knowledge to narrative: Educators and the changing museum.* Smithsonian Institution Press.

Substance Abuse and Mental Health Services Administration (SAMHSA). (2014). *SAMHSA's concept of trauma and guidance for a trauma-informed approach.* https://www.samhsa.gov/resource/dbhis/samhsas-concept-trauma-guidance-trauma-informed-approach

Tolley, R. (2020). *A trauma-informed approach to library services.* ALA Editions.

Treisman, K. (2021). *A treasure box for creating trauma-informed organizations: A ready-to-use resource for trauma, adversity, and culturally informed, infused and responsive systems – Volumes I and II.* Jessica Kingsley Publishers.

Weinberg, A. (2020). *A culture of safety: Building a work environment where people can think, collaborate and innovate.* Spoke & Wheel.

Part V

Virtual Museums

Chapter 28

The Art of Teaching in the Museum:
A Proposition for Pedagogy of Dissensus

Lisbet Skregelid

Education within art museums and galleries has transformed throughout the last decades: from traditional guided tours and one-way communication to dialogue, active participation and interaction and long-lasting partnerships – for example, between museums and schools – to enhance meaningful engagement with art (Dysthe et al., 2012; Myrvold & Mørland, 2019). Experimental, sensory and arts-based educational approaches now emerge in the art museum as well as outreach approaches to a range of social communities (Christensen-Scheel, 2019).

When it comes to arts-based educational methods applied to museum education, this is an area in progress and a site for experimentation. So what does it mean? Does it mean to make some art in the museum in a workshop area that is more or less related to the art exhibited? Does it mean engaging artists to do their art, relating it tightly or loosely to the exhibitions and inviting the audience into their practice?

Arts-based educational approaches in the gallery and museum space are understood in many different manners and unfold in a variety of ways. This chapter is a contribution to what I see as arts-based approaches to education. In this way, I seek to extend current knowledge about how art and art theory can inform teaching in general and in the sites of art museums and galleries in particular. As a point of departure and for investigation, I focus on a university course in visual arts education, for which I have been responsible since 2004, to explore how art itself and art theory are useful sources when doing education in the museum and gallery space.

Arts-based approaches in the museum space

During the last twenty years, we have witnessed a growing interest in education amongst artists and an educational turn in the arts field with exhibitions, seminars, conferences and art projects that make use of education as a leitmotif (Bishop, 2012; Helguera, 2011; Wilson & O'Neill, 2010). To connect art and education in museums and galleries, new approaches are being initiated in these spaces.

I have many times witnessed projects where the artist is asked to respond with a workshop to an exhibition that has no connection to their practice. I have also seen artists engaged in the gallery and museums space initiate some kind of practice that is disconnected from any exhibitions. There are some examples where the artists themselves are invited to engage with the audience in workshops. We see artist-in-residencies in museums, artists doing artist talks and so on. Sometimes artists are invited as art educators to give a workshop that is very much related to the art exhibited and still closely connected to the artist's own artmaking. For all forms of engagement, the digital format opens new possibilities in this regard. Museums and galleries can commission artists and invite them to do something related to their art independently whether there is an ongoing exhibition or not: for example, making us respond to the art from our homes across the world. Throughout the last year, art museums and galleries have in various ways tested out different formats.

Despite all this, arts-based approaches to education in the museum space remain very much unexplored.

The pedagogy of dissensus

I believe that the characteristics of art and art theory can productively inform teaching in art museums and galleries. In my research, I keep returning to the term "dissensus" by the French philosopher Jacques Rancière (2009, 2010) as it has proven to be relevant in educational contexts. Rancière (2009) sees art as dissensus, a rupture in what we can perceive with our senses. He makes use of dissensus to state what art can be and what art can do. He sees dissensus as "an organization of the sensible where there is neither a reality concealed behind appearances nor a single regime of presentation and interpretation of the given imposing its obviousness on all" (p. 48). He also states that dissensus breaks with habitual forms of imagination and contributes to new ways of seeing, hearing and sensing. In my teaching and research, a key context for dissensus is the art museum space (Skregelid, 2016, 2020, 2021).

When dissensus is used as an educational approach, regular ways of teaching are challenged and possible disruptions of the expected are offered. The unforeseen and uncertainties are welcomed. The pedagogy of dissensus may lead to resistance and also to changes in perceptions and attitudes, or what I frame as "events of subjectivation" (Skregelid, 2020, p. 163). So what happens when we make use of the dissensual characteristics inherent in the art itself to guide education in the art museum?

Realizing the pedagogy of dissensus

For sixteen years, as part of my position at the University of Agder, Norway, I have been responsible for teaching groups of students having work practice in Sørlandet Artmuseum (SKMU), Kristiansand. In the art museum space, the students plan, realize and reflect on workshops for their fellow students and students from primary, secondary and upper secondary school. Teaching with the students in the museum and workshops by the students themselves have become a laboratory for exploring, playing and experimenting. This has contributed to establishing an art education methodology that I have realized over the years is very much inspired by the art we are surrounded by and indeed, art in general. In the following section, I offer an overview of how the pedagogy of dissensus is acted out in my teaching by outlining the premise I find to be important for ensuring that the pedagogy I call for can take place.

Practising the ignorant schoolmaster

What strikes me every year is the level of radicalness and playfulness in the workshops the students make for their fellow students and invited pupils. I ask myself – how can this happen when they have so little knowledge about art education? The students are in the first semester of their first year of study when they have a week of work practice. In my introduction to our week in the museum, I could have shared my own knowledge and others' research from this field. However, I always start from the knowledge *the students* have about being a visitor in a museum or gallery setting. By doing this, I realize the premise of equality that is deeply rooted in Rancière's philosophy. The unconventional ideas on education presented in *The Ignorant Schoolmaster* (1991), where a teacher can teach students something the teacher does not know, also inform my construction of educational dissensus. It is about regarding the not-so-experienced or even inexperienced as a resource.

Often the students' experiences with educational activities in museums and galleries are very limited. When asking them about what makes a visit to an art exhibition exciting and inspiring, they often refer to what does *not* work so well. They mention a lot of talking from the guide about facts and too many artworks included in a guided tour. Rather, they prefer to explore the exhibition on their own as part of the visit. Many say they would like to have a dialogue and discussion about the art, and if possible be involved in some kind of activity. The students also mention the importance of an engaged guide, who manages to keep attention on the artworks by asking questions and inviting activities they find relevant, and who also initiates discussions about the art and issues the art touches upon.

Throughout the years, I have practised or actually *been* the ignorant schoolmaster in the museum. Instead of teaching the students about strategies for encountering the art they have explored themselves, I encourage them to make use of expertise they already have and to include their abilities: for example, to play music and perform theatre in their forming of workshops. During the pandemic, we oscillated between in-person and virtual visits as conditions changed. When lockdown prevented us from being physically present in the museum, we moved online. As I had no prior knowledge about online art education in the museum, I had to rely on the exploration of the students. I did not have to act like the ignorant schoolmaster; I was totally unfamiliar with this. Thereby, I made students investigate what already exists in online art educational programmes and present their discoveries to each other, thus initiating a discussion on what works well and what does not work so well. From here, they started planning their own projects.

Equality, relationality and performativity in third space

Some students imagine there is a true meaning inherent in the art they encounter. They want to search for the intention of the artist and believe that this intention must be communicated to others. I hold back my own knowledge, however, and I always try to establish a free and democratic space for different associations and responses to appear, so we begin by encountering one artwork together as a group to help students initiate their inquiry.

Since first entering the field of art educational research, I have been very much inspired by the Scandinavian researchers Helene Illeris (2002) and Venke Aure (2011) when shaping the educational structure for the workshop in the museum. Both argue for approaches to art education inspired by relational aesthetics (Bourriaud, 2002). This means acknowledging the importance of the *encounter* between the art and the spectators instead of focusing merely on the art *or* the spectator. They also emphasize different performative methods, including sensory and bodily responses, when encountering art. Their theories on relational and performative approaches to art education correspond to Rancière's principle of equality of intelligence (2009) and the ways he sees the aesthetic regime of art (2004). Rancière (2009) believes that what art does or can be is not a matter of transmitting messages, making models of how to behave or learning how to understand art. The intention of the artist or the teacher can never be fully anticipated. Instead, he sees the artist (as well as the researcher and teacher) as a constructor of scenes where the participant spectators develop their own translations "in order to appropriate the 'story' and make it their story" (Rancière, 2009, p. 22). It is here, between intention and translation, between balance and imbalance, connections and disconnections, the term dissensus becomes central to Rancière's thinking. The dissensual characteristic of art contributes to new ways of seeing, hearing and sensing and creates a third space for encountering the art.

The hook and affect as guides and principles

Instead of directing the students to work with a particular exhibition, I ask them to explore all the exhibitions in the museum and pay attention to particular shows or artworks that they connect with in one way or another. This attention can either reflect that the viewer likes it a lot, or it can be a result of disgust and aversion. It can also be the fact that they question the art and want to explore it further by making an educational workshop. This strategy is inspired by Illeris's (2005) call for using fascination as a driving force, also referred to as "the hook" (p. 237). Aure (2011) also argues for bringing passion and sensory knowledge into the making of art educational projects in the museum. The students then share their preferences and from there, the groups of three to four students are established.

An educational approach that has a fascination and bodily responses as points of departure connects with the term "affect" and how it is used in relation to art: for example, by Canadian philosopher and social theorist Brian Massumi (2015). Affects are moments of intensity and bodily sensations. Affect is a form of relationship and a form of cognition in which two parties mutually influence each other without this influence taking place consciously and intentionally: "When you affect something, you are opening yourself up to being affected in turn, and in a slightly different way than you might have been the moment before" (Massumi, 2015, p. 110). The way I have described dissensus as something that cannot be planned is thus related to affect. Affect is an experience that just happens.

Using fascination and affect as guiding forces and productive points of departure for making educational projects often also infuses the different projects the students make with the affective – performative and bodily connections – as evident in the examples I provide in this chapter.

Embracing openness and the risk of experimentation

I ask the students to make a memorable trip to the museum for those who will be involved, be they fellow students or invited pupils from various local schools. At this stage, I often remind them to consider what is *not* engaging: for example, a traditional guided tour. For our virtual visit in the spring of 2021, I gave the students the following keywords: *digital, experimental, varied, inclusive, engaging*, and a time frame of 20–30 minutes. In the physical museum space, they normally have more time, ranging from about one to two hours, to explore these keywords.

The openness and the high level of freedom in the assignment are meant to encourage them to experiment, but it might also be challenging. Some students find it very difficult to get started. They might also be anxious about doing it well enough. By confronting the students with the unknown, and by contributing to a movement into a space of uncertainty, I believe that the students' conceptions of art and art education can be re-arranged. With support from Dutch educational theorist Gert Biesta (2017, 2018) and British art educational researcher Dennis Atkinson (2011, 2018), I have advocated for the potentialities in art by bringing disturbance into education but also by doing unconventional teaching in the classroom. In my research, these theorists and their theories on the subject and their interruptive teachings have inspired my way of seeing dissensus as a premise for subjectivation and as something that can be initiated.

Sharing students' art education projects

Autumn 2020: Encountering art with art (in person)

One of the exhibitions that many of the students chose to work with in the autumn of 2020 was a display of investor Nicolai Tangen's art collection. Nine local artists were invited to respond to artworks they had chosen from this collection along with their own artistic production. In the museum, each of the invited artists got their own room to present their encounter with art and to share a dialogue formally, thematically or conceptually. The exhibition varied in form, content and materiality and inspired the students to create arts-based educational projects that made the encounters with art engaging for their fellow students. Each of the projects I refer to here shares a performative educational approach.

One room that caught the students' attention consisted of a scenography called *Absence* by the local performance artist and theatre director Laura B. Vallenes. She was responding to artworks by Norwegian photographer Per Barclay. According to Vallenes, it was the mix of beauty and horror that attracted her to Barclay's images as this corresponds with her own artistic complexity (Sørlandet Artmuseum, 2020). One of the student groups invited us into this space by asking us to sense the room and absorb the atmosphere, followed by writing a poem on a little piece of paper for ten minutes. We were then told to hand in the poem, and we were each given another's poem to read aloud anonymously. We then discussed how easily the words came to us, even though most of us were not used to writing poems. The reading of poems also became a performance in itself. Another group who chose to work with this part of the exhibition translated a poem written by the artist that was placed in the room, and then the students acted it out like a performance in the scenography of Vallenes as an introduction to their art educational project for their fellow students.

Another student project using elements of performance put chairs in front of the artworks. By the chairs, the students placed one question for every artwork that addressed various senses, such as *What do you smell? What do you hear?* Like a game of musical chairs, we had one minute in the chair in front of every artwork. At the signal of the students in charge of the project, we changed chairs. In the end, we compared what we had written about some of the artworks.

Another group of students chose to work with an ongoing exhibition at that time, a solo show by the Norwegian modernist Gunnar S. Gundersen, whose art is non-figurative, hard-edged and colourful. This group of students invited their peers to participate in this abstract art with them. After a short guided tour, they let their fellow students explore the exhibition on their own. They then asked the students to choose one artwork to respond to either by drawing, making a story or by making a bodily response to it. I am not sure whether the student in Figure 28.1 was aware of the corresponding colours in the artwork and in her clothes, but the interactivity between her appearance, Gundersen's abstract art and the museum space is amazingly related.

Spring 2021: Relationality on zoom (virtual)

We had planned to be in the museum in March 2021 and had already invited primary and secondary schools to take part in the projects of the students, as we do every year.

Figure 28.1: Arny Helene Orre, Stine Marie Andersen Byberg, Elena Spiridonidi, *New approaches to abstract art*, 2020. From the exhibition *Gunnar S. Gundersen: A Groundbreaking Modernist* at Sørlandet Artmuseum, 2020. Gunnar S. Gundersen, *Komposisjon (Composition)*, 1957. Oil on panel. 150 x 100 cm. Copyright: Gunnar S. Gundersen/BONO 2021. Photo by Lisbet Skregelid. Copyright: Lisbet Skregelid, 2021.

But due to increasing numbers of COVID-19 infections, we had to change plans and hold the museum project online. I encouraged the students to do some research on this matter and then share it with the rest of the group. All the research material consisted of good and not-so-good examples from national and international museums and galleries. We discussed student findings and formed an archive of digital art educational projects that functioned as a resource. Since we were online, I decided that we could just as well make use of all the possible art out there instead of limiting ourselves to the art in Sørlandet Art Museum. Interestingly, as the lockdown had created a need for socializing, the students made projects that included relationality as an important element.

One group based their project, called *Inspired to Hope*, on the works of Japanese avant-garde artist Yayoi Kusama. She is known for using polka dots in her art and often makes large installations that people can walk into, where entire rooms and sculptures are covered with circles. The students wanted to bring us together by creating a room like the ones we see in Kusama's installations, even though we were separated in our different homes. In advance, the students asked us to prepare ourselves for the online session by making dots on different coloured paper. In one part of the project, we were asked to stick these dots on the wall behind us to make one space for all of us (Figure 28.2). Kusama's poem about the coronavirus from 2020 was also read out.

Another group that related their project to relational aesthetics more explicitly sent us a Facebook invitation to a party some days before their art educational project was to be realized. In the invitation, we were given instructions to dress up and have a drink and a nice meal prepared. When we entered their party (still on Zoom), we were welcomed and the guiding questions were shared in the opening speech: *You may ask, what has partying to do with art? Maybe this form of art mediation is just a smart way to be allowed to have a drink, in the middle of the day?* In the speech, the students shared they had started to get bored because of not being able to socialize; therefore, they wanted us to join them at their party with art as an overall frame of reference. After the speech, it was time for a vernissage. Here we were invited to explore a virtual exhibition of partying that they had curated themselves (Figure 28.3).

Art educational workshops inspired by the art itself

I have many more examples: both from the museum space in the years since 2004 and from the recent online projects. Common to all the projects is experimentation and willingness to break out of habitual ways of visiting art. This intentionality relates to how I see educational dissensus as a praxis that aims to challenge regular ways of teaching. All the projects also make use of artistic elements or make the art run through the educational form of the workshops. Throughout the years, the students have made projects we could not have imagined beforehand, expanding our understanding of how

Figure 28.2: Victoria Malmin Helleberg, Oline Hortemo Hareland and Arny Helene Orre, *Inspired to hope*, 2021. Photo by Lisbet Skregelid. Copyright: Lisbet Skregelid, 2021.

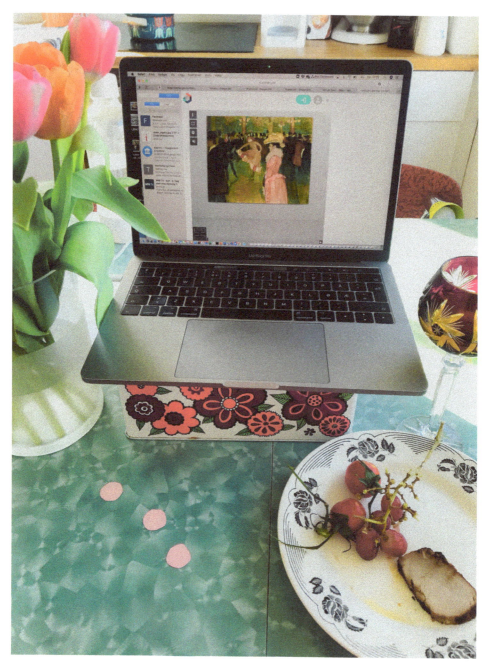

Figure 28.3: Erica Solvoll, Franciszek Piasecki and Iben Kuhn, *The whole evening in 30 minutes*, 2021. Photo by Lisbet Skregelid. Copyright: Lisbet Skregelid, 2021.

pedagogical framing can affect how we encounter the art. My own notions of education in the museum have widened, more lately within the digital domain of art museum education. There is no doubt some rearrangements and events of subjectivation have taken place and will continue to take place for both teachers and students.

References

Atkinson, D. (2011). *Art, equality and learning: Pedagogies against the state*. Sense Publishers.
Atkinson, D. (2018). *Art, disobedience, and ethics: The adventure of pedagogy*. Springer.
Aure, V. (2011). *Kampen om blikket: En longitudinell studie der formidling av kunst til barn og unge danner utgangspunkt for kunstdidaktiske diskursanalyser* [Doctoral dissertation, Stockholm University]. http://urn.kb.se/resolve?urn=urn:nbn:se:su:diva-48277
Biesta, G. J. J. (2017). *Letting art teach*. ArtEZPress.
Biesta, G. J. J. (2018). What if? Art education beyond expression and creativity. In C. Naughton, G. Biesta, & D. C. Cole (Eds.), *Art, artists and pedagogy* (pp. 11–20). Routledge.
Bishop, C. (2012). *Artificial hells: Participatory art and the politics of spectatorship*. Verso.
Bourriaud, N. (2002). *Relational aesthetics*. Les presses du reel.
Christensen-Scheel, B. (2019). Sanselige møter eller kritisk tenkning? Formidling i samtidens kunstmuseer. In C. B. Myrvoll & G. E. Mørland (Eds.), *Kunstformidling. Fra Verk til Betrakter* (pp. 22–46). Pax.
Dysthe, O., Esbjørn, L., Bernhardt, N., & Strømsnes, H. (2012). *Dialogbasert undervisning: kunstmuseet som læringsrom*. Fagbokforlaget.
Helguera, P. (2011). *Education for socially engaged art: A materials and techniques handbook*. Jorge P.
Illeris, H. (2002). *Billede, Pædagogik og Magt: Postmoderne Optikker i Det Billedpædagogiske Felt*. Samfundslitteratur.
Illeris, H. (2005). Young people and contemporary art. *International Journal of Art & Design Education, 24*(3), 231–242.
Massumi, B. (2015). *The power at the end of the economy*. Duke University Press.
Myrvold, C. B., & Mørland, G. E. (Eds.). (2019). *Kunstformidling. Fra Verk til Betrakter*. Pax.
Rancière, J. (1991). *The ignorant schoolmaster: Five lessons in intellectual emancipation*. Stanford University Press.
Rancière, J. (2004). *The politics of aesthetics*. Continuum.
Rancière, J. (2009). *The emancipated spectator*. Verso.
Rancière, J. (2010). *Dissensus on politics and aesthetics*. Continuum.
Skregelid, L. (2016). *Tribuner for dissens: En studie av ungdomsskoleelevers møter med samtidskunst i en skole- og kunstmuseumskontekst* [Doctoral dissertation, University of Oslo].
Skregelid, L. (2020). A call for dissensus in art education! *International Journal of Education Through Art, 16*(2), 161–176. https://doi.org/10.1386/eta_00024_1

Skregelid, L. (2021). Zoom in on dry joy – Dissensus, agonism and democracy in art education. *Education Sciences*, *11*(1), 28. https://www.mdpi.com/2227-7102/11/1/28/htm

Sørlandet Artmuseum. (2020). Kunstnermøte. Kunstnere fra Agder møter Tangen-samlingen. https://www.skmu.no/utstillinger/kunstnermote-sorlandskunstnere-moter-tangen-samlingen/

Wilson, N., & O'Neill, P. (2010). *Curating and the educational turn*. Open Editions.

Chapter 29

The Virtual of Abstract Art: Museum Educational Encounters With Concrete Abstraction

Heidi Kukkonen

I sit on the floor of a large museum room, next to a group of children. I am observing a visit to the Gunnar S. Gundersen – Groundbreaking Modernist exhibition at Sørlandets Art Museum, a regional museum in Kristiansand, Norway. The guide in front of us is telling about the life of this Norwegian painter. We are looking at a large abstract painting with strong, black lines and complex forms. A boy tilts his head to the left, and says, "From this angle, the image looks like a machine..." Others follow the boy's example and tilt their heads to the left, looking at the painting. Then the boy gets on his feet and looks at the painting by slowly tilting his whole upper body to the left. For a brief moment, he is standing on his left leg and balancing his arms wide on his sides like an airplane, eyes fixed on the painting.

By following participatory observation methods with an approach inspired by new materialisms, I observe eight such groups of 10- to 12-year-old children (altogether 145 visitors) on a visit to Sørlandets Art Museum, where they encounter abstract art from the Norwegian modernist painter Gunnar S. Gundersen (1921–1983). The groups participate first in a guided tour with dialogue-based museum educational practices and then visit a digital installation, curated by me and created by the Serbian artist Mirko Lazović in collaboration with the museum. The user-generated installation mediates Gundersen's philosophy of concrete art, inspired by the Swedish artist Olle Bonniér's writings. When visitors enter the room, an image projected on the wall begins to move and transform according to the visitors' movements. The visitors can play and interact with the changing and dynamic composition inspired by Gundersen's *Black Sun* (1967).[1] When I observed the groups, the students began intuitively dancing, singing and playing with the installation. When the children encounter the paintings on the guided tour and interact with the digital installation, the *virtual* abstract art actualizes through discursive and affective routes.

In recent decades, only a handful of studies have been made about museum educational practices with abstract art; these studies focus on meaning-making through language, such as a dialogue in a gallery space or other text-based learning tools (Dima, 2016; Hubard, 2011; Pierroux, 2005; Scott & Meijer, 2009). The situation described above, where the boy balances his body in front of the painting like an airplane, illustrates how abstract art can invite museum visitors not only for verbal interpretation but for movement and multisensory experiences (Figure 29.2). With an approach inspired by new materialisms (Bolton, 2004;

Kontturi, 2018) my focus in this chapter is on the bodily and material aspects of encounters with abstract art.

The purpose of this chapter is to shed light on the *virtual* of abstract art, a concept informed by Gilles Deleuze (1988/2018). I theorize our encounters with Deleuze's theory about the *virtual* and *actual* based on Henry Bergson's philosophy. Matter and objects are not only physical and *actual* but also *virtual* (Deleuze & Parnet, 1977/2002). In *Bergsonism*, Deleuze explains that *virtual* is past time, coexisting with the present, like codes that unfold themselves in the present moment (Deleuze, 1988/2018). Time is not understood as an external force but through action and matter as continuous, immanent and inevitable change. Deleuze (1988/2018) explains that the *virtual* does not mean the opposite of the *real*, but the opposite of the *actual*. Both virtual and actual are real.

In front of an artwork, the materiality suggests and urges us to action, like codes unfolding themselves, but the *virtual* is *actualized* only in lived experience. When I observed the groups with abstract art, the children used their bodies in unexpected ways to view the paintings from different angles and to express themselves in conversations with abstract art. This opened a flow of imagination among the students. I suggest that the virtual can be thought of as all the different ways a work of art can be experienced and actualized, both through language and bodies. I study how the virtuals of abstract art actualize on the guided tour and with the digital installation.

Exploring theory-practice

I have organized this chapter into four parts. In the first part, I introduce my methodological groundings. While my research design is situated in qualitative research and participatory observation methods (Szulevicz, 2020), my approach is influenced by new materialisms (Bolton, 2004; Kontturi, 2018). In the second part, I depict my curatorial plan for the digital installation, which the children visited after the guided tour. Instead of building a representation, I create a space where the visitors explore the philosophy of Gundersen's concrete art, which was inspired by the Swedish artist Olle Bonniér (Bonniér, 1948; Kokkin, 2020). In the third and fourth parts, I analyse how the virtuals of abstract art actualize in the encounters, with concrete examples from the observations.

Gunnar S. Gundersen's art has been called by many names: abstract, non-figurative, concrete and constructivist (Kokkin, 2020). As often pointed out, there is no consensus about the art form's terminology in art history (Kokkin, 2020; Varnadoe, 2006). I use different terms throughout the text, and my decision in each case comes from the motivation to help the reader understand the text. In addition, I intentionally play with the paradoxical relationship of *abstract* and *concrete* in the text to emphasize the paradoxical nature of abstract art.

Participatory observation with new materialisms

The groups participated first on a guided tour at the *Gunnar S. Gundersen – Groundbreaking Modernist* exhibition. The guided tour followed dialogue-based practices (Dysthe et al., 2012), focusing on art historical and biographical information intended to open the students' intuitive interpretations and bodily expressions. After the guided tour, the groups had a workshop where they created abstract art and then visited the digital installation in small groups. Since my focus is on the encounters with abstract art, I have decided not to include the workshop in this text.

The data for this chapter was collected by following participatory observation methods (Szulevicz, 2020; Warming, 2007). When the groups arrived at the museum, they were informed who I was and asked if I could observe the visit. Since I did not know the groups beforehand, and the visitors did not expect a researcher to participate in the guided tour, I took a less visible role during the observations. My role can be described as "observant as participant" (Warming, 2007). Most of the time I silently watched, taking notes, but on some occasions I was actively participating in the situation. For example, the students or the guide would spontaneously engage me in a conversation, or I would ask a short question during the visit. When I observed the groups at the museum, I paid special attention to their movements and other bodily aspects of the visitors. In addition to writing, I drew sketches on the sides of the pages to document their movements. I paid close attention to "not let the textual and discursive powers […] override the material and corporeal intensities" (Kontturi, 2018, p. 45).

Sometimes the students tried to express their thoughts but could not find the words. They started to gesture with their hands and bodies to express themselves. I suggest that the students found an *affective* route for the virtuals to actualize. Affect – for Canadian philosopher Brian Massumi, who bases his theory of affect (2015) on Deleuze and Guattari's and Baruch Spinoza's writings – is not an emotion but intensity and "the *virtual* co-presence of potentials" (p. 5). The artist and theorist Simon O'Sullivan (2001), building on Massumi, writes that *affects* are "reactions in/on the body on the level of matter," and they can be described as "extra-discursive" and "extra-textual" (p. 131). However, the verbal and bodily expressions are often enmeshed in each other, and I regard the discursive and affective lines of actualization as simultaneous instead of exclusive or opposites. Affect does not (always) happen *outside* of words, but *beyond* and *in-between* the discursive or structure. After all, language too has an affective register (O'Sullivan, 2001).

Kontturi (2018) writes that new materialisms take the "vital matter" of art into consideration (p. 14). She says that representational thinking risks a disregard for the unpredictable and creative materiality of art, particularly given that "the movement of art threatens to be reduced to meanings alone – and often to meanings that are already constituted, already known" (Kontturi, 2018, p. 28). Barbara Bolton (2004) makes the case that "representationalism" still dominates our contemporary way of thinking (pp. 12–13). Representation, according to Gilles Deleuze, is formed of opposition, identification, analogy and resemblance (1968/2001).

The curatorial plan in the digital installation

After the guided tour, the groups visited the digital installation in small groups. The purpose of the digital installation was to mediate Gunnar S. Gundersen's art and philosophical ideas about abstract art.[2] From the first meeting onwards, Mirko Lazović and I agreed not to create a representation or a simple copy of Gundersen's work but to generate a space where the visitors could explore abstract art through action and movement. Instead of asking what the artworks represent, I wanted to ask what the artworks can do – or what we can do with them.

The curatorial plan can also be seen in the light of the virtual and actual. Here, I am also loosely paralleling the concepts of *abstraction* and *concrete* together with *virtual* and *actual*. We would build abstract potential (*virtual*) which could then be concretized (*actual*) by the visitors in their own ways and premises. I wanted to curate "an open solution" where the children are helped to get started, but where the outcome or action is not pre-described. I did not want to give ready-made answers about what abstract art is but to provide a space where the visitors can test and experiment with the question themselves with open activities.

It was decided to use Gundersen's concrete philosophy as a starting point in the digital installation. While the museum communicated with Lazović mostly about technical matters, my role as a curator was to provide information about Gunnar S. Gundersen and the context for the project. *Concrete art* came to Norway after the Second World War from Sweden and France, and the international movement was influenced by Bauhaus, suprematism and neoplasticism in Europe (Gjessing, 1998). According to Jan Kokkin, Norwegian art historian and curator of the Gundersen exhibition, Gundersen was influenced by the Swedish artist Olle Bonniér's writings about concrete art (Kokkin, 2020).

Bonniér's text *Naturavbildning. Abstraktion. Konkretion. En begrepsutredning* [Depicting nature. Abstract. Concrete. Investigation of the concepts] (1948) is considered "a manifesto for concrete art in Sweden" (Kokkin, 2020, p. 74). Bonniér writes that art is born through the connection between the image and the spectator. An artwork is concrete when it is perceived only as itself, not as a representation of natural or abstracted forms. He emphasizes that a painting should have a dynamic composition that creates movement to challenge the spectator's perception and make the eyes wonder. The ambivalent image is undergoing continuous change and has a rhythmic matter (Bonniér, 1948). In this case, the digital installation takes place in a darkened room (Figure 29.1). Two projectors project an image on the wall inspired by Gundersen's art, with forms and metallic colours referring to Gundersen's *Black Sun* (1967). When a visitor enters the room, the installation recognizes the body of the visitor, and a circle appears on the wall. The circle starts to move according to the visitor, drawing a trace, making it possible for the visitors to "paint with their bodies" in the space and to interact with the changing and dynamic composition. Some of the elements in the installation have twists and randomness programmed into them to interrupt the visitors: for example, poking and following the visitor's circle to challenge the visitor to move and play.

Figure 29.1: *The digital installation.* I point at the orange circle that depicts my movements in the space. Photo by Heidi Kukkonen. Copyright: Heidi Kukkonen, 2020.

Virtuals actualizing through differentiation and affects

We are sitting on the floor of a dimly lighted museum space. There is excited movement in the group: A girl is wiggling her legs on the floor and a boy next to her is slowly waving his upper body from side-to-side, his eyes on the guide. The guide says that the paintings around us are called concrete, and that they do not represent anything. When the children are asked what they think, multiple hands are raised. "I can see stones; they are in someone's tummy!" says a boy about a painting in front of us. "It is like Olaf's face in Frozen.*" A girl turns towards the back wall and says, "That one looks like a pelican standing on one foot." The guide looks thoughtful. "Wow, you have a great imagination…."*

    Throughout the guided tours, the children pointed at figures in the non-figurative, explaining with words and showing with their bodies how the images reminded them of something familiar. These situations opened a flow of imagination among the children. Even if the activity seems to be based on resemblance and therefore representation (Deleuze,

1968/2001), I argue that the flow of imagination is based on *differentiation*, a character of *virtuality* (Deleuze, 1988/2018). The same painting is suddenly seen from multiple perspectives, each different from the next. The conversation takes a turn to the unknown and the ambiguous in these moments, moving towards a philosophical realm where there are no fixed answers.

This ambiguity and uncertainty might also create discomfort. There were occasions during the observations where the students described the undecidability and the "lack" of fixed answers in abstract art as bothersome or annoying. However, these comments were the key moments that led towards engaging and critical conversations of what and how art can be. I suggest that we should stay and play in the realm of uncertainty – it can be an excellent site of learning for its potential to break old patterns and think anew, to reject tunnel vision and binary thinking and to cope better with the unpredictability of everyday life. Abstract art is a safe and fun way to expose children (and adults) to contradictions and ambiguity. In addition to uncertainty as an important site of learning, such conversations can have other educative benefits, too. According to Dysthe et al. (2012), a dialogue that opens into wondering, counter-perceptions and further reflection promotes democracy and multivocality in the group.

The guide asks what the students think about the oil paintings around us. A girl answers, "They are abstract, and there is not always something particular in the image, you just make it and…" She tries hard to say what she thinks, but she does not seem to find the right words. She makes gestures with her hands in the air, messy circles and scribbles, as if she was intensely painting in the air. A similar situation happens when we have gathered to look at an oil painting called Snake and Bird (1948). A boy says that it looks like a snake in a box, but he, too, struggles to find the right words. He starts to make snake-like movements with his arms, keeping his eyes fixed on the painting.

When the students got engaged in the conversation while looking at the paintings, many began to use their bodies to find new ways to look at the images and express themselves. This created an extra-discursive and affective route to actualize the virtuals of the paintings. In one of the observations, a girl is leaning her body from side-to-side while sitting on the floor and watching a painting (Figure 29.2). Then she gets on her back, lies a moment on the floor and lifts her body slowly up with her arms and hands. She looks at the painting with her head hanging upside down and describes the lines in the image, "The water is moving! Look!"

Here the painting is not only "read" and seen as an example of an art historical canon, but experienced and experimented with movement. Even if the activities focused on verbal conversations, the children used their bodies intuitively and sometimes unexpectedly in the conversations. However, the exhibition architecture itself can stop and start a dialogue (Dysthe et al., 2012). Since the groups were large and each room had a large number of paintings on the walls, there was not always much room for the children to move around, and the children were reminded several times during the guided tour to be careful and to keep a distance from the artworks. The exhibition architecture might hinder the bodily expressions from happening and, therefore, the virtuals from actualizing.

The Virtual of Abstract Art

Figure 29.2: Heidi Kukkonen, *Illustration*. On the left, the boy is balancing his body like an airplane. In the middle, the girl is lifting her body up from the floor while looking at a painting. Copyright: Heidi Kukkonen.

Failures or experiments? Dancing with the digital installation

Three students enter the dark room where the digital installation takes place, and the orange circles mirroring their movements appear on the wall. After a while, they notice that the circles follow their movements and leave traces on the background. All three are silently standing in a line, legs wide apart. When they place their weight from one foot to the other, the wooden floor makes creaky sounds. They begin to play with the sounds by putting as much weight as they can on the front leg. The rocking movement from one leg to the other becomes a dance, and they throw their hair up and down in the same rhythm, as if they were in a concert. The circles and elements are violently shaking on the wall.

In many of the observations, the students begin to intuitively dance in the room. In the situation described above, the dancing happened without words. The students followed silently each other's movements and experiments. The virtuals of the digital installation are actualized not only in direct connection with the literally *virtual* body of the digital installation but in relation to other bodies in the room and the materiality of the space, such as the creaky wooden floor. In one of the observations, a girl began to sing while she danced, and the others joined in her singing while they danced a choreography that they all seem to be familiar with. The *virtual* can therefore not only actualize but the actions create more virtuals as the students follow and interrupt each other's movements.

A girl enters the room and walks towards the moving image on the wall. Then she turns around and looks curiously straight to the projectors. She studies her clothes, covered by the projected images. She looks mesmerised, watching her own hands and body in the light, and slowly touches her sweater where the elements are vibrating.

Brian Massumi (2015) writes that experimental measures can make it possible to access more of the *virtual*: "we can access more of our potential at each step, have more of it actually available" (pp. 5–6). In the encounter described above, the girl is playing with the installation in an unexpected way. Instead of facing the moving image on the wall, she looks in the opposite direction – straight into the projector, breaking the expected pattern of the situation. She then uses her own body instead of the wall to study the projected images. This can be seen as a "failure" in understanding how the installation works or as an experiment leading to something new, yet another virtual actualized in the situation. Similar actions happened many times with the children, something I had not anticipated as a curator. These situations encouraged me to let go of some of the control, to trust the children and to let the museum's educational situations unfold at their own pace without constant guidance and instructions.

Conclusions

"Reading" abstract art on a guided tour awakens a representational conflict and creates a flow of imagination among the children, affording a safe opportunity to encounter uncertainty and ambivalence. Staying and playing in the realm of uncertainty can help us to break old patterns and to think anew, to reject tunnel vision and binary thinking and to cope better with the unpredictability of everyday life. We learn to see things from others' perspectives: counter-perceptions promote democracy and multivocality in the group. In-between, beyond and outside of the discursive structure, the *virtual* abstract art actualizes through the intuitive movements and bodily expressions of the children. With the digital installation, the children are playing, dancing and singing, actualizing the *virtual* and digital materiality of the installation – or as one of the students says during her visit, "You can make art with your body!"

Notes

1. Gundersen, G. S. (1967). *Black Sun* [Painting, acrylic on canvas]. Sørlandets Art Museum, Kristiansand, Norway. https://www.skmu.no/utstillinger/gunnar-s-gundersen-en-banebrytende-etterkrigsmodernist/
2. The installation was part of a larger exhibition that I curated for the museum. The museum applied and received funding for the exhibition from AKO Foundation.

References

Bolton, B. (2004). *Art beyond representation: The performative power of the image.* I.B. Tauris.

Bonniér, O. (1948). Naturavbildning. Abstraktion. Konkretion. En begrepsutredning. *Prisma, 1948*(2), 88–95.

Deleuze, G. (2001). *Difference and repetition* (P. Patton, Trans.). Continuum. (Original work published 1968)

Deleuze, G. (2018). *Bergsonism* (H. Tomlinson & B. Habberjam, Trans.). MIT Press. (Original work published 1988)

Deleuze, G., & Parnet, C. (2002). *Dialogues II* (H. Tomlinson & B. Habberjam, Trans.). Continuum. (Original work published 1977)

Dima, M. (2016). Value and audience relationships: Tate's ticketed exhibitions 2014–15. *Tate Papers, 25.* https://www.tate.org.uk/research/publications/tate-papers/25/value-and-audience-relationships

Dysthe, O., Bernhardt, N., & Esbjørn, L. (2012). *Dialogbasert undervisning – Kunstmuseet som læringsrom.* Fagbokforlaget.

Gjessing, S. (1998). Figur og rom i norsk etterkrigskunst [Painting]. *Fokus 1950.* Valdres Trykkeri.

Hubard, O. (2011). Illustrating interpretative inquiry – A reflection for art museum education. *Curator: The Museum Journal, 54*(2), 165–179. https://doi.org/10.1111/j.2151-6952.2011.00079.x

Kokkin, J. (2020). *Gunnar S. Gundersen: Norwegian post-war modernist.* Arnoldsche.

Kontturi, K. (2018). *Ways of following: Art, materiality, collaboration.* Open Humanities Press.

Massumi, B. (2015). *Politics of affect.* Polity Press.

O'Sullivan, S. (2001). The aesthetics of affect. Thinking art beyond representation. *Angelaki, 6*(3), 125–135. https://doi.org/10.1080/09697250120087987

Pierroux, P. (2005). Dispensing with formalities in art education research. *Nordisk Museologi, 2,* 76–88. https://doi.org/10.5617/nm.3316

Scott, M., & Meijer, R. (2009). Tools to understand: An evaluation of the interpretation material used in Tate Modern's Rothko Exhibition. *Tate Papers, 11.* https://www.tate.org.uk/research/publications/tate-papers/11/tools-to-understand-an-evaluation-of-the-interpretation-material-used-in-tate-moderns-rothko-exhibition

Szulevicz, T. (2020). Deltager observation. In S. Brinkmann & L. Tanggaard. (Eds.), *Kvalitative metoder. En Grunbog* (pp. 97–115). Hans Reitzels forlag.

Varnedoe, K. (2006). *Pictures of nothing – Abstract art since Pollock.* Princeton University Press.

Warming, H. (2007). Deltagende observation. In L. Fuglsang, P. Hagendorn-Rasmussen, & P. Bitsch Olsen (Eds.), *Teknikker I samfundsvidenskaberne* (pp. 314–331). Roskilde Universitetsforlag.

Chapter 30

Projection-Based Augmented Reality for Visual Learning and Creation in Contemporary Art Museums

A Visual Essay

Rocío Lara-Osuna and Xabier Molinet

Projection-based augmented reality (PBAR) techniques offer the possibility to transform flat and three-dimensional surfaces into dynamic interactive displays. This is possible through video mapping software (Figure 30.1), which enables the control and arrangement of projected images in interactive installations (Roldán et al., 2019). This software allows for the connection of different image-capturing devices that can be controlled by the audience to facilitate visitors' immersion and active engagement, fostering an active visual learning experience based on "discursive communication" (Kwastek, 2013, p. 133). We share three examples of installations based on PBAR that were developed in different contexts and with different visual learning objectives to demonstrate the versatility of the approach for museum education.

Dialoguing with Brossa

This example was exhibited in the annual exhibition *Arte para aprender* [Art for learning] (https://www.arteparaaprender.org/) held at the Museum CajaGranada (Granada, Spain) in 2018. For this interactive projected piece, a closed-circuit video installation (Parfait, 2016) was designed with the intention of encouraging visitors to learn about an original work of Joan Brossa (1970) by inserting themselves inside and around the artwork (Figure 30.2).

The installation sought to achieve an interactive image (Martín Prada, 2018) in which the audience, in addition to dialoguing with the work and the rest of the spectators, became an active subject and a fundamental component for a complete understanding of the artistic piece (Figure 30.3).

Figure 30.1: Rocío Lara-Osuna and Xabier Molinet, *Photo essay*, 2021. Composed of two photos by Rocío Lara, 2018.

Figure 30.2: Rocío Lara-Osuna and Xabier Molinet, *Photo essay*, 2021. Composed of three photos by Carmen Ortiz, 2018 and Rocío Lara, 2018.

Picto-luminic-tactile hands

The second interactive installation was part of the *From Mittens to Barbies* workshop (TATE, 2018), held at TATE Liverpool (United Kingdom) in 2018. Another closed-circuit video installation was designed with the intention of highlighting the observation of everyday objects using microscopic cameras and beaming captured images over hand sculptures (Figure 30.4).

Projection on plaster surfaces created a pictorial effect through lighting, transforming the appearance of volumetric pieces. Furthermore, microscopic images projected over the hands provoked the curiosity of visitors, generating a visual connection with the sense of touch, thanks to amplified textures (Figure 30.5).

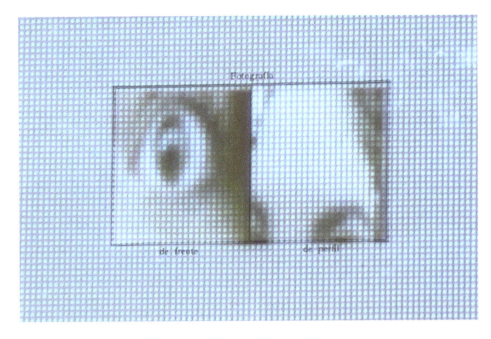

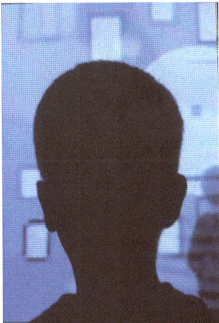
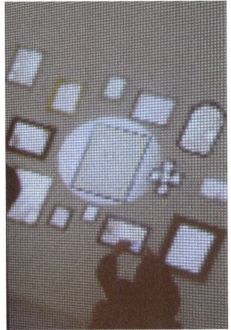

Figure 30.3: Rocío Lara-Osuna and Xabier Molinet, *Photo essay*, 2021. Composed of a photo by Rocío Lara (top), 2018, and two photos by Medardo Cardona, 2018.

Figure 30.4: Rocío Lara-Osuna and Xabier Molinet, *Photo essay*, 2021. Composed of a photo by María Avariento (top) and two photos by Rocío Lara, 2018, including two indirect visual quotations of the piece *El muñeco* [*The doll*] (Rubio Fernández, 2014).

A "Valdeloviewfinder" inside the gallery

The third example was installed at the Hatch Art Gallery in Vancouver (Canada), as part of the collective exhibition *Inhabiting/Living Space* (Shield & Cloutier, 2020). In this case, a special viewfinder inspired by the optical developments in Val del Omar films (Val del Omar, 2019) activated audience participation (Figure 30.6). The tool, composed of a crystal ball and a metal structure that holds a fixed webcam, offered a distorted vision of the pieces exhibited. Images captured by the camera were projected in real time in the exhibition space, so visitors could explore themselves and reconsider the artworks on exhibition by re-viewing them with a different perspective, strengthening a public exchange of the visual details they discovered (Figure 30.7).

Figure 30.5: Rocío Lara-Osuna and Xabier Molinet, *Photo essay*, 2021. Composed of two photos by Rocío Lara, 2018, including an indirect visual quotation of the piece *El muñeco* [The doll] (Rubio Fernández, 2014).

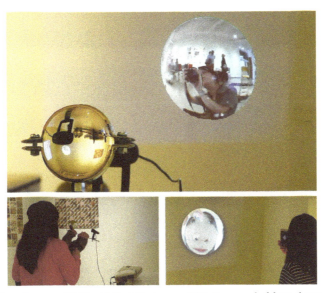

Figure 30.6: Rocío Lara-Osuna and Xabier Molinet, *Photo essay*, 2021. Composed of three photos by Rocío Lara, 2019.

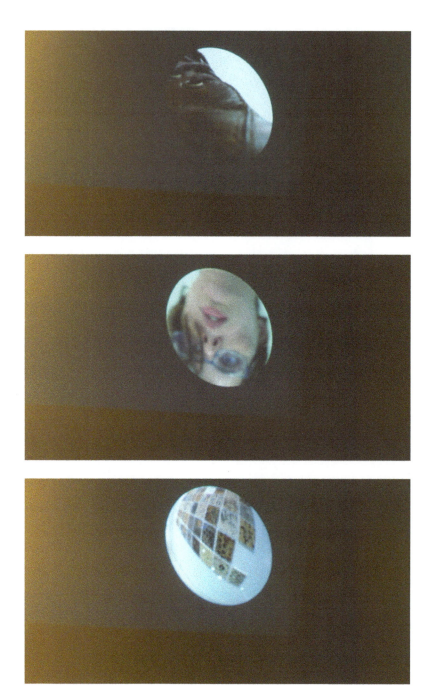

Figure 30.7: Rocío Lara-Osuna and Xabier Molinet, *Photo essay*, 2021. Composed of three photos by Rocío Lara, 2019, including an indirect visual quotation (bottom image) of the piece *A Meter of Territory* (Castillo-Inostroza, 2019).

Concluding comments

These three installations exemplify how through PBAR, spectators can become indispensable creators along with the artist, moving from passive consumption towards fully active and creative aesthetic involvement. This way of conceiving interactivity enables spectators' feedback and aesthetic "response-ability" in terms of how John Cage defined it (1973, p. 10) so that open experiences can be achieved and pursued to facilitate dialogue as the basis of interactivity in museum contexts (Witcomb, 2006).

References

Brossa, J. (1970). *Sin título* [Untitled]. [Serigraphy]. 700 × 500 mm. Museo Caja Granada, Granada.
Cage, J. (1973). *Silence*. Wesleyan University Press.
Castillo-Inostroza, J. (2019). *A meter of territory*. [Photographs]. 100 prints of 100 × 100 mm. Hatch Art Gallery.
Kwastek, K. (2013). *Aesthetics of interaction in digital art*. The MIT Press.
Martín Prada, J. (2018). *El ver y las imágenes en el tiempo de Internet*. Akal.
Parfait, F. (2016). Welcome! On Dan Graham's opposing mirrors and video monitors on time delay. In S. Bianchini & E. Verhagen (Eds.), *Practicable: From participation to interaction in contemporary art* (pp. 469–477). The MIT Press.
Roldán, J., Lara-Osuna, R., & Gonzalez-Torre, A. (2019). The project "Art for Learning Art" in contemporary art museums. *International Journal of Art and Design Education*, 38(3), 572–582. https://doi.org/10.1111/jade.12245
Rubio Fernández, A. (2014). *El muñeco* [The doll]. [Plaster sculptures]. Museo CajaGranada and Centro Cultural Valey de Castrillón.
Shield, A., & Cloutier, G. (2020). Inhabiting/living space. In G. Cloutier, P. Ding, T. Kukkonen, A. Shield, & A. Sokolowski (Eds.), *MAKING Proceedings | InSEA 2019 World Congress* (pp. 855–856). InSEA Publications. https://online.fliphtml5.com/yxjyl/idnn/#p=860
TATE. (2018). *From mittens to Barbies: International arts-based education research – workshop at Tate Liverpool | Tate*. https://www.tate.org.uk/whats-on/tate-liverpool/workshop/mittens-to-barbies
Val del Omar, J. (2019). *Val del Omar: Elemental de España* [Val del Omar: Elementary of Spain]. [Recordings on 5 DVDs]. Cameo Media S. L.
Witcomb, A. (2006). Interactivity: Thinking beyond. In S. Macdonald (Ed.), *A companion to museum studies* (pp. 354–361). Blackwell Publishing Ltd.

Chapter 31

Co-imagining the Museum of the Future: Meaningful Interactions Among Art(efacts), Visitors and Technology in Museum Spaces

Priscilla Van Even, Annika Wolff, Stefanie Steinbeck, Anne Pässilä and Kevin Vanhaelewijn

The museum space and its multiple purposes and meanings

For quite some time, museums have been exploring the potential of technologies and tools for visual literacy education, visitor engagement and exhibition curation, among other things. The COVID-19 pandemic and ensuing lockdowns have, however, accelerated the digitization of museums and intensified the focus on the use of (digital) technological interventions and tools within museums. This trend is mainly received with enthusiasm and excitement by visitors, researchers and museum professionals, but the use of technology should be handled with a certain caution. Technology can be supportive, but it can also become a distraction from the initial and actual purpose (Van Even & Vermeersch, 2019). We inquire in this chapter into how we can establish meaningful interactions among visitors, art(efacts) and technology within the museum space of the future, unlocking the potential of using technology so that it functions as an enabler instead of a barrier.

To dig deeper into these interactions, we first direct attention to the purposes and meanings of museums. The museum space has acquired multiple meanings and purposes throughout time. Where once the museum setting tended to focus on collecting and storing objects, since the eighteenth and nineteenth centuries, the use of object-based information for educational purposes became the dominant function in the museum space. Modern museums have turned into places of learning, where education and training may take place through both formal and informal processes (Günay, 2012).

The purpose of contemporary museums is now to collect, preserve, classify, document, exhibit and curate artefacts and treasures that – depending on the type of museum – have cultural, artistic, historical or scientific significance in order to educate people, support their self-directed learning and last but not least, inspire them. After this fast-forward journey, we are of course tempted to imagine and explore the possible purposes and concepts of the future museum space from the perspective of technology. Will technological change have an impact on the museum concept? And, specifically of interest in our research, how can and will technology be used in a museum setting to support these purposes? What will new technology bring about?

To try and answer these questions, we first discuss the future museum co-imagined through the eyes of youngsters as part of a project in 2018 called RETINA (RE-thinking Technical Interventions to Advance visual literacy of young people in art museums) and connect this project with the notion of meaningfulness. We contrast this with insights from a co-creation workshop in 2021, with museum professionals and researchers, on contemporary uses of technology and their potential role, the supportive and distractive functions of technology, technological enablers and barriers and co-imagined future scenarios (dystopian and utopian). Reflecting on these different perspectives, we end with some conclusions on the possible role of technology within museums of the future.

The future museum co-imagined and co-designed by youth

Our co-imagining of the future museum with youngsters builds further upon insights from three case studies in the RETINA research project of the KU Leuven University in Belgium, which took place in 2018. This project explored how digital tools can enhance the visual literacy skills of young people in art and design museums by organizing two- to five-day co-design sessions with children (aged 10–14 years) in three museums – Ludwig Forum in Germany, Design Museum Gent in Belgium and M Leuven in Belgium – to develop low-tech prototypes for visual literacy tools for the museum of the future (Figure 31.1). This participatory approach included different stakeholders (young visitors in the design process and museum professionals in the evaluation and reflection follow-up) and brought in their different perspectives on digital tools, visual literacy and the future role of museums.

Interestingly, despite the co-designing taking place in different museums with different groups, we found common characteristics with the low-tech prototypes to enhance visual literacy skills and visitor experiences. When we looked at the museum of the future through the eyes of youngsters, we saw there was a strong attraction towards the s(t)imulation of different senses (multisensorial), an experience instead of an information orientation, a focus on contextualization (which exceeds a mere historical background) and an attraction to technological tools with an interactive component. These findings hint at a possible paradigm shift in the future museum concept and purpose and show us how children perceive meaningful interactions with technology.

We did discover, however, some (possible) negative side-effects of using technology during these sessions; namely: (1) some museums do not want to (over) stimulate and actually want to be a place where visitors take time and slow down to *really* look at works; (2) there is a thin line between engaging education experiences and entertainment, and devices often start to become the focus instead of the art(efact); (3) a more nuanced point: interactive tools are attractive, but there are several degrees in interactivity and participation that suggest passive engagement, and sometimes the tool itself is the focus and medium of interaction instead of stimulation for communication between people. In this way, the technology does not necessarily distract from the art(effect), but it lacks a sufficient social component.

As a result, the role of technology in the museum space appeared to be ambiguous in the RETINA project and directed our attention to the importance of a meaningful interaction between museum visitors, technology and art(efacts). Experiences from the RETINA project have shown us that interactions between technology and visitors that lack this element of

Figure 31.1: Co-designing prototypes in the Ludwig Forum Museum, 2018.

meaningfulness can easily lead to a distraction from what we actually want to achieve. In the worst case, technology rather becomes a replacement for art(efacts). There is a danger that the technology becomes the object of interest itself and the primary attraction for visitors. Therefore, meaningfulness should be considered crucial when exploring technology uses and potentials.

Meaningful interaction components

In our case, the interactions we seek are captured by the term "meaningful." To inquire how we can establish a meaningful interaction among museum visitors of all age groups, art(efacts) and technology, we first need to better understand what constitutes the different components of a meaningful interaction.

In the work of Mekler and Hornbaek (2019), we can distinguish different meaning components that can support us in developing user-friendly technology, namely (1) connectedness (connected to the self and the world), (2) purpose (sense of aims, goals and directions), (3) coherence (comprehensibility and making sense of one's experiences), (4) resonance (feeling and intuition) and (5) significance (value and importance).

Based on our experience, some other crucial components can be added to Mekler and Hornbaek's framework that are more context-specific to the museum setting and relate to the visitor experience and the orientation towards art(efacts). Therefore, we suggest (6) collaboration and participation, (7) discovery and (8) authenticity.

Visitors do not always want technology to tell them where to go or what to look at, but rather more meaningful use of technology may be found in the ways in which it fosters collaboration (Sharples et al., 2014) or allows for serendipitous encounters and knowledge discovery (Buchanan et al., 2020). Collaboration and a participatory orientation can be seen as a form of action in which the museum audience plays an active role, and visitors thus participate in the construction of critical meaning-making within a curated process. Different kinds of activities can lead to a participatory approach, such as stories and storytelling or immersive technologies, which merge the physical world with a digital or simulated form of reality. Visitor or audience participation and collaboration, combined with storytelling, is a process of critical interpretation and sense-making of various perspectives, voices and points of view captured in art(efacts). In a museum context, curation of such a process is crucial because interpretation conveys a logical, intuitive and emotional understanding of socio-cultural aspects and actions (Bruner, 1990). A participatory orientation invites audiences to rethink the museum as an interactive space where they can engage as visitors with open-ended questioning (generative questioning), which underpins reflection and investigation of social and cultural assumptions.

Authenticity is also a crucial component. When contemplating the potentials of digital interventions in museums, a central element is how these may affect visitors' experience of the authentic nature of the museum and art(efact) representations. This desire for authentic encounters goes beyond wanting to see and interact and engage with "real" things. It is increasingly connected to audiences wanting a meaningful experience, which satisfies their emotional needs. Thus, the question becomes if and how museums can implement digital interventions that enhance the authentic nature of their exhibitions while supporting the development of meaningful interactions and experiences for visiting audiences. One example of a digital intervention that can enhance an authentic meaningful experience with a participatory orientation is the use of immersive technologies such as virtual reality, augmented reality and mixed reality technologies in exhibitions.

All these components should be considered when incorporating digital technologies in museum settings. When one of the components is absent, technology will become more of a distraction and a barrier rather than a supporter and an enabler. This fragile line between distraction and support is further explored in the following scenarios.

The future museum co-imagined by museum professionals and researchers

In our search for a meaningful use of technology in the (future) museum space, we organized a follow-up co-creation workshop in May 2021 with museum professionals, technology developers and researchers to co-imagine the future museum with different stakeholders. This co-creation workshop took place on Miro, an online whiteboard and visual platform. We asked the participants to brainstorm and share their past work experiences and future ideas during interactive brainstorms and discussions on curation, education and visitor experience. This approach adheres to the principles of participatory methodology, as does co-designing, where you develop *for* people *with* people (Ehn & Badham, 2002). We engaged the different stakeholders – professionals with work experience in museum education, research, curation and technology development – in conversations during the co-creation workshop and added to this set of ideas on how technology is used to look through different professional lenses.

Contemporary uses of technology: Support or distraction?

In the first part of the co-creation workshop, all the co-creators of the museum of the future gave us several examples of current technology uses they were familiar with, and they gave multiple examples of best practices with a high "meaningfulness" level. These practices were based on exhibition experiences: for example, augmented reality immersion of a Van Gogh exhibition in Brussels. We also asked about experiences with technology they disliked and queried what technology cannot replace. Based on these examples, we generated several characteristics for both positive and negative technology uses.

Supportive and supplementary functions and technology enablers

According to museum professionals and researchers, technologies and tools can be used to engage people with art(efacts) and scientific data in new ways. To establish a meaningful engagement with the technology, it was recommended that people be allowed to insert their own narrative as well. This approach leads to visitor involvement and brings in an element of openness.

Another additional and enriching function is to use technology to s(t)imulate sensorial experiences and include the different senses when looking at an artwork or artefact. In the RETINA project, we also found that multisensorial experiences with a s(t)imulation function offer value since they bring (an) art(efact) to life and make the interaction a "lived experience" wherein contextualization and a sense of authenticity can take place.

The use of technology can also assist with knowledge translation practices and offer further conceptualization. Some participants considered facilitating independent knowledge construction as a desirable condition. Technology can offer visitors the possibility of going deeper into the background or additional information and can even include items that are not in the museum's collection. As discussed earlier, immersive technologies can help create an "authentic experience" and make the knowledge translation process easier: for example, putting an artefact in the original setting with its original colours. Furthermore, it is difficult to visualize knowledge such as geographical mobility, cultural exchange and trade on static carriers like text boards. This can be better achieved with digital screens that offer the possibility to present this dynamically.

The aesthetic experience of artefacts can also be enhanced using supportive technologies. For example, we can "restore" a decayed artefact to its former glory without material reconstruction by, for example, augmenting its original state via a mobile app. This has the advantage of keeping the original artefact intact in the condition it was originally found, adding a broader archaeological context to experiencing the artefact.

Digital technology assists in increasing inclusivity and accessibility in the museum: for example, for people who are visually impaired. It can help overcome cultural and linguistic barriers – such as using an audio guide in multiple languages – to make the museum more inclusive. Also, through digital exhibitions, the museum can be made accessible even for those not able to visit the museum physically.

During the workshop, we identified several technology enablers that should help the museum achieve its supportive goal. It was identified that this vision of technology should be part of the general strategic management of a museum concerning where and why technology should be applied. Only through such an integrative approach on all levels of management does the museum make sensible decisions, both in the short and long run, on how to implement these technologies. According to participants, museum management should also pay attention to the sustainability of the technologies they wish to implement.

Another aspect of this strategy concerns the inclusion and participation of different stakeholders: management, curators, visitors, educators and technology developers.

Furthermore, the museum needs dedicated technology experts in their staff team, who oversee the complete processes of technologies in the museum and are aware of new advances in technologies.

Distractive elements, barriers and shortcomings

The use of (more) technologies, especially digital technology, can create a tension with the art(efacts). Often, new technologies are accompanied by a strong belief that they will enable more participation, provoke more sensations and increase fascination. However, we should not forget that originally, the objects of the exhibition themselves were the very reason to attract visitors. The art(efacts) should not become an excuse to deploy new technologies. In such a technocratic paradigm, the role of the museum and the meaning of art(efacts) could become endangered.

Technologies can also prevent people from interacting with each other and museum staff. Technology is not intended as a replacement for the experience of an art(efact) itself, nor is it a substitute for real social encounters, nor can it replace the authenticity of things. A virtual exhibition cannot replace the actual museum visit although it can address issues of accessibility to some degree.

Another distraction is that a museum budget might be tempted to overspend on technologies that perhaps do not deliver the expected results. Investing in "traditional" resources that are not part of a hyped-up trend – such as more staff or educational resources and ventures in general – might actually give the results a museum is seeking.

During our co-creation activities, we identified several barriers to good and meaningful use of technology. The most obvious is that the technology itself can become a barrier when it is not user-friendly. Also, technologies are easily prone to be impersonal, in contrast to a museum guide. A different but possibly related barrier is seen when a given technology leads to a lack of participation or even a form of pseudo-participation. The level of participation can depend on the type of tool or technology being used. Some enable a higher form of interactivity than others: for example, an explanatory video leaves little room for interactivity while a touch screen can offer several exploration options. Therefore, we need to reflect on their characteristics to distinguish which are more participatory-oriented than others.

The economic barrier must also not be forgotten. Museums lacking the funds needed to invest in new technologies may need to outsource this activity, which is not always desirable if the museum wants to remain sovereign. Moreover, outsourcing may not lead to strategies that are long-term oriented or sustainable when the museum staff lacks the competence to maintain these technologies.

Technology does not just offer new possibilities but also introduces limitations, as discussed earlier. We must remain aware of both possibilities and limitations to create sensible uses for these technologies. A possible misuse happens when a technology adds nothing new to the knowledge translation or experience of a collection and the museum space as such.

Future scenarios

A dystopian view

The first group of dystopian scenarios we distinguished is included in Figure 31.2 (red squares). During the co-creation workshop, some participants discussed the possibility that technology becomes a pure distraction that serves entertainment to the detriment of cultural enrichment. In the worst case, technology transforms the museum into a kind of amusement park. One vision sees that artefacts are substituted by technology in the museum. In this future, authenticity is replaced by simulation and meaning by entertainment. When thinking back on the meaning components, we can conclude that this use of technology lacks vision, purpose and resonance.

The second group (black squares) voices a similar concern, but this goes deeper, revealing the digitization of humanity itself. In this dystopian vision, human life is reduced to or

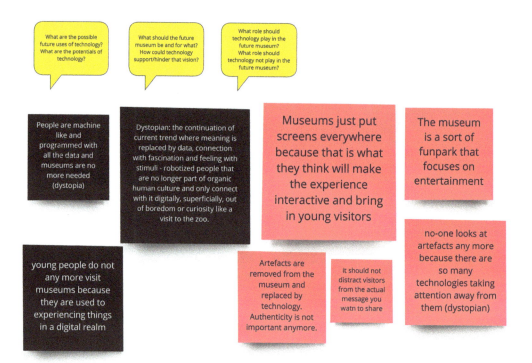

Figure 31.2: Future dystopian scenarios on Miro.

mediated by data. Because in such a future, digitization has become part of the psychology of people, all experiences are reduced to digital information, which is independent of physical space. Clearly, the meaning component of connectedness is missing in this technology vision.

A utopian view

Two main scenarios can be discerned in the utopian future of the museum (Figure 31.3). The first category (yellow squares) speaks of a future where technology enhances, stimulates or augments the experience and connection people have: both with their cultural heritage and with museum collections, through involving the different senses in a positive and enjoyable way that encourages creativity and engagement. In this scenario, hidden qualities are brought within reach with the help of technology.

The second group of scenarios (green squares) speaks of a personal involvement with the museum and its collections. Technologies help bring in voices from outside the museum and cultivate a culture of responsibility and ownership among a broader public. This

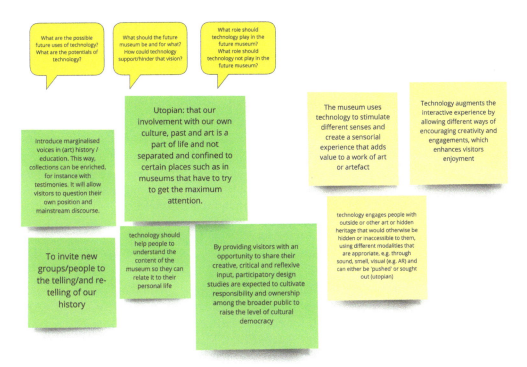

Figure 31.3: Future utopian scenarios on Miro.

"cultural democracy" encourages self-reflection and critical thinking within its population. In its most evolved form, the museum experience is no longer confined to the walls or a particular collection: it becomes part of daily cultural life. The lived experience of culture does not make the museum obsolete; on the contrary, it makes an authentic experience of the museum natural.

Concluding reflections

In this digital era, museums must reinvent themselves and walk new pathways whereby they explore new purposes and concepts of the museum space. Technology plays a prominent role in this transformation and has a strong influence on the experience of visitors, curation practices and education. These tools and interventions can be used to engage people with art(efacts) and scientific data in new ways, stimulate sensorial experiences and assist with knowledge translation practices. They should, however, be supportive of the purposes of the museum and not distract from the art(efacts).

In this chapter, we have discussed the interaction among art(efacts), technology and visitors in the museum space to find ways to keep this interaction meaningful. To establish these conditions in the museum setting, we need user-friendly technology that incorporates different meaning components such as connectedness, purpose, coherence, resonance, significance and discovery. Moreover, we need to make sure that the orientation towards art(efacts) remains authentic and participatory. Different and sometimes conflicting visions of the future museum have been expressed by stakeholders who participated in the research. We cannot exclude the possibility that different museums will take on different future scenarios, just as they do today. The common ground between the different scenarios is to be found in the conviction that people need real interaction with objects, with other people and with the world. This includes all our senses, meaningful dialogues and lived experiences.

We conclude this chapter with a question that we stumbled upon during our study that demands further research: How does the museum type (for example, a natural history museum versus a design museum) have an influence on the use of technology, and would there be different requirements to establish a meaningful interaction?

Acknowledgements and contributions

We would like to thank all the participants of the co-creation workshop who contributed to the insights of this study but did not author this chapter: Klara Hermans (RMAH, Belgium), Annelien Verbeeck (MIM, Belgium), Charlotte Van Peer (M Leuven, Belgium), Sofie Vermeiren (M Leuven, Belgium), Eslam Nofal (Maastricht University, Netherlands), Marije Nouwen (KU Leuven, Belgium), Charmaine Zammit (University of Malta), Raphael Vella (University of Malta) and Jennie Schaeffer (Västmanlands läns museum, Sweden).

Also, a special thanks to Bieke Zaman (KU Leuven, Belgium) who reviewed the setup of the co-creation session and Lode Vermeersch (KU Leuven, Belgium) who was part of the RETINA project team.

References

Bruner, J. (1990). *Acts of meaning*. Harvard University Press.

Buchanan, S. A., Sauer, S., Quan-Haase, A., Agarwal, N. K., & Erdelez, S. (2020). Amplifying chance for positive action and serendipity by design. *Proceedings of the Association for Information Science and Technology, 57*(1), e-288. https://doi.org/10.1002/pra2.288

Ehn, P., & Badham, R. (2002, June 23–25). Participatory design and the collective designer. In T. Binder, J. Gregory, & I. Wagner (Eds.), *Proceedings of the Participatory Design Conference*, Malmo, Sweden (pp. 1–10). https://ojs.ruc.dk/index.php/pdc/article/view/235

Günay, B. (2012, October 5). Museum concept from past to present and importance of museums as centers of art education. *Procedia – Social and Behavioral Sciences, 55*, 1250–1258.

Mekler, E., & Hornbaek, K. (2019, May). A framework for the experience of meaning in human-computer interaction. In *Proceedings of the CHI Conference on Human Factors in Computing Systems* (pp. 1–15). https://doi.org/10.1145/3290605.3300455

Sharples, M., FitzGerald, E., & Mulholland, P. (2014). Weaving location and narrative for mobile guides. In K. Drotner & C. Schrøder (Eds.), *Museum communication and social media* (pp. 187–206). Routledge.

Van Even, P., & Vermeersch, L. (2019). Visual literacy, young people and art and design museums in an era of images: The RETINA Project. In L. Vermeersch, E. Wagner, & R. Wenrich (Eds.), *Guiding the eye: Visual literacy in art museums* (pp. 51–61). Waxmann.

Chapter 32

Immersive Museum Technologies in Turkey and Future Projections in the Field

Ceren Güneröz and Ayşem Yanar

A museum is considered a non-profit, permanent public institution in the service of society and its development. As such it acquires, conserves, researches, communicates and exhibits the tangible and intangible heritage of humanity and its environment for the purposes of education, study and enjoyment (ICOM, 2007). Museums hold artefacts and specimens in trust and work to safeguard diverse memories for future generations, aspiring to guarantee equal rights and access to heritage for all people. Ideally, museums are participatory and transparent; they work in active partnership with and for diverse communities to collect, preserve, research, interpret, exhibit and enhance understandings of the world, aiming to contribute to human dignity and social justice, global equality and planetary wellbeing.

With changes in the definition of a museum's purpose currently underway, the relations established and conducted with the society it serves come to the fore, as do the levels of accessibility (Watson, 2007). Accessibility for museums is the practice of making a museum's sections accessible to all people, which includes making museum websites usable by as many people as possible. Museum websites can play a crucial role by educating the public and representing diverse aspects of culture through a museum's exhibits. The accommodations made for audiences increase a museum's appeal for all who visit, in-person or online, and thus enhance the museum's inclusiveness. Creating an accessible museum that integrates accessibility into every aspect of its operations – governance, management, human resources, education, the registration or collections and curatorial departments, visitor services, information technology and security – is a requirement for contemporary museums. For example, without that broad commitment, a museum might have an accessible building but no accessible exhibits – or vice versa (Montsho, 2020; Poria et al., 2008).

Accessibility and museum technologies

Involving people of all ages in cultural institutions through accessibility is the key point of today's inclusion policies. The changing role of the museum, as embodied by exhibition design that fuses rigorous education with entertainment, interactivity, play and participation (Olesen et al., 2020; Wang & Lei, 2016), triggers a vivid discussion both in academia and the public sector. It is essential to ensure that all programmes, activities and events are also accessible to museum staff and stakeholders, not just the audience and visitors. Equal access must be provided to everyone who wants to use a museum's facility or to research its collections. Cultural programmes must be fully accessible and inclusive to children, women, all citizens with disabilities and adults, including elderly people and cultural minorities. Cultural service organizations need to set an example for their constituents by making their facilities, meetings, websites, print materials and activities fully accessible and inclusive to everyone.

For ICOM's Key Concepts of Museology (Desvallés & Mairesse, 2010), the term "mediation" is preferred as a synonym for interpretation. Mediation implies a whole range of actions beyond interpretation, carried out in a museal context to build bridges between that which is exhibited (seeing) and the meanings these objects and sites may carry (knowledge). In the twenty-first century, museum personnel recognize that carefully designed new technologies may provide visitors with relevant and tailored information and serve to enhance the interpretation of, and engagement with, object-rich collections (Lehn & Heath, 2005). Thus, museum themes should be harmoniously combined with digital content to communicate exhibition content effectively and, at the same time, provide a personally meaningful experience to visitors (Vaz et al., 2018).

Mobile applications, augmented exhibitions, online museum tours and gaming experiences offer immersive and often stunning experiences for visitors. Virtual reality technologies promise to offer an intense, enjoyable experience, but the cost in time, effort and resources can prove to be overwhelming (Lepouras & Vassilakis, 2005). Nonetheless, such technologies are viewed as critically important in enhancing the museum's role as an educational venue – supporting mediation with the interpretation of exhibits and increasing the public appeal of museums.

Museums are exploring the potential of new technologies in their spaces for allowing new scenarios of storytelling and interaction with the exhibitions. In education, the importance of museums is emphasized in emerging concepts of efficiency in education, gaining experience, environment, interaction and constructivism. Due to the wide range of educational options, we firmly believe that the museum can contribute to the mental, physical and emotional development of individuals.

Museums as cultural sites are effective venues for storytelling, with staff eager to craft and distribute new stories in new ways. The likes of augmented reality (AR) and virtual reality (VR) are being used by institutions around the world to make history feel more present both inside and outside the museum space. A number of museums make use of images, sounds and video together, aiming to complement existing presentations and create a memorable exhibition. In Marseille, at the MUCEM Museum of Mediterranean and European Civilizations, each exhibition gallery is supported with video displays, touch screens and kiosks. That museum also uses AR technologies in several sessions, enabling a virtual overlay of educational or entertaining content without modifying the physical space, thus creating a new layer through which to connect with visitors (Murphy, 2018). In another example, in 2019 the Prado Museum in Madrid introduced its first innovative 360-degree immersive experience.

Building on such immediate experiences, digital collections involve another type of technology use in the museum. Digital collections are about being accessible, and digital exhibitions are the easiest and fastest solutions for museums to reach audiences. The Metropolitan Museum of Art in New York made the decision to digitize over 380,000 images from its collection. The Kremer Museum announced a VR experience in 2017, featuring more than 70 Dutch and Flemish seventeenth-century paintings photographed between 2500 and 3500 times. Using the "photogrammetry" technique to build one ultra-high resolution visual model for each painting, this technology allows visitors to enjoy a deeply immersive experience with the paintings. In Japan, in 2018, the Digital Art Museum was launched by the ultratechnologists teamLab; that museum is completely filled with digital works.

Mobile applications are also commonly used in museums, with new applications for the world's largest museums enhancing visitor experiences of vast galleries and stunning collections, with more details as well as information about exhibitions and museum events. Such applications have been provided in both free and paid formats, and select museums are known to offer multiple applications for one location. With the current abilities of smartphones, the use of mobile devices in museums has developed rapidly as demonstrated by renowned establishments such as the Louvre and the American Museum of National History, among others. For instance, *ology* – the most famous app of the American Museum of National History – has been used by teachers for more than twenty years (Kovavisaruch et al., 2015).

Turkish museums in the twenty-first century

Technology use in Turkish museums can be traced to the early 1990s, with private museums leading contemporary museology practices. By the 2000s, it was clear that the understanding and practices of museology had changed. When private museums are compared to state museums today, their internet sites and use of technology continue to demonstrate an advanced infrastructure in a way that visitors can easily follow. Private museums such as Sabancı Museum, Istanbul Modern Art Museum and Pera Museum have endorsed using the internet in museology (Barlas Bozkuş, 2014). Subsequently, in 2006, the Ministry of Culture and Tourism established a Technology Development Branch to transfer its cultural heritage assets to the virtual environment. With the application launched by the Ministry, more than 40 museums – including the Museum of Anatolian Civilizations (European museum of the year winner in 1997), the Topkapi Palace Museum, the Ephesus Museum and the Museum of Troy (European museum of the year winner in 2020) – can be visited online with a 360-degree panoramic view. Several museums in Istanbul and special ancient sites of Troy, Assos, Ephesus and Knidos in the Aegean Region are included in these projects (Çıldır & Karadeniz, 2014).

The Ministry also participates in international cultural heritage projects such as the Museum with No Frontiers (MWNF). MWNF is a kind of virtual museum project that builds bridges through cultural history and contributes to peace initiatives through greater access to knowledge and understanding. MWNF promotes an entirely new, inclusive vision of history that highlights and celebrates the interconnections, cross-fertilizations, exchanges and cooperation between cultures in areas as diverse as archaeology, art and culture, economy and social life. Turkey participated in that project with twenty museums (Museum with No Frontiers, 2021).

Within this educational landscape, interactive technologies, simulation, presentation and exhibition designs have also increased in the museum galleries of Turkey. In 2012, the Ministry started reconstruction works in sixteen museums to renew them in accordance with contemporary museum approaches. These museums include Aksaray Museum, Adana New Archaeological Museum, Bitlis Ahlat Museum, Çanakkale Museum of Troy, Hatay New Archaeological Museum, Şanlıurfa Archaeological Museum, Haleplibahçe Mosaic Museum and Archaeopark, Göbeklitepe Reception Center, Uşak Archaeological Museum and Van-Urartu Museum. In 34 new museums, there are projects aiming to address audience perception by using visuality and related technological facilities, informed with scientific content and new museum architectural design.

Immersive museum technologies in Turkey

For a long time, the term "immersion" has been almost exclusively linked to the gaming industry. However, it also refers to a broad spectrum of experiences – from literature and music to learning (Derda, 2020). Immersion can also be linked to exhibitions, where it is defined as a multisensory experience that "transports" visitors to a different time, place or situation and makes them active participants in what they encounter (Gilbert, 2002).

Mortensen (2010) describes an immersion as one that creates a three-dimensional world by distorting the feeling of time and place, all the while integrating visitors into the experience. Immersion then describes the feeling of being submerged in a completely different reality: one able to grasp, absorb and engross our attention and perception (Gilbert, 2002). That is why, in museology, immersion is a new dimension of design that needs to be taken into consideration. Gilbert (2002) identified that museum professionals are motivated to create experiences that are more interactive, generating a new and potentially competitive leisure-time option more memorable and engaging and finally more effective in making meaning and communicating content – all integral for museums' success. According to Muthiah and Suja (2013), immersive events can create lasting impressions and favourable memories. Immersive methods, with their interactive and engaging possibilities, offer a new aesthetic experience and spectatorship while transcending the human–technology relationship (Bartlem, 2005). It is clear that they are important for museums' identity-building, perception-shaping and marketing efforts, while also playing an important role in word-of-mouth advertising (Popoli & Derda, 2021).

Museum technology projects have been initiated to establish technological infrastructure for several museums and ruins associated with the Ministry since 2000. Within the context

Immersive Museum Technologies in Turkey and Future Projections in the Field

of those projects, the agenda is to construct brand-new pay-desk infrastructures, Internet Protocol cameras and advertisement display networks, as well as modern ticketing practices.

The most common museum technology is the development of a digital information guide and audio headphone systems. Practices providing more interactive museum experiences have been adopted by the Eskişehir Archaeology Museum, Gaziantep Zeugma Museum, Kayseri Seljouk Museum, Galata Mevlevi Dervishes Lodge Museum, Adana and Mersin Archaeology Museums and others – such as installed systems for various visual effects, live painting practice, 3D information systems, stratified holograms, virtual practices, touch screens, digital books, thematic simulations and virtual workplaces. On the Ministry website, virtual visiting practices to some important historical places such as museums, palaces, mosques and fortresses are shared. Among these practices are panoramic tours and virtual museum gallery visits, especially important during closures because of the COVID-19 outbreak. These applications have proven crucial for audiences.

Some AR applications exist in museums, but most are not yet mobile. One example of its technological shift to AR is the *Antalya Exposition* (2016), which presents its visitors with a virtual tour of an ancient Hittite Village (Figure 32.1). To make visitors experience the changes of the seasons in an old Anatolian village, touch screens and kiosk controls – installed in the exhibition hall – are designed to enable interactivity.

Figure 32.1: A view from an old Hittite village. Animation, *Antalya Exposition*, 2016. Photo by Ceren Güneröz.

The Topkapi Palace Gun Collection is another example of enrichment with museum technologies. Various themed short animations and films about the Ottoman military and weapon culture are displayed on an LCD TV information screen. Additionally, 3D holograms of the most famous Ottoman army figures of the Janissary, Cavalryman and Mariners – along with a large map and an LCD TV which contains miniature recreations about several wars – are among the most popular attractions of the museum. Scenes from miniature books written and illustrated in manuscript workshops in Ottoman palaces have been transformed into digital animation by Sabancı Museum, İstanbul. The applications in the museum offer extended information about the art of books and calligraphy in comprehensive collections for museum visitors. Other applications using AR techniques especially aim to attract children and young people to the museum. As well, an interactive game in the museum reflects the historical places of Istanbul, and it can be played on the touch screen. The museum digitized some objects and created interactive exhibits to demonstrate handwriting and making pottery, which was transferred to AR systems for ease of accessibility. Thus, traditional arts are combined with technology. Several such digital tools about traditional Turkish arts were developed for ethnographical museums in Turkey. For example, touch screens at the Çorum Archeological Museum guide visitors on burial ceremonies (Figure 32.2).

Another key example of virtual workshops is that of digital marbling, which requires specific adaptations to reflect traditional marbling methods and techniques; however, these can be easy to learn and perform in a traditional manner (Gazziro et al., 2018). Functionality is the most important factor in maintaining the art of marbling as well as other traditional arts. It needs to be reinterpreted according to the conditions of the period. That is why, as a traditional art in several Turkish Museums, marbling has already been incorporated through digitization. These virtual workshops aim to create a functional sample for edutainment activities for audiences. An example of this may be found in the Ottoman Archives Museum, which started to use a digital marbling application in 2015. When visitors enter the relevant hall in the museum, they come across a full-fledged marbling set with its dyeing boat, tragacanth, brushes and paints in various colours on the touch screen. The main goal of the workshop is to introduce visitors to marbling, which is one of the rare Ottoman arts. This workshop also allows marbling artists to discuss the techniques of the application. VR apps and games for different platforms like Steam and Sony VR have also been developed for museums dedicated to traditional marbling. Museum audiences can create their marbling art pieces as if they were in a traditional workshop.

Our final example, *A Green World for Future Generations*, is an exposition that opened in Antalya in 2016. It aimed to develop environmental awareness, increase audience sensitivity to related issues and transfer knowledge to new generations. The main target audience is children, and one of the most important themes, "children and flowers," was located within the Agriculture Biodiversity Museum, which focused on "nurturing the future." After 10,000 years of agricultural and horticultural development, today people are dependent on cultivated plants. Fewer and fewer species are cultivated every day, and this fact – together

Figure 32.2: Touch screens showing Hittite Civilisation Burial ceremonies, Çorum Archeological Museum, Turkey. Photo by Ceren Güneröz, with the permission of REO-TEK Digital Museology.

with climate changes – puts at risk not only biodiversity but also food security for the future. Short films are held in the leaf-shaped structures of the museum. The development and agricultural technologies of agriculture from the past to present in the museum are the "living wall" technology, which encourages visitors to walk through the history of agriculture, accompanied by visuals as immersive technological applications.

Conclusion

The museum profession has a clear didactic role to play in cultivating awareness of such matters within the digital community by presenting material on the internet using the museum platforms. It is also within the power of the profession to increase public understanding of the internet's utility in providing access to museum resources. By adopting a proactive stance on "born-digital activity" and on anything presented as an internet/virtual/online museum, the professional community will be securing its ability to forge the shape of the museum as it expands ever further into the boundless digital realm (Karp, 2004, p. 50).

Accessibility to museums for all peoples of all ages and abilities has been an issue for many years. Museums have opened their displays to the public as opposed to their previous exclusive dedication to scholars. However, their interpretative provision was purely focused on educational outcomes. In the twenty-first century, technology has a place in art, affecting and shaping it in every respect. By blending art with technology as coexistence – such as the presentation of thoughts and actions in a different way – the development of new art forms in museums is more visible. Recently, in addition to exhibiting in these areas (especially with an emphasis on technology), video installations attract the attention of visitors through their interactive applications. New technologies make it easier to access cultural heritage sites.

Online exhibitions have an important place among the audience-development strategies of museums. According to Reino et al. (2007) regarding the use of technology, people were generally satisfied without the availability of touch screens; nevertheless, a high percentage of visitors would have appreciated them in both museums mentioned above.

Museums can offer technologically enhanced facilities to the public as a source of richness, using visual culture elements with the help of posters, billboards, TV and internet advertisements to promote these technologies. In addition, they can cooperate with large companies and brands in the technology marketplace, forming partnerships to expand the scope of leading-edge technological innovations. They can access technology funding by searching national and international projects. These initiatives will increase the technological opportunities of museums and their accessibility. For new museum projects in Turkey, a set of studies has begun to address visitor perceptions and provide educational opportunities (İşçi et al., 2020). As a result, the museums of Turkey are becoming more "people-oriented" through the use of contemporary technology.

References

Barlas Bozkuş, Ş. (2014). Rethinking nationalism in the case of conquest museum. *Global Media Journal*, *4*(8), 1–12.

Bartlem, E. (2005). Immersive artificial life (A-life) art. *Journal of Australian Studies*, *28*(84), 95–107. https://doi.org/10.1080/14443050509387995

Çıldır, Z., & Karadeniz, C. (2014). Museum, education and visual culture practices: Museums in Turkey. *American Journal of Educational Research*, *2*(7), 543–551. https://doi.org/10.12691/education-2-7-18

Derda, I. (2020). Immersion, so what? From engagement to immersion in sports activations. In P. Godlewski & P. Matecki (Eds.), *Sports marketing: Professional management in sports* (pp. 39–55). Gdansk University of Physical Education and Sport.

Desvallées, A., & Mairesse, F. (2010). *Key concepts of museology*. Armand Colin.

Gazziro, M., Gois, J. P., Gonzales, C. T., & Rodrigues, J. F., Jr. (2018). A computational method for interactive design of marbling patterns. In *2018 17th Brazilian Symposium on Computer Games and Digital Entertainment (SBGames)* (pp. 1–109). https://doi.org/10.1109/SBGAMES.2018.00010

Gilbert, H. (2002). Immersive exhibitions: What's the big deal? *Visitor Studies Today*, *5*(3), 10–13.

ICOM. (2007). *Museum definition*. https://icom.museum/en/resources/standards-guidelines/museum-definition/#:~:text=%E2%80%9CA%20museum%20is%20a%20non,of%20education%2C%20study%20and%20enjoyment

İşçi, C., Güzel, B., Maktal Canko, D., İşçi, T., & Moroğlu, F. (2020). Müze deneyimi: Yönetim ve ziyaretçi perspektiflerinin karşılaştırılması. *Turizm Akademik Dergisi*, *7*(1), 29–45.

Karp, C. (2004). Digital heritage in digital museums. *Museum International*, *56*(1–2), 45–51.

Kovavisaruch, L., Sanpechuda, T., Chinda, K., Wongsatho, T., Chaiwongyen, A., & Wisadsud, S. (2015). Museum's pool: A mobile application for museum network. *Portland International Conference on Management of Engineering and Technology* (pp. 1230–1235). https://doi.org/10.1109/PICMET.2015.7273028

Lehn, D., & Heath, C. (2005). Accounting for new technology in museum exhibitions. *International Journal of Arts Management*, *7*(3), 11–21.

Lepouras, G., & Vassilakis, C. (2005). Virtual museums for all: Employing game technology for edutainment. *Virtual Reality*, *8*, 96–106.

Montsho, G. (2020, January 22). *Making museums accessible to those with disabilities*. MuseumNext. https://www.museumnext.com/article/making-museums-accessible-to-those-with-disabilities/

Mortensen, M. F. (2010). Designing immersion exhibits as border-crossing environments. *Museum Management and Curatorship*, *25*(3), 323–336.

Murphy, A. (2018). *Technology in museums: Introducing new ways to see the cultural world*. Museums+Heritage. https://advisor.museumsandheritage.com/features/technology-museums-introducing-new-ways-see-cultural-world/

Museum with No Frontiers. (2021). *About the project*. http://sharinghistory.museumwnf.org/about.php

Muthiah, K., & Suja, S. (2013). Experiential marketing – A designer of pleasurable and memorable experiences. *Journal of Business Management & Social Sciences Research*, *2*(3), 28–34.

Olesen, A. R., Holdgaard, N., & Laursen, D. (2020). Challenges of practicing digital imaginaries in collaborative museum design. *CoDesign*, *16*(3), 189–201. https://doi.org/10.1080/15710882.2018.1539109

Popoli, Z., & Derda, I. (2021). Developing experiences: Creative process behind the design and production of immersive exhibitions. *Museum Management and Curatorship*, *36*(4), 384–402. https://doi.org/10.1080/09647775.2021.1909491

Poria, Y., Reichel, A., & Brandt, Y. (2008). People with disabilities visit art museums: An exploratory study of obstacles and difficulties. *Journal of Heritage Tourism*, *4*(2), 117–129.

Reino, S., Mitsche, N., & Frew, A. (2007). The contribution of technology-based heritage. In M. Sigala, L. Mich, & J. Murphy, (Eds.), *Information and communication technologies in tourism* (pp. 341–352). Springer.

Vaz, F. I. R., Fernandes, O. P., & Veiga, R. C. A. (2018). Interactive technologies in museums: How digital installations and media are enhancing the visitors' experience. In F. M. J. Rodgriues, Q. M. C. Ramos, S. J. P. Cardoso, & C. Henriques (Eds.), *Handbook of research on technological developments for cultural heritage and e-tourism applications* (pp. 30–53). IGI Global.

Wang, Q., & Lei, Y. (2016). Minds on for the wise: Rethinking the contemporary interactive exhibition. *Museum Management and Curatorship*, *31*(4), 331–348. https://doi.org/10.1080/09647775.2016.1173575

Watson, S. (2007). *Museums and their communities*. Routledge.

Chapter 33

A New Pedagogy of Museology? Innovative Changes in Museum Education for Cultural Heritage, Social Communication and Participation: A Case Study

Renata Pater

At the onset of the COVID-19 pandemic, schools, universities, cultural institutions, museums and theatres all closed. In Poland, most of professional life, school teaching, art and culture quickly moved online. Many daily activities in the virtual space have been intensified, from basic shopping to using medical services, maintaining contact with family and even playing music with others. While experiencing this difficult time of physical separation, many cultural institutions, including museums, were forced to take steps to develop and support novel relationships with the public. The new pandemic-related educational challenges have shown that a number of intermediary and communication practices of museums need to be rethought and redesigned. Physical distancing, restrictions when it comes to face-to-face meetings, mask-wearing and a strict hygienic regime, as well as closures of public and social spaces, were only some of the obvious challenges.

During the pandemic in Poland, the Ministry of Culture and National Heritage – along with the National Institute of Museology and Protection of National Collections and the Forum of Museum Educators – developed a set of rules for educators conducting classes in museums.[1] During this demanding period, many museum employees became unemployed, placing further pressure on museums in general as cultural institutions. The aim of this chapter is to reflect on museum education during this prolonged crisis, which not only forced museums to establish a presence in cyberspace but also opened new possibilities for diverse groups of visitors, providing much-needed support for maintaining good physical and mental health of the population.

Next steps: The educational and technological turn

The question is, what will be the lingering effects of the pandemic? What new forms of activity will museums initiate in different regions of the world? Applications developed by various companies include algorithms that are supposed to make it easier for us to communicate and establish new social and personal contacts.[2] The extent to which new acquaintances were made in this way will become permanent habits of mind depending on many factors and conditions. The technological-educational turn has simultaneously affected all recipients of "prefigurative culture" (Mead, 1970). The youngest generation of users moves in this environment more efficiently, often assisting their parents and grandparents. The time of the pandemic resulted in social media becoming an environment for education and social relations, as was assumed by turn-of-the-century researchers (Meier & Reust,

2000; Zacharias, 2000), along with a deepened social turn to cultural museum cyberspace in the form of digitized collections (Dittwald, 2011). During the pandemic, face-to-face interactions with audiences were minimized and reduced to small, intimate groups, often shifting to areas surrounding the museum environment in response to the needs of the local community. In Poland, many museums have turned in this direction; conferences are held and projects were undertaken that address the issue of building a community around the museum. An example of this approach is a museum think-tank: museums and neighbourhoods.[3]

Innovation in education or new museum pedagogy?

Nowadays, the role of educational initiatives developed in museums internationally and locally (in Poland, Eastern Europe) is growing dynamically (Pater, 2016; Pater & Karamanov, 2020). New proposals are set out for audience involvement in the context of making tangible and intangible cultural heritages both available and accessible (Macdonald, 2015). Art has become an important medium for reconciliation and mediation between generations (Hubard, 2015). Dynamically developing new technologies are becoming incorporated into exhibition spaces, serving as new tools for learning the content of museum collections and their objects. Through games and play, the interactive contexts of exhibitions are extended to the internet. The nature of museum-based learning processes is gradually changing, inviting the viewer to interact and discover meanings through experimentation. The proposed activities provide a forum for expressing opinions, asking questions and even involving the museum community in curatorial work on the development of new exhibitions (Piontek, 2015; Simon, 2010).

Museum educators are establishing increasingly close relationships with local residents by building a community around the museum. Practical activities implementing the museum participation paradigm in Poland are presented in the "Atlas muzealnej partycypacji" (Atlas of Museum Participation) by Katarzyna Jagodzińska.[4]

In Poland, an intensive development of museology took place after the overthrow of communism by the Solidarity movement in 1989. Joining the European Union in 2004 significantly enabled the development of innovative educational activities.[5] In 2006, the Social Forum of Museum Educators was established, which became an initiator of practical changes in Polish museum education and a support link for educators and museum animators.[6] Established in 2011, the National Institute of Museology and Collections Protection has raised the prestige of the "Sybilla" competition, in which prizes are awarded for the most important museum events of the year, including in the category of museum education. (Information on the initiatives awarded in 2011–2020 is available on the competition website.[7]) In 2015, the First Congress of Polish Museum Professionals took place with a focus on the state and future of Polish museology. Among the key topics, museum education was discussed as a separate section.[8] The changes that have taken place in museum education in the last half century indicate the growing social impact of museums in the educational, intergenerational and intercultural dimensions. Research on museum education stresses its growing social and educational role (Hein, 1998; Hooper-Greenhill, 2007; Meier & Reust, 2000; Nettke, 2015; Szeląg, 2019).

The social significance of a museum is fundamentally expressed in its accessibility for social groups with different needs (children, adolescents, adults, disabled and socially excluded). "Accessible museum" is also one of the tabs in the Education section of the Museum of Modern Art in Warsaw website, which addresses content and people with various disabilities.[9] Many museums have introduced and developed online educational activities on the web. The attractiveness of museum collections and the authentic, original "power" of individual objects that have an impact on the viewer's emotions have been extended to didactic multimedia tools, designed to help viewers understand cultural phenomena on many levels. This is also one form of an "accessible museum."[10]

Opening cultural education, not only in cyberspace

The dynamic development of cultural education has also found its place in the museum. In Poland, several new museums have been created; some of them are under construction but still carry out educational activities, such as the Polish History Museum.[11] During the pandemic, this proved to be both necessary and helpful.[12] Museums with digital collections can offer new activities to audiences in the virtual space much more easily and quickly:[13] this was especially the case when schools were closed during the lockdown, and parents were required to take over care of their children and support them in remote learning.[14]

By moving completely to the internet, school education had to be open to new opportunities and suggestions delivered directly to the children's doorsteps.[15] For example, the Museum of Krakow held an online meeting on its educational proposal, "The power of the Internet (in) education" (18 January 2021). It has also produced films and held web-based competitions for learners. As expressed by the slogan – "At the Krakow Museum, we focus on education!" – education is part of that museum's activities, and it has offered a host of lessons online.[16] Building links between museums and the public through the internet has become a sign of recognizing the needs of different social groups and an invitation to participate in novel forms of interaction. Educational programmes in Poland, offered in English and Ukrainian as well as Polish, have been aimed at different intercultural communities also, to help people overcome the difficulties of social isolation, loneliness and helplessness they experienced during the pandemic. The multicultural community of Krakow was invited to participate in the "listening to the city" project, with the artistic documenting of life in the pandemic: "We are describing, documenting the city and telling stories about Krakow. We are listening to Krakow. Home studio. Home-made storytelling" (Niezabitowski, 2021). The project ended with an exhibition.[17] The Tatra Museum's (Muzeum Tatrzańskie) educational blog was created with local residents in mind, but during the pandemic it also sparked interest among Poles living abroad.[18] Similar internet activities offered by the Polish museums have met with interest in various parts of the world.[19]

In a way, the limitations imposed by the pandemic forced museum professionals to undertake new tasks for which they had no time before, such as virtual exhibitions.[20] New suggestions for "listening" to the museum and "listening in" to the stories about the museum have proven to be useful. Muzeum Cricoteka in Krakow offered a sound-collecting walk through the city. "Kantor tu jest" [Kantor is here] is a story of the city seen with the artist's eyes, inspired by the art of Tadeusz Kantor. The museum also offered a form of "artistic walks" to audiences staying at home during lockdown.[21] Suggestions for activities during museum closures and winter holidays were sent out by museums all over Poland. On the website of the National Institute of Museology and the Protection of Collections, parents, teachers and guardians could find the full programme of *Winter Holidays with the Museum 2021*.[22] The continued presence of cultural heritage in cyberspace required a great deal of effort by educators, museum professionals and IT specialists. Classes were also supported in the form of remote collaboration, by meetings in chat rooms and webinars. In this way, meetings could be held when that would not have been possible before the pandemic.[23] The virtual collaborative platform discussions, preceded by presentations of museum activities, inspired new projects and helped establish issue-based collectives.[24]

Museum education, as presented in its new dimension in cyberspace, is becoming a particular form of delivery open to the actual needs of both local and global communities. The temporal dimension is important. Museums continue to play a key role in cultural, aesthetic, artistic and historical-humanistic (and humanitarian) education. The past finds its dimension in museum collections, stories and the provenance of the individual object. We are creating the future today by using museum collections and objects (museum education) to build good intergenerational relations and understand our own history and existence more fully.[25]

The global pandemic has shown us how quickly we can find ourselves in unexpected situations. Physical confinement and isolation triggered the need, or even the urge, to open up to our closest neighbours. In this context, art turned out to be a liberating medium in the Polish experience. The activities initiated by artists in their residences became not only local balcony concert events but also a new way of establishing relations. The language of music and the visual arts contributed significantly to the building of a community of values (Olbrycht, 2019; Żuk, 2016; Żurakowski, 2011). The performances of artists supporting doctors, nurses and health services involved in the relief effort were a special sign of solidarity and a spontaneous expression of understanding and thanks. Videos circulating on the internet at the beginning of the pandemic showed just how much everyone needs good relationships with other people to be able to overcome the fears and prejudices, the loneliness of forced physical isolation and the difficulties of times of reduced health or illness. Museums around the world have responded to this situation. In Poland, cultural institutions have taken various actions, supported by aid programmes launched by local governments and state authorities. Educators encouraged the public to participate in social culture with invitations to virtual exhibitions, concerts, public readings and creative involvement with art. The time of the pandemic revealed new possibilities via new forms of artistic communication, connecting through art and with art. But most of all, it was art that became a bridge to unity, helping us live through this difficult time.[26]

Online meetings in the space of museum collections at least partly compensated for our inability to meet face-to-face. An invitation to interpret the cultural heritage of our ancestors in different historical periods is, in fact, an invitation to creatively wrestle with reality and to continue examining oneself in the difficult art of living. In 2020, the European Commission and Europa Nostra honoured 24 exemplary achievements from eighteen European countries. The permanent exhibition at the European Solidarity Centre in Gdansk was the only Polish winner of the European Heritage Award/Europa Nostra 2021 and was recognized in the category of education, training and awareness raising. The exhibition uses modern display techniques and a participatory approach. During the pandemic, the European Solidarity Centre offered residents of the city walks and meetings organized in different languages.[27]

Open and holistic education in the twenty-first century

Contemporary educational spaces created in museums, art galleries, science centres and theme parks in Poland and beyond enjoy great popularity, attracting the interest of audiences of all ages. In art galleries, science centres and museums, education is delivered holistically through interactive exhibitions. Relevant examples can be found at the Copernicus Science Centre, Zachęta National Gallery of Art, Warsaw National Museum and the Museum for Children in the State Ethnographic Museum, as well as many others.[28] The goal is to holistically address the multiple interests and cognitive capacities of human beings (Commandeur et al., 2015). It is proposed that museum activities take place by means of independent, autonomous choices of different learning paths, ways of experiencing exhibits and objects, learning about phenomena and solving problems (Hein, 1998). This principle also applies to cyberspace, where viewers can navigate and select educational programmes by themselves, guided by their own individual interests. Further examples of activities can be found at the Copernicus Science Centre and the Polish Song Museum.[29]

Art in museum education – Education as a museum-based art of humanization

In Poland, we are witnessing a significant shift: Contemporary art enters into a performative relationship with the viewer in the virtual realm. Establishing interactions encourages cooperation, reflection, the awe of beauty and, above all, critical thinking (Dutton, 2020; Kwiatkowska-Tybulewicz, 2016).[30] Museum pedagogy relies on skillfully introducing the viewer to the diversity of art worlds and developing socio-cultural competencies. In this context, education through art is defined as a process aimed at finding understanding and establishing a value-oriented dialogue (Olbrycht, 2019; Zalewska-Pawlak, 2017; Żurakowski, 2011).[31]

As a site of informal education, the contemporary museum is a meeting place, a third shared space beyond home or school/work, which is both recognizable and important in the local community as well as the "global village" of cyberspace (Mendel, 2017; Zacharias, 2000). Characteristic of the second decade of the twenty-first century is the participatory dimension of cultural institutions and the social engagement of museums in lifelong education (Fuchs, 2015). Emerging activities addressing existential themes and issues such as time, happiness, closure, isolation, enslavement and cultural or social mores – in the broad context of exhibitions, collections and more – today significantly broaden the definition of the museum as an institution that functions actively in cyberspace as well as actual space.

In this new museum pedagogy, learning takes place in a dialogic encounter between agents. It is learning in relationship with another person, with the object and its content values; it is also a mutual and empathic kind of learning. To some extent, this marks a return to the ancient Greek idea of the *museion* as a learning community. The particularly relevant contemporary meta-competence of "learning" encompasses all processes created for the acquisition of social and civic competencies, new knowledge and skills and taking up new approaches. Humanistic education is understood in Poland as cultural education in and through the museum (Nettke, 2015; Szeląg, 2019). Acquiring and developing cultural competencies strengthens the intrinsic motivation to change and discover new opportunities and realize one's full potential. The effectiveness of non-formal education is significant in this regard; a museum is a place that actively supports not only preschool and school education processes but above all offers competence-based education for different audiences in the process of lifelong learning (Commandeur et al., 2015; Hooper-Greenhill, 2007; Pater & Karamanov, 2020). It supports creative development in formal and informal education by developing manifold competencies. This challenge is being taken up by museums and art galleries across the world as they become spaces for dialogue and reasoning and for the persistent discovery of truths about the world, oneself, the other and the reality around us. The future of the museum is in constant dialogue with its audiences, where a sense of agency resides in the understanding of the "new" *paideia* – on the different paths of real life and in cyberspace (Archer, 2013; Olbrycht, 2019).

The experiences of recent years have shown how quickly the world around us can change. Polish museums have developed quite intensively in the last decade, but the pandemic radically accelerated these changes. Currently, museologists and educators are discussing what new dimensions may emerge within the museum during the post-pandemic period.[32] The new *paideia* of the museum appears today as a "common good," the essence of which is the development and deepening of humanity's relationship with others in the world of art and culture and of the diverse communities of the global village. "The act" defines humanity in an ethical and axiological dimension, showing the dignity of a person as a doer (Wojtyla, 1969/2020). Cultural education in Poland, expressed through the activities of museum educators, is an important challenge for the formation of humanistic values, the protection of cultural heritage and the peaceful continuation of generations. Hopefully, museum education in Poland will continue to develop and become more accessible to everyone through virtual space.

Notes

1. https://www.gov.pl/web/kulturaisport/edukacja-muzealna-stacjonarna-w-warunkach-pandemii--dobre-praktyki?fbclid=IwAR0kHdtdT0uCwHTv3puDkFjsJhxzRQk4QUUDyrlJ6r2RC5I-KICJdrkGXAc
2. For example, see https://www.startupgrind.com/blog/the-future-of-dating-is-artificial-intelligence/
3. https://polin.pl/pl/muzealny-think-tank-muzea-sasiedztwo-publikacja
4. https://muzeumpartycypacyjne.pl/o-atlasie/
5. https://www.gov.pl/web/kulturaisport/inwestycje-muzealne---nasze-wiano-na-100-lecie-odzyskania-niepodleglosci
6. http://edukacjamuzealna.pl/
7. http://konkurssybilla.nimoz.pl/2013
8. http://kongresmuzealnikow.pl/
9. https://artmuseum.pl/pl/edukacja/muzeum-dostepne; https://artmuseum.pl/pl/news/kolekcja-dostepna-w-etr
10. https://muzeumslaskie.pl/pl/dostepnosc/; https://muzeumslaskie.pl/pl/kategoria/warsztaty-online/; https://wirtualne.muzeumgdansk.pl/
11. https://muzhp.pl/pl/p/247/muzeum-online; https://muzhp.pl/pl/p/1/przedszkola-szkoly
12. https://www.youtube.com/watch?v=DM0tPju2oqI&list=PLskSDJDNQbHndjpGf-WURCNTSYl75TY5s; https://zbiory.mnk.pl/pl/strona-glowna
13. Valuable initiatives of museum education and cultural heritage interpretation have been undertaken by the Malopolska Institute of Culture. During the pandemic, an online conference was held: "Museums are closer than you think," at which a new version of the portal "Virtual Museums of Malopolska" was inaugurated. https://muzea.malopolska.pl/pl/strona-glowna. The "education" section provides suggestions for children, adults and teachers.
14. Twelve modern museum buildings were built: https://www.architekturaibiznes.pl/12-gmachow-muzeow,2949.html; Muzeum Józefa Piłsudskiego w Sulejówku, Muzeum: https://muzeumpilsudski.pl/zajecia edukacyjne-dla-szkol-i-przedszkoli/- Muzeum II Wojny Światowej w Gdańsku: https://muzeum1939.pl/edukacja.html; Muzeum Fryderyka Chopina: https://muzeum.nifc.pl/pl/muzeum/edukacja//12_edukacja-online
15. https://zbiory.mnk.pl/pl/strona-glowna
16. https://muzeumkrakowa.pl/lekcje?type_online=on. During the pandemic, city residents were invited to "listen to the city" and document its different perspectives through any method of artistic expression. The project resulted in an exhibition. https://muzeumkrakowa.pl/edukacja
17. https://muzeumkrakowa.pl/edukacja; https://www.facebook.com/muzeumkrakowa/
18. https://muzeumtatrzanskie.pl/blog-edukacja/

19. This information was obtained by interviewing museum educators at the listed museums.
20. https://muzeumslaskie.pl/pl/kategoria/warsztaty-online/
21. https://www.cricoteka.pl/pl/kantor-tu-jest-spacer-dzwiekowy-po-krakowie/
22. http://muzealnictwo.com/2020/12/ferie-z-muzeum-2021/
23. "Sztuka edukacji – Fotografia w działaniu" [The Art of Education – Photography in Action] https://sztukaedukacji.zacheta.art.pl/, The Annual Conference of the Forum of Museum Educators, "Museum and Education in Times of Change," took place online on 14 December 2020. http://edukacjamuzealna.pl/?s=Spotkanie+online+liderek+i+lider%C3%B3w+edukacji+muzealnej
24. Museum educators were invited to remote classes held by the author, introducing students to online activities. Meetings with educators supported our discussions with virtual walks around exhibitions, which would have otherwise taken place in the museum. A series of "Museum Animator in the Local Community" classes were visited by educators from the Cricoteka Museum, the Museum of Modern Art in Warsaw, the Tatra Museum in Zakopane and the MOCAK Museum in Krakow. This showed us a new possibility for teaching to be conducted at the Jagiellonian University, in collaboration with various museums.
25. Map of e-museums in Poland: https://www.e-muzeum.eu/
26. The Ministry of Culture, National Heritage and Sport launched the Culture on the Web programme: https://www.gov.pl/web/kulturaisport/kultura-w-sieci
27. https://ecs.gda.pl/europa-nostra-2021
28. Examples include an exhibition, "co dwie sztuki to nie jedna" [two arts are better than one]: https://zacheta.art.pl/pl/wystawy/co-dwie-sztuki-to-nie-jedna; https://zacheta.art.pl/pl/edukacja/dzieci; a mobile exhibition, "Umysł przyłapany" [Captured Mind] Centrum Nauki Kopernik (Copernicus Science Centre): https://www.kopernik.org.pl/wystawy-objazdowe/umysl-przylapany; https://www.kopernik.org.pl/edukacja; an exhibition for children, "W muzeum wszystko wolno" [In the museum anything goes], The National Museum in Warsaw: http://www.mnw.art.pl/wystawy/w-muzeum-wszystko-wolno-wystawa-przygotowana-przez-dzieci,195.html; at the Museum for Children: Eureka, czyli odkrywam! [Eureka! I'm making a discovery] An exhibition about philosophy and art; for children aged 4–10: https://ethnomuseum.pl/wystawy/eureka-czyli-odkrywam/ https://www.youtube.com/watch?v=bHtMETqScp8; The State Ethnographic Museum in Warsaw: Nocowanki dla dzieci [Night in the museum for children]: https://www.youtube.com/watch?v=yZF9ggX7_D8
29. The Copernicus Science Centre offers attractive exhibitions for visitors to explore online: https://www.kopernik.org.pl/wystawy; https://www.kopernik.org.pl/edukacja. At the Museum of Polish Song in Opole, this was the museum's educational offering for the school year 2020–2021: https://muzeumpiosenki.pl/edukacja/oferta-edukacyjna-na-rok-szkolny-20202021_715.html
30. https://artmuseum.pl/pl/news/muzeum-online; https://www.mnw.art.pl/multimedia/swieta-2020/filmowe-warsztaty-zabawki-choinkowe/
31. https://msl.org.pl/wydarzenia-online/; https://www.mnw.art.pl/multimedia/filmy/domowe-warsztaty-dla-najmlodszych/ #Zostań w domu. Sztuka przyjdzie do Ciebie [#Stay at home. Art will come to you]: https://www.gov.pl/web/kulturaisport/zostan-w-domu--

sztuka-przyjdzie-do-ciebie; https://msl.org.pl/edukacja-online-jako-medium-tworczosci-panel-live-z-udzialem-publicznosci/
32. Museum of the Future in the Museum of Art in Lodz (a discursive cycle): https://msl.org.pl/muzeum-przyszlosci-04-perspektywy-/; https://pages.facebook.com/StowarzyszenieMuzealnikowPolskich/

References

Archer, M. S. (2013). *Człowieczeństwo. Problem sprawstwa* (A. Dziuban, Trans.). NOMOS.

Commandeur, B., Kunz-Ott, H., & Schad, K. (Eds.). (2015). *Handbuch Museumspädagogik: Kulturelle Bildung in Museen*. Kopaed.

Dittwald, A. M. (2011). Kanadyjska Galeria Narodowa. Aspekty digitalizacji muzeum. *Muzealnictwo, 52*, 274–284.

Dutton, D. (2020). *Instynkt Sztuki. Piękno, zachwyt i ewolucja człowieka*. Copernicus Center Press.

Fuchs, M. (2015). Ästhetische bildung und kulturelle bildung. In B. Commandeur, H. Kunz-Ott, & K. Schad (Eds.), *Handbuch museumspädagogik: Kulturelle bildung in museen* (pp. 109–113). Kopaed.

Hein, G. (1998). *Learning in the museum*. Routledge.

Hooper-Greenhill, E. (2007). *Museums and education: Purpose, pedagogy, performance*. Routledge.

Hubard, O. (2015). *Art museum education: Facilitating gallery experiences*. Palgrave Macmillan.

Kwiatkowska-Tybulewicz, B. (2016). *Wychowawcze aspekty sztuki współczesnej. Z perspektywy pedagogiki krytycznej*. Wydawnictwo Uniwersytetu Warszawskiego.

Macdonald, S. J. (2015). Revolutions, turns and developments in museum education: Some anthropological and museological reflections. In B. Commandeur, H. Kunz-Ott, & K. Schad (Eds.), *Handbuch museumspädagogik: Kulturelle bildung in museen* (pp. 95–105). Kopaed.

Mead, M. (1970). *Culture and commitment: A study of the generation gap*. Doubleday & Company.

Meier, T. D., & Reust, H. R. (2000). *Medium museum. Kommunikation und vermittlung in museen für kunst und geschichte*. Paul Haupt.

Mendel, M. (2017). *Pedagogika miejsca wspólnego. Miasto i szkoła*. Wydawnictwo Naukowe Katedra.

Nettke, T. (2015). Was ist museumspädagogik? Bildung und vermittlung in museen. In B. Commandeur, H. Kunz-Ott, & K. Schad (Eds.), *Handbuch museumspädagogik: Kulturelle bildung in museen* (pp. 31–42). Kopaed.

Niezabitowski, M. (2021). Historia dobrze opowiedziana ... Czy COVID-19 nauczy nas słuchać miasta? *Muzealnictwo, 62*, 163–172.

Olbrycht, K. (2019). *Edukacja kulturalna jako edukacja do wzrastania w człowieczeństwie*. Wydawnictwo Uniwersytetu Śląskiego.

Pater, R. (2016). *Edukacja muzealna – muzea dla dzieci i młodzieży*. Wydawnictwo Uniwersytetu Jagiellońskiego. https://doi.org/10.4467/K9529.26/e/16.16.4789

Pater, R., & Karamanov, O. (2020). Museum education in the context of socio-cultural changes in the countries of Eastern Europe (using the examples of Poland, Ukraine and Russia). *Muzeológia a kultúrne dedičstvo, 8*(2), 17–30. https://doi.org/10.46284/mkd.2020.8.2.2

Piontek, A. (2015). Partizipative ansätze in museen und deren bildungsarbeit. In B. Commandeur, H. Kunz-Ott, & K. Schad (Eds.), *Handbuch Museumspädagogik: Kulturelle Bildung in Museen* (pp. 198–206). Kopaed.

Simon, N. (2010). *The participatory museum*. Museum 2.0. https://participatorymuseum.org

Szeląg, M. (2019). The progressive museum vs. museum education and museums in Poland. *Zeszyty Artystyczne. Edukacja muzealna, 34*, 121–133.

Wojtyła, K. (2020). Osoba i czyn. In T. Styczeń, W. Chudy, J. W. Gałkowski, A. Rodziński, & A. Szostek (Eds.), *Karol Wojtyła. Osoba i czyn oraz inne studia antropologiczne*. Wydawnictwo KUL (pp. 43–344). (Original work published 1969)

Zacharias, W. (2000). *Interaktiv. Medienökologie zwischen Sinnenreich und Cyberspace. Neue multimediale Spiel-und Lernumwelten für Kinder und Jugendliche*. KoPäd Verlag.

Zalewska-Pawlak, M. (2017). *Sztuka i wychowanie w XXI wieku*. Wydawnictwo Uniwersytetu Łódzkiego.

Żuk, G. (2016). *Edukacja aksjologiczna. Zarys problematyki*. Wydawnictwo Uniwersytetu Marii Curie-Skłodowskiej.

Żurakowski, B. (2011). *Kultura artystyczna w przestrzeni wychowania*. Wydawnictwo Uniwersytetu Jagiellońskiego.

Biographies

Jaanika Anderson is a director of research at the University of Tartu Museum in Estonia. Her interests include history of museums and museum education, collection-based teaching methods and contemporary museology.

Jackie Armstrong is an associate educator, Visitor Research and Experience at MoMA. Jackie works cross-departmentally on research and evaluation, centring audiences' voices. Lived experiences and research of trauma also inform Jackie's work, including the Artful Practices for Well-Being initiative. She holds an MA in museum studies from the University of Toronto and has completed studies in ancient art and archaeology, anthropology and tourism management systems.

Maria Avariento-Adsuara is an adjunct professor of art education in the Faculty of Humanities and Social Sciences at the University of Jaume I in Castellon, Spain. Her interests include artistic methodologies of teaching in art education, visual a/r/tography and creation of graphic work through printing and engraving.

Marie-France Berard is a lecturer at the University of British Columbia in Vancouver, Canada. Her interests include art museum education and mediation, contemporary arts' pedagogical potential, curriculum studies, critical approaches to art education and post-qualitative research.

Lilly Blue is head of learning and creativity research at the Art Gallery of Western Australia, and an interdisciplinary artist, educator and researcher working with poetic pedagogies, classroom-based studio practice and curatorial activism. She conceives and collaborates on projects that amplify the experience of children and other marginalized groups as critical and valuable in activating ethical futures.

Bruno de Oliveira Jayme is an assistant professor in curriculum, teaching and learning in the Faculty of Education, University of Manitoba. He is a Brazilian queer activist and art educator, working in the areas of arts and social justice, community museums and art galleries.

Kremena Dimitrova is an illustrator-as-historian, lecturer in visual culture and practice-based Ph.D. researcher in decolonizing history through comics at the University of Portsmouth in the United Kingdom. She specializes in socially engaged and site-specific creative interventions and visual storytelling in the heritage sector, with a focus on unearthing hidden and marginalized narratives.

Laura Evans is a distinguished teaching professor and the director of the Art Museum Education Certificate at the University of North Texas in Denton, Texas. Evans received her Ph.D. in art education with a museum studies specialization at the Ohio State University, her MA in museum studies at the University of Toronto and her BA in art history and English at Denison University, Granville, Ohio. Evans has worked in museums from Australia, to Washington, DC to New Zealand.

João Pedro Fróis is a guest researcher at the Medical School of the University of Lisbon and a research affiliate of the Center for Phenomenological Psychology and Aesthetics, University of Copenhagen. As of 2014, he has been a fellow of the International Association of Empirical Aesthetics IAEA and served as its vice-president for Portugal and Spain. His main interests lie in the psychology of aesthetics, creativity and the visual arts.

Sue Girak, Ph.D., is a primary visual arts specialist and lectures in teacher education in Perth, Western Australia. She encourages collaborative artmaking and environmentally sustainable art practices in the classroom. Sue is committed to applying arts-led research in her classroom to give children greater autonomy in their artmaking.

Shaun Grech, Ph.D., is a senior academic consultant on Disability Inclusive Disaster Risk Reduction with CBM and director of The Critical Institute (Malta). He is also an honorary associate professor with the Department of Health and Rehabilitation Sciences at the University of Cape Town, an affiliate associate professor in the Department of International Relations at the University of Malta, and editor-in-chief of the international journal *Disability and the Global South (DGS)*. He is also co-editor of the book series Palgrave Studies in Disability and International Development.

Ceren Güneröz is an associate professor. She worked as an intern at Frankfurt and Hamburg Children's Museums and Miami Children's Museum. She completed an MA in museum education and Ph.D. in fine arts education at Ankara University. She also studied as an exchange student at Goldsmiths College and then completed an MA at Başkent University Museology Department.

Riikka Haapalainen (Ph.D., B.Ed.) is a professor of contemporary art research at the Academy of Fine Arts (Uniarts Helsinki) in Finland. Haapalainen's research and teaching interests include theories of avant-garde and contemporary art, participatory and social processes in art, exhibition pedagogy and critical museum research.

Jan Hogan is a senior lecturer and coordinator of the drawing and printmaking workshops at the School of Creative Arts and Media, University of Tasmania, Australia. Her research interests include place-based, practice-led research, museum studies, drawing and printmaking.

Maria Huhmarniemi is an associate professor at the University of Lapland, Faculty of Art and Design. She engages with questions concerning the North and environmental issues such as the relationship between people and nature and environmental responsibility.

Jasmin Järvinen works at Solutions for Sustainability team at Aalto University, Finland. She holds an MA, and her interests at the moment include intersectional and equal work practices and boosting students and the university community towards a sustainable future.

Timo Jokela is a professor of art education at the University of Lapland in Finland and the University of Arctic's chair of art, design and culture. He leads the thematic network on Arctic Sustainable Arts and Design (ASAD). His theoretical studies, artistic activities and art-based action research projects focus on relationships among Northern cultures, art and nature.

Lars Emmerik Damgaard Knudsen is an associate professor in the Faculty of Arts at Aarhus University in Denmark. His interests include out-of-school learning, museum education, theory and practice, phenomenology and arts-based research.

Anniina Koivurova, DA (Art and Design), is a professor of art history at the University of Lapland. Previously she worked as a university lecturer in art education and as a regional curator at the Rovaniemi Art Museum. Currently, she is researching children's drawings from a reconstruction era of Lapland and an association of Finnish expressionist artists called the October Group (Lokakuun ryhmä).

Tatiana Kravtsov is a doctoral candidate in the Faculty of Art and Design at the University of Lapland in Finland. Her research interests include art-based research methods, traditional and contemporary handicrafts in the Arctic, creative tourism, ecological sensibility and connectedness with nature.

Heidi Kukkonen is a Ph.D. research fellow at the University of Agder, Norway. She studies museum educational situations with abstract modernist art and new materialist theory-practice in her Ph.D. project.

KUNST:form is a Copenhagen-based curator-duo consisting of **Lene Crone Jensen** and **Hilde Østergaard**. They have a background as curators, educators and consultants at art institutions such as Rooseum Centre for Contemporary Art (Sweden), Louisiana Museum of Modern Art (Denmark), Nikolaj Kunsthal (Denmark) and the municipality of Gentofte (Denmark). Lene has worked as the director of Copenhagen Art Festival and Göteborgs Konsthall (Sweden), and today works as a senior curator at the independent art space, Skovhuset Art & Nature (Denmark). Hilde works as an exhibition curator at the National Gallery of Denmark. Through KUNST:form, their goal is to spark change through participatory art exhibitions.

Richard Lachapelle is a professor in the Faculty of Fine Arts at Concordia University, Montreal, Canada. His research interests include museums, museum education, adult education, time-based media and studio production.

Marilyn Lajeunesse has worked in the museum field for over 30 years, namely at the Montreal Museum of Fine Arts, Education and Wellness Department. Her expertise includes how arts can contribute to well-being, accessibility and inclusion. She developed the award-winning "Sharing the Museum" programme in 1999, co-designing programmes with community groups underserved by the cultural sector and contributing to numerous research papers.

Rocío Lara-Osuna is a postdoctoral researcher and teacher at the University of Granada, Spain. She holds a degree in fine arts and a Ph.D. in arts and education. Her artistic and research production focuses on the use of projection-based augmented reality for the development of arts-based teaching methods, following the didactic proposals of the Spanish filmmaker Jose Val-del-Omar.

Rolf Laven is a professor, Ph.D., artist and researcher in Vienna (University College of Teacher Education, Academy of Fine Arts & University of Applied Arts). He studied sculpture and art education at art academies in Maastricht/NL and Vienna/A. Laven is chair of the Professional Association of Austrian Art and Design Educators (BÖKWE) and a board member of EASLHE (European Association Service Learning in Higher Education).

Keven Lee is an interdisciplinary artist (dance and ceramics) and a lecturer at the School of Physical and Occupational Therapy, Faculty of Medicine and Health Sciences at McGill University, where he completed his graduate degrees. His doctoral research focused on understanding experience through the use of critical and existential phenomenology, combined with Dewey's pragmatism.

Stephen Legari is a registered art therapist and a couple and family therapist. He holds an MA in art therapy from Concordia University and another MA in couple and family therapy from McGill University, where he won the award for clinical excellence. He has worked with a range of populations in numerous clinical, educational and community contexts. Since 2017, Legari has been a programme officer for art therapy at the Montreal Museum of Fine Arts, a full-time museum-based art therapy programme that includes therapy groups, research collaborations, internships and a community art studio.

Abbey MacDonald is a senior lecturer in arts education for the School of Education at the University of Tasmania, Australia. Abbey works with social justice, arts industry and philanthropic organizations looking to collaborate with education transformation stakeholders. She is president of Art Education Australia, the peak national body for visual art education in Australia.

Tanja Mäkitalo is an MA student in art education in the Faculty of Arts at the University of Lapland, Finland. Her research interest is in enhancing well-being through art and nature in art-based activities and developing art museum pedagogy.

Attwell Mamvuto is a senior lecturer in the Department of Art Design and Technology Education (Faculty of Education) at the University of Zimbabwe. His research interests include the art curriculum, art pedagogy and assessment and teacher education.

Ricardo Marín-Viadel is a professor of art education in the Faculty of Fine Arts and Faculty of Education, University of Granada (Spain). His interests include art education, arts-based educational research and visual and social a/r/tography.

Jaime Mena is an assistant professor of visual arts education at the University of Granada, Spain. His research focuses on visual arts-based research methods, arts-based educational methods and museum education. He has worked as head of education at Centre Pompidou Málaga and the State Russian Museum branch in Málaga.

Xabier Molinet is an assistant professor in the Faculty of Education at the University of Granada, Spain. His Ph.D. explored the visual relations between students and their educational spaces. His current interests include arts-based research, photography and lighting, photographic explorations of territory and arts-based teaching and learning.

Ángela Moreno-Córdoba is a Ph.D. student in the arts and education doctoral programme at the University of Granada, Spain. Her interests include art education, educational research based on the visual arts, museum mediation and analysis of children's photography.

Dónal O'Donoghue is a professor and head of the School of Education at the National College of Art and Design, Dublin, Ireland. He studies contemporary art, curatorial practice and education, with a particular interest in contemporary art's pedagogical potential, educative quality and distinctive capacity to function as a mode of scholarly inquiry and research. He is the author *of Learning to Live in Boys' Schools: Art-Led Understandings of Masculinities* published by Routledge in 2019. Dr O'Donoghue is a distinguished fellow of the National Art Education Association. He currently serves as past senior editor (2021–2023) of *Studies in Art Education*.

Melanie Orenius (MA, Arts) works as curator of education at Amos Rex Art Museum in Finland and as an independent artist and writer. Her interests include gentle, critical, intersectional and anti-colonialist art pedagogy and public programmes.

Patricia Osler (Ph.D.) is an art educator and the director of Academic Research for the Convergence Initiative, Montreal. Her research interrogates the neuroscience of creativity, drawing upon a transdisciplinary practice that aims to deepen understanding and awareness of arts-based approaches, art-as-research and emergent pedagogies in museum education.

Andrew Palamara is the gallery coordinator of the Emmanuel Art Gallery and CU Denver Experience Gallery at the University of Colorado, Denver. He has previously worked in education at the Cincinnati Art Museum, Dallas Museum of Art and MASS MoCA. He holds a BFA in graphic design and illustration from Belmont University and a MA in art education from the University of North Texas.

Paloma Palau-Pellicer is an associate professor of art education in the Faculty of Humanities and Social Sciences at the University of Jaume I in Castellon, Spain. Her interests include artistic methodologies of teaching in art education, arts-based research, visual a/r/tography, and theory analysis and criticism of fine arts.

Melissa Park is an associate professor at the School of Physical and Occupational Therapy, Faculty of Medicine and Health Sciences, at McGill University with a background in art history, occupational science/therapy and anthropology. Her participatory and ethnographic research uses a critical and narrative phenomenological and aesthetic theoretical framework.

Anne Pässilä is a senior researcher at LUT University, Finland. She specializes in applying arts-based initiatives and arts pedagogy to support innovation and development processes in the public, private and third sectors. She has extensive experience in front-line workplace engagement in research-based theatre as a support in developing shared understanding in the context of practice-based innovation management.

Renata Pater is an associate professor at the Faculty of Philosophy, Institute of Education of the Jagiellonian University in Kraków, Poland. Her research interests include education theory, cultural pedagogy, aesthetic education, theory and practice of museum education and educational partnership in competency education. Author of the 2016 book *Edukacja* *muzealna – muzea dla dzieci i młodzieży* [Education in Museum – Museums for Children and Youth] and numerous articles, Dr Pater is also a producer of museum and art education projects in Poland and abroad (Germany, Switzerland and Austria) and a member of the Polish Educational Research Association.

Guadalupe Pérez-Cuesta is a researcher in the Department of Visual Arts Education at the University of Granada, Spain, and museum educator at the Alhambra. His research interests include arts-based research methods, teachers' identity and museum education.

Dominik Porczyński is an assistant professor in the Institute of Sociology at the University of Rzeszów in Poland. His interests include sociology of art, museum studies, past presencing, regional identity and regional education.

Tiina Pusa (Doctor of Arts) is a head of the art education (MA) major in the Department of Art and Media at the Aalto University School of Arts, Design and Architecture, Finland. Pusa's doctoral thesis (2012) was situated within the discourse of phenomenological research in art education. Her present interests consider queer issues in the context of art education and the societal and political role of a teacher.

Annalise Rees is an Australian visual artist with expertise in drawing and drawing-based methodologies. Her practice is frequently collaborative and cross-disciplinary. With a focus on process, Rees often works directly in response to the site, exploring the act of drawing as a fundamental method of enquiry for encountering the unknown and unfamiliar.

Benjamin J. Richardson is a professor of environmental law at the University of Tasmania, Australia. His scholarship includes the role of aesthetics and the arts in environmental policy and governance.

Deborah Riding is a visiting research fellow at the University of Chester, UK. She has worked in gallery education for over twenty years, managing and delivering programmes for a range of audiences. Deborah's research interests are around collaborative practices in galleries; her doctoral thesis, *Challenging the Rules of Engagement*, focused specifically on the co-creation of knowledge in the public art museum.

Joaquín Roldán is a professor of art education in the Faculty of Fine Arts and Faculty of Education at the University of Granada, Spain. His interests include art education, aesthetic education, arts-based educational research and a/r/tography.

Andrea Rubio-Fernández is an associate professor of art education in the Faculty of Education at the University of Oviedo, Spain. Her work focuses on arts-based teaching methodologies and a/r/tography.

Paola Ruiz-Moltó is an assistant professor of art education in the Faculty of Humanities and Social Sciences at the University of Jaume I in Castellon, Spain. Her interests include bio(art), sound art and artistic methodologies of teaching in art education.

Lise Sattrup, Ph.D., is a pedagogical consultant at Skoletjenesten, Danish Knowledge Centre for Education in Museums and other external learning environments in Denmark. Her interests include museum education, democratic education and art pedagogy.

Anita Sinner is a professor of art education at the University of British Columbia, Canada. She works extensively with stories as pedagogic pivots, with an emphasis on creative geographies in education. Her recent edited collections (short titles) are *Living Histories* (Garnet & Sinner), *Community Arts Education* (Lin, Sinner & Irwin) and *A/r/tography: Essential Readings and Conversations* (Irwin, Lasczik, Sinner & Triggs).

Emilie Sitzia holds a special chair at the University of Amsterdam and is an associate professor of cultural education in the Department of History at the University of Maastricht. She specializes in the impact of art on audiences and word/image interdisciplinary studies.

Lisbet Skregelid is a professor in the Faculty of Fine Arts at the University of Agder in Norway. Her interests involve art education in and outside formal education and arts-based research. In a range of contexts, she explores how art and art theory can inform teaching – what she calls "pedagogy of dissensus."

Stefanie Steinbeck is an educational anthropologist exploring the world(s) of museums. She is particularly interested in visitor experiences and embodied meaning-making experiences when meeting historical pasts.

Anniina Suominen, Ph.D., is a professor of art pedagogy at Aalto University in Finland. Her experiences of practising and living in two different academic systems and cultures (Finland and the United States) have provided a perspective that influences her scholarship and assessment of the state of democracy and solidarity in contemporary Finnish arts education at different levels.

Ronna Tulgan Ostheimer has worked in the education department of the Clark for more than eighteen years, first as the coordinator of community and family programmes and then, for the past thirteen years, as director of education. Her goal as a museum educator is to help people understand more fully that looking at and thinking about art can expand their sense of human possibility. Before coming to the Clark, Tulgan Ostheimer taught at the Massachusetts College of Liberal Arts in the education department. She holds an Ed.D. in psychological education from the University of Massachusetts and a BA in sociology and American studies from Hobart and William Smith Colleges.

Priscilla Van Even is a philosopher, (museum) educator, communication scientist and anthropologist. She is a researcher in the Meaningful Interactions Lab at KU Leuven (Belgium) and specializes in science communication, participatory science, visual literacy and research methodology. She also holds a position as a museum guide.

Kevin Vanhaelewijn is an archaeologist with an anthropological approach who focuses on the meaningfulness of historical research. He also holds a degree in management and specializes in complexity thinking and user experience design. Furthermore, he is an art educator and a museum guide.

Susana Vargas-Mejía is an art educator, art historian and artist from Colombia. She is currently the director of Communications and Digital Strategy at the Bogotá Museum of Modern Art – MAMBO. Her research interests include museums, social media and art education and arts-based research methods.

Raphael Vella is a professor of art education at the Faculty of Education, University of Malta. His recent research focuses on sustainability issues in art education, socially engaged art, art education in Malta, contemporary artistic practices and curating. He is also a practising visual artist and curator.

Wolfgang Weinlich, Ph.D., is a professor at the University College of Teacher Education, Vienna (Pädagogische Hochschule Wien). He graduated from the Academy of Fine Arts, Vienna and has been working as an art educator since 2005. His work focuses on art didactics and digital media, empowerment through art didactics and service learning.

Boyd White is an associate professor in the Department of Integrated Studies in Education, Faculty of Education, McGill University. His teaching and research interests are in the areas of philosophy and art education, the latter particularly focused on the topic of aesthetics and art criticism. Dr White is the author of numerous journal articles, text chapters and five books. He was editor of the *Canadian Review of Art Education: Research and* Issues for several years and has served as a reviewer for a number of journals and educational research organizations. He is retired as of August 2023.

Emily Wiskera has worked in museum education since 2011, with a specialized focus on accessibility and working with diverse populations. As an interpretation specialist at the Dallas Museum of Art, Wiskera develops interpretive materials for the museum's collections and special exhibitions. She is passionate about creating dynamic and equitable experiences with art that encourage visitors to create, reflect, share and connect.

Annika Wolff is a researcher at LUT University in Finland. Her specializations are in co-design and human–data interaction – at the intersection of complex data, machine and human learning. Her research focuses on how people make sense of, interact with and design from complex data.

Aysem Yanar graduated from Ankara University's Ph.D. programme in Home economics. She has been working as an associate professor on the conservation and restoration of cultural properties at Ankara University, Faculty of Fine Arts. Her academic interests include cultural heritage, traditional arts and geographical indication. She also completed her MA at Başkent University Museology Department.

Esra Yildiz received her BA in environmental engineering (Istanbul Technical University) and sociology (Istanbul University) and MA degrees (Istanbul Technical University) in art history. She pursued her postdoctoral studies at the Humboldt University of Berlin and EHESS (Paris). She teaches visual culture, contemporary art history and cinema at İstanbul Bilgi University and is the director of the cultural management MA programme. She worked as an exhibition, research and publication coordinator for various exhibitions organized at Santralistanbul. She is also the director of the documentary films *A Shadow Among Pages: The Second-Hand Bookseller Vahan* (2010) and *Stateless* (2021).

Index

A
a/r/tography 116, 277, 297–302, 417, 422, 423, 424
Aalto 28, 419, 423, 424
ableism 51
Aboriginal *see* Indigenous
academia 395
accessibility 7, 151, 248, 256, 386, 387, 395–97, 400, 402, 409, 420, 425
activism 210, 211, 218, 227, 417
actor(s) 93, 98, 146, 239
actualization 223, 361
adaptations 68, 400
addiction 339
administration 145, 146, 315
adolescents 144, 334, 409
adult(s) 131, 133, 145, 190, 196, 237, 299, 301, 320, 364, 396, 409, 420
advocacy 53
Aegean 397
aesthetic(s) 18, 21, 64, 65, 68–71, 98, 139, 140, 163, 165–67, 169, 170, 178, 189–91, 196, 201–03, 211, 223, 224, 251, 348, 377, 386, 398, 410, 418, 422, 423, 425
affect 8, 18, 52, 91, 266, 290, 291, 361, 363–65
Africa 131
Afro-futurism 333
Afrontamento 148
agency 42, 115, 127, 139, 177, 236, 333, 337, 412
agonism 356
agriculture 402

Ahmed, Sara 290, 291, 293, 294
AI (artificial intelligence) 413
Alhambra 279, 423
allegory 92
allyship 27
Alzheimer's 6, 287–89, 291, 294
amateur 29
ambiguity 311, 364
America 39
amnesia 72
Amsterdam 424
anachronisms 19
analogy 282, 361
ancestors 131, 279, 337, 411
anecdote 195–96
Anglophone 265
Ankara 79, 81, 418, 426
anonymity 19
Anthropocene 35, 122, 283
anticolonialism 220
anticonsumption 220
apparatus 77, 147
apprentice 182
apps 400
AR (augmented reality) 385, 396, 420
Arab 15, 21, 323
archaeology 128–30, 251, 398, 417
Archaeopark 398
architecture 93, 96, 103, 146, 166, 211, 217, 218, 364, 423
archive 105, 352
Arctic 113–16, 119, 419

Armenian(s) 77, 79, 82
armour 21
art and design 382, 419–21
art dream 225
artefact 28, 32, 51, 70, 96, 126–31, 133, 139, 147, 152, 153, 155, 170, 178, 202, 224, 236, 238, 248, 250, 381, 386, 388, 395
artezpress 355
arts-based xiv 51, 114, 116, 163, 212, 218, 219, 275, 277, 345–46, 350, 419–25
art-based action research (ABAR) 115, 116, 120, 419
artist 6, 15, 18, 22, 23, 44, 46, 56, 63, 64, 66, 67, 69, 70, 71, 83, 91, 93, 94, 98, 113, 116, 117, 119, 143, 145, 147, 152, 156, 157, 165, 178, 179, 183, 189, 190, 195, 196, 201, 202, 217–19, 229, 240, 266, 268, 275, 276, 308, 309, 310, 312, 314–16, 320, 345, 346, 348, 350, 361, 377, 400, 410, 419, 423, 425
artisan 66
artistas 99
artivist 30, 33
artistic-based teaching 167–70
assemblage(s) 53, 63, 65, 68, 263, 266–69
asylum 16
asynchronous 158
atelier 113
atrium 229
atrocities 78, 84
audience xiv 3, 4, 7, 20, 27–29, 33, 39, 43, 44, 46, 52, 63, 64, 67, 71, 151, 158, 177–82, 185, 189, 196, 210, 217, 218, 229, 237, 299–302, 307, 315, 316, 319, 345, 371, 384, 385, 395, 399, 400, 402, 408–412, 417, 423, 424
audioguide 386
augmented reality 385, 396
Australia 18, 61–71, 418, 419, 421, 423
Austria 97, 223, 227, 423
Authorship 63, 64, 167, 308
Autism 296
Autobiography 322
Autónoma 172

Avantgarde 227, 232, 352
Axiological 412

B

Baccalaureate 163
Bakhtin, Mikhail 139, 148
Bal, Mieke 69, 94, 266
Barcelona 289, 296
barclay 350
Baroque 20
barrier(s) 23 381, 385, 387
Bauhaus 362
Beauty 8, 65, 115, 117, 122, 140, 146, 189, 191, 192
Bedouin 58
Behaviour 15, 64, 71, 115, 236, 239, 327
Belgium 382, 390, 391, 425
belief(s) 22, 71, 115, 229, 314, 335, 387
belonging 31, 40, 169, 287, 331
benefactors 250
benevolence 23
benign 93
Bergson, Henri; bergsonism 360
Berlin 3, 81, 84, 96, 426
Betweenness 218
Bhabha, Homi 85
Bias 52, 337
Bildung 415, 416
Biesta, Gert 349
billboards 402
binary 29, 179, 181, 364, 366
biodiversity 67, 70, 115, 402
blindness 139
blog 409
blueprint 34
bodies xiii 4, 9, 16, 21, 119, 131, 263, 267, 268, 293–95, 319, 321, 332, 360–65
Bogotá, Columbia 91
Bolton, Barbara 359–61
bombing 79
bondage 42
bonds 115
border(s) 15–17, 23, 44, 82, 91, 231, 235, 237

Index

Bosnia 93, 96
Bottega 19
boullée 270
boundaries 22, 39, 44, 56, 63, 145, 152, 158, 250, 266
Bourdieu, Pierre 22, 145, 239
Bourriaud, Nicolas 348
Braidotti, Rosie 66
brain 323
brainstorm 385
branch 119, 251
Brazil xiv 51, 53, 54
breadth 64, 67
Britain 40, 42, 239
Brussels 385
Budapest 96

C

cabinet 251
cacophony 324
calligraphy 400
camera(s) 80, 210, 215, 218, 372, 374, 399
camerawork 212
camouflage 289
campaigns 47, 338
Canada 3, 6, 128, 287, 374, 417, 420, 424
Canon 364
canvas 53, 184
capital 21, 22, 151, 236, 240
capitalism 312
caregiver(s) 6, 287, 292
Carpathian 237
carpet(s) 282
Cartesian 128
cartography 43, 44
Cassell 35, 197
catalogues 179, 267
catastrophe 217
category 21, 288, 289, 408, 411
cathedral 247, 251, 254–57
cavalryman 400
çavdar 84
cave 113
ceded 242
cell 331
cemetery 79, 211
censorship 18
centre 16, 28, 33, 98, 126, 167, 242, 267, 277, 280, 289, 294, 295, 300, 311, 315, 411
centralization 302
centrum 414
centimetres 131, 169
century 15
ceramics 277, 420
chalk 35
characterization 43
Chester, United Kingdom 423
children 8, 28, 39, 42, 79, 105, 133, 142, 144–47, 155, 165, 171, 182–85, 189–96, 202, 203, 219, 224, 226, 227, 229, 240, 248, 252–56, 334, 337, 359, 360, 362–64, 366, 382, 396, 400, 409, 414, 417–19, 421
childhood 3, 113
China 263, 264
choreography 365
chromatic 276, 282
chronotope 139, 140, 147
cinema 144, 426
circa
   1600s 129
   1700s 129
   18th century 39, 42
   1800s 129
   19th century 283
   1900s 129
      1950s 105, 141
      1960s 143, 211
   20th century 280
   2000s 397
   21st century 39
circuit 371, 372
citizens 51, 78, 81, 239, 247, 310, 396
civic 22, 239, 412
Čižek, Franz 227
classicism 335
classification 24

class 22, 56, 145, 195, 209, 217, 218, 223, 225, 227, 229, 241, 249, 254, 310, 407, 414
classrooms 184, 189, 191, 193, 195, 250, 278, 349, 417, 418
clay 32, 103, 169, 280, 282
clergy 247
clichés 69
climate 63, 189, 196, 310, 402
coda 294–95
codes 140, 239, 283, 360
codesign 425
coercion 18
coexistence 402
cognition 32, 349
coherence 169, 203, 319, 325, 384, 390
Coimbra 147
collaborations 27–30, 33, 42, 64, 70, 71, 120, 126, 134, 140, 155, 156, 180, 189–91, 196, 225, 249, 275, 287, 308–11, 313, 325, 326, 331, 334–36, 338, 359, 384, 410, 414, 421
collage 105, 211, 212, 216, 217, 219
collections xiii, xiv 5–8, 10, 28, 65, 69, 114, 116, 119, 120, 125, 139, 140, 142, 156–58, 166, 167, 177, 182, 183, 189, 190, 195, 201, 203, 205, 227, 237, 248, 250, 251, 253, 254, 256, 263, 279, 334, 345, 349, 389, 395–97, 400, 408–12, 417, 424, 425
Colombia xiv 91, 92, 96, 99, 425
colonialism 7, 20, 32, 51, 335
colour 20, 40, 42, 117, 227, 282, 350, 362, 386, 400
comics 39, 42–44, 46, 418
commemoration(s) 41 44, 79, 80, 91, 94, 96, 97
commons 3, 6, 22, 30, 114, 119, 155, 179, 211, 235, 276, 312, 315, 334, 336, 382, 390, 399, 412
communism 408
community xiii, xiv 5, 7, 51, 52, 54, 56, 57, 63, 70, 71, 82, 115, 116, 141, 146, 147, 151, 152, 155, 156, 163, 165, 167, 169–71, 181, 182, 203, 219, 238, 239, 249, 250, 276, 310–12, 334–37, 402, 408–10, 412, 417, 419–21, 424

competence 151, 387, 412
computer 391, 403
concept 5, 9, 15, 17, 44, 82, 93, 94, 96, 97, 106, 115, 116, 129, 144, 147, 151, 152, 166, 170, 178, 180, 189, 192, 196, 202, 223–25, 227, 230, 231, 265–68, 276
conceptualization 44, 386
conflict(s) 7, 30, 71, 77, 78, 79, 84, 91–94
connect 63, 69, 71, 99, 156, 209, 264, 269, 282, 321, 322, 323, 325, 332, 345, 348, 381, 396, 425
constructionism 163, 170, 171
constructivism 396
contemporary 9, 19, 21, 39, 41, 44, 64, 65, 70, 92, 96, 103, 118, 120, 140, 147, 157, 163, 166–70, 178, 179, 189, 191, 201, 202, 209, 223, 229, 230, 248, 250, 264, 268, 280, 334, 337, 361, 369, 381, 382, 385, 397, 398, 402, 411, 412, 417, 419, 421, 424–26
continent 3, 5, 15, 16
contingent 43, 63
continuum(s) 269, 309, 312, 316
contours 289
convention 4, 128, 181, 182
convergence 4, 128, 316, 321
Copenhagen 126, 210, 308, 311, 313, 418, 420
copyright 104, 143, 144
Coronavirus 352 (*see also* COVID-19)
Corpus 54, 127
countermemory 99
counter-narrative 51, 57
coup 77, 79, 81
COVID-19
    closure 399
    isolation 13
    pandemic 156
craft 225, 294, 310, 321, 396
crisis 189, 324, 407
criteria 127, 168, 224, 278, 315
critic 94, 308, 314
crítica 172
criticality 29, 210
crystallization 146

cubism 227
cultivate 6, 23, 177, 223, 389
cultura *see* kunst
enculturalization 229
curation
curator 5, 15, 63, 64, 66, 178, 179, 182, 185, 193, 196, 300, 308, 314, 316, 362, 366, 419, 422, 425
curatorship 51
curricula 71, 155, 156, 237, 238, 241–42, 247, 250, 252, 310
cyber
cyberspace 8, 407–12
cyborgs 186

D
dance 323, 365, 420
Denmark 126, 209, 419, 420, 424
decolonization 41, 44, 46, 177
deconstruct 146, 216
decorative 250, 282
dehumanization 15, 17, 22, 42
delegitimize 18
Deleuze, Gilles 56, 63, 69, 266–69, 360, 361, 364
dematerializing 217
dementia 295, 296
democracy 7, 57, 84, 147, 364, 366, 390, 424
demystify 151
Denmark 126, 209, 419, 420, 424
deprovinzialisieren 232
destabilization 287
destruction 41, 65
deterritorialization 57
Dewey, John 190, 202, 319, 320
diagram 158, 269
dichotomies 42
difference 130, 131, 140, 180, 181, 211, 215, 217, 218, 223, 224, 312, 314
diffraction 32, 181
digital xiii 8, 20, 40, 45, 158, 195, 264, 279, 323, 346, 349, 352, 355, 359–63, 365, 381, 382, 384–86, 389, 390, 396, 397, 399, 400, 409, 425
dilettante 29

diorama 72
disability 418
discourses xiv 52, 54, 66, 77, 78, 139, 144, 178, 179–81, 196, 212, 235, 239, 266, 267, 299, 300, 423
discrimination 8, 22, 33, 77
disease 287
disempowerment 53
dissens 355
dissensus 346–49, 352, 424
dissertation 263
dissonance 71
divinity 23
documentary 80, 84, 323, 426
drawing xiv 19, 67, 68–71, 105, 156, 169, 180, 191, 201, 202, 209, 210, 224, 264, 276, 289, 333, 350, 362, 419, 422, 423
dual 64, 184
Dutch 349, 397
dystopian 382, 388–89

E
ecology 310
education xiv 4–10, 21–23, 27, 40, 64, 91, 94, 96–99, 114, 115, 118–20, 125, 133–134, 139, 141, 142, 144–47, 151, 152, 154, 157, 159, 163, 166, 167, 177–81, 190, 191, 209, 223–25, 231, 236, 242, 248, 251, 256, 275, 314, 315, 320, 345, 348, 413, 418, 419, 421, 422, 425
edutainment 400
egalitarian 46
Egypt 27, 28, 31, 32
Eisner, Elliot 166
elite 151, 239, 263, 287
emancipation 42, 52
emergence 65, 78, 290
emigration 18
emotion 28, 30, 32, 33, 44, 98–99, 105, 115, 275, 282, 321, 361, 409
empathy 6, 16, 94–95, 98–99, 115, 147, 316, 320
empower 5, 56, 154, 179
enable 32, 70, 117, 154, 189, 210, 230, 387, 399

encounter xiv 3, 4, 6, 18, 21, 40, 63, 64, 66, 67, 70, 98, 103, 106, 131, 147, 169, 182, 190, 196, 229, 230, 263, 265, 267–69, 287, 294, 316, 348, 350, 355, 359, 360, 361, 366, 398, 412
enculturalization 229
enslavement 42, 44, 412
entanglement 67, 71
entrepreneurship 113, 118–20
environment 27, 31, 52, 55, 57, 63, 65, 66, 71, 114, 192, 194, 236, 249, 320, 324, 396, 400, 407, 424
epicentres 151
episode 54
epistemological 170, 177, 180–82, 185
equality 9, 31, 39, 40, 312, 347, 348, 395
era 40, 91, 105, 311, 390, 419
erasure 69, 70
Estonia xiv 7, 247–52, 256, 257, 417
etching 195
ethics 20, 21, 269
Europa 411
event(s) 15, 18, 22, 56, 57, 79, 80, 82, 83, 93, 145, 169, 180, 201, 210, 230, 231, 239, 269, 311, 322
evocation 212
evolution 145, 334, 338
excavations 129
exhibitionist 186
exposition 400
expression 30, 52, 83, 106, 142, 144, 169, 211, 226, 227, 248, 267, 282, 312, 361, 364, 366, 410, 413
extinction 65, 67–70
extremists 80

F
façade 165, 312
facilitation 30
fairy 66
faith 20
fake 220
family 40, 53, 57, 113, 248, 252, 254, 279, 337, 407, 420, 424

FARC 91
felt 21, 53, 57, 92, 117, 142, 196, 201, 292–94, 331, 333, 336, 337
feminism 30
festival 71, 80
fiction 143, 275
fieldnotes 263, 288
figure 21, 39, 142
film 18, 77, 80, 84, 211, 240, 264, 336, 400, 409, 426
Finland 27, 28, 105, 115, 418, 419, 421–25
fixities 18
flexibility 156, 248
fluid 16, 63, 177, 263, 264
flux 185
fold 118, 276
fotografia 172 (*see also* photography)
Fotografisk 308, 310, 314, 315 (*see also* photography)
fragmentation 109
France 265, 277, 323, 362
Frankfurt 418
Freire, Paulo 52, 55, 142
frieze 227, 230
frottage 69, 105
futurism 227

G
gallery 18, 21, 54–56, 65, 67, 113, 114, 177–85, 189, 190, 192, 193, 196, 263, 264, 268, 269, 288, 333, 334, 345, 347, 359, 374–76, 399, 423
gaming 396, 398
gaze 32, 33, 279, 280
gender 27, 29, 30, 56, 331, 337, 338
generative 266, 268, 384
genocide 64, 91
genre 143
gent 382
geography 56, 143, 254
geology 250
Germany 93, 239, 382, 423
gestalt 133
Giroux, Henry 22

globalization 16, 236, 248
glow 227
Goodman, Nelson 139
graffiti 263
Granada 164, 165, 169, 275, 277, 278, 282, 371, 420, 421, 423
graphite 105, 169
Greece 139
greening 122
grief 28, 32, 33
groundbreaking 351, 359, 361
Guattari, Felix 266
guerrilla 91
Gundersen, Gunnar S., 126, 350, 359, 362
gutter(s) 43

H
habitus 22
Halifax 58
Hamburg 418
handicrafts 419
handwriting 400
harassment 53
Haraway, Donna xiv 66, 181
Harmonization 77
hate speech 13–23
headphone(s) 195, 324, 399
hegemony 41, 179
Helsinki 28, 418
heritage xiii 79, 103, 106, 151, 157, 171, 205, 283, 321, 395, 405–15
hermeneutisch 232
heroes 42, 239
herotopia 211
heterogeneous 224, 226, 229
Hispanic 23
historia
historiography 47, 48
historiophoty 48
Hobart 65, 67, 424
holism 133
holograms 399, 400
homeland 239

hominids 131–33
Honduras xiv 161–71
horizon 56, 140
horror 350
hybrid 42
hypothesis 140

I
icon 21
ideation 278
ideology 80, 81, 146, 251
Illeris, Helene 209, 210, 217, 218, 219, 348
illness 410
imaginarium 314
immanence 269
immigrant 8, 33
impact 9, 40, 70, 78, 98, 133, 147, 157, 177, 178, 189, 190, 196, 209, 239, 319, 321, 323, 326, 409, 424
imperialism 263
impressionism 53
imprisonment 83
improv 333
impulse 182
incarceration 99
inclusion 22, 23, 46, 163, 225, 249, 334, 337, 386, 420
incognita 192
index 23, 47, 59, 171
indigenous 9
individuality 337
inequalities 236
infancy 157, 159
infrastructure 397–99
inhumanity 13–23
injustice 23, 28, 58, 331
ink 264, 268
innovation(s) xiv 99, 157, 402, 408–09, 422
inscription 129
installation(s) 17, 91, 92, 97, 126, 128, 142, 165, 168, 169, 192, 195, 196, 217, 263–65, 268, 279, 280, 311, 315, 324, 359, 362, 366, 371
institute(s) 29, 256, 423

instrumentalization 20, 146
integrity 171
intensification xiii 16
intercesseurs 266–67
interdependence 116, 309
interdisciplinary 39, 46, 116, 147, 180, 225, 247, 276, 300, 417, 420, 424
interface 154, 158
interlocutor 3–5, 238, 239, 241
intern(s) 256, 418
internet 18, 20, 397, 402, 408–10
intersectionality 33
interstices 32
intervention(s) 8, 9, 39, 41, 117, 142, 146, 166, 169–71, 180, 211, 265, 275–80, 282, 283, 309, 311, 312, 314, 381, 384, 390, 418
interwar 227, 240
intuition 166, 384
inversion 275
Islam 79
isolate 13 (*see* COVID-19)
Istanbul 79, 82, 397, 400
Italian 28
Iteration 13, 68
Itso, E. B., 307, 310–13, 316

J
jamming 209
Japan 397
jigsaw 177, 180
judgement(s) 30, 40
junctures 14–23
justice xiii 16, 28, 81, 82
juxtaposition(s) 20, 22, 66, 212, 264, 267

K
kaiserliche 247
kantor 410, 414
kapitał 243
Karlsplatz 228
kin 72
kindergarten 163, 219, 240, 253

kinetismus 227
king 47, 206
kingdom 4, 41, 372, 418
kiosk(s) 396, 399
Knappett 127–29
Køs 209, 210, 217–19
Kultur 231
Kunst 225, 308–312, 315, 420
kunstdidaktiske 355
KUNST:form 308–311
Kurdish 77, 79–82
Kuttner 43

L
l'amour 145
l'art 148
l'internationale 34
laboratories 142
Lapland 103, 105, 113–115, 117, 419, 421
Latour, Bruno 31, 236
lawsuits 77
learn 4, 21, 41–44, 113, 131, 140, 166, 177, 179, 203, 209, 210, 235, 237, 238, 240, 242, 276, 323, 335, 366, 371, 400
legacies 41
legitimacy 179, 218, 307
leisure 247, 252, 253, 398
leitmotif 146, 345
Leuven 382, 390, 391, 425
Levinson 224, 231
lifelong 248, 252, 412
lifeworld 224, 227, 230, 321
Lisbon 141, 418
literacies 153
littering 66
Liverpool 169, 177, 178, 184, 372
lobby 16, 103
lockdown(s) *see* COVID-19
London 4, 39, 40, 42
Louvre 397
lutruwita, Tasmania, Australia 61–71
lyric 219

M

macro 279
Madrid 396
mainstream 225
makers 31, 32, 334
Malta xiv 15, 16, 18–21, 390, 418, 425
mambo 425
manifesto 362
manifold 412
map 43, 44, 46, 143, 158, 211
marbling 400
marginalization 8, 32, 333, 335
maritime 257
Marseille 319, 323, 396
martyr 20
martyrdom 16
mask 119, 407
massacre(s) 78, 80, 81
Massumi, Brian 290, 292–294, 348, 349, 361, 366
materialism 30, 115, 359–361
matter 66, 69, 70, 129, 140, 167, 242, 333, 348, 360, 418
Mattingly, Cheryl 287, 289
matura 238
maximalism 20
Mbembe 84
mechanism(s) 94, 236, 309, 315
media 51, 57, 224, 311, 315
mediators 84, 256, 265–69
megalopolis 140
melancholy 279
mémoire 85
mentorship 197
metanarrative 70
metaphor 19, 105, 166, 264, 266
method 55, 105, 127, 134, 142, 203, 287, 311, 413, 423
metropolis 129
Mexico 16
migrants 15, 20
migration 22
milieus 266, 269

military 77, 79, 81, 251, 400
mind-set 127
miniature 400
mirror 15
misogyny 18, 19, 21
mnemonic 78
mobilization 49–58, 155
modalities 145, 265
mode(s) 15, 212, 224, 230, 231, 264, 267, 308, 332, 421
modernism 113
Montreal 6, 128, 129, 131, 287, 420–422
monument(s) 78, 79, 82, 91–94, 96
mosaic(s) 54, 55
mosque 399
Mostar 96
motifs 264
motto(s) 142, 269, 279
Mouffe 22, 30
multiculturalism 77
multimedia 157, 212, 265, 268, 409, 414
munari 142
mural 164, 169, 264
museal 396
musealization 244
museologists 265, 412
museumification 81
Muslim(s) 19, 80
myriad 52, 53, 71
mythology 254, 311
myths 15

N

naïve 314
narration 33, 325
nationalism 236
nature 3, 5–8, 15, 43, 114, 419, 421, 385
negative 71, 78, 241, 319, 323, 382
neocoloniality 17
neoliberalism 8
neoplasticism 362
Netherlands 390
network(s) 54, 127–29, 152, 399

neurodiversity 334
newcomers 103
niche 98
nichtminimalistischen 232
non-human 115, 120, 128, 267
non-living 290, 295
normative 27, 29, 30, 32
Norway 346, 359, 362, 419, 424
Novice 182
numeracy 193
nurture 3, 7, 70, 133, 190

O

object 28, 30–32, 41, 53, 66, 91, 99, 125, 127, 128, 133, 153, 170, 210, 217, 224, 248, 250, 290, 292, 384, 412
objectification 42
Obrist, Hans Ulrich 4
Obstacles 241
offline 18, 22
online 17, 18, 20–22, 151, 155, 156, 158, 254, 256, 326, 332, 347, 352, 385, 395, 402, 409, 411, 414
openings xiii, xiv 27, 52, 53, 147, 178, 182, 288, 349, 352, 409–411
oppression 21, 23, 29, 30, 32, 51, 52, 53, 56
opus 267
orchestra 103
organization(s) 30, 31, 81, 155, 180, 241, 309, 315, 346
Ortiz, Carmen 372
Oslo 355
ossification 287
Österreichischer 225
Other 15, 52, 55, 65, 70, 71, 80, 82, 84, 91, 93, 98, 114, 131, 133, 155, 214, 215, 412
outbreak 399
outsider 52
outsource 387
overpackaging 387

P

pädagogik *see* pedagogy

pädagogische 425
pain 33, 93, 331
painting 16, 17, 19–21, 53, 114, 117, 227, 238, 263, 264, 268, 335, 359
paleoanthropology 133
palettes 326
palimpsest 68
pandemic *see* COVID-19
panorama 79
Paquin, Maryse 265
paradigm xiv 181, 182, 224, 231, 322, 387, 408
paradox 64, 70
parfait 371
Paris 426
parodies 144
pathologies 251
patriotism 19, 239
patrons xiv 335
paucity 125
pavilions 288
peace 13, 91, 94, 96, 98, 99
peacebuilding 100
pedagogy 6, 8, 22, 28–30, 82, 96, 103, 111–20, 151–54, 156, 181, 209, 224–25, 299, 300, 315, 316, 343–355, 419, 421, 422, 424
pedestrians 133
pencils 105, 169, 333
performance(s) 43, 67, 69, 70, 113, 140, 143, 155, 166, 210, 211, 212, 236, 254, 279, 350, 410
period(s) 20, 40, 77, 79, 129–131, 145, 148, 264, 320, 400, 407
perspective xiv 30, 52, 98, 115, 146, 194, 209, 225, 238, 333, 334, 335, 337, 364, 366, 381, 382, 384, 413, 424
Perth 191, 418
Pharaoh 121
phenomena 287, 409, 411
phone(s) 210, 215, 337
photography; photogrammetry; photomontage 116, 117, 211, 277, 397, 414, 421
play 7, 52, 67, 84, 97, 133, 240, 312, 347, 359, 362, 364, 365, 395, 402, 408, 410

Index

plinths 91
pluralism 197
poem 40, 212, 350
poetization 212, 217–19
Poland xiv 96, 235, 236, 239, 241, 242, 406, 408, 423
police 79, 31
polychrome 279, 282
populace 151
porcelain 129
portal 413
portrait(s) 117, 119, 143, 144, 279
portray(als) 15
Portugal 140–44
positionality xiv 20
possibilities xiv 8, 22, 55, 67, 140, 211
poverty 16, 53, 163
power 20, 27, 31, 51, 54, 57, 77, 94, 166, 167, 181, 193, 224, 267, 275, 310, 402, 409
practitioner 46, 68, 190
pragmatism 224, 420
praxis 178, 352
presence 8, 9, 42, 84, 194, 264, 275, 407, 410
principle(s) 18, 126–29, 133, 142, 209, 218, 314, 336, 348–349, 385, 411
printmaking 419
priorities 63, 71, 155, 224, 311
prison 81–82
privilege 29, 32, 66, 310, 332, 334
process xiv 15, 22, 28–30, 33, 41, 43, 44, 46, 63–67, 105, 117, 119, 127, 129, 166, 169, 170, 181, 182, 185, 196, 201, 203, 218, 219, 223, 224, 236, 269, 310–312, 319, 320, 324, 411, 423
prochoice 21
procurement 249
programme 6, 144–46, 151, 155, 156, 185, 189, 191, 421
prohibition(s) 31, 32
projection-based augmented reality (PBAR) 369–77, 420
projections 39, 43, 126, 144, 264, 372, 393–402, 420

Prösler 236
protocols 156, 399
prototypes 133, 382, 383
provocation(s) 21, 22, 67, 94, 192
proximity 22, 31, 69, 289
Prussian 126
psychiatry 296
psychoanalyst 142, 240
psychomotor 320
PTSD 339
publics 7–9, 18, 40, 44, 57, 84, 91, 141, 145, 183, 190, 308
punctuate 288
pupil(s) 156, 249, 252, 257, 349
purpose (of museum) 248
purging 18

Q

quadrangle 311
quadrants 98
qualification 154
qualität xiii 58, 237, 293, 360
quantum 185
Quebec 128
queering 27, 30, 33
questionnaires 58
quilt 279
quizzes 155, 157

R

racialization 17
racism 7, 16, 18, 21, 51
Rancière, Jacques 346, 348
ratio 224
recolonize 42
reconciliation 77, 78, 82, 84, 96, 98, 408
recycle 84
refugees 16, 18
regime(s) 346, 348, 407
reindeer 116
relationality 32, 63, 64, 66, 275, 348, 350–52
religion 15

rematerializing 211
remote 113, 151, 409, 410, 414
render 19, 22, 64
renovate 23
repertoire 310–12, 314–16
repetition 289, 293, 315, 316, 323
repository 139, 183
representationalism 361
reproductions 15, 16, 19–21, 132, 182, 189, 192–95, 264
republic 77, 79, 84, 252, 257
resemblance 361, 363
reservations 218
residency 156
resilience 65, 182
resonance 30, 40, 290–93, 384, 388, 390
resource(s) ix 21, 114, 154, 155, 159, 315, 347, 395, 396, 402
restoration 248
rethink 9, 29, 39, 99, 157, 384
retraced 331
reverberate 292
revisionist 39
revitalize 46, 119
revolution 142
rhetoric 29
rhythm 33, 288, 365
rituals 270
Roca, José 94
Rogoff, Irit 178, 210, 218
romanticized 189
Rovaniemi 103, 104, 419
ruins 93, 103, 105, 130, 398
rupture xiv 69, 96, 180–182, 346
Russia 113, 126, 257

S
Sarajevo 96
Särestöniemi 113–16, 118, 119
scaffolded 191
scale 66, 319, 325
Scandinavian 348
scenario(s) 96, 97, 149, 295, 390, 396

scene(s) 131, 183, 184, 212, 279, 282, 309, 310, 314, 332, 334, 348, 400
scenography 350
scepticism 314, 316
sceptre 166
schizophrenia 58, 72, 270
school(s) 7, 57, 96, 144–47, 151, 156, 163, 165–68, 216, 219, 237, 242, 412
science xiii 51, 65, 143, 225, 249, 252, 266, 411, 422, 425
Scotland 47, 58
sediment 129
seminal 312
semiotext 270
senior(s) 179, 334, 418–422
sensation(s) 69, 292, 321, 349, 387
sense 4, 7, 20, 30, 52, 69, 71, 94, 99, 117, 145, 170, 182, 195, 217, 239, 288, 293, 312, 324, 335, 336, 350, 412, 424, 426
Serbian 359
serendipity 391
series 44, 55, 65, 117, 131, 168, 179, 192, 229, 261–69, 311, 331, 414, 418
serigraphy 377
settlement(s) 113, 128, 129
sexism 51
sexuality 30
signage 278, 326, 333
simulacrum 144
site 9, 13, 57, 65, 78, 80, 82, 84, 96, 129, 412
situ 97, 253–254
sketches 30, 132, 276, 361
slave 42
slavery 39–41, 46
slippage 65, 66, 71
Slovak 243
smartphones 397
SMCA (Serralves Museum of Contemporary Art) 140–143, 145–47
socialization 287
sociosemiotics 127–128
sociedad 171, 284
software 371

solidarity 28, 30–33, 408, 410
sound 54, 126, 195, 213, 227, 229, 280, 292, 324, 334, 365, 396, 424
soundscapes 227
souvenir 19
sovereign 15, 309, 387
Soviet 248
Sowa 224, 229–231
Spain 166, 201, 275, 279, 299, 371, 417, 418, 420–424
Specialization 418, 425
species 67, 68, 70, 131, 400
specimens 68, 250, 395
spectacle 166, 264
spectator(ship) 9, 96, 211, 212, 218, 276, 277, 300, 348, 362, 371, 377
spectrum 398
Spinoza 361
squatter(s) 311, 312
staff 28, 29, 31, 32, 154, 157, 159, 180–182, 192, 267, 333–37, 387, 396
stage 21, 237, 238, 316, 319, 334, 349
stakeholders 152, 334, 338, 382, 385, 386, 390, 395, 421
standards; standardized 51, 96, 154, 247, 268, 310, 326
standpoint(s) xiv 56, 57, 129
state 15, 23, 52, 54, 61–71, 77–81, 224, 225, 236, 269, 346, 397, 408, 410, 424
statue 41
stereotypes 337
stewardship 66
stigmatization 287
Stockholm 355
storyteller 5
stratagems 125
stratification 145
student 116, 218, 225, 226, 241, 278, 279, 311, 350, 418, 421
studio; studiorum 154, 189, 190, 192, 194, 257, 334–36, 417, 420, 421
subalterns 33
Subcarpathia 238

Subjectivation 346, 349, 355
subversion 146
supersurvivors 339
suppression 79
suprematism 362
surface(s) 103, 105, 132, 292–94, 371, 372
sustainability xiv 56, 120, 147, 386, 419, 425
Sweden 362, 390, 420
Switzerland 423
sybilla 408
symbiosis 66
symbolism 97, 128, 129
sympathetic 71
symposia 157
synergies 43
synthesis 236, 278
Szántó, András 3–5

T
tableaux 126
taboos 57
tactics 98
tagging 294
Talboys, Graeme K., 248, 253
tale(s) 275
Tate 177, 178, 184, 372
teacher 8, 57, 120, 142, 144, 147, 151, 154–56, 159, 163, 170, 181, 192, 209, 225, 229, 241, 249, 254, 276, 280, 418, 423
teamlab 397
technology 79, 225, 379–391, 395, 397, 399, 402
template 266
tempo 227
tenet 128
tension 15, 65, 66, 69, 94, 140, 178, 180, 217, 289, 290, 291, 387
terrain 46, 70, 178, 210, 211, 217, 218, 220, 315
territorialities 266
testimony 77, 98
textile 225
texting 331
texture(s) 20, 86, 103, 105, 372
theatre(s) 59, 240, 249, 347, 350, 407, 422

theologies 23
theoriebildung 232
things 3, 18, 20, 34, 41, 44, 52, 54, 170, 194, 195, 215, 223, 238, 263, 266, 267, 269, 289, 312, 326, 331, 334, 335, 366, 381, 385, 387
threshold 65, 66, 331
tirant 205, 284
tografía 171, 284, 414
tokenism 312, 316
tonality 288, 293
torture 20, 81
touch 30, 31–32, 131, 238, 268, 275, 347, 366, 372, 387, 396, 399, 400, 401, 402
touch screens 387, 396, 399, 400, 401, 402
tour 6, 21, 27, 29, 116, 125, 157, 190, 195, 227, 249, 268, 285, 287–95, 333, 337, 347, 349, 350, 359, 360, 361, 362, 363, 364, 366, 396, 399
tourist xiv 113, 115, 120, 140, 143, 237, 252, 282
toxicity 66
trace 9, 22, 39, 40, 241, 275, 292, 362, 365
trade(s) 236, 386
tradition ix, xiv 4, 5, 6, 7, 28, 32, 51, 57, 64, 68, 69, 91, 92, 93, 94, 96, 113, 115, 120, 140, 143, 144, 146, 152, 154, 167, 178, 180, 190, 192, 194, 195, 229, 239, 249, 264, 300, 308, 323, 345, 349, 387, 400
trafficking 156
tragacanth 400
tragedies 32, 91
transcend 4, 22, 115, 230, 398
transform 9, 22, 23, 33, 52, 54, 55, 56, 63, 64, 66, 78, 81, 83, 103, 113, 114, 117, 119, 120, 145, 152, 157, 250, 263, 275, 279, 282, 293, 294, 321, 324, 359, 371, 372, 388, 390, 400
transition 237, 248
transmodernity 23
transparency 182–84, 331, 335–336, 338
transphobia 18
trauma 7, 78, 79, 84, 329, 331–38
travel 17, 54, 56, 113, 131, 143, 279
trend 300, 381, 387
triad 320

triangulation 312
trivializations 224
Turkey xiv 75, 77–84, 393, 395–402

U
undoings 15
ugliness 18, 19, 66
United Kingdom 4, 41, 372, 418
Ukraine 237
Ultratechnologists 397
unbuild 33
uncertainty 177, 181, 182, 311, 349, 364, 366
undergraduate 276
unfold 44, 309, 314, 345, 360, 366
unlearning 32, 34, 180
urban 71, 209, 211, 316
utopian 4, 225, 382, 389

V
Valdeloviewfinder 374
Valencia 201, 205
vallance 63
value 4, 29, 31, 32, 44, 55, 56, 63, 64, 65, 66, 67, 70, 71, 72, 93, 96, 103, 114, 139, 145, 152, 153, 166, 170, 171, 177, 180, 191, 196, 205, 229, 239, 249, 251, 269, 295, 307, 309, 312, 314, 320, 333, 335, 384, 386, 410, 412
variations 169, 218
venue(s) 79, 96, 253, 396
verbatim 54
verdict 80
vernacular 66
vernissage 352
versatility 371
verso 23, 24
victim(s) 16, 80, 91, 93, 98
video(s) 54, 93, 98, 125, 158, 265, 311, 323, 324, 371, 372, 376, 387, 402, 410
Vienna 97, 225, 226, 227, 420, 425
viewfinder 374
viewpoint 98
village 399, 412
villamil 170

villareal 282
vinyl 301
violations 77
violence 15, 16, 17, 18, 20, 77, 78, 79, 81, 84, 91, 93, 96, 97, 98, 99, 163, 331
virtual reality (VR) 385, 396
visibility 81, 139, 146, 182, 191, 230, 315
visitor 3, 7, 8, 9, 18, 28, 29, 31, 52, 54, 55, 56, 57, 91, 94, 98, 99, 103, 106, 113, 114, 120, 125, 126, 127, 133, 140, 145, 146, 153, 154, 166, 167, 169, 177, 182, 185, 195, 202, 225, 226, 227, 235, 242, 248, 250, 252, 253, 254, 265, 266, 275, 276, 277, 279, 282, 287, 300, 302, 309, 319, 321, 322, 323, 324, 325, 326, 331, 332, 333, 334, 335, 336, 347, 359, 360, 362, 371, 372, 374, 381, 382, 384, 385, 386, 390, 396, 397, 398, 399, 400, 402, 403, 407, 417, 424, 425
vistas 145, 181
visualization 105
vocabulaboratories 316
vocabulary 30
voice(s) 9, 18, 31, 51, 53, 65, 79, 93, 99, 139, 177, 179, 182, 185, 187, 189, 190, 191, 192, 193, 194, 195, 212, 214, 263, 288, 293, 308, 324, 333, 334, 335, 337, 338, 384, 388, 389, 417
void(s) 210, 215, 218
voivodeship 236
volunteer 334
Vygotsky 55, 59

W

walk 43, 54, 91, 94, 96, 97, 129, 131–33, 291, 312, 324, 352, 366, 390, 402, 410, 411, 414
wander 117, 289, 333, 334
war(s) 78, 79, 91, 92–93, 96, 97, 98, 103, 105, 126, 239, 240, 247, 362, 400
warehouse 184
warrants 55
Warsaw 409, 411, 414
wasteland 211
wealth 40, 226, 310
weaponization 20

weave 322
web 8, 125, 156, 157, 409, 414
webcam 374
Weber, C. 250, 258
website 7, 140, 169, 277, 335, 395, 396, 399, 408, 409, 410
welfare 115
wellness 287, 420
welt 231 (*see also* world)
weltanschauung 232
whiteboard 385
Wien 226, 227–228, 425 (*see also* Vienna)
wilderness 64
window(s) 199, 288, 294, 334
wisdom 333
wissenschaftliche 232
witness 52, 70, 77, 78, 80, 81, 84, 119, 129, 139, 229, 230, 294, 345, 411
wonder 3, 182, 217, 250, 263
workshop(s) 27, 28, 30, 31, 32, 33, 53–54, 55, 58, 65, 83, 103, 105, 106, 113, 116–120, 142, 144, 145, 168, 179, 180, 190, 192, 195, 196, 211, 216, 218, 227, 242, 268, 287, 311, 312, 314, 315, 334, 345, 346, 347, 352–355, 361, 372, 381, 385, 386, 388, 390, 400
worldview xiii 115, 120, 139
woven 282, 322, 323, 335, 337

X

xchanges xiii

Y

Yearbook 121, 206
youth 8, 28, 33, 66, 227, 240, 382–384
YouTube 99, 413, 414
Yugoslavia 96

Z

Zembylas 98, 100
Zimbabwe xiv 151–59
zone(s) 20, 56, 58, 223, 230
Zoom 350–52
Zwischen (*see* between)